ANSWERS

TO

TOUGH
QUESTIONS

FROM EVERY BOOK OF THE BIBLE

Answers to Tough Questions

from Every Book of the Bible

From Every Book of the Bible

A Survey of Problem
Passages and Issues

J. Carl Laney

kregel
PUBLICATIONS

Grand Rapids, MI 49501

Cover design: Alan G. Hartman
Book design: Nicholas G. Richardson

Library of Congress Cataloging-in-Publication Data
Laney, J. Carl.
  Answers to tough questions from every book of the Bible / J. Carl Laney.
      p.   cm.
  Includes bibliographical references.
  1. Bible—Criticism, interpretation, etc. 2. Bible—Miscellanea. I. Title.
BS511.2.L35   1997   220.6—dc21   96-53071
                                          CIP

ISBN 0-8254-3094-1

Printed in the United States of America

1 2 3 / 03 02 01 00 99 98 97

To my students at Western Seminary
whose questions inspired my search for answers.

CONTENTS

INTRODUCTION

Since 1975 I have had the privilege of teaching Bible on a seminary level. In preparation for my lectures I have interacted with many tough questions that arise in Bible study. Over the years I have made a personal study of each of the major interpretive and background questions to help my students deal with these issues. This book will enable Bible students, including pastors, Sunday school teachers, and Bible study leaders, to benefit from this research.

Kinds of Questions

There are many different kinds of questions that we encounter when reading the Bible.[1] The ones I'll address in this book concern:

- *Archaeology:* How do we account for the archaeological evidence that biblical Ai was not occupied when Israel entered Canaan (Josh. 8:18–27)?
- *Authorship:* Who wrote the book of Genesis?
- *Background:* What was the stigma associated with being a "Samaritan" (John 4:9)?
- *Ethics:* Does the story of Rahab's lie provide a biblical basis for situation ethics? Is it sometimes right to lie (Josh. 2:1–7)?
- *History:* What was the date and the duration of the conquest (Josh. 11:16–18)?
- *Inerrancy:* Was Paul in error when he said that "twenty-three thousand" people died (1 Cor. 10:8; compare Num. 25:9)?
- *Interpretation:* Who were the "sons of God" who took wives from the daughters of men (Gen. 6:2)?
- *Literature:* What is the "documentary theory" of the Pentateuch?
- *Miracles:* What actually happened on the day when "the sun stood still" (Josh. 10:12–14)?
- *Quotations:* How does Matthew see Jesus' sojourn in Egypt as a fulfillment of Hosea 11:1, "Out of Egypt did I call My son" (Matt. 2:15)?
- *Science:* Is there any biblical evidence for the evolutionary hypothesis (Gen. 1:12)?
- *Synoptic:* In comparing Matthew 4:1–11 with Luke 4:5–12, how do we account for the different order of events in the Temptation?
- *Textual*: Should the story of the adulterous woman be considered part of the original text (John 7:53–8:11)?
- *Theology:* What does it mean to be made "in the image of God" (Gen. 1:27)?

Presuppositions

We all operate on the basis of certain presuppositions or generally accepted facts. I'd like to share my presuppositions with you so you will understand my approach to Bible difficulties. These presuppositions are the basis for my work in answering questions and interpreting difficult texts.

1. The Bible is the inspired Word of God (2 Tim. 3:16).
2. The Bible is true and without errors (John 17:17).
3. There are passages in Scripture that are hard to understand and interpret (2 Peter 3:16).
4. Many of the difficult passages can be clarified through careful study.
5. The Scripture is best interpreted by the literal (normal), historical-grammatical method.[2]
6. Believers are dependent on the ministry of the Holy Spirit to clarify and illuminate the text (John 16:13; 1 John 2:27).
7. The best solutions are those that reflect the most clear, straightforward interpretations of the text.
8. There are some questions for which we don't have answers from the Bible (Ps. 35:11).
9. Learning to live with unanswered questions is an exercise of Christian faith (Heb. 11:3).

Problem Solving

How do we go about solving problems in Scripture? There are many different kinds of problems that have peculiar issues to be resolved. Here is a general overview of the steps that I have followed in answering the questions found in this book.

Identify the Problem

The first step is to determine what kind of problem we have encountered. Is it textual, theological, or an issue of ethics? It is helpful to state the problem in the form of a question. For example, Did Jesus endorse pacifism when He said, "Do not resist him who is evil" (Matt. 5:39)?

Examine the Text

The second step is to determine exactly what the text of Scripture says. Sometimes the problem is in the translation or the result of our superficial reading of the text. If you have the training, consult the original text. Sometimes a problem can be resolved simply through a closer reading of the text, as in the case of the supposed execution of Achan's children (Josh. 7:22–26).

Consider the Options

In dealing with the problem of lack of archaeological remains at Ai during the time of the conquest (compare Josh. 8:18–27), there are several options that we might consider. First, the Bible is wrong in reporting that the Israelites conquered Ai. Second, Ai has been wrongly identified and should be found elsewhere. Third, Ai has been properly identified, but remains from Joshua's day have yet to be uncovered.

Propose a Solution

After considering the possible solutions, we must select one that is consistent with our presuppositions and has the greatest support. In dealing with the question of whether or not Jesus was mistaken when He referred to the mustard seed as the smallest of all seeds (Matt. 13:31), the conclusion that He *was* mistaken is not consistent with the Bible's teaching that Jesus is God. God doesn't make mistakes. So, we propose another solution. Jesus was talking about the kinds of seeds that are sown and cultivated. He was not making a universal scientific statement about all seeds. In proposing a solution, it is important to keep in mind such hermeneutical principles as "analogy of Scripture" and "preference for the clearest meaning" of the text.

Keep an Open Mind

After selecting the best solution to the problem, don't close your mind to further study. You never know when you will discover an additional insight that will shed new light on the subject. I remember when I lectured on an interpretive problem one day. Several of my students raised some insightful questions about my solution. After class, I went back to my study and poured over the matter again. I discovered that there *was* a better solution. The class interaction had demonstrated the weakness of my view. At the next class period, I told my students to throw away their previous notes, and I taught the subject again. In discussing the controversial Qumran Scrolls, William LaSor wrote, "We have nothing to fear from truth; only ignorance can hurt us. . . . New truths always challenge old opinions. But new truths never destroy old truths; they merely separate truth from falsehood."[3] I admire people who are willing to change their opinions when confronted with new truth.

Stepping-Stones

The solutions that I have offered in this book are not intended to serve as the final answers to all the difficulties of the Bible. But I do hope that they serve as stepping-stones in your research and study of God's Word. The answers presented here are based on careful research. They are consistent with a high view of Scripture. But they are also the well-researched opinions of one fallible man. My words are temporal and fallible. Only God's Word is eternal and infallible. As Isaiah reminds us, "The grass withers, the flower fades, but the word of our God stands forever" (Isa. 40:8).

J. CARL LANEY

Endnotes

1. While there are many designations for God in the Bible, there is one name by which He has identified Himself. This is the name Yahweh, the "memorial-name" by which God wanted to be remembered for all generations (Exod. 3:15). Jews have traditionally avoided the use of God's name for fear of misusing it, and Christians have followed in this pattern. Although the name Yahweh may be unfamiliar to some readers, its biblical significance calls for its use in this book (see Exod. 3:13–15).

2. Literal interpretation means that we will interpret the words in light of their normal usage. We will be alert to figures of speech and metaphors but will seek the literal meaning behind the figure.

   Historical interpretation means that we will consider the historical background in seeking to interpret a passage. This includes geographical, cultural, and archaeological material that may provide insight into the meaning of the text.

   Grammatical interpretation means that we will consider the grammar and syntax of the original language in determining an interpretation.

   The literal (normal), historical-grammatical method of interpretation recognizes that the Bible contains different kinds of literature—historical, poetic, wisdom, etc.—for which specialized interpretive principles apply. For further study, see Gordon D. Fee and Douglas Stuart, *How to Read the Bible for All It's Worth* (Grand Rapids: Zondervan, 1981), 2–9.

3. William S. LaSor, *The Dead Sea Scrolls and the New Testament* (Grand Rapids: Eerdmans, 1972), 27.

OLD TESTAMENT

GENESIS

Authorship

Who wrote the book of Genesis?

Genesis is an anonymous book, but the evidence suggests that it was written by Moses. The author was well acquainted with the land of Egypt, as Moses certainly was. His education in Pharaoh's court would have prepared him for writing such a book. Several texts attribute the Torah to Moses (compare Exod. 17:14; Deut. 31:9, 14), and this term may include Genesis as well. Jesus' reference to the law of circumcision (John 7:22–23) as being given by Moses (Gen. 17:12) suggests that He believed in the Mosaic authorship of Genesis.

Affirming the Mosaic authorship of Genesis does not preclude his use of other source materials. While God could have directly revealed to Moses the stories of the patriarchs, Moses could have drawn from earlier records to write this book.

Genesis 1:1–3

Does Genesis 1:1–3 describe the original Creation or a later refashioning of the earth?

There are three basic interpretations of this important text. According to the *gap theory*, Genesis 1:1 describes the original, perfect Creation. But between verses 1 and 2 there is a gap of many years. During this period, Satan fell and the earth underwent a cataclysmic change as a result of God's judgment. Verse 2 is interpreted to describe the chaotic condition of the universe (Isa. 24:1; 45:18; Jer. 4:23–26) after the fall of Satan (Isa. 14:9–14; Ezek. 28:12–15). According to the view, verse 3 refers to God's first step in the process of reconstructing and reforming the judged earth. This view is motivated by a desire to harmonize the Genesis account of Creation with the evolutionary theory, which requires vast geologic time periods. The main flaw in the gap theory is that the Hebrew syntax links the verses in such a way that does not allow for a gap between verses 1 and 2.

A second interpretation of the Creation account is known as the *re-creation theory*. According to this view, the account of the original Creation is not recorded in the Genesis record. Original Creation happened long before Genesis 1:1. After original Creation, Satan fell, and the original creation fell under divine judgment. Millions of years passed as the lifeless earth aged. Then God began to reform or refashion the earth (Gen. 1:1) from its judged and chaotic state. Genesis 1:1 describes, then, a new beginning, not an absolute beginning. Like the gap theory, this view leans heavily on hypothesis and speculation, depending more on what is *not* revealed than on what the text actually declares.

The third view interprets Genesis 1:1–3 to describe *original Creation*. Verse 1 records that God the Creator, on the first day of original Creation, made the material heavens and earth. Verse 2 contains three circumstantial clauses that describe the condition of the earth as it was until God began to form the original material into its present form. The earth was in a perfect yet unfinished state during the first part of the first day of creation. These clauses imply no imperfection but merely describe the earth as unformed and unfilled early in that first day of Creation. Verse 3 shows the manner in which God worked— by His word—and records God's first step in the process of bringing the universe into its present form.

Both the *gap theory* and the *re-creation theory* leave us with no clear word from God concerning the original perfect Creation. This would seem unusual in light of the Scripture's emphasis on God as Creator (John 1:3; Col. 1:16; Heb. 11:3). The original Creation view avoids the tenuous speculation of the other views and the arbitrary distinctions between John 1:3 and Hebrews 11:3 (original Creation) and Genesis 1:1–3 (re-creation). This view has the advantage of being the most clear and straightforward interpretation of the text.

Genesis 1:5

Were the "days" of the Creation account twenty-four-hour days as we know them?

The Genesis record of Creation indicates that each step in the process was completed in one "day" (*yom*) for a total of six days. Some biblical scholars have argued for a figurative use of the term "day" in Genesis 1. According to this view, the six days of the Creation account were long ages (millions of years), not the normal twenty-four-hour days. This theory is closely linked with the evolutionary hypothesis, which demands long periods of time for mutation, natural selection, and the adaptation of living beings.

The *day-age theory* is supposedly based on the figurative use of *day* in the Hebrew Scriptures. While there are examples of such usage in expressions like "the day of the LORD" (Mal. 4:5), the context must be considered in determining the meaning of any word. Second Peter 3:8, "with the Lord one day is as a thousand years," is often quoted in support of the theory. But note the comparison "as" *(hos)* that Peter employs. Peter is not saying that a day *is* a thousand years. Within the context of the passage, Peter is explaining that what seems to involve a long time from the human temporal viewpoint is "as" a day from an eternal perspective.

In the Genesis Creation account, each of the six days is described as including "evening and morning." This suggests to the reader that normal, twenty-four-hour days are in view. Throughout the Hebrew Scriptures, the term *yom*, "day," is never used figuratively when it has a number attached ("fourth day," "fifth day"). In the command to keep the Sabbath, the people are instructed, "Six days you shall labor and do all your work . . . for in six days the LORD made the heavens and the earth " (Exod. 20:9–11). The comparison demands that "six days" mean the same thing in both cases. And no one would argue the day-age theory for the human work week. We can be sure that the earliest readers of Genesis understood the Creation account to refer to normal, twenty-four–hour days. That is the best approach for readers today as well.

Genesis 1:12

Is there any biblical evidence for the evolutionary hypothesis?

According to the evolutionary hypothesis, life on this earth began about 4.5 billion years ago when chemicals in the sea, acted upon by sunlight, formed themselves into one or more simple-celled organisms. These organisms have since developed by the natural selection of favorable mutations into all living and extinct plants and animals, including human beings. There are several variations of this hypothesis. *Theistic evolutionists* believe that this long and gradual process took place under the controlling direction of a supernatural Being. This view represents an attempt to harmonize modern science with a belief in God as Creator. *Progressive creationists* believe that God directly created the first life and also major stages of life throughout geologic history. But they believe that extensive evolution has taken place over vast periods of time within these major created groups of living beings.

In my understanding, the Bible is totally lacking in evidence for the evolutionary hypothesis. This theory is contradicted by the Genesis account, which reveals that all living things were created in six days and reproduced "after their kind" (1:12, 21, 24). The biblical evidence allows for variation of these kinds into races and breeds but not for the subsequent, evolutionary development of new kinds. Beagles and bulldogs, dachshunds and great danes all belong to the same "kind." They are dogs. According to Genesis 1:24, they will always reproduce dogs. No dog will ever become a horse or grow extra legs to better enable it to chase cats.

The fact that there was no evolutionary development of the human race is demonstrated by the fact that God *first* created Adam, and *then* Eve (2:7, 22). Evolutionists have to deny the biblical record that God made Eve from Adam's rib (v. 22). According to the evolutionary viewpoint, they would have evolved together.

As a scientifically oriented university student, I came to accept theistic evolution as the best way to recognize the authority of both science and Scripture. During my first year at seminary, my evolutionary viewpoint was challenged as I studied the biblical record. After reading many books on the subject, I came to the conclusion that as a Christian my ultimate source of authority is the Bible. After reading Hebrews 11:3, I decided that I must accept the biblical account of Creation by faith, even though I still had some questions.

Further research on the Evolutionary Hypothesis led me to the discovery of major flaws. I found that the hypothesis is founded on two basic presuppositions: (1) mutation and (2) natural selection. Mutation is the basis for changes in the genetic structure of the organism. Natural selection means that animals that experience changes for the worse will die. Animals that experience beneficial changes will survive and reproduce. But we might ask, Can the evolutionists or naturalistic scientists show one example of a mutation that ever increased on a genetic or observable level the complexity of the species? The answer is no. There simply have not been any.

Variations that do occasionally appear (through gene recombination and mutations) are less complex and represent a weakening of the organisms within these specialized varieties. Further objections to the evolutionary hypothesis should be considered. First, the viewpoint contradicts the second law of thermodynamics, which states that all spontaneously occurring action takes things from order to greater random (disorder). The theory of evolution holds just the opposite.

Second, many complex, multipart organs cannot function until they are complete. The human eye would have no reason to improve by mutation unless the muscles, lens, and retina all worked in the first place.

Third, the absence of transitional forms is a major objection to the theory. While thousands of transitional forms should be expected, all plants and animals may be classified into groups with which they share distinguishing features. Although transitional forms should appear in the fossil record, major groups of plants and animals appear suddenly, and no intermediate types are found. Certain similarities in groups of animals can be explained as evidence of a common Designer not a common ancestor.

Genesis 1:27

What does it mean to be made "in the image of God"?

Although Genesis teaches that humankind was made in the "image" of God, nowhere are we told in Scripture exactly what this means. Hence, there is a lot of debate on the subject. Theologians agree that this resemblance to God makes humankind unique among God's creatures. No animal is said to be made in God's image. Theologians also agree that this resemblance to God is not physical, since "God is spirit" (John 4:24) and has no material body.

Usually the image of God in humans is explained in terms of the immaterial aspects of our persons that we share with God—human intellect, emotion, and will. Others suggest that this image refers more specifically to the spiritual qualities that are shared by God and humankind.

In answering this question, I have found help from a statement by Charles Ryrie: "The image of God involves man's being given dominion over the earth and his capacity for moral action, both of which have been disturbed by the entrance of sin so that he has lost his dominion and corrupted his moral abilities."[1] A look in the text of Genesis seems to confirm Ryrie's suggestion. Notice in the Genesis account that God fills, subdues, and rules His creation. Humankind is given the same obligation—to fill, subdue, and rule (Gen. 1:28). Humankind's capacity to fill, subdue, and rule in a godlike manner has been disturbed by the entrance of sin and the corruption of human moral abilities.

Genesis 3:16

What is the "desire" that a wife will have for her husband?

As part of the judgment on the human race for the original sin of our ancestors, Adam and Eve, God said to the woman, "Yet your desire shall be for your husband, and he shall rule over you" (Gen. 3:16). A proper interpretation of this statement is the basis for a biblical understanding of the relationship between husbands and wives.

There are three traditional views regarding the woman's "desire." (1) *Sexual.* A wife's sexual desire for her husband will be so strong that she will be ready to face the pain of childbearing to satisfy it. (2) *Psychological.* The desire makes a woman willing to be a slave of a man and is the expression of her psychological dependence upon her husband. (3) *What her husband desires.* The wife will desire only what her husband desires, and she will have no command over herself. The rule of the husband is viewed as punishment for sin. None of these three views pass the test of biblical consistency or human experience.

The way to a proper understanding of this passage is through making a comparison of Genesis 3:16 and 4:7.[2] These Hebrew texts are precisely the same except for appropriate changes in person and gender:

> Yet your desire shall be for your husband, and he shall rule over you (Gen. 3:16).

> And its [sin's] desire is for you, but you [Cain] must master it (Gen. 4:7).

In Genesis 4:7, sin's desire is to enslave Cain—to possess or control him, but the Lord commands Cain to overpower sin and master it. An active struggle is implied.

A comparison between Genesis 3:16 and 4:7 suggests that the wife has the same sort of desire for her husband that sin has for Cain—a desire to possess or control. In the marriage relationship, this desire disputes the headship of the husband—the leadership God has assigned him in the home. As the Lord tells Cain what he should do, that is, master or rule sin, so the Lord states what the husband should do, exercise authority over the wife.

The words of Genesis 3:16 mark the beginning of the battle of the sexes. As a result of the Fall, husbands no longer rule easily. Sin has corrupted the willing submission of wives. A husband must struggle to exercise leadership and authority in marriage. A wife's desire is to control her husband—to usurp his divinely appointed headship—and he must exercise authority and leadership, if he can.

The two clauses of Genesis 3:16 are antithetical and should be translated:

> And your desire to control shall be to your husband, *but* he should master you.

The wife's desire is to contend with her husband for headship in their relationship. Consequently, the husband must actively seek to rule and exercise authority over his wife. Conflict in the home resulting from the curse can be reduced under the new covenant when a Christian husband loves his wife sacrificially and a Christian wife respects her husband's leadership in the home (Eph. 5:22–28).

Genesis 4:17

Where did Cain get his wife? Did he marry his sister?

This is one of those questions for which the Bible does not provide an answer. Possible suggestions include: (1) Cain married his sister, a younger daughter of Adam and Eve; (2) God created a wife for Cain as he did for Adam; (3) Cain married a woman from another family—a family not related to Adam. The objection with this last suggestion is that it contradicts the clear teaching of Scripture that traces the human race back to Adam (Luke 3:23–38; Rom. 5:12–19; 1 Cor. 15:45–49). It is possible that Cain married a niece—a daughter of his murdered brother Abel. Ultimately, we must admit that there is no biblical answer to this question. The writer of Genesis evidently did not consider this information essential to the communication of the message of his book.

Genesis 6:2

Who were the "sons of God" who took wives from the daughters of men?

This is a classic question of Bible interpretation for which four interpretations have been proposed.

Apostate Sethites: According to the Sethite view the "sons of God" were descendants of Seth—the godly line—who intermarried with the depraved descendants of Cain. The perversion that God judged was the pollution of the godly line of Seth by religiously mixed marriages. The progeny of the intermingling are said to be wicked tyrants. The major problems with this view are (1) the absence of the use of the term *sons of God* for believers in the Old Testament and (2) the failure to explain the origin of the giants and mighty men through religiously mixed marriages.

Angelic Creatures: According to the angel view the "sons of God" were fallen angels that took on human bodies to cohabit with beautiful women of the human race. The perversion was the intrusion into the human race by angels, which resulted in progeny that were monstrous giants. The major problems with this view are (1) the words of Christ in Matthew 22:30 stating that angels do not marry, and (2) the psychological and physiological problems of angelic marriages.

Ambitious Despots: According to this view the sons of God were despotic chieftains of Cainite descent who married a plurality of wives in order to expand their dominion. The progeny of these marriages were dynastic rulers. Problems with this view include (1) the absence of evidence that a monarchial system of rulers had been established in the line of Cain, and (2) the question of why something so familiar as kingship should be expressed so indirectly.

Humankind in Marriage: In his commentary on Genesis, Sailhamer has presented a creative solution to an old problem.[3] He argues that Genesis 6:1–4 returns to the theme of marriage (2:24) and reminds the reader that the sons and daughters of Adam greatly increased in number, married, and continued to have children. The major difficulty is how the reader is to account for the great evil mentioned in 6:5. Where did this come from if not 6:1–4? It seems that the greatness of the judgment (world flood) demands something extraordinary as its cause. The "wickedness of man" mentioned in 6:5 does not seem sufficient cause for world judgment.

Since all Scripture is God-breathed and profitable (2 Tim. 3:16), it would seem that God would have believers understand the truth of Genesis 6:1–4. To say that the passage is unintelligible is an approach no student of the Word should take. It would be best to make a tentative conclusion on the basis of present evidence and trust that further research will eventually shed new light on the problem. I suggest that the angel view, advocated by the rabbinical writers and earliest church fathers, is the best tentative interpretation. The expression *sons of God* is used exclusively in the Old Testament for angels (Job 1:6; 2:1; 38:7). The New Testament writers seem to refer to the angelic sin of Genesis 6 in 2 Peter 2:4 and Jude 6–7. While all four positions have problems, it appears that those of the angel view can be most satisfactorily resolved.

1. While Christ stated that angels do not marry (Matt. 22:30), His point in the context is that the marriage relationship is limited to this earth and has no purpose in heaven where there is no procreation. Jesus was speaking generally of the state of things in heaven without making reference to a perversion that took place on earth.

2. While there are psychological and physiological problems with angelic marriage, such problems are found in connection with other supernatural occurrences in the Bible. Angels ate food in the presence of Abraham (Gen. 18:1–8) and were desired by the men of Sodom (19:1–5).

The severity of God's judgment—the destruction of the human race—suggests the unusual and unprecedented nature of the sin. The intermarriage of human and angelic creatures seems to answer best to the severity of the judgment.

Genesis 6:4

Who were the "Nephilim"?

The answer to this question depends upon one's answer to the previous question, Who were the sons of God? The Hebrew root nph may mean "to fall" or may mean "to fall upon." The Nephilim were those who had "fallen" or those who "fall upon" others. The Nephilim were either contemporaneous with the marriages of 6:2 or were the offspring of those marriages. The latter seems to be suggested by the fact that the word "were" (Gen. 6:4) can best be translated "arose." The term "Nephilim" is used in Numbers 13:33 of the Anakim, who were people of great stature. The interpretation that best corresponds with Numbers 13:33 is that of strength and prowess. The Nephilim were apparently the unnaturally large offspring of the fallen angels and mortal women whose marriages are referred to in Genesis 6:2.

Genesis 6:15

How big was the ark?

The ark that God instructed Noah to build was more like a barge than a ship. Its dimensions are given in "cubits," a unit of measure that approximates 18 inches. On this basis the size of the ark can be calculated as 450 feet long, 75 feet wide, and 45 feet high. The total capacity of the ark would be 1,400,000 cubic feet. This capacity is equivalent to 520 railroad box cars! Genesis 6:16 tells us that the ark had three decks, providing the boat with 101,250 square feet of space.[4] Whitcomb points out that two of every species of air-breathing animal in the world today could be housed in half this available deck space. So there would have been plenty of room for Noah's family, food, the five additional representatives of the animals that could be used for sacrifice (Gen. 7:2), and those that have become extinct since the flood. Contrary to popular thinking, the passengers on the ark did not suffer from lack of space!

Genesis 7:6

Was the flood a worldwide or local occurrence?

While some have argued that the flood was a regional disaster, the following biblical and literary evidence indicates that it was a worldwide event:
  1. *The depth of the water*. The Bible records that all the mountains of the earth were covered (Gen. 7:19).
  2. *The death of all creatures*. The Bible records that all living creatures on the surface of the earth perished (Gen. 7:21).
  3. *The duration of the flood*. The flood lasted over one year (371 days), much longer than would be the case with a regional flood.
  4. *The need for the ark*. Had the flood been only a local event, God could have directed Noah, his family, and the animals to migrate to a safe place.
  5. *The testimony of Peter*. The apostle Peter compares the flood with the

final destruction of the world (2 Peter 3:3–7). Since the latter is clearly universal, we would understand the former to be as well.

6. *The purpose of the flood.* The flood was designed by God to destroy all humankind because the earth was corrupt and filled with violence (Gen. 6:5–7, 11–13).

7. *The literature of other cultures.* With some variations, the account of a great, universal flood is part of the mythology and legend of almost every culture on earth. The Hopi Indians of the American Southwest and the Incas high in the Peruvian Andes have legends of a great flood covering the land and wiping out virtually all life on earth. The ancient Babylonian *Epic of Gilgamesh* tells of a husband and his wife who built a boat and became the sole survivors of a universal flood.

Genesis 9:25

Why did God curse Canaan for Ham's sin?

Genesis 9:20–25 records that after the flood, Noah drank an excess of wine, became drunk, and lay uncovered in his tent. Ham saw the nakedness of his father and reported it to his two brothers, Shem and Japheth, who entered the tent backward and covered their father. When Noah awoke he realized what had happened and prophetically cursed Canaan, Ham's son, and blessed Shem and Japheth. We wonder why Noah cursed Canaan instead of Ham. There are four basic answers to this problem.

Ham's Punishment Transferred to Canaan: According to this view, Canaan was cursed because his father, Ham, had already been blessed (9:1). Since a curse cannot rest where a blessing has been bestowed, Ham was punished by the curse being set upon his youngest son.

Ham Cursed, Not Canaan: Some have suggested that the words, "Cursed be Canaan," should be understood to mean, "cursed be the *father* of Canaan." The original reading was "Ham" but was changed to "Canaan" to conform with the fact that the Canaanites were subjugated by the Israelites in the conquest.

Canaan Cursed for His Own Sin: In order to justify the curse on Canaan, it has been suggested that Canaan was an accessory to his father's sin. It is hypothesized that Canaan saw Noah's nakedness and told Ham.

Canaan's Descendants Cursed, Not Canaan Himself: Ross has argued rather convincingly that the curse was on Canaan's descendants, not Canaan himself.[5] Ross points out that Ham had no respect for his father's nakedness and that this constituted a major step toward moral abandon (compare Lev. 18:2–23). Noah saw in Canaan the evil traits that characterized his father, Ham. This moral abandon and sexual perversion marked Canaan's descendants as well (vv. 24–30).

The curse, then, is not directed against the man Canaan, but against the Canaanite people—the descendants of Canaan many generations later. The Canaanites were to suffer the curse of conquest—not because of the sins of

Ham but because they themselves acted like their ancestor, Ham, with moral abandon. The curse on Canaan's descendants was a prophecy and a judgment that was fulfilled in the conquest of the land by Joshua.

Genesis 17:13

Why did God choose "circumcision" as the sign of His covenant with Abraham?

The English word *circumcise* is derived from the Latin, meaning "to cut around." This refers to the removal of the foreskin of the male penis. This is a common practice among many African, South American, and Middle Eastern peoples, including Jews and Muslims.

The Lord introduced the practice of circumcision to the Hebrews as the sign of His promise to Abraham (Gen. 17:10–14). Circumcision is commanded in the law codes of the Old Testament (Exod. 12:48; Lev. 12:3) and was practiced by the Hebrews (Exod. 4:24–26; Josh. 5:2–7). The rite of circumcision was a sign that one was a member of the covenant community of Israel, that one was separated from the world and dedicated to God's will. Among the Jews it was a mark of distinction. The uncircumcised were viewed with contempt.

Ethnocentrism blinded many descendants of Abraham to the real meaning of the rite, and it became an external practice without any spiritual content. Therefore, Moses and Jeremiah spoke of "circumcision of the heart" (Deut. 10:16; 30:6; Jer. 4:4; 9:25–26). Accordingly, it was not the outward act, but the inward reality for which it stood that counted most with God (compare Rom. 2:28–29). True circumcision is of the heart, not the flesh.

Returning to our question, why circumcision? Why not some other sign (like the rainbow) that is not so hidden and personal? First, circumcision is a sign on the male member, which is consistent with the patriarchal leadership in the Old Testament. The male bears the sign of the covenant and leads the family spiritually. Second, circumcision requires shedding blood. And the shedding of blood is associated with covenant-making in the Old Testament and the ancient Near East. Third, circumcision consecrates the sexual function of the male to the Lord. God placed the Israelites in the middle of a land where people worshiped Baal, Asherah, and Astarte through sexual rites. Cultic prostitution was entrenched in Canaanite worship and culture. By placing the sign on the sexual organ, God was reminding the Israelite males that their bodies were devoted to the Lord and were not to be used in the worship of Canaanite deities, nor were sexual rites to have any place in the worship of Yahweh (compare Exod. 19:15; 20:26).

Genesis 22:2

How could God command Abraham to offer a human sacrifice?

Human sacrifice is clearly condemned in the Torah and throughout the Old Testament (Lev. 18:21). Anyone who offered a child as a sacrifice was to be stoned to death (20:2–5). Nevertheless, human sacrifice was practiced by the Canaanites and by the Israelites as well. Ahaz and Manasseh made their sons "pass through the fire" (2 Kings 16:3; 21:6), a euphemism for infant sacrifice by fire.

Is God calling Abraham to do what He has clearly prohibited? The key to answering this question is to appreciate the fact that this incident in the life of Abraham is designed by God as a test (Gen. 22:1). Abraham did not know it at the time, but the narrator clearly wants the reader to understand that God did not intend for the Patriarch to sacrifice his son.

Kaiser points out that the term *nissah* (test) is used eight times in the Hebrew Bible referring to a testing in relationship to obedience to God's commandments, statutes, or laws.[6] In commanding Abraham to sacrifice his son, God was testing Abraham's faith and obedience. Abraham passed God's test by demonstrating obedient faith when he offered up Isaac (Heb. 11:17–19). God, who never intended for Abraham to sacrifice his son, provided a ram to take Isaac's place on the altar and blessed Abraham for his obedience (Gen. 22:16–18).

Genesis 23:11

If Ephron the Hittite offered to "give" Abraham the field and cave for the burial of Sarah, why did Abraham insist on paying for it?

This is a good example of ancient bargaining. Ephron knew that Abraham needed the field and was politely offering Abraham the opportunity to have it. He knew, of course, that Abraham was a man of integrity and would not take advantage of his generous "gift." Abraham, displaying integrity, offered to buy the field at whatever price Ephron would ask. In the end, Abraham paid four hundred silver shekels for the field and cave at Machpelah.

This kind of bargaining still goes on today in the shops in the Old City of Jerusalem. Don't be surprised if a merchant offers you the merchandise for "free." He knows you will insist on paying for it.

Genesis 30:37–42

Why did Jacob's strange method of getting off-color goats and sheep seem to work? Is there any scientific basis for this?

Jacob made Laban a proposal that his uncle could not resist. He agreed to remain and work for Laban if all the off-color sheep and goats would become his. With few exceptions, sheep are born white and goats are black. Jacob asked for the white and spotted goats and black sheep. Why would he make such an offer? He had a scheme to outwit Laban!

Jacob sought to better his chances of getting off-color animals by placing peeled, white-striped branches before the animals as they mated. This rather devious action was based on superstition and is completely unscientific. This plan could not have effected the markings of the animals. However, God prospered Jacob in spite of this deficiency, and the spotted and striped animals became numerous. God gave Jacob success in spite of himself. Jacob later recognized that his success and prosperity were from God (Gen. 31:5, 7, 9; 33:11).

Genesis 32:24

Why did God allow Jacob to wrestle with Him all night long when the match could have been concluded in an instant?

According to Hosea 12:4, the one with whom Jacob wrestled was an angel. Yet Jacob clearly recognized this one to be divine (Gen. 32:30). The name given to Jacob—*Israel* (he who strives with God)—suggests as well that Jacob wrestled with God. Certainly God could have ended the wrestling match in an instant. Why did He allow it to continue?

The background of the incident is the key. Jacob was returning from Paddan-aram and was "greatly afraid and distressed" (v. 7) over his impending meeting with Esau, whom he had deprived of the birthright. God had assured Jacob of His blessing and protection (28:14; 32:12), but Jacob was still fearful.

During the nightlong wrestling match God was teaching Jacob a lesson. Jacob had nothing to fear. He was wrestling with *God* and winning! Like a father wrestling with his child, God was letting Jacob win. God was letting Jacob win to teach him a spiritual lesson. Jacob has God's promise, presence, and protection. Jacob is powerful enough to wrestle with God and win! As dawn was breaking, God ended the match by touching Jacob's thigh and displaying His power. But He gave Jacob a new name to help him remember that he had nothing to fear. Jacob became Israel, for he had "striven with God" and "prevailed" (32:28).

Genesis 38:9

What was Onan's sin?

When Judah's firstborn son, Er, died childless, Judah instructed his second son, Onan, to marry Tamar, Er's widow. This custom was in keeping with the law of levirate marriage revealed to Israel in Deuteronomy 25:5–10. The term levirate is from the Latin *levir,* meaning "husband's brother." The purpose of this unusual custom was to preserve the name and the inheritance of the dead brother. By legal fiction, the firstborn son of the levirate marriage would be named son of the dead brother and would inherit the dead man's property. This custom provides important background for the answer to this question.

According to the custom of levirate marriage, Onan was responsible to produce a son through Tamar, his dead brother's widow. He knew that the offspring would not be considered legally his and did not wish to perform this levirate duty. To prevent Tamar's conception, Onan practiced *coitus interruptus.* Genesis 38:9 records that he "wasted his seed on the ground, in order not to give offspring to his brother."

Onan's refusal to perform his levirate responsibility was a sin against his family and his brother's widow. Perhaps he was selfishly coveting the firstborn's portion for himself, hoping to inherit the property of the deceased brother (compare Num. 27:8–9). God judged Onan with death not because he practiced contraception but because of his selfishness and greed.

Genesis 49:3–4

Who was Jacob's heir and recipient of the patriarchal promise?

Genesis 49 contains the prophetic blessing of Jacob on his twelve sons. Which one of these sons became his heir and the recipient of the promise first given to Abraham (Gen. 12:1–3)?

Jacob's firstborn son, Reuben, is said to have been disqualified because of his immorality with Bilhah, his father's concubine (35:22; 49:3–4). Jacob's next two sons, Simeon and Levi, were also disqualified because of their excessive revenge against the Shechemites who had raped their sister Dinah (34:25–30; 49:5–7). Next in line for the position as heir is Judah, the fourth son. Genesis 49:10 promises that the "scepter" and "ruler's staff" shall not depart from Judah. These emblems of royalty suggest that Judah became Jacob's heir. This is confirmed by 1 Chronicles 5:2, "Judah prevailed over his brothers and from him came the leader *[nagid]*."

But one might be inclined to ask, Where does Joseph fit in? Didn't Jacob favor him (Gen. 37:3) and adopt his two sons (48:5)? In ancient times, the birthright meant becoming the chief heir and receiving a double portion of the inheritance. In this case, the double portion went to the sons of Joseph, who took his place as tribal leaders in Israel (1 Chron. 5:1). But Judah became the chief heir and inherited the patriarchal promise. He is the ancestor of King David and Messiah Jesus (Matt. 1:2, 6).

Genesis 49:10

What is the meaning of the term "Shiloh"? Is this a messianic prophecy?

Genesis 49:8–10 records Jacob's prophetic blessing on Judah. Here Judah is promised supremacy over his brothers and is likened to a lion that none dare arouse. He is designated as the possessor of royal emblems, "the scepter" and "the ruler's staff . . . until Shiloh comes."

It should first be noted that this "Shiloh" is not a reference to the place where the ark was kept before the capture of Jerusalem (Josh. 18:1), for the spelling of that name is different in the Hebrew. The traditional viewpoint, both of Christian and Jewish interpreters, is that "Shiloh" is a proper designation for the coming Messiah. Recent scholarship suggests that the Hebrew *shiloh* is not a personal name or a title, but the relative pronoun *shi*, a preposition, *le*, and the pronominal suffix *oh* and should be rendered "to whom it belongs." In other words, the scepter and the ruler's staff would remain in the tribe of Judah until the one comes "to whom it belongs."[7] This is a veiled prophecy to the coming of the Messiah, who will rule and reign over His theocratic kingdom.

Endnotes

1. Charles Ryrie, *A Survey of Bible Doctrine* (Chicago: Moody Press), 105.
2. Susan T. Foh, "What Is the Woman's Desire?" *Westminister Theological Journal* 37 (spring 1975): 376–83.
3. John H. Sailhamer, "Commentary on Genesis," *The Expositor's Bible Commentary*, vol. 2 (Grand Rapids: Zondervan, 1990), 76–77.
4. John C. Whitcomb Jr., *The World That Perished* (Winona Lake, Ind.: BMH Books, 1973), 23.
5. Allen P. Ross, "The Curse on Canaan," *Bibliotheca Sacra* (July–September 1980), 223–240.
6. Walter C. Kaiser Jr., *Toward Old Testament Ethics* (Grand Rapids: Zondervan, 1983), 263.
7. Allen P. Ross, *Creation and Blessing* (Grand Rapids: Baker Book House, 1988), 703.

EXODUS

Exodus 1:5

What was the number of Jacob's descendants who entered Egypt?

Exodus 1:5 states that seventy descendants of Jacob entered the land of Egypt while Genesis 46:26 gives the total as sixty-six. To the number "sixty-six" we need to add Joseph, his two sons (v. 27) Ephraim and Manasseh, and Jacob himself, for a total of seventy. Interestingly, the Septuagint version of Exodus 1:5; Acts 7:14, and one Hebrew manuscript from Qumran gives the number as seventy-five. This figure is based on the Septuagint's listing of Joseph's three grandsons and two great-grandsons in Genesis 46:20.

Exodus 1:8

Who was the pharaoh who did not know Joseph?

The Bible does not identify this ruler by name, but it has been suggested by historians that the pharaoh who "knew not Joseph" was Ahmoses I (about 1570–1548 B.C.), who founded the Eighteenth Dynasty and drove the Hyksos, "foreign rulers," from Egypt.[1] He was probably prejudiced against all Semites because of the recent Hyksos (a Semitic people) domination. He instigated oppressive measures against the Hebrews to make sure that Egypt would not fall under foreign rule again.

Exodus 1:19–20

Did God bless the Hebrew midwives for lying?

When the pharaoh instituted his oppressive measures against the Israelites, the Hebrew midwives were instructed to put male babies to death. But the midwives "feared God" and let the little boys live (1:17). When questioned by the pharaoh they explained that the Hebrew women were more vigorous than Egyptians and the babies were delivered before the midwives arrived (v. 19). The narrator then comments, "So God was good to the midwives" (v. 20).

While one might argue that God blessed their lie, the text does not suggest this conclusion. Twice it is stated that the midwives "feared God" (vv. 17, 21). Verse 21 makes it clear that their households were established because "the midwives feared God." The text does not endorse a lie but commends the fear of God and the sanctity of human life.

Exodus 3:13–15

What is the meaning and significance of God's name?

When the Lord told Moses to return to Egypt and report that God had appointed him to lead the Israelites out of their bondage, he raised a legitimate question. What if the people ask, "What is His name?" Moses wanted to be able to validate his call and commissioning by naming the One in whom his authority rested. In Exodus 3:14–15 God revealed to Moses the memorial name by which He wanted to be remembered for all generations. The term I AM is the first person form of the Hebrew verb *hayah*, "to be." God's actual name, translated "Lord," is *Yahweh*. This is the third-person form of the verb *hayah* and could well be translated "He is." The name implies that God is the Self-Existent One. And He exists not for His own sake only, but for the sake of His people!

Why is the name Yahweh so foreign sounding and unfamiliar to us? It began as a matter of reverence for God. Since it was blasphemous to misuse the name of God (Exod. 20:7; Lev. 24:10–23), some Jews figured that it would be better to avoid using it at all. Instead of using the name Yahweh, the Jews substituted the designation *Adonai,* meaning "Lord." Eventually God's name was pronounced only by the high priests during their benedictions on the Day of Atonement. In ancient times it was pronounced distinctly, then later in a whisper, lost among the sounds of the priests' instruments as they accompanied the benediction.[2]

In the 1500s an attempt was made to reintroduce the name of God by combining the name Yahweh with the designation *Adonai.* The composite name appeared as "Jehovah." Sadly, this was an unintentional devaluation of the name of God. Names are important to people, and God's name is important to Him. As God's people, we should know and use His memorial name, Yahweh.

Exodus 3:18

Did God suggest that Moses should deceive Pharaoh by requesting merely a three-day journey into the wilderness?

God directed Moses to return to Egypt and ask the pharaoh to grant the Hebrews the opportunity to make a "three days' journey" into the wilderness that they may sacrifice to Yahweh. It has been suggested that God was instructing Moses to deceive Pharaoh so that the Israelites might escape. Would God encourage deception and lying?

The clear teaching of Scripture is that the Lord is the "God of truth" (Isa. 65:16) and that His people should speak the truth (Eph. 4:15). I suggest what we have here is an example of oriental bargaining. You will see such negotiation taking place in the Old City of Jerusalem where tourists haggle with Arab shopkeepers over the price of an item. The buyer starts low and works up through offer and counteroffer to an acceptable price. And so here, Moses is instructed to ask for a three-day journey as the first step in the negotiations for full release.

Exodus 4:21

Why did God "harden" Pharaoh's heart? Is it right for God to harden people's hearts so that they will not respond?

In His final instructions concerning the Exodus, God told Moses that in spite of the wonders that Pharaoh would see, He would "harden his heart" so that Pharaoh would not let the people go (Exod. 4:21).

It is important to note at the beginning that there are three different expressions used in Exodus regarding the hardening of Pharaoh's heart. First, God would harden Pharaoh's heart (v. 21). Second, Pharaoh would harden his own heart (8:15). Third, Pharaoh's heart was hardened (7:13). Putting these ideas together, I suggest that the hardening of Pharaoh's heart was a divine judgment on the one who was already hardening his own heart against the Lord. Romans 9:17–18 reveals that this was all part of God's sovereign plan for the accomplishment of His will. Although God was judicially involved in the hardening of Pharaoh's heart, Pharaoh was not a mere pawn in some divine game. He stood responsible for his own hardening and rejection of God.

Exodus 4:24–26

Why did God try to put Moses to death?

The passage in question has baffled interpreters throughout the centuries. Moses was on his way back to Egypt to lead the Israelites out of that land when he encountered a *theophany*—an appearance of God. But this wasn't an inspiring event for Moses, for Yahweh "sought to put him to death" (Exod. 4:24). Most interpreters agree that a neglect of circumcision lies at the background of Moses' near-death experience. This is evidenced by the fact that the Lord left Moses alone after the circumcision was performed (v. 26).

The sign of circumcision was instituted by God as the sign of His promise to Abraham (Gen. 17:9–14). Boy babies were to be circumcised on the eighth day after birth. Apparently the circumcision of Moses' son was neglected. This may have been to accommodate the wishes of Zipporah. As a Midianite, she may have wanted to wait until the child was thirteen, as is the custom among bedouin tribes today. The required ritual had been neglected and God was holding Moses responsible (v. 14). This compromise nearly cost Moses his life!

But Moses was apparently too sick to perform the ritual and so Zipporah proceeded to do so. But her revulsion and disgust with baby circumcision is reflected by her words, "You are indeed a bridegroom of blood to me" (Exod. 4:25). Most scholars conclude that these words are spoken to Moses. Allen has proposed that these words are addressed to Yahweh and reflect Zipporah's contempt for the God who required baby circumcision.[3] The expression, "bridegroom of blood," may be rendered "bloody bride-father," indicating that Yahweh was like the circumcisers of Zipporah's culture, demanding circumcision of the groom just before marriage.

When the ritual was completed, Zipporah took the bloody foreskin and "made it touch at his feet" (literal Heb., v. 25). While most conclude that the pronoun "his" refers to Moses, Allen offers the intriguing suggestion that it refers to Yahweh, with whom Zipporah was angry over being forced to perform the circumcision on her child.

Exodus 7:11

How did Pharaoh's court magicians manage to duplicate Moses' miracle of turning his staff into a snake?

Before Moses' second encounter with Pharaoh, the Lord gave Moses the power to perform a miracle that would help Pharaoh recognize that Moses was not someone to ignore. When thrown down, Moses' staff would become a serpent. Unfortunately, the miracle was replicated by Pharaoh's court magicians. How did they do this?

The biblical text does not tell how the staffs of the court magicians became serpents. But numerous suggestions have been offered: (1) optical illusion; (2) slight of hand; (3) charming through drugs; and (4) demonic influence. Several Egyptian scarabs have been found that depict a snake charmer holding up a serpent made stiff as a staff before some observing deities. Whatever the magicians did, it was enough to satisfy Pharaoh and harden his unbelieving heart (Exod. 7:13).

Exodus 7:17–20

Did the Nile River really turn to blood?

The first plague on Egypt was the turning of the waters of the Nile to *dam,* "blood." Was this actual blood with red corpuscles? It has been pointed out by many geologists that an unusually high Nile flood brings tons of red soil down from the mountain highlands of equatorial Africa. The higher the inundation, the deeper the color of the red waters. Following this view, the waters of the Nile were reddish in color but were not blood.

There are several problems with this view. First, it doesn't fully explain the text. The Lord told Moses that this judgment would fall upon the rivers, streams, pools, reservoirs, and water vessels (Exod. 7:19). All water sources, not just the Nile, were affected. Second, the discoloration of the Nile from silting does not normally kill all the fish and render the water "foul" (v. 18). Third, the discoloration of the Nile from silting is a gradual process, not an immediate event that would stun or persuade Pharaoh.

With Davis, I agree that it is not necessary for us to conclude that the water was turned into literal human or animal blood.[4] The point here is that it had the appearance and effect of blood, becoming foul and killing the fish. We don't fully understand how the miracle took place, but that is the nature of miracles.

Exodus 16:14

What was the "manna" that the Lord provided for His people in the wilderness?

During Israel's wilderness sojourn, God provided His people with a desert diet of "manna." The word *manna* is taken from the question raised by the Israelites who first saw it. They asked, *man hu,* literally rendered, "What is it?" This has been brought into English as "manna."

The manna was fine flakes that appeared like frost on the ground (Exod. 16:14). It was amber in appearance (Num. 11:7) and tasted like "cakes baked with oil" (v. 8). It could be baked, boiled, or eaten without any preparation. The provision of manna was from God, not Moses (John 6:32), and was intended to teach the people of Israel an important spiritual lesson: "that man does not live by bread alone, but . . . by everything that proceeds out of the mouth of the Lord" (Deut. 8:3).

Exodus 18:2–6

What happened to Moses' wife?

Exodus 18:2 records that Moses "had sent away" his wife, Zipporah, apparently while he was in Egypt preparing for the Exodus. She, with their two sons, Gershom and Eliezer, had gone back to Jethro while Moses took leadership of the nation of Israel. The passage records how Moses was now reunited with his wife and family at Mount Sinai (vv. 5–6).

The Bible does not tell us why Moses sent Zipporah and the children away. Perhaps the pressures of his ministry were overwhelming and he felt that he could not give his attention to his family at this time. There is no indication from this passage that their separation was permanent or ended in divorce. This is the last mention of Zipporah in the Bible.

Exodus 19:15

Why did God warn the people at Mount Sinai not to "go near a woman"?

As the people of Israel were preparing to enter into a covenant relationship with Yahweh, they were instructed "Be ready for the third day; do not go near a woman." This is correctly understood to be a prohibition against sexual relations. Does this mean that there is something wrong with the sexual relationship of a married couple?

The prohibition must be understood within the context of the Canaanite culture that surrounded the Israelites at this time. At the center of Canaanite religion was the fertility cult. It was believed that the gods Baal, Asherah, and Anath controlled the fertility of the land. The worshipers of these sordid deities would engage in sacred prostitution to encourage the gods and goddesses to copulate and thus bring fertility to the land.

By prohibiting sexual relations at the time of their entering into the covenant with the Lord, Yahweh was emphasizing to His people that sexual activity had no place in the worship of the one true God.

Exodus 20:5

Is it fair of God to punish children for the sins of their fathers?

The second commandment in the Decalogue calls for Israel's exclusive worship of Yahweh. The Israelites were prohibited from making or worshiping idols. The consequences of disobeying this command appears to effect the offspring of the disobedient. The words, "visiting the iniquity of the fathers on the children, on the third and the fourth generations," seem to be an unwarranted judgment on children for sins they were not responsible for—sins committed by their ancestors. This just doesn't seem fair or just.

Often a problem passage can be illuminated through another text of Scripture. For example, Deuteronomy 24:16 records, "Fathers shall not be put to death for their sons, nor shall sons be put to death for their fathers; everyone shall be put to death for his own sin." Ezekiel 18:1–20 and Jeremiah 31:29–30 lend support in affirming the principle of an individual's responsibility for his or her own sin.

In view of these rather clear and direct statements of Scripture, I suggest that Exodus 20:5 is addressing the issue of temporal consequences rather than personal judgment. The one who sins will be judged for the sin. But the consequences of someone's sinful actions may be experienced by friends, family members, and children. A child may suffer fetal alcohol syndrome because of the sinful indulgence by the mother. God holds the mother responsible, but the child inevitably suffers.

Exodus 20:26

What is the issue behind the instruction that a priest not expose God's altar to his nakedness?

This concern for "nakedness" must be set in the context of ancient Canaanite religion where ritual nakedness and sexual activity was an essential feature of the cult. Sex was the primary function of the Canaanite goddesses Astarte, Anath, and Asherah, whose sexual organs are accentuated in the various representations that have been found by archaeologists. Sacred prostitution, as was practiced by Canaanite worshipers, was intended to encourage sexual relations among the gods and goddesses and thus bring fertility to the earth.

The instruction in Exodus 20:26 is intended to emphasize to the Israelites that cultic nakedness has no place in the worship of Yahweh. As a further precaution, Moses instructed the priests to make "linen breeches" to be worn under their robes and cover their bare flesh (28:42–43).

Exodus 21:22

Does this verse provide any biblical basis for the practice of abortion?

Exodus 21:22 is set in the context of the law of retaliation, which was intended to set reasonable limits on the measure of punishment that could be exacted from someone guilty of causing injury to another person. Here a case is considered where a man accidentally strikes a pregnant woman. Some scholars have concluded from this text that the unborn child is merely potential human life. It is concluded that since the punishment for accidentally killing an unborn child is less severe than the punishment for killing an adult, the unborn baby must be considered less than human. According to this view, abortion does not constitute the termination of human life and is not unscriptural.

This view has two major difficulties—one in the interpretation and the other in the application of the text. *Shakol,* the usual Hebrew word for "miscarry" (Gen. 31:38; Exod. 23:26; Job. 3:16) is not used in Exodus 21:22. The verb *yatzah,* translated "has a miscarriage" (NASB) literally means "her children come out" and is customarily used for live births (Gen. 25:26; 38:28–30; Job 3:11; Jer. 1:5). The text clearly speaks of premature birth rather than miscarriage.

It should be noted that the text makes no distinction between harm done to the child and harm done to the mother. Two possible situations are contemplated—an accident in which no harm comes to the mother or child and an accident in which the mother or child is injured. The accident without injury results in a mere fine, probably imposed because of the danger to which the mother and child are exposed. In the case of an accident with some injury— to the mother, her child, or both—the law of retaliation is to be applied.

A second difficulty with the "miscarriage" approach to this verse is in the application to abortion. Even if it could be demonstrated that the text refers to accidental miscarriage rather than premature birth, it could not be used to justify abortion. First, the injury is accidental, not intentional as in abortion. Second, though unintentional, the action was considered wrongdoing and punishable by law. Third, while the text may not expressly prohibit abortion, neither does it grant authority to perform abortion. The sanctity of human life—both born and unborn—is strongly affirmed throughout the Bible.[5]

Exodus 22:25

Does the prohibition against charging interest apply to us?

The prohibition found in Exodus 22:25 is set in the context of the proper treatment of strangers, widows, orphans, poor, or otherwise disadvantaged persons. Within that context, the Lord instructed Israel not to charge interest when loaning money to the poor. The main point here is that the Israelites are not to take advantage of someone's poverty as an opportunity for personal enrichment. If someone needs money to buy bread or clothing, the money was to be loaned interest free.

Collecting interest from a bank on your savings deposit is an investment and a business arrangement from which both parties benefit. Such an arrangement does not take advantage of another's poverty and is not prohibited here.

Exodus 23:28

What were the "hornets" that God sent ahead of His people in the conquest?

In Exodus 23:27–31 the Lord explains the provision He would make to ensure Israel a successful conquest of Canaan. He promises to throw the enemies into confusion and cause them to flee. In addition, He promises to "send hornets" ahead of the Israelites to "drive out the Hivites, the Canaanites, and the Hittites." What were these "hornets"?

Since the bee or wasp was a sacred symbol of the pharaoh, it has been suggested that the hornets refer to the Egyptian army steadily raiding Canaan year after year, weakening the inhabitants before Israel's conquest. However, Deuteronomy 7:20 indicates that the hornet was still future on the eve of the conquest. A more likely interpretation is that the hornets should be understood figuratively in terms of what they represent. Swarms of stinging hornets engulfing unsuspecting people cause panic and flight. In the previous verse, the Lord promises to send His "terror" ahead of the Israelites, throwing the Canaanites into "confusion." Davis notes that fear and panic played a strategic role in the Israelite victories both in Transjordan and Canaan[6] (Num. 22:3; Josh. 2:9, 11; 5:1; 9:24).

Exodus 24:9–10

How is it possible that Moses, the priests, and the elders of Israel "saw the God of Israel" at Mount Sinai?

The Bible is quite clear that "God is spirit" (John 4:24) and possesses no physical body. He is referred to by Paul as the "invisible God" (Col. 1:15; 1 Tim. 1:17). And yet it is recorded in Scripture that certain individuals saw God. Theologians have come to call such events *theophanies*. A *theophany* is simply "an appearance of God." God, who is invisible and without a material body, sometimes chooses to manifest Himself through a vision (Ezek. 1) or in physical form (Isa. 6). I believe that these appearances of God are manifestations of Christ, the second person of the Trinity, before His incarnation.

Moses and the leaders of Israel were privileged to witness a visible manifestation of God. They even saw his "feet" (Exod. 24:10). Moses was later granted the opportunity to see God's "back," but not His face (33:20–23). These words emphasize the immanence of God. Although He is holy and transcendent, He is willing to come near and let Himself be known to His people.

Endnotes

1. *The Biblical World*, 1966 ed., s.v. "Egypt," 211.
2. Alfred Edersheim, *The Temple* (Grand Rapids: Eerdmans, 1958), 310–11.
3. Ronald B. Allen, "A Pericope of Mystery: Who [or What] is 'The Bloody Bridegroom'—Exodus 4:24–26," *Bibliotheca Sacra*.
4. John J. Davis, *Moses and the Gods of Egypt* (Grand Rapids: Baker Book House, 1971), 93.
5. For further study, see my article "The Abortion Epidemic: America's Silent Holocaust," in *Vital Contemporary Issues,* ed. Roy B. Zuck (Grand Rapids: Kregel Publications, 1994), 33–45.
6. Davis, *Gods of Egypt,* 238.

LEVITICUS

Theme

What is the meaning of the term holy, *which is used so frequently in this book?*

The word *qodesh*, "holy," which appears about ninety times in the book of Leviticus, has the basic meaning of "separateness" (Lev. 20:26). Holiness is the opposite of *hol* (profane), meaning "not separate" or "common." That which is holy is marked off, separated, and withdrawn from ordinary use. At its basic meaning *holiness* is not primarily a moral concept, though ethical or moral holiness is often an outgrowth of the idea of separateness. The fact that holiness does not necessarily refer to moral purity is seen in the application of the concept to the Canaanite temple prostitute who was separated for religious service and called a *q'desha*, "holy one" (Deut. 23:18). When holiness means separation to God, a morally righteous being, the concept takes on the implication of moral purity—conformity to God's righteous standards and statutes (Lev. 20:7–8).

Three aspects of holiness occur in relationship to the individual believer. First, there is *positional* holiness based on new birth. Second, there is *final* holiness that takes place when we become glorified like Christ. Third, there is *experiential* holiness that involves the process of conforming our daily lives to our position in Christ.

Leviticus 1:4

What is the meaning of the expression, "to make atonement"?

The Hebrew term *kipper*, "to make atonement," appears 150 times in the Bible, 49 times in Leviticus alone. Early scholars suggested that this word was derived from an Arabic root *(kappara)* meaning "cover" or "conceal." According to this view, atonement involves pacifying God through covering sin. Some scholars have suggested that the word *atonement* is derived from an Assyrian root *(kuppuru)* meaning "to cleanse" or "to wipe clean." This idea seems to suit contexts where the altar or sanctuary is the direct object of the verb and the action results in the cleansing of the holy object. More recent scholarship is suggesting that the word *atonement* is derived from the Hebrew word *kopher*, meaning "ransom" or "ransom price." Accordingly, "to make atonement" means to pay a ransom. Sin and defilement, deserving of judgment by death, is removed by the payment of a ransom through sacrifice. In the ritual of sacrifice, the life of an animal, symbolized by its blood, is exchanged for the life of the worshiper. An innocent life is exchanged for the life of the guilty.

Leviticus 4:20

Did the old covenant sacrifices secure forgiveness of sin?

The sacrifices and offerings of the old covenant expressed a need for the removal of sin that they could not ultimately satisfy. The writer of Hebrews makes it clear that "it is impossible for the blood of bulls and goats to take away sins" (Heb. 10:4). The sacrifices of the old covenant point to the person and work of Christ, who offered Himself as a better and final sacrifice (9:13–14; 10:10).

The old covenant sacrifices expressed the faith of the Israelites who looked to God for forgiveness and cleansing from sin. While the old covenant sacrifices did not secure forgiveness, they constituted an expression of faith and were token payment for sin, which God accepted until the better and final sacrifice—Christ's blood—could be offered. When God accepted a sacrifice and granted forgiveness to an old covenant believer, it was as if God were saying, "That is enough for now. One day the penalty for sin will be paid in full." There was forgiveness of sin through the old covenant sacrifices, but Christ's blood ultimately paid the penalty for sin that God demanded.

Leviticus 10:1–11

What was the sin of Nadab and Abihu that cost them their lives?

Leviticus chapter 10 is set in strong contrast with chapters 8–9. In 8:4 we read that Moses "did just as the LORD commanded him." In 9:10 we read that Aaron did "just as the LORD had commanded Moses." Now in 10:1 we read that Aaron's sons, Nadab and Abihu, did something that the Lord "had not commanded them." The nature of their sin is not fully explained. After the Lord sent fire from heaven to consume the sacrifice on the altar, Nadab and Abihu put fire in their firepans and "offered strange fire before the LORD." Suddenly, fire came from the presence of the Lord and the two sons of Aaron were burned to death.

Most commentators suppose that their sin consisted in the fact that they did not take the fire for the incense from the incense altar. However, this was never commanded and the requirement is only inferred from the priest's offering on the Day of Atonement (Lev. 16:12). The context is the key to the problem here. The shouting of the people (9:24) may have encouraged Nadab and Abihu to take some personal liberties, offering incense at an improper time and in an improper manner. The fire they offered is called "strange" in the sense that it was unauthorized. This offering was their own little improvement on what God had prescribed.

Moses explains the basis for the judgment in verse 3. The Lord said, "By those who come near Me I will be treated as holy, and before all the people I will be honored." Apparently these young men failed to treat God as holy and so God demonstrated His own holiness through judgment. While the judgment seems rather severe, that is probably because we don't fully appreciate the seriousness of God's holiness. Defending His reputation for holiness required more than a slap on the wrist. The deaths of Nadab and Abihu leave us in awe of the awful holiness of God.

The prohibition against using any intoxicating drink while ministering before the Lord (10:9–10) may offer a small clue as to the reason for Nadab's and Abihu's failure. Those who perform holy service before the Lord must do so with clear minds (Prov. 20:1; compare 1 Tim. 3:3).

Leviticus 11:1–23

Why were the people of Israel prohibited from eating certain foods?

When God created the animals, He created them equal. The Creation account in Genesis makes no distinction between clean and unclean animals. But at the time when Noah was preparing the ark, God instructed him to take on the ark seven pairs of every "clean animal" and one pair of those that are "not clean." This was so that there would be animals for food and for sacrifice after the flood (Gen. 8:20; 9:3).

The distinction between the clean and unclean animals is elaborated in the Mosaic Law. Those designated clean animals are the ones that have split hoofs and chew the cud (Lev. 11:2). Certain other animals, birds, and fish are forbidden, including the pig, the vulture, and eels. These regulations may have promoted healthy living, but health needs were not God's primary motivation in giving these commands. These regulations were intended to set Israel apart as a people distinct from the idolatrous nations that surrounded them. These regulations must be understood in the light of later revelation, like the vision of Peter (Acts 10:11–16) and Mark's comment on the words of Jesus, "Thus He declared all foods clean" (Mark 7:19).

Wenham points out that as soon as all nations could belong to the people of God, "those food laws which had symbolized Israel's election and served to separate her from the nations became irrelevant."[1]

Leviticus 12:2

Why would childbirth render a woman unclean under the old covenant?

From an Old Testament perspective, children are regarded as a blessing from the Lord (Pss. 127:3; 128:3 and the following verses) and barrenness is considered a reproach (Gen. 30:24). If children are such a blessing, then why is childbirth defiling?

The answer to this question must be traced to the fall of humankind and the curse that came upon Adam and Eve. Recall that as a consequence of their sin, pain and suffering would accompany motherhood, and birth would be ultimately followed by death (3:16–19). Hence, according to the law, everything connected with procreation—including childbirth, menstruation, and seminal emission—rendered people unfit for the performance of their religious duties. The law concerning the uncleanness of a woman after childbirth provided an important teaching lesson for Israel. The uncleanness served as a reminder of Adam's sin and the spiritual uncleanness that it brought to the human race.

It is important to remember that the defilement of childbirth is a ceremonial rather than a moral issue. The defilement relates to the woman's participation in worship not to her moral standing before God.

Leviticus 12:4–5

Why is the period of a mother's uncleanness doubled when she gives birth to a female child?

The text indicates that a mother would be unclean for a total of forty days after the birth of a baby boy (v. 4) but for eighty days after the birth of a little girl (v. 5). It has been suggested that this law was an accommodation to a belief held in antiquity that bleeding continued longer after the birth of a little girl. There appears to be no scientific or medical evidence for this view. One might speculate that the double period of uncleanness relates somehow to a woman's part in the Fall. The fact is, we just don't know a good answer to this question. Perhaps the reason was known and understood by those living in antiquity and we have lost it through time and distance.

Leviticus 13:47; 14:34

How can a garment or a house contract leprosy?

Leviticus 13–14 records the regulations for dealing with leprous persons and things. Leprosy, or Hansen's disease as we know it today, is a neurological disfunction that results in the loss of feeling to body extremities. Deformity occurs when the tissues of these extremities, like the fingers or ears, are damaged and deteriorate due to the inability of the victim to sense any pain.

The term *zara't,* "leprosy," as it is used in the biblical world included all kinds of skin diseases, dermatitis, fungus, and mold. Consequently, there could be leprosy on a garment, an article of leather, the wall of a house, or on a person.

Leviticus 16:10

What is the meaning and function of the "scapegoat" on Israel's Day of Atonement?

Among the sacrifices presented on the Day of Atonement was a live goat that was to be released into the wilderness. The goat is referred to by the Hebrew term *'azazel.* There is quite a lot of debate over the meaning of this word. Some have suggested that *'azazel* was a demon living in the wilderness (Lev. 17:7; Isa. 13:21). According to this view, the goat was not a gift to 'azazel, but the sins of Israel were being sent back to their author. Such a ritual could have been easily misunderstood as a gift to the demon, something clearly forbidden (Lev. 17:7).

It has been suggested that the term 'azazel is based on an Arabic root meaning "to remove," or "rough ground," but Arabic roots are doubtful. I suggest that 'azazel is based on the Hebrew words for "goat" ('ez) and "to go away" ('azal) and simply means "the goat that has gone away." This view is reflected in the Septuagint and Latin Vulgate. It is from this idea that the English "scapegoat" is derived.

Whatever the exact meaning of the term 'azazel, there is no doubt as to the meaning of the ceremony. The function of the goat was to bear away the sins of Israel. The laying on of hands by the priest signified the identification of the goat with the sinful people. The ritual indicated "This goat represents Israel." The confession of sins over the head of the goat signified the transference of sins to the animal. The sins of the people were placed on the back of a substitute. Bearing the iniquities of the people, the goat was led into the wilderness. The Mishnah records that the goat was led to a steep cliff and was pushed over backward to kill it (*Yoma* 6.6). The Mishnah also records that a scarlet cord was tied to the horn of the goat. Another was tied to the door of the sanctuary. When the goat reached the wilderness, the cord turned white to symbolize the promise of purification from sin (*Yoma* 4.2; 6.8; Isa. 1:18). But this miracle ceased forty years before the destruction of the temple. That would be about the time when John the Baptist introduced Jesus with the words, "Behold the Lamb of God who takes away the sin of the world" (John 1:29). The old covenant ritual was soon over because the ultimate Sin-bearer had come.

Endnotes

1. Gordon J. Wenham, *Numbers* (Downers Grove, Ill.: InterVarsity Press, 1981), 34.

NUMBERS

Numbers 1:46

How should we understand the large numbers in the census figures of Numbers?

There are two numberings of the Israelites in the book of Numbers. The first (Numbers 1) is for military purposes, and the second (Numbers 26) is for the purpose of dividing the land. In both numberings, the count includes only males from twenty years old and upwards, and the totals are over six hundred thousand. When we add an equal number of women and at least as many or more children, the number of Israelites in the wilderness can be estimated at around two million.

Many interpreters have been troubled over these large numbers. The objection is usually raised that there would have been simply too many Israelites to have survived for forty years in the wilderness. Therefore, attempts have been made to reduce these figures. It has been suggested by some that the census figures found here are misplaced and actually come from a later period in Israel's history. But would they be "misplaced" six times (compare Exod. 12:37; 38:26; Num. 1:46; 2:32; 11:21; 26:51)? Others have suggested that the figures have been misinterpreted. It is supposed that the Hebrew word translated "thousand" (*'eleph)* should be rendered "a tribal unit." So in the case of Reuben, the text should be interpreted to mean "forty-six tribal units, or 500 people" (Num. 1:21). But the total given in Numbers 2:32 clearly assumes that *'eleph* means a "thousand."

Allen has offered evangelical scholars an intriguing possibility in suggesting that the census figures in Numbers are deliberately exaggerated as a rhetorical device to bring glory to God and point to the fulfillment of God's promise to multiply the descendants of Abraham.[1] He suggests that the actual count of the Israelite warriors may have been around sixty thousand, but this was multiplied by a factor of ten to "celebrate the work of the Lord." Allen argues from 1 Samuel 18:7 that a rhetorical use of numbers is not out of keeping with literal (normal) interpretation.

A major problem with this viewpoint is the payment of the half-shekel temple tax as recorded in Exodus 38:25–26. Moses was required to collect one-half shekel from each of the Israelite males for the support of the tabernacle. They collected a total of 301,775 shekels, which amounts to 603,550 half shekels. This is the exact number provided by the census found in Numbers. To suggest that the collection was exaggerated to agree with exaggerated census figures is pushing the limits of literal interpretation.

It is my suggestion that we accept the large census figures in Numbers as they are given. Are the figures unreasonable? Of course! How could two million people survive for forty years in the wilderness? The answer: Only by God's miraculous provision of manna and water was such survival possible in a dry and barren wasteland. I agree with Allen that the numbers celebrate the work and provision of God, but there is no indication within the text itself that suggests they were exaggerated. If God can provide for sixty thousand, He can provide for six hundred thousand! That is the nature of our miracle-working God!

Numbers 3:6–10

What is the relationship between the priests and the Levites?

Both the priests and the Levites are descendants of Jacob's son Levi. But God designated Aaron and his sons to serve as priests, representing the people in sacrificial worship of Yahweh. Of the descendants of Levi, only those who are also descendants of Aaron may serve as priests. The rest of the male members of the tribe of Levi were designated to assist the sons of Aaron in the service of the tabernacle and later the temple. The priests are responsible for officiating at the sacrifices. The Levites were the priests' helpers.

Numbers 4:3

Numbers 4:3 indicates that the Levites were to serve from age thirty and retire at the age of fifty. How do we reconcile this with Leviticus 8:24, which indicates that they were to begin service at age twenty-five?

Serving as a Levite was a very significant responsibility. Numbers 8 records how Levites were separated from members of other tribes, purified, and ordained into service. It was their awesome responsibility to cover and carry the articles of the tabernacle. One mistake could cost a careless Levite his life (compare 2 Sam. 6:4). It would, therefore, be appropriate to be well trained before entering into Levitical service. I suggest that the Levites began their training at age twenty-five and assumed the full responsibility for their office at age thirty.

Numbers 5:11–31

What is this strange ritual that was required for a woman suspected of adultery? Why was this ritual important?

This passage provides a test for a man who suspects his wife of committing adultery. If he has not caught her in the act of adultery, how can he prove her guilty? If she is innocent, how can she be vindicated and the suspicion of her husband dispelled? This strange ritual provides the solution.

The text directs the man who suspects his wife of defiling herself through adultery to take her to the priest with a small grain offering. The suspect wife is then taken before the Lord in the tabernacle. Her hair is undone and some of the grain offering is placed in her hand. Then the priest makes a pronouncement that if she is innocent, she will come to no harm. But if she is guilty, her thigh will "waste away" and her abdomen will "swell" (Num. 5:21). She is then required to drink water that has been mixed with dust from the floor of the tabernacle. If no harm comes to her, then her husband can be assured that she was innocent of the suspected adultery. If guilty, "her abdomen will swell and her thigh will waste away, and the woman will become a curse among her people" (v. 27). In addition, it appears, she will be barren and childless (v. 28).

The Code of Hammurabi addresses a similar situation, requiring the suspected wife to throw herself into the river.[2] The survival of the wife would prove her innocence.

In his helpful commentary on Numbers, Wenham has pointed out that the key to understanding a society's fundamental values is its ritual system.[3] He suggests that if we do not understand the ritual system of a people, we do not understand their deepest beliefs and values. In a lengthy discussion on the essence of ritual, Wenham argues that Old Testament rituals express religious truths visually as opposed to verbally.[4] Rituals are the ancient equivalent to television, modes of communication between the human and divine worlds in Bible times. But better than television, they are an interactive, two-way channel of communication. On one hand, they are "dramatized prayers," expressing people's deepest hopes and fears. On the other hand, they are "dramatized divine promises or warnings," declaring God's attitude toward human beings.

With this understanding, we have a better appreciation of the powerful teaching medium the Lord provided in the ritual for the suspected adulteress. The message is clear: No matter how secret or hidden, God knows and judges sin. The ritual provides a means of exposing the adulteress and punishing her sin. Although this text does not address the issue, the male adulterer would be equally accountable according to the law (Lev. 20:10).

The detailed ritual procedures in Numbers 5 are designed to show the seriousness of the sin of adultery and of God's holy demand for sexual purity. While this ritual was part of the old covenant, the principles taught here are abiding. Hebrews 13:4 reminds us, "Let marriage be held in honor among all, and let the marriage bed be undefiled; for fornicators and adulterers God will judge."

Numbers 11:31–34

Why did God send a severe plague on the Israelites after providing them with quail?

In response to the complaint of the people about their desert diet of manna, the Lord sent them a provision of quail. But while "the meat was still between their teeth," the Lord sent a severe plague and many died.

It has been suggested that the reason for the plague was the people's neglect of proper food preparation. Leviticus 17:14 prohibits the eating of blood. Perhaps the people were in such a rush to eat they did not make sure that the blood was drained from the meat. While this is a reasonable possibility, the text suggests another interpretation. The place is named Kibroth-hattavah, "the graves of greediness." This suggests that the problem was their greed. Perhaps the people doubted the adequacy of the provision and rushed in a greedy manner upon the quail, each one trying to get more than his neighbor. Greed is clearly sinful (Rom. 1:29; Eph. 5:3). Jesus called for contentment (Luke 3:14) and warned, "guard against every form of greed" (12:15).

Numbers 12:1

Who was "the Cushite woman" whom Moses married? And what happened to Zipporah?

The designation *Cushite* is derived from Cush, the first son of Ham (Gen. 10:6), who was the ancestor of the people living in the southern Nile valley (Ethiopia). There are two basic views regarding the Cushite woman whom Moses married. According to ancient Jewish tradition, she was none other than Zipporah, a native of Midian. In support of this view, it is argued that Habakkuk 3:7 uses the terms "Cushan" and "Midian" as synonyms. Allen has suggested that the term *Cushite* may have been used to express contempt for Zipporah's swarthy skin due to her Midianite ancestry.[5]

The second view interprets "the Cushite" to be someone other than Zipporah. According to this view, Zipporah died or was divorced by Moses. Shortly afterward, Moses entered into a second marriage with someone of whom Aaron and Miriam did not approve. Another variation of this view is that Moses took another wife in addition to Zipporah.

The text does not provide us with sufficient detail to say what happened to Zipporah or to identify the Cushite with certainty. But the designation "Cushite" seems to distinguish her from Zipporah, a Midianite. The objection raised by Aaron and Miriam appears to have been based on recent circumstances—probably Moses' new marriage to a dark-skinned Cushite. The marriage itself would not have been wrong. God had forbidden the Israelites to marry the Canaanites (Exod. 34:16) but had said nothing about Cushites. While the complaint of Miriam and Aaron focused on Moses' marriage, Numbers 12:2 reveals that their jealousy was the basic cause of the criticism.

Numbers 12:9–10

Why was only Miriam judged with leprosy when both she and her brother Aaron had made the complaint?

Both Aaron and Miriam challenged Moses' sole right to speak for God to the people (Num. 12:1–2). And both were subjected to the Lord's angry rebuke (vv. 5–9). But we wonder why only Miriam was judged with leprosy.

The answer is found in Numbers 12:1 where the Hebrew text reads, "and she spoke." This makes it clear that Miriam was the chief instigator in the complaint. Aaron appears to have followed her leading in taking up the issue. Both were to blame, but Miriam had greater responsibility for this challenge of Moses' authority.

Numbers 13:33

Did the "Nephilim" (see Gen. 6:4) survive the world flood? How do we account for their presence in Canaan?

When the spies returned from searching out the land, they reported fearfully, "There also we saw the Nephilim." The Nephilim appear for the first time in Genesis 6:4 as the offspring of the unions that marked the climax of human wickedness on earth. The Nephilim were large-bodied individuals who were known for their strength and prowess.

There are three possible understandings of Numbers 13:33. First, this is a reference to some of the same individuals as introduced in Genesis 6:4. But it would have been impossible for them to have survived the flood. Indeed, the purpose of the flood was to destroy all life on earth (Gen. 6:17, 21). Second, this is a reference to other Nephilim who appeared on the earth after the flood. The Bible does mention giants like Og king of Bashan (Deut. 3:11) and the Philistine Goliath (1 Sam. 17). But nowhere are these giants called "Nephilim." Third, the spies are making an exaggerated allusion to the Nephilim of Genesis 6:4. Panicking over the apparent dangers of the conquest, they call the people of Canaan "the Nephilim." This is a clear case of hyperbole—exaggeration to emphasize a point. This is evident from the previous verse in which they describe Canaan as "a land that devours its inhabitants" (Num. 13:32). There were no Nephilim in the land, but to a people who viewed themselves to be "like grasshoppers," the inhabitants of Canaan looked as threatening.

Numbers 15:22–29

What does Moses mean when he refers to an "unintentional" sin? Doesn't sin by nature involve intent?

In Numbers 15:22–29 Moses records God's gracious provision for atonement in cases of unintentional sin. Various expressions are used to describe such a sin (vv. 22, 24, 27). The basic idea of these expressions is that someone has made an error, gone astray, or committed an inadvertent sin. Such a sin is distinguished from the sin done defiantly (literally with a "high hand"), for which there is no provision of atonement (vv. 30–31).

There are two issues in considering any act of sin—the action itself and the attitude of the person involved. While the act itself is not unimportant, the Lord's greatest concern is with the attitude of the lawbreaker. He distinguishes between the person who unknowingly breaks the law and the person who does so with full knowledge and intent.

An unintentional sin could take place in at least two possible ways—through negligence or as a result of ignorance. An example of the former would be an accidental homicide (35:22–25). Responsibility for an accidental death is less than that for a premeditated murder. An example of a sin of ignorance would be when king Abimelech took Abraham's wife into his harem (Gen. 20:9). Being improperly informed, he thought Sarah was Abraham's sister.

The relationship between the attitude and the act of sin was neglected by the Pharisees of the New Testament. They prided themselves in keeping the letter of the law, but their attitudes were far from pleasing to God. They thought they were free from sin because they had not committed the act of adultery. Jesus said that having lust for a woman—the attitude of adultery—is tantamount to committing the act itself (Matt. 5:27–28).

Numbers 15:32–36

Since the death penalty had been prescribed for Sabbath violations, why did Moses have to bring the case of the wood gatherer before the Lord?

The story of the wood gatherer provides an example of a sin of the "high hand" (Num. 15:30–31). A man was apprehended for gathering sticks on the Sabbath. Some would suggest that the gathering of sticks violated the Sabbath (Exod. 20:8–11) and that Moses consulted the Lord because the mode of punishment had not been prescribed. But stoning was nothing new (19:12–13), and Moses did not need any review on the issue of the death penalty.

Another possibility is that Moses apparently did not regard the gathering of sticks as a violation of the Sabbath (20:8–11). But building a fire would be another matter. The latter was specifically prohibited and the death penalty was prescribed for violators (35:2–3). So why did Moses need to consult the Lord regarding this case? I suggest that until this time there was no legal precedent for a violation of the intent of the law. The man was not building a fire but was apparently planning to do so. The Lord revealed to Moses that the wood gatherer should be put to death. Yahweh regarded the *intent* to sin as equivalent to the sin itself. This principle is confirmed by Jesus in His Sermon on the Mount (Matt. 5:21–28).

Numbers 20:2–13

What was the sin of Moses and Aaron by which they forfeited the privilege of leading the people into the Promised Land?

This text teaches that disobedience can disqualify a believer from opportunities of service and leadership. During the fortieth year of the wilderness wanderings, the people once again murmured because of a water shortage. The Lord instructed Moses and Aaron to *speak* to the rock and it would bring forth water (20:8). Instead, Moses spoke to the people and then *struck* the rock—twice! His words and actions made it appear as though his own efforts had produced the water. God graciously provided water for the people, but Moses and Aaron forfeited the opportunity of leading the people into their land.

The sin of Moses and Aaron appears to be twofold (v. 12). First, they are rebuked because they did not believe God. Their presumptuous unbelief was evidenced by their disobedience to the Lord's clear instructions. Second, they are rebuked for their failure to treat God as holy. Their words and actions did not reflect a high view of God's holiness. Moses and Aaron were guilty of diminishing the reputation of God in the eyes of the people. When the leaders failed to give God the glory He deserved, He manifested His holiness in judgment (v. 13).

Numbers 22:2–38

Was Balaam a true prophet and a believer in the God of Israel?

The character of Balaam has been the subject of much discussion through the years. At times he sounds so pious, as one seeking a word from the Lord (22:8, 18). Yet every mention of him in Scripture condemns him for moral, ethical, and religious faults (Num. 31:8, 16; Deut. 23:3–6; Josh. 13:22; 24:9–10; Judg. 11:23–25; Neh. 13:1–3; Mic. 6:5; 2 Peter 2:15–16; Jude 11; Rev. 2:14).

Balaam was a prophet but one that is completely outside of Israel's prophetic tradition. Specifically, Balaam was a *baru* diviner who claimed the ability to "see" what will happen based on phenomena in nature. Allen comments:

> He is a pagan, foreign national whose mantic acts center on animal divination, including the dissection of animal livers, the movements of animals, and the light of birds. He believed that he had a way with the gods, a hold on them. To him Yahweh was not the Lord of heaven but just another deity whom he might manipulate.[6]

Balaam was invited by Balak to curse Israel. Had he been a true prophet of God he would have known immediately how to answer. But the promised awards were very attractive. And Balaam decided to consult with God in hopes that he might gain some personal benefit (2 Peter 2:15). Even when God said, "Do not go with them; you shall not curse the people" (Num. 22:12), he persisted in pursuing the opportunity with hopes for personal enrichment. Lured by the promise of reward, he kept the negotiations open (v. 19).

God eventually granted Balaam permission to go to Balak with the command, "only the word which I speak to you shall you do" (v. 20). God granted permission for Balaam to go in order to show in a dramatic way His sovereign choice to bless Israel. Although Balaam failed in his attempts to curse Israel, he succeeded in seducing the people to worship Baal of Peor through cultic prostitution with the Midianites (25; 31:16). Although he boasted of being a speaker for Yahweh, his actions reveal Balaam's true character as an unbeliever.

Endnotes

1. Ronald B. Allen, "Numbers" in *The Expositor's Bible Commentary*, ed. Frank E. Gaebelein (Grand Rapids: Zondervan, 1990), 688–91.
2. James B. Pritchard, ed., *Ancient Near Eastern Texts* (Princeton: Princeton University Press, 1969), 171.
3. Gordon J. Wenham, *Numbers* (Leicester, England: Inter-Varsity Press, 1981), 26.
4. Ibid., 29–30.
5. Allen, "Numbers," 797.
6. Ibid., 888.

DEUTERONOMY

Authorship

Who wrote the book of Deuteronomy?

The Mosaic authorship of Deuteronomy is evidenced by several factors. First, Deuteronomy 31:9 explicitly states, "Moses wrote this law" (see also 31:24). Second, the Jews of Jesus' day believed that Moses wrote Deuteronomy (see Matt. 22:24; Mark 10:3–4; 12:19). Third, Jesus refers to Deuteronomy 24:1–4 as the commandment of Moses (Matt. 19:7). The unity and authenticity of Deuteronomy as a Mosaic book are confirmed by the fact that its structure conforms to that of the suzerain-vassal treaties of the fifteenth to thirteenth centuries B.C.

Chapter 34 was obviously written by someone other than Moses since it records the account of Moses' death. Early Jewish tradition suggests that this chapter was written by Joshua.

Mosaic authorship of Deuteronomy is rejected by many scholars who relegate it to the time of King Josiah (640–609 B.C.). It is argued that the publication of Deuteronomy as a pseudo-Mosaic book was the basis for King Josiah's great reform (2 Kings 22–23).

What is the "documentary theory" of the Pentateuch?

The documentary theory of the Pentateuch, also known as the "documentary hypothesis," affirms that the Pentateuch (Genesis through Deuteronomy) contains a compilation of selections from several different documents written at different times and places long after the time of Moses. The four main documents include:

J (850 B.C.) The "Jahwist" document was written by an unknown writer in the southern kingdom of Judah who portrayed or referred to God in anthropomorphic terms. This writer had a prophetlike interest in ethical and theological reflection and used the divine name Yahweh.

E (750 B.C.) The "Elohist" document was written by an unknown writer in the northern kingdom of Israel. This writer was more objective in style and tended to focus on concrete particulars and used the term *Elohim* to refer to God.

D   (621 B.C.) The "Deuteronomic" document was composed, possibly
     under the direction of the high priest Hilkiah, at the time of
     Josiah's reform. The document focuses on the temple,
     encouraging the people of Judah to abandon their local
     sanctuaries. The document was strongly influenced by the
     prophetic movement.

P   (500 B.C.) The "Priestly Code" was composed in various stages
     from the time of Ezekiel to the time of Ezra. The P document is
     concerned with the origins and institutions of Israelite worship.
     It shows special interest in genealogical lists, sacrifices, and
     rituals.

According to critical scholars, an unknown editor combined J and E into a
single document (JE) about 650 B.C. D was added to JE about 550 B.C., and P
was added to JED about 430 B.C.

The first step toward the construction of the documentary theory was the
work of Jean Astruc, a French professor of medicine, who suggested in his
Conjectures (1753) that Moses may have used two prior written sources—an
Elohist and a Jahwist document. J. G. Eichorn was the first professional scholar
to adopt this approach. In his three-volume work (1780–83) he extended the
analysis to the rest of the Pentateuch. Wilhelm de Wette (1805) tried to prove
that Deuteronomy was a pious fraud concocted by Josiah and Hilkiah in order
to centralize all worship in Jerusalem, thus establishing the D document as
the latest of the three. In 1853 Hermann Hupfeld divided up E into earlier and
later works, the earlier to become known as the "Priestly Code" (P). Karl H.
Graf argued in 1866 that the legal portions of P were exilic.

In his *History of Israel* (1878), Julius Wellhausen applied the principle of
natural evolution to Israel's religion. Wellhausen presented such plausible
arguments for his views on the documentary theory that it was popularized
under his name, the Wellhausen hypothesis. The theory has continued to
undergo modification, but the majority of critical scholars today accept the
basic approach set forth in Wellhausen's classic work.

The documentary hypothesis is plagued with problems, the most noteworthy
of which I will mention here. First, the underlying problem with the
documentary hypothesis is its basic antisupernatural approach to Scripture.
According to advocates of this view, the Pentateuch contains the fallible words
of humans, not the infallible words of God. The Mosaic authorship of the
Pentateuch is denied and the history recorded there is considered unreliable.
The documentary hypothesis is inconsistent with an evangelical approach to
Scripture (compare 2 Tim. 3:16–17; 2 Peter 2:20–21).

Second, the documentary theory is plagued with circular reasoning. The
critic posits the conclusion that the Pentateuch has literary strands that are
recognizable and have consistent features. Studying the text, he assigns each
strand its peculiar features. Then he "finds" the features in the biblical text,
assigning each portion of the Pentateuch to a JEDP document. The whole
process of discovering literary features and isolating documents is circular.

Third, the theory has been undermined by advances in form criticism, particularly study of the fifteenth–thirteenth century suzerain-vassal treaty, which points to the literary unity of Exodus and Deuteronomy. The fact that Deuteronomy and portions of Exodus follow a regular form including elements set forth in contemporary treaties indicates that these books are literary units, not bits and pieces of different literary documents.

Fourth, the argument that narrative literature can be divided up on the basis of various designations for deity is quite weak. Frequently the J document uses Elohim, and the E uses Yahweh. There are other reasons for using different designations—variety, fuller description, context reflecting a particular attribute. The fact that one God can have many names is abundantly evident in Ugaritic literature.

Finally, the parallel passages, also called "doublets," need not point to two different literary strands or traditional accounts. Genesis 1–2 contains one Creation account, not two. Chapter 1 presents in a general way the creation of the universe while chapter 2 focuses on the creation of man and woman. This technique of recapitulation was widely practiced in ancient Semitic literature.

Deuteronomy 14:22–29

What was the practice of tithing under the old covenant?

The law of tithing called for giving a tenth of one's produce or income to support the temple, priesthood, and other noble causes. The purpose of tithing was to remind the people of Israel that everything they had came from the Lord and ultimately belonged to Him.

The Bible's teaching on tithing is found in three principle passages. Leviticus 27:30–33 sets forth the principle of giving "a tithe of the land" to the Lord. Numbers 18:21–32 requires the Israelites to give a tithe to the Levites, who had no land inheritance. The Levites are then to give a tithe of the tithe to the priests. Deuteronomy 14:22–29 describes a tithe that is to be eaten by the offerer with his family at one of the feasts in Jerusalem and a tithe that was to be given to the poor every third year.

The rabbis struggled with the differences between these texts and decided that they were complimentary rather than contradictory. The *first* tithe was given to the Levites as stated in Numbers 21 (Deut. 14:7). A *second* tithe was taken to Jerusalem to be used in worship and celebration (vv. 22–26). A *third* tithe was given every third year to provide for the stranger, the orphan, and the widow (vv. 28–29). Modern interpreters have debated the matter of multiple tithing. Critical scholarship has suggested that there was just one tithe, which was variously used at different times in Israel's history. Since Deuteronomy 14 mentions all three tithes within one context, it suggests that multiple tithing was the practice in Israel.

Tithing was only a part of the religious dues of the Israelites. In addition, there was the sin offering, the thank offering, the firstfruits of the crops, the firstborn animals, redemption of the firstborn child, the half-shekel temple tax, annual wood gathering, and the freewill offerings. Grant concludes that "the sum total of religious obligations levied upon the people by various Old Testament codes was nothing short of enormous."[1]

While tithing is advocated by many Christians today, most are not thinking of the Old Testament tithe that would amount to around twenty-five percent. The New Testament pattern is proportionate giving, "as he may prosper" (1 Cor. 16:2). Paul challenges believers to give as each one "has purposed in his heart; not grudgingly or under compulsion; for God loves a cheerful giver" (2 Cor. 9:7).

Deuteronomy 21:15–17

Does this text suggest that polygamy was lawful in the Old Testament period?

Polygamy, although contrary to God's original pattern of one woman for one man (Gen. 2:24), was certainly practiced in the biblical period. Abraham took Hagar in addition to Sarah. Jacob married two sisters. Deuteronomy 21:15–17 is one of several texts (see Exod. 21:7–11; Lev. 18:18; 2 Sam. 12:7–8) that seem to support polygamy. Here we find a law that protects the inheritance rights of the firstborn son of an unloved wife. The man in question has taken a second wife, whom he loves, and has had a son by her. Can he rightfully deny his firstborn the inheritance rights in favor of his son through his loved wife?

It is argued here that Moses would not have legislated upon the case of a man with two wives if having two wives was unlawful. However, legislation on an issue does not necessarily imply its approval. Deuteronomy 23:18 legislates upon the wages of a harlot but does not authorize harlotry.

More careful study of the text indicates that Moses is legislating for a man who has had two wives in succession, the second after the first one died. The Septuagint, Latin Vulgate, Samaritan Version, and Jewish Targum all follow this opinion. Kaiser points out that to insist that both wives are living would be asking the imperfect verb form to bear a load it was not meant to carry.[2] This law envisions a situation in which a man has a son by his first wife. After her death, he remarries and has another son. Since he loves his second wife more, he wants to give her son the inheritance rights. God prohibits this. The legislation protects the inheritance rights of the firstborn.

Deuteronomy 24:1–4

Is divorce and remarriage authorized by this text? And what is the "indecency" for which the man divorces his wife?

This passage has often been used to argue for divorce and remarriage in cases of immorality. Unfortunately, the structure of the passage has not always been reflected in English translations. We have here an example of biblical case law. The first three verses describe the case, specifying the conditions for which the command in verse 4 applies. It is important to remember that the presentation of the case does not in itself constitute divine approval.

In this case Moses describes a man who divorces his wife and she remarries. Then her second marriage ends either by death or divorce. The command that is applicable is given in verse 4. A man may not remarry his former wife, if she has in the meantime been married to another man. Even though her second husband divorces her or dies, she may not be reunited in marriage to her first husband. To do so would be "an abomination before the LORD" and "bring sin on the land" (Deut. 24:4).

The rabbis debated the meaning of the term *indecency*. Literally, the Hebrew *arvat dabar* means "the nakedness of a thing" or "a naked matter." This term is used in Deuteronomy 23:14 as a euphemism for excrement. The "indecency" apparently refers to some shameful or repulsive act short of adultery, since adultery was punishable by death (22:22–24) not divorce. The indecency was the basis for the man's divorcing his wife but is not presented in this text as legitimate grounds for divorce.

Endnotes

1. F. C. Grant, *The Economic Background of the Gospels* (New York: Russell & Russell, 1973), 97.
2. Walter C. Kaiser Jr., *Toward Old Testament Ethics* (Grand Rapids: Zondervan, 1983), 187.

JOSHUA

Joshua 2:1–7

Does the story of Rahab's lie provide a biblical basis for situation ethics? Is it sometimes right to lie?

Some Christians have appealed to the story of Rahab in defense of a righteous lie. After hiding the two spies under stalks of flax on her roof, Rahab told the king's men that the Israelites had left the city and she did not know where they went (Josh. 2:5). Does her lying provide biblical justification for lying?

Several key hermeneutical principles are helpful in responding to this question. First, it is important to remember that the Bible often records what God does not necessarily approve. Second, divine approval of an individual in one aspect or area of life does not mean there is divine approval in all aspects of character or conduct. Third, application should be made on the basis of what the Bible obviously blesses or commends, not on every detail of the passage.

Putting these principles into application, I suggest that the Bible recorded the story of Rahab without implicit approval of her lying. There is no evidence in the text that God approved or blessed her lie. What the Bible clearly commends is Rahab's faith, not her falsehood! Hebrews 11:31 records that it was "by faith" that Rahab did not perish along with the rest of the Canaanites at Jericho. Although a Canaanite and a harlot, she had come to believe in Yahweh, the God of Israel (Josh. 2:11).

As a new believer from a very immoral background, she told a lie. But her example at this point does not provide a legitimate ethical basis for telling a lie. We serve a "God of truth" (Ps. 31:5) who exhorts us to "speak the truth" (Zech. 8:16; Eph. 4:15, 25). To justify lying in order to save a life implies that God has so few resources at His disposal that He needs us to lie to rescue someone from a difficult situation. Certainly God is greater than that!

Jesus called for constant honesty, without hedging or modifying the truth (Matt. 5:33–37). This does not mean that we must tell all that we know. I need not tell a crazed man with a gun that my wife and children are hiding in the closet! At the same time, there does not seem to be a biblical justification for lying. Because God is truth, He regards all lies as sinful—contrary to His character. Believers should speak the truth always and trust in God's protective care.

Joshua 3:14–17

How do we account for Israel's crossing of the Jordan River at flood stage?

Joshua 3:14–17 records how Joshua led the people to the banks of the Jordan and across the river into Canaan. The biblical text records that as the priests with the ark of the covenant stepped into the river, the waters "rose up in one heap, a great distance away at Adam," enabling the people to cross. "Adam" is identified with Damiyeh, about nineteen miles upstream from Jericho. The crossing took place in the spring of the year, during harvest, when the Jordan River is at flood stage (3:15). It is during this time of year that the snow is melting on Mount Hermon and filling the channel of the Jordan with an overabundance of water. While the river could be easily forded during the dry season, this was impossible in the spring when the river overflows its banks.

Some have suggested that what we have here is a natural occurrence resulting from a landslide that blocked the flow of the Jordan. On several occasions in history, a landslide along the steep banks blocked the river's flow. History records that the river was blocked for sixteen hours in 1267 and for twenty-one hours in 1927. But does this interpretation of the event give full recognition of the text that records that the people crossed "on dry ground" (v. 17)? And could a landslide have blocked the channel during a time when the river "overflows all its banks" (v. 15)?

I suggest that what we have here is nothing less than a miracle. This is suggested by the fact that the event occurred at flood stage (v. 15) and that the people crossed "on dry ground" (v. 17). The response of the Canaanites also suggests that this was a supernatural rather than a natural occurrence. The Canaanites heard how the Lord had "dried up the waters of the Jordan" and they were terrified (5:1).

Joshua 4:1–20

How many stone memorials were set up by the Israelites?

The Israelites have always had a fondness for signs and symbols that commemorate God's mighty acts and that teach future generations what He has accomplished. In Joshua 4 the people are instructed to take up stones from the Jordan River to perpetuate the memory of the miraculous crossing. The NIV indicates that they took up twelve stones from the middle of the Jordan, where the priests with the ark had stood, to set up a memorial at Gilgal (Josh. 4:8–9). The NASB translation records that they "took up twelve stones from the middle of the Jordan" (v. 8) and "set up twelve stones in the middle of the Jordan" (v. 9). This would suggest that there were two memorials—one at Gilgal and the other in the Jordan River. Which is the preferred interpretation?

The text clearly indicates that a memorial of twelve stones was set up at Gilgal (v. 20). Was there also a memorial in the river? Verse 9 would indicate so. The text records that Joshua "set up" *(qum)* twelve stones "in the middle of the Jordan." The words, "they are there to this day," would suggest that at least until the time of the writing of Joshua, the stone memorial was still visible when the Jordan ran low. The translators of the Septuagint understood that the stones set up in the river were different from the stones set up at Gilgal. They add the word *allous* ("other") in verse 9 to indicate that these stones were different from the ones already mentioned.[1]

The text indicates that two, twelve-stone memorials were set up by the Israelites. The memorial at Gilgal commemorates *what* happened, and the memorial in the Jordan commemorates *where* it happened.

Joshua 5:13–15

Who is the "captain" who appeared to Joshua on the eve of the conquest of Canaan?

As Joshua was preparing for his first battle with the Canaanites, he had a strange encounter with a man holding a drawn sword. Not being one to be intimidated by a stranger, Joshua stepped forward and asked him to identify himself, "Are you for us or for our adversaries?" The stranger responded, "No, rather I indeed come now as captain of the host of Yahweh" (5:14). Who was this visitor?

First, the visitor identifies himself as "captain," a term translated "prince" in Isaiah's reference to the "Prince of Peace" (Isa. 9:6). Second, he identifies himself as commander of "the host of Yahweh," usually understood as a reference to God's angelic army. Third, he is one whom Joshua considered worthy of worship. Joshua bowed down before the visitor. Finally, the words of verse 15, "Remove your sandals from your feet," is precisely parallel to Moses' encounter with God in Exodus 3:5.

Indications from the text suggest this passage records a *theophany*—an appearance of God (compare Gen. 16:7–13; Exod. 3:5; Judg. 6:11–24; 13:3–23). At the beginning of the conquest, Joshua had an encounter with God, reminding him that this was the Lord's battle. The Lord would lead and give victory as the Israelites followed by faith.

Joshua 6:17–18

Would a righteous and just God command the total destruction of the men, women, and children of Canaan?

One of the troubling issues of the conquest is God's command that Joshua and the Israelites utterly destroy the Canaanites living in the land. In Deuteronomy 20:16 Yahweh declares, "In the cities of these peoples that Yahweh your God is giving you as an inheritance, you shall not leave alive anything that breathes."

There are two purposes evident in God's command for the destruction of the Canaanites. First, it was intended to punish the inhabitants of the land for their wickedness. Several biblical texts link the conquest of Canaan with the sin and iniquity of the Canaanites (Gen. 15:16; Lev. 18:25; Deut. 9:5). Tragic as it was, the conquest was a much deserved judgment on a very wicked people. And the children suffered the consequences of their parents' sin. Second, the conquest was intended to preserve Israel's purity by preventing involvement with the Canaanites and their wicked ways (Lev. 18:24–30). Deuteronomy 7:2–5 warns of the moral and spiritual consequences of involvement with the Canaanites.

In responding to this question it is important to emphasize that the conquest of Canaan was no ordinary war. The Israelites were engaged in a holy war, executing God's judgment on the wicked Canaanites. The conquest of Canaan is the righteous response of a holy God to sin.

Joshua 7:22–26

How can the killing of Achan's children be justified?

During the conquest of Jericho, Achan violated the ban and took some of the things that God had ordered to be destroyed. Achan was identified by drawing lots (see Prov. 16:33) and confessed to his sin. Although it is reasonable that Achan should be punished, it is hard to justify the stoning of his children. Various attempts have been made to resolve this issue.

It seems unlikely that they would have been punished because of Achan's sin since the punishment of children for the sin of their father is specifically prohibited by Deuteronomy 24:16. It is more reasonable to suggest that they reaped the natural consequences of Achan's sin, as in Deuteronomy 5:9. But a stoning seems beyond the realm of natural consequences. There is direct punishment involved in an execution. Some commentators have speculated that the children were punished for sharing in Achan's sin. Living in the same tent, they could not help be accomplices. Perhaps the children helped hide what Achan had taken.

There is another alternative that is suggested by the Hebrew text and supported by rabbinic interpretation. The Hebrew text of verse 25 reads, "And all Israel stoned him with stones; and they burned them with fire." The rabbinic interpreters recorded in the Talmud understood the text to mean that they "stoned him," Achan, and "burned them," the stolen goods. This interpretation would harmonize nicely with God's instruction that the material remains of the city of Jericho be destroyed (Josh. 6:17). According to this view, Achan's sons and daughters (7:24) were taken only "as witnesses" to the execution site (Talmud *Sanhedrin* 44a). Achan and his stolen goods were stoned, burned, and buried, but the children were spared.

Joshua 8:18–27

How do we account for the fact that biblical Ai was not occupied when Israel entered Canaan?

Archaeological excavations at et-Tell, a site that has been traditionally identified with biblical Ai, reveal that there is a long occupational gap between

2200 B.C. and 1000 B.C. This means that the site was not occupied when the
Israelites entered Canaan in 1406 B.C. A leading Israeli archaeologist
comments, "This lack of any Late Bronze Canaanite city at the site or in the
vicinity contradicts the narrative in Joshua 8 and shows that it was not based
on historical reality."[2] How should we interpret this data?

Some interpreters have suggested that the battle recorded in Joshua 8
actually took place at Bethel, but the story became associated with the ruins
at et-Tell. Others suggest that the narrative of the conquest of Ai is an etiological
story that developed to explain the ruins at et-Tell. It has also been suggested
that Ai was simply a military outpost of Bethel and that Joshua 8 is really the
story of the conquest of Bethel, not Ai. However, the text clearly presents Ai
as an inhabited city with a king.

Believing that the Bible is accurate in its account of the conquest of Ai, we
are left with two possible conclusions. First, it is possible that Ai has been
identified correctly but the archaeological evidence has been misinterpreted.
Second, Ai has been incorrectly identified; we should look for the biblical
site elsewhere. It is important to remember that archaeology is not an exact
science and that material remains are subject to varying interpretations. While
the location of Ai is uncertain, there is no question as to its conquest as recorded
in Joshua 8.

Joshua 10:12–14

What actually happened on the day when "the sun stood still"?

Something very unusual happened as Joshua was pursuing the Amorites
(Canaanites) who had attacked the city of Gibeon. As the enemy fled down
the ascent of Beth-horon toward the Aijalon Valley, Joshua prayed, "O sun,
stand still at Gibeon, and O moon in the valley of Aijalon." And the next verse
records, "So the sun stood still and the moon stopped, until the nation avenged
themselves of their enemies" (10:13).

There are three basic interpretations of Joshua's long day.

1. *Poetic Interpretation.* According to this view, the account of the battle
and the long day contains poetic imagery and should not be taken literally. It
only *seemed* like the sun stood still because the day was long.

2. *Total Eclipse.* One biblical scholar has suggested that the word translated
"stand still" should be rendered "be eclipsed," based on the use of the root in
astronomy texts found in Babylon.[3] This would involve a technical use of the
Hebrew verb *amad.* An eclipse would have provided shade and cooling relief
not only to Joshua's troops, but also to the enemy.

3. *Prolongation of Light.* This view interprets the passage literally. Because
of the long day, Joshua was able to complete the battle before darkness set in.
There is some debate among proponents as to exactly how this might have
happened. It has been suggested that the long day was caused by a slowing of
the earth's rotation due to a comet passing near the earth. Another explanation
is that the longer day occurred as a result of the earth tilting on its axis. Since
the slowing or tilting of the earth would result in cosmic upheaval, Davis has

proposed that the long day was caused by refraction of light, extending the sun's rays on a local level.[4] This view is consistent with Scripture and seems to best account for the uniqueness of the day ("no day like that before it or after it," v. 14).

In the final analysis, we don't know how God answered Joshua's prayer and extended the day for the Israelites. We must be content to live with a mystery. That is often the case with biblical miracles.

Joshua 11:16–18

What was the date and the duration of the conquest?

The date of Israel's conquest of Canaan is debated. Many archaeologists and historians argue for a 1290 B.C. exodus from Egypt and a 1250 conquest of Canaan. The major argument in favor of this view is the discovery of major destruction and burning of cities in Canaan around 1250 B.C. The archaeologists are quick to conclude that the ashes found represent the conquest of Canaan by Joshua. However, the biblical text does not record that Joshua burned the cities that he captured. He burned Jericho (6:24), Ai (8:19), and Hazor (11:11). Joshua 11:13 records that Hazor was the only city the Israelites burned during the northern campaign. I suggest that the burned level discovered by the archaeologists may represent destructions that took place during the time of the judges, for the biblical evidence leads us to date the conquest around 1406 B.C.

According to 1 Kings 6:1, Solomon began to build the temple in the fourth year of his reign, 480 years after the Exodus. Solomon reigned forty years (970–931 B.C.), and the fourth year of his reign would be 966 B.C. Using 966 B.C. as a base, the date of the Exodus can be calculated by going back 480 years to 1446 B.C. The forty-year wilderness wanderings would then place Joshua's conquest in the year 1406 B.C.

Other biblical and archaeological data serve to confirm this date. First, in Judges 11:26, Jepthah reminds the king of Ammon that the Israelites had been in Ammon for three hundred years. Since Jephthah's judgeship can be dated no later than 1100 B.C., Israel's arrival in Transjordan could be no later than 1400 B.C. Second, the Amarna Letters (about 1400–1366 B.C.), mention the Habiru (apparently etymologically equated with "Hebrew") as invading southern and central Palestine. Abdi-Hiba, governor of Jerusalem, wrote numerous letters to Pharaoh Akhenaten (1375–1353 B.C.) to request aid against the encroaching Habiru if the region was to be saved for Egypt. Third, John Garstang's excavation (1930–36) at the site of Jericho resulted in the discovery of a violent destruction that could be dated to around 1400 B.C. More recent study of the pottery, stratigraphic considerations, and carbon-14 dating all serve to confirm to correctness of the biblical date—1400 B.C.[5]

We often think of the conquest of Canaan as a quick campaign that lasted several months. But the biblical text records that Joshua "waged war a long time" with the kings of Canaan (Josh. 11:18). Careful calculation indicates that the conquest of Canaan took approximately seven years to complete.

Caleb was forty at the time the spies were sent into the land (1445 B.C.) and eighty-five at the time of Joshua's division of the land (14:7–10). This means that the final division of the land took place around 1400 B.C., six or seven years after the 1406 B.C. crossing of the Jordan into Canaan.

Endnotes

1. M. H. Woudstra, *The Book of Joshua* (Grand Rapids: Eerdmans, 1981), 92.
2. Amihai Mazar, *Archaeology of the Land of the Bible* (New York: Doubleday, 1992), 331.
3. Robert Dick Wilson, "Understanding 'The Sun Stood Still,'" *Princeton Theological Review* 16 (1918), 46–54.
4. John J. Davis, *Conquest and Crisis* (Grand Rapids: Baker Book House, 1969), 69–70.
5. Bryant G. Wood, "Did the Israelites Conquer Jericho?" *Biblical Archaeology Review* (March–April 1990), 44–57.

JUDGES

Setting

How does the period of the judges fit between the conquest and the monarchy?

The period of the judges covers about 325 years, from 1375 B.C., the death of Joshua, to 1050 B.C., the beginning of the monarchy and the anointing of King Saul. The problem is that if all the terms of service performed by the judges are totaled, they amount to 410 years. This is about 85 years too long when we seek to fit this period between the conquest and the monarchy.

The solution is that many of the careers of the judges overlapped or were contemporaneous. The judges did not rule over all the land but over particular areas of Israel. Two judges could have assumed leadership in different areas at the same time. The lesser judge Tola may have served at the same time as Jair (Judg. 10:1–3). The Hebrew word translated "after" in verse 3 can be rendered "with." Judges 10:7 implies that Jephthah, who was occupied with the Ammonites to the east of the Jordan, and Samson, who was concerned with the Philistines on the west, were contemporaneous in their activity.

Judges 2:10–17

How can we account for the rise of idolatry among the Israelites after the death of Joshua?

Judges 2:10 records that there arose another generation after Joshua "who did not know the LORD, nor yet the work which He had done for Israel." The Israelites soon broke their covenant with Yahweh and fell into idolatry, worshiping the male and female gods of Canaan. There were two key factors in this spiritual apostasy. First, it appears that the older generation failed to teach the younger generation the great things that Yahweh had done. Children grew up in families that neglected their educational responsibility as set forth in Deuteronomy 6:6–9.

A second factor in the spiritual apostasy of the Israelites was the very seductive nature of Canaanite worship. The fertility-cult worship practiced by the Canaanites was founded on the belief that the gods were created by an act of reproduction. Worshipers believed that plants, animals, and children came about as a result of the sexual relations of the gods. To encourage the gods to copulate and thus fertilize the land, the priests and priestesses of the cult practiced "imitative magic." They engaged in sacred prostitution in order to cause the gods to lust and to desire sexual relations. These rituals would be performed in a temple or in the shelter of a grove of trees. One can easily imagine how the Israelites quickly became ensnared by this sexually stimulating and exciting new form of worship. The altar dedicated to the worship of the true God, Yahweh, was soon forgotten.

Judges 2:13

Who are the gods of Canaan?

Two of Canaan's gods are mentioned in Judges 2:13. Others are introduced elsewhere. El (9:46) was the supreme god of the Canaanite pantheon. He was prominent in early Canaanite theology but was later displaced by his son, Baal. Although he did continue to exist as a father-god, he played a role of lesser importance than such heroes as Baal.

Asherah (6:25) was the chief consort of El in Canaanite theology. She served as a mother-god and was associated in the biblical period with Baal (3:7). She was the chief god of Tyre, the hometown of Jezebel (compare 1 Kings 18:19).

Baal was the son and successor of El. His name simply means "lord." Of the gods of Canaan, he was the most directly involved with humankind. He was a fertility god whose domain was the sky. In Canaanite literature he is referred to as "the rider of the clouds." The name Baal is sometimes qualified by a place-name to represent a local manifestation of the chief Canaanite god (Num. 25:3; Josh. 11:7; Judg. 3:3). In sculptures Baal appears with a horned helmet. In one hand he grasps a club or a mace and in the other a spear embellished with leaves, which may portray lightning and vegetation. In Aramean sculptures he stands on the back of a bull.

Anath (Judg. 3:31) was a fertility god who was a sister-cohort of Baal. The sexual union of Baal and Anath was thought to be responsible for rain and the fertility of the soil.

Ashtaroth (in NASB; Astaroth in the KJV) is the plural form of "Ashtoreth" (Greek Astarte) who served as both a female god of fertility and of war. Ishtar was her Assyro-Babylonian counterpart, while Aphrodite was her counterpart in classical Greek mythology.

The names Anath, Asherah, and Ashtaroth are all related to sex and fertility and were often interchanged to the point where the female gods were no longer differentiated.

Judges 3:9

What is the relationship between Othniel and Caleb?

The descriptive phrase, "Othniel the son of Kenaz, Caleb's younger brother," used here and in Judges 1:13, could mean that either Kenaz or Othniel was Caleb's younger brother. However, the Massorete scholars clearly believed that Othniel was Caleb's brother and made a division in the Hebrew text between "son of Kenaz" and "brother of Caleb."[1] The problem is that Caleb is elsewhere called the "son of Jephunneh" (Num. 32:12; Josh. 14:6) while Othniel is called the "son of Kenaz" here and in 1 Chronicles 4:13. How can the two be brothers if they have different fathers? The likely answer is that Othniel was Caleb's younger half-brother. They had the same mother but different fathers.

Judges 6:36–40

Was Gideon's use of the fleece a valid method for determining the will of God?

Judges 6:14 records God's clear command to Gideon regarding the Midianites: "Go in this your strength and deliver Israel from the hand of Midian. Have I not sent you?" In response, Gideon asked for a "sign" that it was God who was speaking to him (v. 17). God gave him the requested sign, causing fire to spring up from a rock to consume a sacrifice (v. 21).

But Gideon questioned God on this matter. He asked for the sign of the fleece to determine if God would deliver Israel as He had spoken (vv. 36–37). God gave him the sign he requested. The fleece was wet from dew while the ground remained dry. Not quite convinced, Gideon asked for yet another sign! This time, the fleece was to be dry and the ground wet with dew. Once again, God gave Gideon the sign he requested.

Many people seek the will of the Lord by following Gideon's example of casting out a fleece. Is this kind of action supported by Scripture? I suggest that it should not be followed as an example in seeking the will of the Lord. God's directive had been given to Gideon (v. 14), and the victory had been promised (v. 16). Gideon was testing God to find out if He meant what He said. This was an improper test of God's faithfulness to His own promises. We might wonder why God seemed to honor Gideon's request for the second and third sign. Perhaps this illustrates the fact that God meets us where we are, even when we are struggling and are weak in faith.

Judges 11:30–31

What was the fate of Jephthah's daughter?

Before Jephthah went into battle against the Ammonites he vowed to the Lord that when he returned in peace he would offer to the Lord as a burnt offering whatever came out of his house to meet him. When he returned from battle, he was met by his daughter—his only child! Jephthah resolved to keep his rash vow, and his daughter willingly complied. What was the fate of Jephthah's daughter—death by human sacrifice, or devotion to temple service?

Death by Human Sacrifice

Many scholars believe that Jephthah offered his daughter as a burnt offering to Yahweh. The following arguments are offered in support of this view:

1. The Hebrew word *'olah* (11:31) always has the idea of "burnt offering" in the Old Testament.

2. Jephthah was the son of a heathen prostitute and may have been acquainted with Canaanite cultic worship of this kind current in Transjordan (Lev. 18:21; 20:2–5).
3. Human sacrifice was carried out by the king of Moab (2 Kings 3:26–27) and later by Israelite kings (2 Kings 31:6; 2 Chron. 28:3).
4. Jephthah was capable of such violence, as demonstrated by his execution of forty-two thousand Israelites (Judg. 12:6).
5. Verses 37–40 imply there is no hope for children in the future for Jephthah's daughter because of her impending death.

Devoted to Temple Service

Other scholars believe that Jephthah devoted his daughter to the service of God for the rest of her life in perpetual celibacy at the tabernacle. Advocates for this view offer the following arguments in support of their position:

1. Exodus 38:8; 1 Samuel 2:22, and Luke 2:36–37 reveal the fact that such devoted women did serve in the central sanctuary.
2. Human sacrifice was contrary to Mosaic Law and Israelite practice (Lev. 18:21; 20:2–5; Deut. 12:42; 18:10).
3. Jephthah was filled with the Spirit of God (11:29), and it is unlikely that a Spirit-filled man would carry out such a wicked act in clear violation of God's law.
4. No priest would have been willing to officiate over such a sacrifice. If Jephthah had tried to do it himself, certainly the people of Gilead would have objected.
5. In verse 31 the conjunction (waw) can just as well be translated "or." In other words, Jephthah's vow made allowance for his daughter, promising to give her to God in lifelong tabernacle service if she should be the first to greet him.
6. The fact that the daughter bewailed her virginity for two months points to the idea of a celibate life of temple service. Had sacrifice been her fate, she would have mourned the brevity of her life, not her virginity.
7. The statement that she "knew no man" would be meaningless if she had been put to death (11:39).
8. A possible translation of commemorate (lament KJV) in 11:40 is "talk to," indicating that the daughter was still alive. The translations "commemorate" or "lament" are based upon the assumption that she died.

While one could argue for either position, the hermeneutical principle of preference for the clearest interpretation would lead us to the conclusion that Jephthah probably sacrificed his daughter. This appears to be, as Kaiser says, "the most natural reading of the text."[2] While some scholars have tried to suggest that Jephthah gave himself an alternative to sacrifice with the Hebrew particle waw in verse 31, 'o is the Hebrew particle of choice. The fact that Jephthah's daughter wept for her virginity (v. 37) should not be interpreted that her life was spared. The statement simply heightens the tragedy of the situation.

We must be quick to point out, however, that God would not have approved such a vow or the sacrifice. The sacrifice of a human life was contrary to Mosaic Law (Lev. 18:21; 20:2–5; Deut. 12:31; 18:10) and to sound moral principles.

It may be that this narrative is included in Judges by the author as another illustration of the moral and religious chaos that characterized the period of the judges (Judg. 21:25).

Judges 19:29–30

Why did the Levite dismember his concubine and send her body parts throughout Israel?

Judges 19 records the extent of moral degradation among the Israelites who had adopted a Canaanite morality. What took place at Gibeah has striking parallels to the events that occurred with Lot in Sodom (Gen. 19). When the men of Gibeah sought to have sexual relations with the Levite, they were offered his concubine. The unfortunate woman was found dead the morning after the homosexual men of Gibeah had abused her through the night. The Levite then dismembered her body and sent the parts throughout Israel. Saul later did a similar thing with his oxen when seeking to muster Israel to defeat the Ammonites (1 Sam. 11).

The grisly tokens sent to the Israelites served both as a warning and a challenge. They were a shocking warning of the deep immorality into which the nation had fallen. And they constituted a challenge to punish the guilty men of Gibeah and make things right. The distribution of the concubine's body parts served to awaken Israel from its moral lethargy and unite the tribes to face their moral responsibility (Judg. 20). The outrage that occurred at Gibeah stood as a monument of wickedness for centuries to follow (Hos. 9:9; 10:9).

Endnotes

1. Leon Wood, *Distressing Days of the Judges* (Grand Rapids: Zondervan, 1975), 165.
2. Walter C. Kaiser Jr., *Hard Sayings of the Old Testament* (Downers Grove, Ill.: InterVarsity Press, 1988), 104.

RUTH

Ruth 3:4

What is the background of the custom of uncovering the feet, as Ruth was instructed to do with Boaz?

In seeking a husband for Ruth, her daughter-in-law, Naomi instructed Ruth to go to the threshing floor at night, uncover the feet of Boaz and lie down. This custom was obviously known and understood by Boaz but is strange and obscure to modern readers. There is no basis for interpreting this as an immoral proposal. That would be contrary to the godly characters of Ruth, Naomi, and Boaz.

In the ancient world, a position at the feet signified submission. When Joshua defeated the five kings of the Amorites in his southern campaign, he invited the commanders of his army to put their feet on the necks of the kings. Then Joshua charged his men to be courageous because God would give them victory over their enemies (Josh. 10:24–25). Psalm 110:1 uses the same imagery when Yahweh says to the Messiah, "Sit at My right hand, until I make Thine enemies a footstool for Thy feet."

Lying down at the feet of Boaz was an act of submission. Ruth was placing herself under the authority of Boaz. She then expressed verbally what she had demonstrated symbolically. Her words in verse 9, "so spread your covering over your maid," served as a request for the protection and security of marriage (see Ezek. 16:8).

Ruth 4:1–6

What was required of the near kinsman, and why was the nearer kinsman unwilling to redeem Ruth?

According to ancient custom, the near kinsman *(goel)* was to serve as a protector of family rights. First, the kinsman was responsible to protect family property, purchasing it to avoid having it sold outside the family (Lev. 25:25–28; Jer. 32:6–15). Second, the kinsman was to protect persons, like Ruth, making sure that she would be cared for and that her husband's name would not be forgotten (Lev. 25:47–55; Deut. 25:5–10). Third, the kinsman was to serve as a protector of blood, making sure that blood vengeance against a murderer was not neglected (Num. 35:16–25; Deut. 19:4–12; Josh. 20:1–9). In the case of Ruth, it was the second function that was required, the protection of Naomi and Ruth.

When confronted with his kinsman responsibility by the elders gathered at the city gate, the nearer kinsman at first consented. He was willing to buy the field of Naomi and keep the property in the family. But then he was informed of his further obligation—to marry Ruth and raise up a son to bear the name of the first husband and inherit the property (4:5). At this point, the offer seemed less attractive. To marry Ruth and redeem the property would jeopardize his own inheritance. Perhaps he did not want to invest in property that would not remain in his own family and belong to his own children. It is even possible that he hoped to inherit the property himself (see Num. 27:9). Either way, in declining, the nearer kinsman cleared the way for Boaz to act.

Ruth 4:9–10

How does Boaz illustrate Christ as our "Kinsman-Redeemer"?

The book of Ruth teaches that redemption requires a kinsman-redeemer. The qualifications and functions of the kinsman-redeemer are illustrated in Boaz, who is typical of the Lord Jesus Christ. The kinsman-redeemer had to be a blood relative to have the right of redemption, even as Christ was a blood relative of human beings through the virgin birth (John 1:14, 1 Tim. 2:15). The kinsman-redeemer had to have the resources to purchase the inheritance, even as Christ had the resource of His own precious blood (1 Peter 1:18–19). The kinsman also had to have the resolve to redeem, just as Christ laid down His life of His own volition (Mark 10:45).

Ruth 4:21–22

How was it possible for David, the great-grandson of a Moabite, to serve as king, build an altar, and worship in the assembly of the Lord?

According to Deuteronomy 23:3, no Moabite or any of his or her descendants for ten generations could enter the assembly of Yahweh to worship or to serve God. David was a third-generation descendant of a Moabite, yet he became king of Israel, built an altar, and sacrificed to Yahweh (2 Sam. 24:25)! The moral law of God is always binding, but Jesus pointed out that human need sometimes transcends the letter of the ceremonial law. He appealed to the fact that David ate the showbread that was only for the priests and that the priests broke the law by making bread on the Sabbath for the temple (Matt. 12:1–8).

The book of Ruth shows that the law of God is not to be trifled with. Elimelech left the land of promise and consequently lost his life. His sons died as well. But the book also demonstrates that there may be an exception to the ceremonial law of God based on faith and loyal love. Ruth, the Moabitess, demonstrated faith and covenant loyalty to God. The prohibition against Moabite participation in worship was superseded by the principle of faith.

1 SAMUEL

1 Samuel 1:1

Elkanah, the husband of Hannah, is called "an Ephraimite," yet he is named in 1 Chronicles 6:26–27 as a descendant of Levi. How is this possible?

Elkanah is clearly a descendant of Levi. The term "Ephraimite" refers to his geographical location not his ancestry. He lived in Ramah (1:19), in the territory of Ephraim.

1 Samuel 1:28

Does this passage lend support to baby dedication as is practiced in many churches today?

This is not baby dedication as is commonly practiced among Christians today. The word translated "dedicated" literally means "made him over to." In fulfillment of her vow, Hannah was giving her child completely and irrevocably to the Lord. From this point on Samuel would live in Shiloh under the supervision of Eli, the high priest. Samuel would receive visits from his mother only once a year. This is far different than the custom of baby dedication.

Rather than dedicating babies, perhaps churches should dedicate new parents, encouraging them to raise their children in a godly manner.

1 Samuel 6:19

How could 50,070 people have looked in the ark and been judged by the Lord? It seems that the deaths of some would have deterred the others from looking into the ark.

The number 50,070 is doubted even by conservative scholars and probably represents a scribal error in transmission.[1] The number 50,000 is absent in three Hebrew manuscripts. The figure given by the Jewish historian Josephus is 70 (*Antiquities* 6.16), which is reasonable and probably correct.

1 Samuel 8:21–22

In response to the persistent demands of the people, the Lord instructed Samuel to appoint the Israelites a king. Was this the will of God for Israel?

It is important to distinguish three aspects of the will of God. God's *sovereign* will is what God decrees to come to pass. It includes all things (Eph. 1:11) and is irresistible and immutable. We do not regard this as fatalism, for God is involved and concerned, and people are responsible for their actions. God's *preceptive* will is what He prescribes or prefers. This aspect of the will of God includes His moral desires as revealed in His Word (Exod. 20:1–17). Finally, God's *permissive* will refers to what the Lord permits even when it is not in conformity with His prescribed will. God may permit sin, though it is not in keeping with what He prefers.

Was it God's will for Israel to have a king? The answer is "yes!" Prophecies dating back to Moses indicate that this was God's plan (Gen. 49:10; Num. 24:17; Deut. 17:14–20). The fact that the monarchy was actually instituted indicates that it was part of God's sovereign will—His decree. But was it God's will that they acquire a king in the manner in which they were doing it? No. The people were rejecting the kingship of Yahweh (1 Sam. 8:7) and were motivated by a desire to be "like all the nations" (v. 20). Nevertheless, God allowed this to take place, because it was within His permissive will for the nation.

There is application for us. When believers are in God's sovereign will but out of His preceptive will (that is, disobedient), then they alone are responsible for their actions. God is sovereign, but people are responsible. With respect to sin and evil, God wills to permit it (see Gen. 50:20; Acts 2:23) but not to effect it, for He is not the author of evil (James 1:13).

1 Samuel 10:1

What is the significance of Samuel's anointing Saul with oil?

In biblical times anointing with oil signified a consecration or setting apart for service. The anointing of a ruler was actually a religious act that established a special relationship between God and the king, who then served as His anointed representative and ruler over His people.[2] Even though Saul became David's enemy, David refused to lift up his hand against "the Lord's anointed" (1 Sam. 24:6). Although David may have lost his respect for King Saul, he never lost his respect for God, whom Saul represented.

1 Samuel 13:8

When was Saul instructed to wait in Gilgal seven days for Samuel?

Verse 8 presents us with a chronological problem that takes us back to Saul's first anointing (1 Sam. 10:1–8). At that time Saul was commanded by Samuel to proceed to Gilgal and to wait there for him seven days in anticipation of Samuel's sacrifice (v. 8). First Samuel 13:8 obviously refers to the same event. Some commentators suggest that the events of 10:8–13:14 took place in a period of seven days, but that seems rather forced and unnecessary. Liberal scholars argue that the statement in 10:8 is misplaced and belongs elsewhere.

I suggest that Saul had agreed after his anointing by Samuel to meet at

Gilgal for sacrifice and worship prior to any major engagement with the Philistines (v. 8). The agreement had apparently been made about two years earlier (13:1–2). But rather than waiting for Samuel as he had been instructed, Saul offered the burnt offering himself in order to unify the people and prepare them for war (v. 9).

1 Samuel 15:35

How does the statement "Samuel did not see Saul again" harmonize with the encounter recorded in 1 Samuel 19:24?

First Samuel 15:35 indicates that Samuel did not "see" Saul again for the rest of his life. Yet Saul was with Samuel at Ramah (19:24). The key to this apparent discrepancy is that the Hebrew verb translated "to see" can mean "to give attention; take heed; or regard with interest." The point is that as God was through with Saul as king, so was Samuel. Samuel did not have regard for Saul as king for the rest of his life.

1 Samuel 16:2

Did God suggest that Samuel lie about his real purpose in going to Bethlehem to anoint a new king?

When the Lord instructed Samuel to go to Bethlehem to anoint a new king to replace Saul, the prophet was concerned for his own life. This concern was not unwarranted in light of Saul's spiritual degeneracy and violent temper (see 18:11). The Lord simply gave Samuel another reason to go to Bethlehem. He was to take a heifer and offer a sacrifice to the Lord (16:2). In order to avoid arousing the suspicions of Saul, the anointing would be performed while Samuel officiated at a sacrifice. If questions arose about his Bethlehem visit, Samuel could simply explain that he was there to sacrifice to the Lord.

1 Samuel 16:14

How should we understand the reference to "the evil spirit from the Lord" that terrorized Saul?

The "evil spirit from Yahweh" has been understood in various ways: (1) demonic possession as divine punishment; (2) demonic attack or influence; (3) an evil messenger like the one sent to entice Ahab (1 Kings 22:20–23); or (4) a spirit of discontent created by God in the heart of Saul (compare Judg. 9:23). Since Saul appears to have been a believer (see 10:6, 9), it is unlikely that he would have been demon-possessed. The contrast with the "Spirit of Yahweh" in the first part of the verse would rule out the spirit-of-discontent view. The verse should probably be understood to mean that God sovereignly appointed a demon, one of Satan's emissaries (see Matt. 12:24), to torment Saul. This might have been intended by God to drive Saul to his knees so that he might look to the Lord for help. The verse points to the fact that God is sovereign over all spiritual powers—even Satan and his assistants.

1 Samuel 17:55

Why did Saul not know David's family name since David had been serving as court musician (1 Sam. 16:18–23)?

Saul had promised 1 Samuel 17:25 that whoever defeated Goliath, he would "make his father's house free in Israel."

Saul knew David as his court musician but had apparently forgotten the name of David's father. He needed this information in order to reward David's family for the victory.

1 Samuel 28:8–14

How should we explain the appearance of Samuel before Saul and the witch of En-dor?

Saul was facing a critical battle with the Philistines and sought out a medium to help him determine the outcome. In the Hebrew, the phrase translated "medium" literally reads "a woman who is a mistress of necromancy," that is, one who consults the dead to determine the future. Under the cover of darkness, Saul traveled to En-dor and asked the medium to bring up the prophet Samuel from the dead (28:11).

The medium carried out Saul's instructions, but, rather than using the tricks of her trade to deceive Saul, she was very much surprised to see an old man appear whom Saul identified as Samuel (v. 14). The appearance of Samuel has been interpreted in various ways by scholars and theologians. Some have suggested that the appearance of Samuel was *psychological*—in the mind of Saul. There are two arguments against this view: (1) the woman also saw Samuel (v. 12); and (2) Saul actually talked with Samuel (v. 15). The church fathers held the view that a *demon impersonated Samuel* and appeared to Saul. But the message recorded in 28:16–19 would have hardly come from a demon. Still others have concluded that the medium was a *fraud* and tricked Saul into thinking that he saw Samuel. Yet the medium was surprised by Samuel's appearance (v. 12), and that would not have been the case had it been planned.

It seems best to follow the view held by the rabbis that the text records a *genuine appearance* of Samuel that God Himself brought about. There are at least five arguments in favor of this interpretation.

1. The medium was surprised, indicating that something happened that she was not expecting (v. 12).
2. Saul identified the figure as Samuel and bowed down in respect for the prophet. It is unlikely that Saul, who knew Samuel so well, would have been deceived by an impersonation.
3. The message Samuel spoke was clearly from God (vv. 16–19).
4. The biblical text itself says that the figure was Samuel (vv. 12, 15–16). It is clear that the author, under divine inspiration, intended the readers to understand that Samuel actually appeared to Saul.
5. A similar appearance of men from the dead took place when Moses

and Elijah appeared at Christ's transfiguration (Matt. 17:3). There is nothing inherently difficult with God bringing about a posthumous appearance of Samuel the prophet.

1 Samuel 31:12

Why were the bodies of Saul and his sons burned by the men of Jabesh-gilead?

Cremation was not the customary practice of the Hebrews. The burning of a body was usually reserved for criminals (see Josh. 7:25). Perhaps the bodies of Saul and his sons were burned because they had been mutilated or were badly decomposed. Verse 13 records that the bones were gathered and properly buried.

Endnotes

1. John J. Davis, *Biblical Numerology* (Grand Rapids: Baker Book House, 1968), 87–88.
2. Roland De Vaux, *The Bible and the Ancient Near East* (Garden City, N.Y.: Doubleday, 1967), 152–66.

2 SAMUEL

2 Samuel 1:5–10

How do we harmonize the Amalekite's report of Saul's death with the account of Saul's suicide in 1 Samuel 31:1–7?

While 1 Samuel 31 makes it clear that Saul committed suicide, the Amalekite claims to have found Saul wounded on the battlefield and to have killed him at the king's own command. There are two possible interpretations of the account. One possibility is that Saul attempted suicide but failed, and the Amalekite simply finished him off. The problem with this approach is that 1 Samuel 31:4–5 indicates that Saul died by falling on his sword.

It is more likely that Saul died as recorded in 1 Samuel 31:1–6 and that the Amalekite's story was a fabrication. The Amalekite apparently sought recognition from David or some reward for slaying Saul. As a mercenary soldier or battlefield looter (2 Sam. 1:8), he came across Saul's body and took Saul's crown and bracelet (v. 10) to substantiate his story and thus ingratiate himself to David. David apparently believed the Amalekite's story and had him executed on the basis of his own testimony of having slain Yahweh's anointed—something David had refused to do (1 Sam. 24; 26).

2 Samuel 5:9

What is the meaning of the term "Millo"?

The term "Millo" is derived from the Hebrew word translated "to fill." Hence, Millo has the idea of a place that is filled, a mound or a terrace. Some archaeologists have suggested that the term refers to terraces on the eastern slope of the City of David that served as supports for the buildings above. Others suggest that the term refers to an artificial fill required to overcome a depression in the saddle between the City of David and the Temple Mount. The Millo formed an important part of Jerusalem's defenses (1 Kings 9:15; 2 Chron. 32:5), but the exact location has not been identified with certainty.

2 Samuel 5:13

What accounts for David taking more wives?

The multiplication of David's wives was in direct violation of God's commands for the king (Deut. 17:17) and reflects David's failure to obey the

Lord. While love and lust may have been factors in David's actions, the marriages were more likely intended to enhance David's political standing among the nations of his day. In ancient times, international treaties and alliances were usually sealed by the marriage of a king's daughter to the other participant in the treaty. This served to unite the royal houses and solidify the relationship between the nations. This cultural background, no doubt, accounts for many of David's and Solomon's wives.

2 Samuel 8:4

How many horsemen did David capture when he defeated Hadadezer? First Chronicles 18:4 gives a larger number.

Second Samuel 8:4 records that David captured seventeen hundred horses from Hadadezer. But 1 Chronicles 18:4 gives the figure as seven thousand horsemen. How do we reconcile these figures?

The reference to seventeen horsemen in 2 Samuel 8:4 is apparently a scribal error in transmission, for the Septuagint and 1 Chronicles 18:4 indicate that the text should read "one thousand chariots and seven thousand horsemen." It has been suggested that the word for chariotry *(rekeb)* was inadvertently omitted by a scribe in copying 2 Samuel 8:4, leaving a reading of "one thousand and seven thousand horsemen." A later scribe then reduced the "seven thousand" to seven hundred, thus leaving a reading of seventeen hundred horsemen." In all probability, Chronicles contains the correct figures.

2 Samuel 11:2

Was Bathsheba behaving immodestly when David saw her bathing?

Archaeologists have discovered that Israelite houses during the Old Testament period traditionally had an enclosed courtyard that was considered part of the house. The courtyard was often the location of a cistern, a basin for collecting rainwater. Bathsheba, bathing at night, perhaps by lamp light, was actually "inside" her house. But her courtyard could be seen from the roof of David's house at a higher elevation. Bathsheba might have been more careful, knowing that she did not have the highest house on Mount Zion. But David, looking down from above, should have respected her privacy and turned away.

2 Samuel 12:23

Did David expect to see his child in heaven? Does this verse teach the salvation of infants?

God revealed to David that the child that he and Bathsheba had conceived in adultery would die (2 Sam. 12:14). When the child became sick, David fasted and mourned. But when the child died, David arose and ate food. Questioned by his servants about his behavior, David explained, "Now he has died; why should I fast? Can I bring him back again? I shall go to him, but he shall not return to me."

These words have been used by many to comfort grieving parents, assuring them that children who die in infancy are taken to heaven. Careful examination of the verse, however, indicates that David was not really speaking to the issue of afterlife but of the inevitability of death. The point of the verse is that there is no reason for continuing fasting, for the child had died. David's child could not return to life and activity, but David would someday join his son in death. Where did David expect to be at death? Psalm 6:4–5 and 16:10 indicate that David anticipated going to *sheol* (the grave), the place of the dead.

Where should we look for comfort when dealing with the death of an infant? While God has not chosen to reveal to us the eternal state of those who die in infancy, there is comfort in knowing that God is incomprehensibly righteous, loving, and just. We may have confidence that He will do what is right. Our comfort in a time of sorrow is in the character of our sovereign God.

Our Lord Jesus has a great love for children. When some women brought their children to Jesus so that He might lay hands on them and pray, the disciples rebuked them. But Jesus said, "Let the children alone, and do not hinder them from coming to Me; for the kingdom of heaven belongs to such as these" (Matt. 19:14). The character of God and the love of Christ for little ones leads me to believe that those who have died in infancy are in heaven with Jesus.

2 Samuel 12:31

What did David do to the Ammonites?

Second Samuel 12:26–31 records how David captured Rabbah and defeated the Ammonites. There are two interpretations of verse 31 regarding David's treatment of the Ammonites. Some interpreters believe that David imposed *hard labor* on the captives. However, the view would require us to emend the words "pass through" to "toil at." But this approach would contradict 1 Chronicles 20:3, which indicates that the Ammonites were cut with saws. Others believe that David imposed *cruel death* on the captives in accordance with Ammonite ways (1 Sam. 11:2; Amos 1:13). This view is probably correct, as confirmed by 1 Chronicles 20:3. The action may have been taken against only those warriors who resisted.

2 Samuel 14:27

This verse indicates that Absalom had three sons, but in 2 Samuel 18:18 he states, "I have no son to preserve my name." How should we understand these statements?

The text of 2 Samuel 14:27 states quite clearly that Absalom had three sons. The reference in 18:18 could be taken as a contradiction, but there is an alternative. Absalom's words, "I have no son to preserve my name," may be interpreted to mean that he had no son who could carry on the family name. The sons of Absalom are never named and may have died in infancy.

2 Samuel 15:7

Did Absalom's rebellion take place in the last year of David's reign?

Second Samuel 15:7 records that "at the end of forty" years Absalom went to Hebron to proclaim his kingship. The number forty could refer neither to the age of Absalom nor to the year of David's reign. The latter is unlikely since David reigned forty years and the rebellion probably would not have taken place in the last weeks of his reign.

It appears that the "forty years" is a scribal error in transmission and should read "four years," in keeping with the Septuagint, the Syriac, and Josephus's *Antiquities* (7.196). The four-year period began either with Absalom's return from Geshur (14:23) or his reconciliation with David (14:33).

2 Samuel 18:9

Where did we get the view that Absalom was caught in the tree by his hair?

The tradition that Absalom was caught by his hair comes from Josephus (*Antiquities* 7.239), but this suggestion makes sense in light of the comment about Absalom's long hair in 2 Samuel 14:26.

2 Samuel 19:24–30

Why did David rebuff Mephibosheth and divide Saul's land between Mephibosheth and his servant Ziba?

When David was returning from exile after Absalom's revolt, he was met at the Jordan by Saul's crippled son Mephibosheth. David asked why he had not followed David when Absalom usurped the throne. Mephibosheth, exhibiting the conventional signs of mourning, explained how he had been deceived by his servant and rests the matter with David's wise and just judgment. David's decision was to divide Saul's land between Mephibosheth and Ziba. There are three possible explanations for David's actions.

First, it is possible that David simply did not understand the facts of the case and made a poor judgment. Second, in light of Ziba's explanation (2 Sam. 16:1–4), he did not believe Mephibosheth to be totally innocent. Third, David may have been trying to repay Ziba for his earlier kindness (vv. 1–2) and simply forgave his deceit regarding Mephibosheth.

2 Samuel 21:19

Who slew the giant Goliath?

Second Samuel 21:19 attributes the slaying of Goliath to Elhanan, in contradiction with the account of David's victory recorded in 1 Samuel 17:50. There are at least three possible solutions to this problem. First, there could have been two giants by the name of Goliath. Second, Elhanan and David may be different names for the same person, just as Solomon was also known by the name Jedidiah (2 Sam. 12:25). Third, there has been a scribal error in transmission and the text should read, "Elhanan . . . killed the *brother of Goliath*." This third view is supported by the parallel account in 1 Chronicles 20:5.

2 Samuel 24:1–10

What led David to numbering of the people and why was this sinful?

Second Samuel 24:1 suggests that the numbering was prompted by the Lord, while 1 Chronicles 21:1 indicates that it was prompted by Satan. These references reflect two aspects of the same incident. Although Satan actually instigated the pride and rebellion that led to the numbering of the people, God permitted Satan to exercise that influence so that His divine plan might be carried out. A similar situation is recorded in Genesis 50:20 where Joseph explains that while his brothers did evil against him, God used those actions to accomplish good.

Why was the numbering of the people sinful when God had commanded a similar census earlier in Israel's history (compare Num. 1:1–3)? Josephus speculates that David's error was in forgetting to collect the half shekel for every head counted (compare Exod. 30:12–13; *Antiquities* 7.318). It is also possible that David had been commanded not to number the people but did so anyway. Perhaps the sin was in David's own lack of faith in God's protective care over the nation. He may have been trusting in himself and the military strength he could muster rather than in the Lord.

2 Samuel 24:16

What does it mean that the Lord "relented" (KJV "repented") of the calamity He was about to bring on Jerusalem?

The clear teaching of Scripture is that God does not change His mind or character (1 Sam. 15:29; James 1:17). The term *relented* (Hebrew, *naham*) is an expression of God's sorrow concerning evil, as in Genesis 6:6. God's character and attitude toward sin does not change. But He may change His approach toward sinful people based on a change in their attitude. Whereas God will manifest wrath and judgment on sinners, He demonstrates mercy and forgiveness toward the repentant.

1 KINGS

1 Kings 1:1–4

What kind of relationship did David have with Abishag, and why does the text record that David had no intercourse with her?

King David lived before the time of central heating and electric blankets. In his old age, when he could not keep warm, his servants provided him with Abishag, a lovely young maiden who "became his nurse." The word *nurse* is somewhat misleading. The Hebrew word is derived from the verb meaning, "to be familiar with," and refers to someone who stands in an intimate relationship with another person. Abishag slept with David to keep the king warm.

Verse 4 records that David did not have sexual intercourse with Abishag. Why is this intimate detail revealed? Perhaps it is intended to illustrate David's physical decline (that is, impotency). But more likely, this point is noted to show that Abishag was not David's wife or concubine and explains how Adonijah could ask for her as a wife (1 Kings 2:17) in light of the prohibition of Deuteronomy 22:30.

1 Kings 2:17–24

Why did Bathsheba and Solomon view Adonijah's request for Abishag so differently?

After Solomon took the throne, Adonijah asked Bathsheba to speak to the king about taking Abishag as his wife. Bathsheba seemed accepting of the proposal and brought the matter to her son Solomon. But King Solomon was outraged and declared, "Ask for him also the kingdom. Surely Adonijah will be put to death today" (1 Kings 2:22, 24).

In touch with the cultural clues of his day, Solomon no doubt recognized that appropriating the royal harem was a recognized method of laying claim to the throne (2 Sam. 16:21). He interpreted Adonijah's request as an indication of Adonijah's persistent pursuit of the Judean throne. Bathsheba, on the other hand, may not have considered the request inappropriate. In her view, Abishag could not be considered David's wife or concubine since he had not known her intimately (1 Kings 1:4). From Adonijah's perspective, he may have been innocent of any further attempts at the throne but made a foolish request that cost him his life. On the other hand, he may have been seeking to outwit both

Bathsheba and Solomon in laying claim to the throne, but the plan failed. In any case, the results were the same. Adonijah was executed and Solomon's throne was established.

1 Kings 3:2–4

What was Solomon doing sacrificing at a high place?

A "high place" was an elevated platform used by the Canaanites to offer sacrifices to their gods. The Lord clearly instructed the Israelites that these cultic worship centers were to be destroyed when they entered the land (Num. 33:52). Yet we find that the Israelites were using high places to worship Yahweh after the destruction of Shiloh (see 1 Sam. 9:12–14; 10:5, 10). It seems that high places were generally forbidden by the Lord, but in the absence of a tabernacle or central sanctuary, Yahweh accepted high places dedicated to true worship.

1 Kings 7:23

Are the measurements of the bronze sea an example of an error in Scripture?

Among the bronze vessels prepared by the skilled metal worker Hiram was a bronze sea. The measurements of this item have raised a question regarding the accuracy of Scripture. The text records that it had a five-cubit diameter (15 feet) and a thirty-cubit circumference (45 feet). At first, that does not seem possible. A basic rule of geometry is that the circumference is equal to *pi* times diameter. But 45 feet times *pi* (3.14159) comes to 14.3 feet, not 15! Is this evidence of an error in Scripture?

In the first place, it should be noted that the author is simply providing a general description of the bronze sea. It would be unwise and unfair to demand geometrical precision of a general description. But it is possible to provide a reasonable explanation of the data. Perhaps the sea had an outer lip and the 15 feet was measured from this point, whereas the interior diameter amounts to 14.3 feet. It is also possible that the thickness of the sides accounts for a difference between the interior and exterior measurements. These are reasonable explanations of the apparent conflict. There simply is not enough information to say that this verse contains an error.

1 Kings 11:30–36

At the division of the kingdom, did one tribe go unassigned?

When Ahijah predicted the division of the kingdom, he dramatically tore his new robe into twelve pieces and gave ten to Jeroboam. This was symbolic of the division of the kingdom and the apportioning of the twelve tribes. Then, regarding Solomon, the Lord declared, "but he will have one tribe, for the sake of My servant David and for the sake of Jerusalem" (1 Kings 11:32). What happened to the twelfth tribe?

The one tribe that was promised to Solomon was the tribe of Benjamin. This is evident from 1 Kings 11:36, where the Lord declared, "But to his son I will give one tribe, that My servant David may have a lamp always before Me in Jerusalem." Since Jerusalem was in the tribal territory of Benjamin (Josh. 18:16), the promise of this tribe would guarantee the preservation of Judah's capital. The tribe of Judah is not mentioned in the division since the loyalty of David's own tribe would have been assumed.

There are no tribes missing from the division. The southern kingdom received the tribes of Judah and Benjamin (1 Kings 12:21). The northern kingdom received the tribes of Reuben, Gad, Asher, Naphtali, Manasseh, Issachar, Zebulun, Dan, Ephraim, and Simeon (2 Chron. 15:9; 34:6).

1 Kings 11:4

How can this passage say that David was wholly devoted to the Lord when he was guilty of adultery and murder?

The very first allusion to David in Scripture refers to him as "a man after His [God's] own heart" (1 Sam. 13:14). David's spiritual integrity and walk with God is repeatedly referred to as an example for others to follow (1 Kings 3:14; 9:4; 11:6). And yet David was by no means perfect. His sins and failures were many. But in spite of these problems, his heart was always tender toward the Lord (see Pss. 32 and 51). Furthermore, David did not gain divine favor or approval because of his blameless character but because of his great faith in God. Although none of us is perfect, we can—by personal faith—be people whose hearts are fully devoted to our God.

1 Kings 15:1

What principles should we employ when synchronizing the reigns of the kings of Judah with the reigns of the kings of Israel?

The principles we employ were first presented in an article by Edwin R. Thiele,[1] professor of religion at the University of Chicago. In his research, Thiele managed to account for all the chronological data in Kings and Chronicles without wholesale emendation of the Masoretic text. His methodology and conclusions were later expanded into a book, *The Mysterious Numbers of the Hebrew Kings* (University of Chicago Press, 1951). The major principles essential to a proper understanding of Hebrew chronology are summarized here.

1. *Two Methods of Reckoning the Years of a King's Reign*

In Assyria, Babylon, and Persia, when a king came to the throne the year was called the king's accession year, and the first year of his reign was reckoned from the first day of the year after the king assumed the throne.

The nonaccession-year method of dating reckoned the king's first year from the day he first came to the throne. The new king's first year would also be the last year of the former king. The nonaccession-year system is always one year greater than the year of reign according to the accession-year method.

For example, Gerald Ford succeeded Richard Nixon in July 1974. According to the nonaccession-year system, 1974 was Ford's first year. According to the accession-year method, 1974 was Ford's accession year and his first year did not begin until 1975.

Based on the chronological data found in the Scripture, Thiele has determined conclusively that at the division of the monarchy (931 B.C.) the northern kingdom adopted the nonaccession-year method, and the southern kingdom continued using the accession-year system. This situation prevailed until the reign of Jehoram of Judah, who was allied with the northern kingdom through his marriage to Athaliah, Ahab's daughter, and who adopted Israel's nonaccession-year system in 848 B.C. Later, in the days of Jehoash and Amaziah (796 B.C.), both kingdoms shifted to accession-year dating, perhaps due to the growth of Assyrian influence.

It should be noted that throughout the history of the divided monarchy, Israel and Judah used their own systems to synchronize with the neighboring kingdoms regardless of the systems their neighbors employed.

2. *Two Methods of Computing Regnal Years*

A second principle essential to a proper understanding of the chronology of the Hebrew monarchy is that two methods of computing regnal years were in use by the Israelites during the period of the divided monarchy. While the religious year was reckoned from Nisan to Nisan (Exod. 12:2), the civil year began in the autumn and went from Tishri to Tishri (compare Lev. 23:24).

Citing evidence from 1 Kings 6:1, 37, Thiele demonstrates that Solomon's regnal year was computed from Tishri, and that his successors in the southern kingdom computed their regnal years on the basis of a Tishri-to-Tishri year.

In the northern kingdom, Jeroboam adopted the practice of a spring new year as it was observed in Egypt and Mesopotamia rather than follow the custom observed in the rival kingdom of Judah (compare 1 Kings 12:2–3, 20, 32–33; 15:1).

3. *Reigns Not Always Figured from the Official Accession Year*

Often there were coregencies where a particular king ruled with his father. Such a precedent was set by David when he had Solomon anointed king before his death (1 Kings 1:39; 2:1). Unless one posits the existence of coregencies, the overlapping years might be understood as consecutive and the history of the nation would be inaccurately extended. The coregencies commenced with the first, rather than the accession year of the king.

4. *Synchronisms with Extrabiblical Sources*

The entire system of Old Testament chronology for the kings of Israel and Judah can be interlocked at vital points with the astronomically verified absolute chronology of the Assyrian eponym lists (name lists that recorded the officials who held the office of *Limmu* during a particular year in Assyria's history). The lists give not only the names, but also principal events of the year, such as the eclipse of June 15, 763 B.C.

Some of the important dates established by the eponym lists are the Battle of Qarqar (853 B.C.), the tribute of Jehu to Shalmaneser III (841 B.C.), the western campaign of Tiglath-pileser III (743 B.C.), the conquest of Samaria (722 B.C.), and the attack of Sennacherib on Jerusalem (701 B.C.).

Applying Thiele's principles to these dates, we are able to determine that the date of the disruption of the monarchy was 931 B.C. From this crucial date the chronologer may count up or down to determine other important dates in Israel's history. Having laid out Thiele's principles, I will refrain from repeating the research here, which can be found in his helpful, updated volume, *A Chronology of the Hebrew Kings.*[2]

1 Kings 21:19; 22:37–38

Is Elijah guilty of a failed prophecy regarding the place where the dogs licked up Ahab's blood?

In 1 Kings 21:19 Elijah predicted, "In the place where the dogs licked up the blood of Naboth the dogs shall lick up your blood, even yours." Later, in 1 Kings 22:37–38 we read that after Ahab's death his body was brought to Samaria. There, by the pool of Samaria, his chariot was washed out and "the dogs licked up his blood." If Naboth was stoned to death at Jezreel (21:1–16), how could Elijah's prophecy about Ahab be fulfilled at Samaria?

This certainly seems like a clear contradiction. But several points should be noted. First, the text does not state explicitly where Naboth was stoned. First Kings 21:13 simply says that his accusers took him "outside the city." It is possible that they could have taken him as far as Samaria for execution at the capital. Second, the text does not state where the dogs licked up the blood of Naboth. It is only assumed that this happened at Jezreel. It is possible that his body was taken to Samaria for verification by Jezebel and that the dogs licked up his blood there. Whatever the case, the author of 1 Kings did not perceive any contradiction in his account and presents the account of the dogs licking up the blood of Ahab as a fulfillment of Elijah's prophecy. What seems to be a discrepancy to the twentieth-century reader was apparently not a problem to the ancient author.

1 Kings 22:22

How should we understand God's use of a "deceiving spirit" to entice Ahab to battle?

In 1 Kings 22, after Micaiah's prediction of Ahab's defeat at Ramoth-gilead, this true prophet of God presents a vision that explains why the false prophets have predicted Ahab's victory. In his vision, the Lord questions, "Who will entice Ahab to go up and fall at Ramoth-gilead?" (v. 20). An evil spirit volunteers, "I will go out and be a deceiving spirit in the mouth of all his prophets." Micaiah concludes by declaring to Ahab, "Now therefore, behold, the LORD has put a deceiving spirit in the mouth of all these your prophets; and the LORD has proclaimed disaster against you" (v. 23).

We should note, first of all, that this is a vision that portrays how Ahab is being deceived by his false prophets. Visions are designed to teach truth through symbols. This vision dramatically demonstrates God's complete sovereignty over His creation. Even evil spirits are under His control and can be used by God to accomplish His sovereign purposes. Second, God did not tell the evil spirit to lie. He simply allowed the spirit to carry on his deceiving work. The work of the deceiving spirit vividly pictures how Ahab was being deluded by his false prophets. Third, this vision does not commend or promote lying. God is truth (Deut. 32:4), and believers are clearly instructed to speak the truth (Exod. 20:16; Eph. 4:25). Finally, it was for the purpose of divine judgment that God allowed Ahab to be deceived by an evil spirit. This is the story of a man who persistently rejected the truth. So God simply permitted the lying spirit to be an instrument for his defeat and death. This is similar to what Paul describes in 2 Thessalonians 2:11–12 where God will send "deluding influence" on those who reject the truth "in order that they all may be judged."

1 Kings 22:48–49

Was Jehoshaphat a willing partner in his ill-fated commercial venture with King Ahaziah of Israel?

Some Bible students have spotted an apparent contradiction between the records of 1 Kings and 2 Chronicles regarding Jehoshaphat's involvement with Ahaziah in a shipping enterprise. Second Chronicles 20:35–36 records that Jehoshaphat king of Judah allied himself with Ahaziah king of Israel to build ships to sail to Tarshish. Then when Ahaziah requested that Jehoshaphat take some of his servants in the ships, Jehoshaphat refused (1 Kings 22:48–49). How do we account for this?

Jehoshaphat's alliance with Ahaziah, son of Ahab, was a compromise with a worshiper of Baal. This relationship was condemned by the prophet Eliezer, who warned of the disastrous outcome of the venture (2 Chron. 20:37). It seems that at this point, Jehoshaphat backed out of the venture and refused to let Ahaziah's servants sail on the ships (1 Kings 22:49). The Lord's judgment on this alliance is evidenced by the fact that the ships were destroyed, apparently by a storm, before they left the harbor.

Endnotes

1. Edwin R. Thiele, "Chronology of the Last Kings of Judah," *Journal of Near Eastern Studies* 3 (1944), 137–286.
2. Thiele, *A Chronology of the Hebrew Kings* (Grand Rapids: Zondervan, 1977).

2 KINGS

2 Kings 2:1

What was the function of the prophets Elijah and Elisha in relationship to the paganism and idolatry of their day?

Elijah and Elisha were prophets representing God as protagonists against idolatry and Baal worship. As speakers for Yahweh, Elijah and Elisha labored diligently to expose the absurdity of Baal worship and to discredit it in the eyes of their contemporaries.

How did they accomplish their purpose? Leah Bronner has effectively demonstrated how the miracles of Elijah and Elisha served as polemics against paganism.[1] Elijah and Elisha were well acquainted with the myths circulating about Baal that attributed to him numerous and varied powers. The Canaanites believed that Baal was the storm and fertility god who bestowed upon humans and upon the land the blessings of fertility. He sent forth lightning, fire, and rain. He gave corn, oil, and wine. He could revive the dead, heal the sick, and bestow the blessing of progeny. Elijah and Elisha wished to liberate the people from these beliefs by showing through their miracles that all the powers ascribed to Baal by Ugaritic mythology are really the attributes of Yahweh only!

At an ancient site in Syria, known as Ugarit, a vast library of cuneiform texts was found by French archaeologists. The texts date from the biblical period and shed light on the culture and religion of ancient times. In Ugaritic sources Baal is shown to be in control of fire and lightning. Many Ugaritic texts refer to Baal as flashing his thunderbolts and having control over fire. The references to the "chariot of fire" (2 Kings 2:11; 6:17) show that Yahweh is the one who controls this element. The fire of Yahweh that fell at Mount Carmel (1 Kings 18:38) and upon the soldiers of Ahaziah (2 Kings 1:10–14) demonstrates conclusively that it is Yahweh who controls fire.

Many Ugaritic texts attest to Baal's dominion over rain. Only with his approval could rain fall and cause the land to prosper. It was this concept of Baal that Elijah wanted to prove false when he began his prophetic ministry by proclaiming, "As Yahweh the God of Israel lives, before whom I stand, there shall be neither dew nor rain these years, except by my word" (1 Kings 17:1). Elisha also demonstrated Yahweh's control over water in healing the waters at Jericho (2 Kings 2:19–22) and predicting the provision of water for the three kings campaigning against Moab (3:17).

The stone reliefs of Baal portray his relation to vegetation and indicate that he has dominion over agriculture and the produce of the land. Baal was closely related to grain. As grain "dies" and is "revived" in the earth, so was the case with Baal. As Baal conquered Mot, the god of death, through the help of fertility goddess Anath, fertility returned to the land and the heavens are said to "rain oil," a metaphorical description of agricultural prosperity due to good rainfall.

The miraculous feeding of Elijah at the brook Cherith demonstrates that Yahweh is the provider of bread (1 Kings 17:6). The miraculous provision of the oil and meal for the widow of Zarephath (2 Kings 1:16), the feeding of Elijah in the wilderness (1 Kings 19:6), the provision of oil to pay the debts of the poor widow (2 Kings 4:1–6), and the miraculous feeding of the hundred men with the twenty loaves (vv. 42–43) all serve to demonstrate that Yahweh is the One who increases oil and multiplies grain. The miracle of providing oil and grain for the widow of Zarephath took place in Phoenicia in order to demonstrate that even in that land it was not Baal but Yahweh who gave oil and meal!

In one Ugaritic text the gift of progeny is apparently given by the chief Canaanite diety El at the request of his son Baal. As the authority of Baal continued to grow, that of El diminished, until by the time of Elijah and Elisha formal consent of El would no longer be necessary. The blessing of Elisha on the Shunamite woman who eventually gave birth to a son (vv. 16–17) shows that not Baal but the prophet of Yahweh is to be approached as an intercessor for children. Yahweh is the one who provides children, not Baal!

The people of Ugarit were well acquainted with the myths relating the dying and rising of Baal. It is quite possible that they believed that Baal, who died and was resurrected, had the power to resuscitate others. Baal's victory over death was regarded by his followers as having dominion over it. The raising of the widow's son (1 Kings 17:17–23), the raising of the Shunamite's son (2 Kings 4:32–37), and the posthumous miracle of the resurrection of the corpse that touched Elisha's bones (13:21) are designed to show that Yahweh controls life and death, not Baal.

Baal is also associated with healing (compare 5:13–27) and with having dominion over the river (compare 11:8–14). Other stories portray Baal as eating and sleeping (compare 1 Kings 18:27). The miracles of Elijah and Elisha demonstrate that the myths ascribing great power to Baal are false. Such powers are Yahweh's only!

2 Kings 2:9

What did the "double portion" promised to Elisha imply?

The meaning of the double portion must be traced to Deuteronomy 21:17 where the expression is used to describe the inheritance of the firstborn. The law required that the firstborn son of an Israelite receive a double portion of the inheritance. When Elisha said, "Let a double portion of your spirit be upon me," he was using the language of metaphor. Quite simply, Elisha was making a formal request to function as Elijah's firstborn—to become the primary heir of his prophetic ministry.

2 Kings 2:23–24

How do we account for the severity of God's judgment on the "lads" who mocked Elisha?

When Elisha was going up to the city of Bethel, he was met by some young men who mocked him, "Go up, you baldhead; go up, you baldhead!" The words "go up" appear to refer to the recent ascension of Elijah. And the term "baldhead" is obviously a reference to Elisha's receding hairline. The words rendered "young lads" refers not to children but to young men. The feminine form of this designation can refer to a girl of marriageable age. The term in verse 24 is used in 1 Kings 12:8 of the young men who counseled Rehoboam.

In the incident recorded here, we are not considering the actions of foolish little children but of responsible young men who should know better. By suggesting that Elisha "Go up" and ascend like Elijah, they were rejecting God's prophet, His anointed representative. The divine judgment that fell upon the forty-two young men was in keeping with the curses of the covenant that God promised on the disobedient (Deut. 28:26).

2 Kings 6:19

Did Elisha lie to the Syrian soldiers that were coming to capture him?

The Syrian (Aramean) soldiers were sent by their king to apprehend Elisha. They surrounded Dothan with the hopes of capturing him but were stricken with temporary blindness in answer to Elisha's prayer. Elisha then informed them, "This is not the way, nor is this the city; follow me and I will bring you to the man whom you seek" (2 Kings 6:19). They were then led by the prophet about ten miles to Samaria where the Lord opened their eyes and they saw Elisha.

Careful review of the facts of this case indicate that Elisha spoke no lie. He simply told the blinded soldiers that they were not going to find the prophet in Dothan, but they would in another place. True to his promise, Elisha led them to Samaria and revealed himself to them there.

2 Kings 19:9

Was Tirhakah, king of Cush, old enough to lead a campaign against Sennacherib in 701 B.C.?

The inscriptions of Sennacherib indicate that his invasion of Judah and siege of Jerusalem occurred in 701 B.C. (2 Kings 18–19; Isa. 36–37). The biblical record of this campaign also mentions the threatenings of "Tirhakah king of Cush" (2 Kings 19:9). But the Kawa Stela 4, which refers to Tirhakah, seems to indicate that the Egyptian ruler was only nine years of age in 701, hardly of age to lead the army that tried to defeat Sennacherib.

Some scholars have theorized that the action with Tirhakah implies a second invasion of Judah by Sennacherib—one not recorded in extant Assyrian annals but which occurred sometime around 680 B.C.

The speculations about a second campaign by Sennacherib have been undermined by a reexamination of the Egyptian texts. Based on more careful study, it now appears that Tirhakah's father, Piankhy, died in 713 B.C. at the very latest, but more likely around 717 or 716 B.C. As Tirhakah was a son of Piankhy, he could not be only nine in 701 B.C., born four to seven years after the death of his father!

A mistake was also made in assigning Tirhakah's age at twenty to the year 690/689 B.C. (mentioned in Kawa Stela 5.17). Actually, he was twenty just after his brother Shebitku's accession to the throne in 702 B.C. Further examination of the Egyptian texts indicates that Tirhakah was twenty or twenty-one years old in 701 B.C., when his brother summoned him to assume leadership in the campaign into Judah. He was certainly old enough to play this responsible role, even though he was not the reigning king. It was common practice in the ancient Orient for writers to refer to people and places by titles and names acquired later than the period being described. Tirhakah would have been king by the time the episode was recorded in Isaiah 36 and 2 Kings 18. Indeed, Egyptian texts refer to him as "His Majesty" (Kawa Stela 4.7–8) at a time when he was only crown prince.[2]

2 Kings 20:11

How could the shadow retreat by ten degrees on the stairway?

When Hezekiah prayed to God about his mortal illness, he was promised another fifteen years of life (2 Kings 20:6). Somewhat doubtful, the king asked Isaiah for a sign of the Lord's healing. After considering the options before him, Hezekiah asked that the shadow on the stairway of Ahaz "turn backward ten steps" (v. 10). God granted the request and "He brought the shadow on the stairway back ten steps."

Since the advance of the shadow is the natural result of the earth's rotation, how could God have stopped the earth and turned it backward to accomplish this miracle? Such a reversal would have had a cataclysmic repercussions! Here we encounter the same kind of problem we faced in Joshua's record of how the sun stood still. It is reasonable to assume that the shadow's reversal was a miracle that occurred on a local rather than a cosmic level. Exactly how God accomplished this wonder remains a mystery—but that's the nature of miracles!

2 Kings 24:6

Did Jehoiakim die in Jerusalem or in Babylon, as indicated by 2 Chronicles 36:6?

Second Kings 24:6 records that Jehoiakim "slept with his fathers," a euphemism for death. The text does not disclose the place of his death. Second

Chronicles 36:6 records that Jehoiakim was taken in bronze chains to Babylon. This passage contains no reference to his release or his death. It is possible that Jehoiakim was eventually released to return to Jerusalem and lived out his life there. On the other hand, he could have died in captivity. The biblical record is simply not explicit on this point.

Endnotes

1. Leah Bronner, *The Stories of Elijah and Elisha as Polemics against Baal Worship* (Leiden: E. J. Brill, 1968), 1–175.
2. K. A. Kitchen, *Ancient Orient and Old Testament* (Downers Grove, Ill.: InterVarsity Press, 1966), 82.

1 & 2 CHRONICLES

Purpose

Why do we need Chronicles if we have the books of Samuel and Kings?
What distinctive contribution does Chronicles make?

The existence of several histories covering the same period suggests to us that the purpose of Chronicles is not simply to record another history of Israel. Some have thought of Chronicles as containing supplemental material. While this is true, it does not account for all the material in Chronicles. In studying the books of Chronicles we discover the author, probably Ezra, is more concerned with the *interpretation* of history than merely with the recording of events. Based on a review of Judah's past, Ezra provides a message for the contemporary generation of Jews concerning how they should live in the future. The books of Chronicles have five distinctive characteristics.

1. *Religious Emphasis.* The writer of Chronicles is concerned mainly with Israel as a religious community. He is especially concerned with religious institutions—the priesthood, the temple, and worship. He intends for the record of Chronicles to preserve the priesthood and proper temple worship and to maintain the ethnic and religious purity of the Jews.

2. *Moralistic Emphasis.* The author is a commentator as well as a recorder, a religious teacher as well as a historian. Chronicles gives spiritual insight into Israel's history and provides many moral lessons.

3. *Levitical Emphasis.* There is a great emphasis on Levitical institutions: the Law of Moses (1 Chron. 22), the ark (13–16), and the Levites and singers (13; 15–16).

4. *Success Emphasis.* The writer is interested in focusing on the success of Judah's kings. There is no reference to David's failures (2 Sam. 1–4; 11–12) or Solomon's failures (1 Kings 11). Saul's reign, Absalom's rebellion, Adonijah's attempt to usurp the throne are all omitted.

5. *Southern Kingdom.* The writer is concerned with the Davidic line of kings. These kings reigned in Judah, the southern kingdom. Chronicles records no history of the northern kingdom except where it relates to Judah. For this reason the Elijah and Elisha stories are absent.

Text

> *What is the relationship of Chronicles to the books of Samuel and Kings?*

There are four different ways in which Chronicles relates to the material found in the books of Samuel and Kings.

1. *Follows Samuel and Kings.* Sometimes we find that Chronicles follows the accounts in Samuel and Kings quite closely. In such cases, Chronicles can be helpful when doing textual criticism.
2. *Paraphrases Samuel and Kings.* Sometimes the writer of Chronicles presents a paraphrase of materials appearing in Samuel and Kings. Compare Solomon's address and prayer of dedication for the temple in 1 Kings 8:12–50 and 2 Chronicles 6:1–42.
3. *Adds Unique Material.* Sometimes Chronicles adds unique material that is not found in Samuel or Kings. Examples include David's dedication of the ark (1 Chron. 16) and preparation for temple worship (22–29), Uzziah's pride and discipline by the Lord (2 Chron. 26), and Manasseh's captivity and repentance (33).
4. *Gives a Different Account.* Sometimes the chronicler gives a slightly different account of the events. It is this category of differences that presents difficulties for those who hold to the inspiration and inerrancy of Scripture. If God's Word is truth, shouldn't two accounts say the same thing?

Differences between Chronicles and the other historical books provide an opportunity for us to search for a satisfactory way to harmonize the events. For example, in 2 Samuel 5:21 it is reported that David and his men "carried away" the idols that the enemy had abandoned. In 1 Chronicles 14:12 it is recorded that the idols were burned with fire. What actually happened? I suggest that the idols were *first* carried away and *then* burned with fire. Geisler and Howe have done an excellent service in proposing solutions to many of the apparent contradictions.[1]

> *Where did the author of Chronicles find the supplemental material for this book?*

Three different kinds of material are cited or referred to by the author.

1. *Prophetic Works*
   Records of Nathan the Prophet—2 Chronicles 9:29
   Prophecy of Ahijah the Shilonite—2 Chronicles 9:29
   Visions of Iddo the Seer—2 Chronicles 9:29
   Records of Shemaiah the Prophet and Iddo the Seer—2 Chronicles 12:15
   Commentary of the Prophet Iddo—2 Chronicles 13:22
   Annals of Jehu the Son of Hanania—2 Chronicles 20:34
   Acts of Uzziah, by Isaiah—2 Chronicles 26:22
   Records of Hozai—2 Chronicles 33:19

2. *Historical Works*
   The Book of the Kings of Israel—1 Chronicles 9:1
   The Book of the Kings of Judah and Israel—2 Chronicles 16:11
   The Book of the Kings of Israel and Judah—2 Chronicles 27:7
   The Records of the Kings of Israel—2 Chronicles 33:18
3. *Works Belonging to the Reign of David*
   The History of Samuel the Seer—1 Chronicles 29:29
   The History of Nathan the Prophet—1 Chronicles 29:29
   The History of Gad the Seer—1 Chronicles 29:29

Endnotes

1. Norman Geisler and Thomas Howe, *When Critics Ask* (Wheaton: Victor Books, 1992), 201–12.

EZRA

Ezra 1:1

What date marks the ending of the seventy-year captivity predicted by Jeremiah?

Ezra indicates that the decree of Cyrus allowing for the return of the Jews came in fulfillment of Jeremiah's prophecy that the Judeans would be in captivity seventy years (Jer. 25:11–12; 29:10). There are two possible ways of calculating the fulfillment of the prophecy. The first method is to date the beginning of the Captivity in 605 B.C. when the Jews were first taken captive to Babylon (Dan. 1:1; 2 Kings 24:1). According to this view, the Captivity would conclude in 536 B.C. when the Jews began work on the second temple in Jerusalem. A second way of calculating the seventy years is from 586 B.C., when the Babylonians destroyed Jerusalem, to 515 B.C., when the rebuilding of the second temple was completed.

While either system works, the prophecy is best fulfilled by the first method. Jeremiah's prophecy concerns the period of captivity rather than the period that the temple would be out of commission. The Jews were first taken captive to Babylon in 605 B.C. Their return to the land—in fulfillment of Jeremiah's prophecy—was marked by the setting up of the temple altar in 536 B.C.

Ezra 1:2–3

Was Cyrus a believer?

The words of Cyrus, "Yahweh, the God of Israel; He is the God who is in Jerusalem," might lead us to conclude that Cyrus was a believer. However, an ancient inscription recording the words of Cyrus tells the rest of the story. In the inscription, Cyrus acknowledges the gods Bel, Nebo, and Marduk. He states that Bel and Nebo wanted him to rule over Babylon. He refers to Marduk as "the great Lord" and states, "I was daily endeavoring to worship him."[1]

The testimony of Cyrus himself suggests that he was a polytheist—a worshiper of many gods. He simply acknowledges Yahweh as one of many gods. The fact that Cyrus was not a believer in the one true God is indicated by the Lord's statement concerning him: "I will gird you, though you have not known Me" (Isa. 45:5). God used Cyrus as an instrument of deliverance, but Cyrus did not know the Lord.

Ezra 1:8

Is Sheshbazzar the same person as Zerubbabel?

There are three main views regarding the identity of Sheshbazzar and his relationship with Zerubbabel. Some expositors argue that Sheshbazzar is simply another name for Zerubbabel. Daniel, for example, had a Hebrew and a Babylonian name (Dan. 1:7). In support of this view is the fact that Zerubbabel is said to have laid the foundation of the temple (Ezra 3:8; 5:2; Zech. 4:9), but in an official letter to Darius, Sheshbazzar is said to have done this (Ezra 5:16). On this basis, it is suggested that the two must have been the same person.

Others have suggested that Sheshbazzar may have been the officially appointed leader (v. 14), whereas Zerubbabel rose up as a popular but unofficial leader at the time of the first return. However, the apocryphal book 1 Esdras in 6:18 states that the temple vessels being returned to Jerusalem were entrusted to Sheshbazzar and Zerubbabel as separate individuals.

The view that is most consistent with the biblical record is that Sheshbazzar preceded Zerubbabel, his nephew. Sheshbazzar was appointed by Cyrus (Ezra 1:8; 5:14) but may have died soon after the return in 537 B.C. Zerubbabel, probably Sheshbazzar's nephew[2] (1 Chron. 3:17–19), was then elevated to the position vacated by his uncle and received the title "governor" (Hag. 1:1, 14; 2:2, 21). This view is supported by the fact that while both men are associated with laying the foundation of the temple in 536 B.C. (Ezra 5:16; Zech. 4:9), only Zerubbabel is associated with completing the project two decades later (Hag. 1:1, 12; Zech. 4:9).

Ezra 4

Is the chronology of chapter 4 confused?

Ezra 4 records the opposition and hostility experienced by the returned exiles as they sought to reestablish themselves in the land. The opposition began in the time of Sheshbazzar and Zerubbabel (536 B.C.) and continued until the days of Nehemiah (444 B.C.).

Verses 6–23 record the opposition experienced by the Jews during the reigns of Ahasuerus (486–464 B.C.) and Artaxerxes (464–424 B.C.). Some scholars have suggested that these verses are chronologically misplaced since they record events that took place fifty to ninety years after the first return. Within the context of Ezra 4, it is better to understand these verses as illustrating that the opposition to the temple rebuilding in 536 B.C. was not an isolated incident. This was simply one of several experiences that the Jews faced at this time. Although Ezra is telling the story of the first return, he is writing about a hundred years later. In telling the story, he simply mentions these two other examples of opposition to show how such experiences were characteristic of the restoration period. There is no chronological confusion here when we carefully consider the context, and understand why Ezra is referring to these later incidents.

Ezra 6:22

Why did Ezra make mention of the "king of Assyria" when he was writing during a time long after the demise of that nation?

Although some have regarded this as a scribal error, the Septuagint also reads "Assyria," and nothing in the Hebrew text suggests a textual problem here. In light of the context, it is apparent that Darius is meant (Ezra 6:1, 12, 14–15). So why is he called "the king of Assyria"?

In Nehemiah 9:32, the designation "kings of Assyria" is used to include Assyrian, Babylonian, and Persian kings. Since the Persians ruled former Assyrian territories, it could be said that Darius was "king of Assyria," just as Cyrus (king of Persia) claimed the title "king of Babylon."

Ezra 10:3

What "law" does Shecaniah refer to in presenting a biblical basis for his suggestion?

The problem facing Ezra was that many of the returned exiles had become involved in religiously mixed marriages. Such marriages had led Solomon into idolatry and apostasy (1 Kings 11). In order to avoid such devastating consequences, Shecaniah suggested that the Jews "put away" their foreign (that is, unbelieving) wives. And he adds, "Let it be done according to the law."

Many conclude that Shecaniah is suggesting divorce on the basis of Deuteronomy 24:1–4. There are two major objections to this conclusion. First, the word translated "put away" *(yatzah)* is not the usual word for divorce.[3] In describing what takes place, Ezra uses none of the common Hebrew words for divorce. Perhaps Shecaniah was thinking of something more like annulment or separation, not divorce in the technical sense. Second, Deuteronomy 24:1–4 does not directly address the issue of divorce. The text in question simply prohibits a particular case of remarriage. Deuteronomy 24:1–4 does not provide a biblical basis for divorce nor does it authorize any divorce procedures.

The problem facing the restoration community was the issue of religiously mixed marriages. There is a law that addresses this matter—Deuteronomy 7:1–4. This law explicitly prohibits intermarriage with an unbelieving person and warns of the idolatry that so often results from religiously mixed marriages. Shecaniah, I believe, was appealing to this law as the basis for the action he suggested to Ezra and the restoration community.

Ezra 10:11–12

Does this passage provide biblical support for a believer to divorce an unbelieving spouse?

Acting on the advice of Shecaniah, Ezra instructed those who had become involved in religiously mixed marriages to "separate" *(badal)* themselves from their unbelieving wives. While some might appeal to this text as providing biblical support for divorce and remarriage, the evidence for this is lacking.

Consider, first of all, that Ezra does not use the normal Hebrew words for divorce. Ezra may have had in mind a temporary separation, perhaps in keeping with the procedures for marrying captive women (Deut. 21:10–14), rather than divorce. Second, Ezra makes no mention of remarriage either for the Jews or the foreign women. While one might conjecture that remarriage took place, this is based on the questionable assumption that this passage refers to divorce. Third, the issue of whether a Christian should divorce an unbelieving spouse is directly addressed by Paul in 1 Corinthians 7:12–13. The apostle Paul clearly says do not send her or him away. Nowhere in Scripture do we find biblical precedent for divorcing an unbelieving spouse.

The steps taken in Ezra 10 were with a view to preserving the religious purity of the returned exiles. Divorce is neither condoned, condemned, or even addressed in this situation. Perhaps this incident was recorded by Ezra to illustrate the challenges facing the restoration community and the tragedies of becoming involved in religiously mixed marriages.

Endnotes

1. James B. Pritchard, *The Ancient Near East* (London: Oxford University Press, 1958), 207.
2. This suggestion is based on the assumption that the "Shenazzar" of 2 Chronicles 3:18 is a variation of the name "Sheshbazzar."
3. Walter C. Kaiser Jr., *Hard Sayings of the Old Testament* (Downers Grove, Ill.: InterVarsity Press, 1988), 142.

NEHEMIAH

Nehemiah 1:11

What were Nehemiah's responsibilities as Artaxerxes' "cupbearer"?

Classical sources provide detailed descriptions of cupbearers in the Persian court. Xenophon (about 430–354 B.C.), the famous pupil of Socrates, describes one of the main duties of the cupbearer as follows: "Now, it is a well known fact that the cupbearers, when they proffer the cup, draw off some of it with the ladle, put it into their left hand, and swallow it down—so that, if they should put poison in, they may not profit by it" (*Cyropaedia* 1.3.9). The apocryphal book of Tobit also sheds light on the position. "Now Ahikar was cupbearer, keeper of the signet, and in charge of administration of the account . . . for Esarhaddon had appointed him second to himself" (Tobit 1:22).

These quotations make it clear that the cupbearer was a man of great responsibility and influence in the Persian court. Only a man of exceptional trustworthiness would be given this post.

Nehemiah 6:15

Could the walls of Jerusalem have been rebuilt in a mere fifty-two days?

Some scholars prefer to follow Josephus, who writes that the rebuilding of the wall took two years and four months (*Antiquities* 11.179). However, the Septuagint and Latin Vulgate both support the reading of the Hebrew text. Fifty-two days is a rather short time for such a project, but even the enemies of the Jews recognized that this work had been accomplished "with the help of . . . God" (6:16).

Nehemiah 7:5–73

How do we account for the differences between the lists of returning exiles in Ezra 2 and Nehemiah 7?

Nehemiah 7:66 agrees with Ezra 2:64 in providing the total number of those who returned—42,360. However, when the individual sums are added, the total amounts to 29,181 in Ezra and 31,089 in Nehemiah. Some have supposed that the lists were from different occasions and that the changes represent growth in the community. Others suggest that the list in Nehemiah contains revisions based on additional information. Still others argue that the discrepancies are due to confusion resulting from the custom of using letters of the Hebrew alphabet to represent numbers. Since the numbers of Nehemiah's list are generally larger, it may be that some of the figures in Ezra 2 were estimates that were later revised.

Nehemiah 8:17

Was the Feast of Tabernacles totally neglected from the days of Joshua until the time of Nehemiah?

Nehemiah 8 records that the entire restoration community gathered in Jerusalem to celebrate the Feast of Tabernacles. Verse 17 records that they "had indeed not done so from the days of Joshua the son of Nun to that day." Does this mean that this important feast was neglected by the Israelites throughout the period of the judges and the monarchy? The word translated "so" is the key to this problem. It can be translated "just so" or "in the same way." Although the Feast of Tabernacles had been observed in the days of Sheshbazzar and Zerubbabel (Ezra 3:4) and on other occasions as well, it had not been observed in such an enthusiastic and God-honoring manner since the days of Joshua.

Nehemiah 10:32

Why did the returned exiles pledge to contribute one-third of a shekel to the temple ministry when the Mosaic Law called for a half shekel?

The Mosaic Law required that every Israelite contribute one-half of a shekel annually to support the temple ministry (Exod. 30:11–16). One commentator suggests that the one-third shekel was offered in *addition* to the half shekel required by Moses.[1] The returned exiles had just gone through some difficult times economically (compare Neh. 5:1–5). Nehemiah may have reduced the amount in light of the economic conditions of the day.

Endnotes

1. Judah J. Slotki, *Daniel, Ezra, Nehemiah* (London: Soncino, 1951), 246.

ESTHER

General

How do we account for the fact that God is never mentioned in the book of Esther?

The lack of any mention of God in the book of Esther has raised questions about the book. Is Esther a secular book, and should it be included in Scripture?

The absence of any reference to God is, I believe, intentional. This is intentional understatement to emphasize the obvious presence of God behind the scenes. Although God is not mentioned in Esther, He is certainly evidenced throughout the book as He providentially protects His chosen people. The book dramatically illustrates how God may use seemingly insignificant events in human affairs to bring about His sovereign purposes. God is powerfully present in the book of Esther, working "all things after the counsel of His will" (Eph. 1:11).

Esther 1:11

Why did Vashti object to her husband's request that she display her beauty at the feast?

After 180 days of feasting with his princes and nobles, Ahasuerus prepared a 7-day banquet for the citizens of Susa. The celebration was no doubt lively! The text notes that "the royal wine was plentiful according to the king's bounty" (1:7). It was on the seventh day, at the end of the festivities when the king's heart "was merry with wine" that Ahasuerus ordered Vashti to appear before his guests. From all indications, this was a rather drunken group before which Vashti was ordered "to display her beauty" (v. 11). Understandably, she was reluctant to participate in such debauchery.

The Talmud gives us an additional clue as to why Vashti refused to display herself as the king requested. While the Bible states that the king ordered her to display herself "with her royal crown," the Talmud and Jewish commentators understood that she was to appear with only her royal crown, that is, naked.[1]

Esther 2:8

Why did Esther participate in the beauty contest to become the new queen?

It is clear from verse 8 that Esther did not volunteer to participate in this contest. Her beauty "of form and face" (2:7) must have caught the attention of the king's officers. Verse 8 indicates that as young ladies were gathered to Susa to begin the contest, "Esther was taken." This would indicate that she had no choice in the matter.

Esther 2:12–15

Did Esther sleep with the king before they were married?

Some people have wondered about Esther's moral standards. Did she have sexual relations with Ahasuerus before the two were married? This question reflects a misunderstanding of the whole selection process. In this polygamous society, participation in the contest meant becoming a member of the harem (2:9), the wives of the king. There were two harems or groups of wives to whom Ahasuerus had access—the harem of the virgins and the harem of the concubines (v. 14). A concubine is a true wife but one of secondary rank. Although the marriage customs of Persian royalty in ancient times were vastly different from today, there appears to have been no moral impropriety on Esther's part. Entering the contest meant becoming a wife of the king.

Esther 2:10, 20

Was it wrong for Esther to hide her Jewish background?

As a Jewish woman, Esther was in a potentially dangerous situation. This was a time when the Jews were being persecuted. Mordecai was certainly familiar with the antisemitic attitudes evidenced by some members of the king's court (3:1–6). Out of concern for Esther he instructed her not to make her ethnic origin known (2:10, 20). Esther wisely followed Mordecai's counsel on this matter.

Esther 4:13–16

Did Esther really want to help her people, or was she simply forced into it?

Some have doubted that Esther really wanted to help her Jewish people. The words of Mordecai in 4:13–14 may suggest that he had to talk her into responding. I believe that Esther recognized the seriousness of the situation and wanted to prayerfully prepare for approaching the king. To enter the king's presence uninvited might cost Esther her life! She asked the Jews in Susa to fast for three days in preparation for her approaching the king. The word *fast* implies that time normally spent in the preparation and eating of food would be replaced with prayer. Esther's words, "If I perish, I perish" (v. 16) is a courageous statement of her submission to God's sovereign will. Esther certainly wanted to help her people but counted the cost and prepared herself for the sacrifice of her life.

Esther 9:6, 15–16

Was it right for the Jews to slaughter five hundred citizens of Susa and thousands more in the provinces of Persia?

Even after the death of Haman, his edict of destruction remained in force for the Jews. But the counteredict that Ahasuerus authorized gave the Jews the right to defend their lives and property in the face of deadly assault (8:11). The book of Esther records that many Persians died in their attack on the Jews. These deaths were not the result of Jewish aggression but of Jewish self-defense! None of the Persians would have died if they had refrained from attacking the Jews. The integrity of the Jews in this matter is emphasized by the repeated statement, "they did not lay their hands on the plunder" (9:10, 15–16). The Jews refused to enrich themselves through their victory over the Persian aggressors.

Endnotes

1. A. Cohen, *The Five Megilloth* (London: Soncino, 1946), 198.

JOB

Theme

Is Job basically a book about the suffering of the righteous?

Job is popularly viewed as a classic study in the problem of suffering, particularly the suffering of the righteous. However, careful study of the book reveals that the problem of suffering is simply the medium through which to deal with an even more significant matter. At the heart of the book of Job is the issue of faith and doubt. In this book the author leads us to consider serious questions: How can Job go on believing God in the face of such circumstances? Would a sovereign, loving, and just God allow an innocent person to suffer such devastating trials? Is it possible to keep our faith in times of trial?

The book of Job shows us that devastating trials need not destroy our faith. With Job, we can learn to minister from a position of pain. Our hope is not in our circumstances or well-being. Our hope must be in God alone!

Job 1:1

What kind of man was Job? Was his suffering due to some hidden fault that the Lord was trying to bring to his attention?

Many commentators have approached the book of Job with the understanding that God was disciplining Job for some hidden fault that he was unwilling to acknowledge. According to this view, Job struggled with his suffering until he came to acknowledge and confess this fault. This viewpoint, I believe, is in contradiction with the clear statement of the first verse. Here the author introduces Job as "a blameless and upright man, fearing God and turning away from evil." This description is twice repeated by the Lord Himself (1:8; 2:3).

Job was not a sinless man, but he was a good man. He was a man of integrity. Not even Satan, "the accuser of our brethren" (Rev. 12:10), could fault his personal conduct. What made suffering so difficult for Job was the seeming injustice of it all. He had done nothing deserving of such discipline. And so he struggled with the issues of faith and doubt.

Job 1:6

Who are the "sons of God" mentioned here?

The Hebrew term *bene elohim* (sons of God) is used only in Job (1:6; 2:1; 38:7) and in Genesis 6:2. Although the Genesis reference is debated, it is clear from the contexts in Job that the reference is to angels. Job 38:7 indicates that before God made humankind, the "sons of God" shouted for joy over His creation of the stars. The angels are referred to as sons of God in the sense that they are His creation.

Job 1:6

Does this verse mean that Satan has unrestricted access to heaven?

Several passages in addition to this verse indicate that Satan has access to heaven. In Zechariah 3:1, the prophet Zechariah had a vision of Joshua the high priest standing before the Lord in heaven, and Satan was there accusing him. Revelation 12:7–9 describes how Satan will one day be thrown down out of heaven to the earth. Revelation 12:10 refers to Satan as accusing believers "before our God day and night." The biblical evidence is clear. Satan does have access to heaven and takes opportunity of that privilege to accuse and slander the saints.

But I would hesitate to suggest that Satan's access to heaven is unrestricted. Certainly he is under God's sovereign authority. Satan's access before the throne of God is only by divine permission. One day that permission will be withdrawn and Satan will be thrown down to the earth (Rev. 12:9). His being cast into the abyss for a thousand years (20:2–3) is merely a prelude to his ultimate destiny—the lake of fire (v. 10).

Job 3:8; 41:1

Does the reference to the dragon monster Leviathan give evidence of ancient mythology in Scripture?

The name "Leviathan" refers to the sea monster Lotan that, according to ancient myth, Baal is said to have killed. The stories about this monster are found in cuneiform texts found at Ras Shamra, Syria, known in ancient times as Ugarit. In the Baal Epic, Leviathan is depicted as an anticreation dragon monster who is a foe of the cosmic order. According to ancient mythology, he could cause an eclipse by twisting himself around the sun.

Readers of the Bible may be surprised that this mythical monster is mentioned five times in Scripture (Job 3:8; 41:1; Pss. 74:14; 104:26; Isa. 27:1). We have here examples of the use of myth in the Bible as poetic image. This is borrowed imagery not borrowed theology. The biblical writers did not believe in the myth of Leviathan any more than the Christian poet John Milton believed in the gods Neptune or Bacchus when he refers to them in his poetry.

The biblical references to Leviathan are always in poetic passages and are used as poetic imagery to depict chaos opposed to the cosmic order. Thus in Job 3:8, Job expresses his wish someone had roused Leviathan on the day of his birth so that he might never have come into existence. Job did not believe in Leviathan. He simply drew from the treasury of ancient myth an image that would enhance his poetry.

Job 19:25–27

Do these words of Job indicate his belief in the bodily resurrection?

This passage has been variously interpreted even by careful, conservative scholars. In spite of his difficulties, Job expresses faith that his "Redeemer" lives. A redeemer (*goel*) in the Old Testament provided protection or legal preservation for a close relative who could not do so for himself.[1] In this context, the redeemer is God Himself, as indicated by the parallel statement, "I shall see God," in verse 26. In verse 25 Job expresses confidence that God will one day take His stand and vindicate him.

When did Job expect to be vindicated by his living Redeemer? Verse 26 can be interpreted to mean that (1) Job would see God in his resurrected body, or (2) he would see God in his afterlife. The key to the proper interpretation of this verse is our understanding of the Hebrew word *min*. Does it mean "in [my flesh]," as the NIV and KJV render it? Or does it mean "from [my flesh]," as the RSV and JB have it? Or does it mean "without [my flesh]," as the ASV and NASB render it?

The basic meaning of *min* is that of separation or removal from a person, place, or circumstance. This may lead us to conclude that Job expected to see God after his spirit has been separated from his body by death. However, his statement in verse 27, "my eyes shall see," would argue against this approach. It appears that Job expected to see God with his own eyeballs. In this context *min* would better be rendered, "from [the vantage point]."[2] Accordingly, Job expected to see God from the vantage point of his future resurrection body.

What is certain from this text is that Job expected God's vindication after death. Job's utterance clearly expresses his faith in an afterlife. While greatly debated, his words may even affirm belief in the biblical doctrine of the bodily resurrection (Dan. 12:2; Luke 24:39; John 5:28–29; Acts 2:31–32; 1 Cor. 15).

Job 42:6

If Job was truly a righteous man (1:1; 2:3), of what did he repent?

At the end of the book, Job is finally satisfied not because of an answer to his suffering, but because he has met God (42:5). He has experienced God in a way that has enabled him to cope with the unanswered question in his life. But if his suffering was not the result of personal sin, of what did Job repent?

Although Job's suffering was not the result of sin, his frustration over his friends' accusations led him to say some wrong things. He went so far as to suggest that God had done him wrong and thus perverted justice (33:10). He was also guilty of complaining against God (v. 13). I suggest that at the end of his experience, Job "repented" (42:6) of accusing God of injustice and repented his complaining attitude.

Endnotes

1. Roy Zuck, *Job* (Chicago: Moody Press, 1978), 89.
2. Gleason L. Archer, *Encyclopedia of Bible Difficulties* (Grand Rapids: Zondervan, 1982), 214.

PSALMS

Psalm 3:1

Are the historical notations in the psalms part of the original text and are they considered accurate?

Thirteen of the psalms contain "superscriptions" that recount the historical settings out of which they were composed. Many other psalms include brief superscriptions mentioning the author and providing directions for use, "For the choir director; on a stringed instrument." These notations are actually the first verse of the psalm in the Hebrew text. There is some debate as to whether they are part of the original psalm or were added by later editors. What matters to us is that they are included in the Hebrew Bible as part of the psalm. That leads me to conclude that they should be regarded as we would any other Scripture. I believe that the superscriptions are reliable and accurately reflect the circumstances of composition.

Psalm 5:5

How is God's "hate" for "all who do iniquity" consistent with His love for sinners (John 3:16)?

The clear teaching of Scripture is that God loves sinners and sent His Son to die in their place. Jesus declared that God "loved" the unbelieving world (John 3:16). Paul declares in Romans 5:8, "But God demonstrates His own love toward us, in that while we were yet sinners, Christ died for us." And yet, God is not pleased with sinners. He certainly hates their sinful actions. But does God "hate" them?

The Hebrew word translated "hate" *(sane)* generally expresses an attitude toward persons and things with which one wishes to have no contact. It can communicate different attitudes ranging from active hostility (Deut. 16:22) to lack of preference for someone (Gen. 29:31). The translation given by Holladay may be helpful. He renders the word, "be unable or unwilling to put up with."[1] This seems to fit the context of Psalm 5:5. While God is committed to sinners and desires them to come to repentance, He is unwilling to put up with those who persist in wickedness. God is opposed to sinners. He separates from the wicked and brings the consequences of their sin upon them.

Psalm 13:1–2

The psalmist often accuses God of neglecting or forgetting His people. How do we account for such expressions of complaint against God in the psalms?

Many of the psalms contain a lament, or complaint, about the severe circumstances the psalmist has experienced. Often the complaint is addressed to God, "How long, O LORD? Wilt Thou forget me forever?" The psalmist does not usually subject himself to twentieth-century expectations of quiet and pious prayer. He cries out to God with a boldness and honesty that often makes conservative Christians a bit uncomfortable.

The psalmists, I believe, maintained a high regard for God. But they knew how to pray and did so powerfully. Like Hannah, they were not afraid to "pour out" their souls before the Lord (1 Sam. 1:15; Ps. 62:8). This is the kind of prayer Paul had in mind when he said, "Be anxious for nothing, but in everything by prayer and supplication with thanksgiving let your requests be made known to God" (Phil. 4:6).

When describing their distress or complaint in detail, the psalmists should not be viewed as grumblers. They are merely taking their concerns before the Lord, their judge and their redeemer. They cry out to God with confidence that He has the power to lift them out of the "miry clay" and put them on a solid rock (Ps. 40:1–2). The complaints are really the preparation for praise— praise offered to God in a time of His apparent absence.

Psalm 22:22

What does the psalmist mean when he promises to "praise" God?

The book of Psalms makes a great contribution to our understanding of praise. The word translated "praise" *(yadah)* in the Hebrew text means literally "to confess publicly" or "to give public acknowledgment." This word is used, in the psalms, of giving public acknowledgment of God's character or activity.

There are basically two kinds of praise appearing in the psalms. *Descriptive praise* declares what God is like, focusing on His attributes. *Declarative praise* recounts what God has done, focusing on His actions. The important thing to remember about the biblical concept of praise is that it has a forum and always occurs in a group. You can thank God in private prayer and worship Him during your devotions, but you can praise God only in public, where others can hear and respond to your statements about Him.

Psalm 34:1

Is there a mistake in verse 1, which mentions Abimelech instead of Achish (compare 1 Sam. 21:13).

The background of Psalm 34 is the incident described in 1 Samuel 21:10–15. There the king of Gath is identified as "Achish." But the superscription of Psalm

34 names him as "Abimelech." Some would simply dismiss this problem as an error in the superscription. But there two better solutions.

One solution is that Abimelech was simply another name for Achish. It was not uncommon in ancient times for people to have two names. Gideon was also named Jerubbaal (Judg. 6:32; 7:1), and Solomon was also known by the name Jedidiah (2 Sam. 12:25). Another possibility is that "Abimelech" was a dynastic title used by Philistine leaders. In Hebrew the name means "father of a king" and is used of three different Philistine rulers in the Old Testament. In David's time, Achish may have been the personal name of Abimelech, ruler of the Philistines.

Psalm 37:25

Should this verse be interpreted to mean that Christians will never go hungry or be forced to beg?

Psalm 37 is good example of a Wisdom Psalm, in which the ways of the righteous and the wicked are set in bold contrast (vv. 9, 22, 29, 34). It is generally observed that the righteous will experience the blessings of life and that the wicked will experience the very opposite. But sometimes this is not true. Righteous Job suffered and saw the wicked enjoying prosperity! But in Wisdom Literature, it is the general truth that is emphasized, not the occasional exception.

In highlighting the blessings experienced by the righteous, David declares, "I have not seen the righteous forsaken, or his descendants begging bread" (v. 25). Similarly, in Psalm 34:10 he declares, "They who seek the LORD shall not be in want of any good thing." In both of these statements, David is referring to the normal consequences of good behavior. Occasionally the reverse might be experienced by a given individual. This is not a matter of the inspiration or inerrancy of Scripture. It is simply the nature of Wisdom Literature, which presents general rules without concern for possible exceptions.

What David affirms in Psalm 37:25 is the fact that God provides for His own. This is generally true in our experience of life. But if for a time He chooses not to provide, I believe He will grant us sufficient grace to go without.

Psalm 42:1

Didn't the sons of Korah die with him when the earth opened up and swallowed the rebels in the wilderness (Num. 16:32)? How could they have authored these psalms?

Korah's servants ("all the men who belonged to Korah," Num. 16:32) died with him, but his sons survived. Numbers 26:11 reports, "The sons of Korah, however, did not die." The descendants of the disobedient Korah became celebrated singers (2 Chron. 20:19) and psalm writers (Pss. 42–49; 84–85; 87–88) in Israel.

Psalm 51:4

What did David mean when he said, "Against Thee, Thee only have I sinned"? Had he not also sinned against Bathsheba and her husband, Uriah.

Of course David had sinned against Bathsheba and Uriah by his adultery and murder. There is no question about that. But David is emphasizing in this statement that all sin—even that which injures another person—is ultimately against God. Adultery violates the divinely intended sanctity of marriage. Murder violates the sanctity of the image of God in a person. A sin against a person is first and foremost a sin against a holy God.

Psalm 58:6

How should we interpret the imprecations in the psalms?

An *imprecation* is a prayer for judgment on one's enemies. This is a leading feature in a number of psalms (7; 35; 58; 59; 69; 83; 109; 137; 139). Many Christians wonder how such prayers can be consistent with the New Testament teaching, "Bless those who persecute you; bless and curse not" (Rom. 12:14).

The key to our understanding of the imprecations is to appreciate their theological basis in the Abrahamic covenant (Gen. 12:1–3). God promised Abraham that he would "curse" those who expressed their hostility against his family and descendants. Thus, the psalmists' imprecations are simply appeals for God to carry out His promised judgment on those who have cursed Israel. These judgments would be in accordance with the very promise and purposes of God.

It is also helpful to understand the stated purposes of the imprecations in the psalms. These give us a divine perspective on the seemingly human and vengeful cries for judgment. The imprecations are intended to:

- establish the righteous (Ps. 7:8)
- cause God to be praised (Pss. 7:17; 35:18, 28)
- help people to recognize that there is a God who judges the earth (Ps. 58:11)
- demonstrate that God is sovereign (Ps. 59:13)
- prevent the wicked from enjoying the same temporal destiny as the righteous (Ps. 69:28)
- cause the wicked to seek the Lord (Ps. 83:16–18)

Christians should understand and appreciate the theological basis for the imprecations. But, like the dietary laws of the Old Testament, these teachings have been superseded by new revelation. Paul admonished the Romans, "Never take your own revenge, beloved, but leave room for the wrath of God, for it is written, 'Vengeance is Mine, I will repay, says the Lord'" (Rom. 12:19). And his words in 2 Timothy 4:14 indicate that Paul practiced what he preached.[2]

Psalm 82:6

What does the psalmist mean when he refers to human leaders as "gods"?

The term translated "gods" *(elohim)* is a plural designation for deity and is customarily translated "God." It can be used of false gods or of the true God, Yahweh. On rare occasions *elohim* is used of those who are god-like in terms of position or authority. An example is seen in Exodus 4:16, which says that Moses would be "as God" to Aaron.

In Psalm 82:6, the term *elohim* is used to refer to human judges or rulers. They could be called gods in the sense that God had given them a position as administrators of His justice. Jesus appeals to this text in John 10:34 when arguing the case for His own deity.

Psalm 117:1

What is the meaning of the expression, "Hallelujah"?

The Hebrew word *hallelujah* is made up of two elements. The first is the verb *praise* represented by the first element, *hallelu*. This is a command to give a vocal and public declaration concerning the greatness or goodness of God. The particular nuance of the Hebrew word is "joyful boasting."[3] The second element in the expression *hallelujah* is a shortened form of the divine name. *Yah* (jah) is short for Yahweh, the revealed name of God in Scripture (Exod. 3:13–15). The word *hallelujah* is an invitation to join in joyful praise because you are excited about the greatness of our God!

Psalm 137:8–9

How can the psalmist pronounce his blessing on those who would dash infants against the rocks?

In Psalm 137:7–9, the psalmist petitions the Lord to remember Israel's foe the Edomites, who attacked Judah when it fell to ravages of Babylon. We are reminded in verse 7 that the Edomites cried out for the total destruction of the city of Jerusalem. The Babylonians complied by destroying the walls and burning the temple.

Now in verse 8 the psalmist pronounces a blessing on the one who would repay Babylon for the evil it had done to Jerusalem. In verse 9, a blessing is pronounced on the one who would destroy the next generation of warriors in the nation of Babylon. We are rightly troubled by the harshness of the words of this verse. Sadly, the dashing of little children was common in ancient warfare (2 Kings 8:12; Isa. 13:16; Hos. 13:16; Nah. 3:10). This prayer for judgment was in keeping with the Abrahamic covenant, which promised a curse on those who cursed Israel (Gen. 12:2–3). As Christians, we can appreciate the covenantal background of Psalm 137 without joining in the blessing declared in verse 9. For a discussion of the imprecations in the psalms, see the answer to the question for Psalm 58:6.

Psalm 139:13–16

What are the implications of this passage in the abortion debate?

In Psalm 139:13–16, David joyfully acknowledges that God intricately wove him together in his mother's womb. God, the Master Craftsman, was actively involved in fashioning David within the womb. This suggests that God had a relationship with David while he was growing and developing before birth.

The unborn child is not just a piece of tissue, but a human being with a potential for human experience. This text is a strong biblical polemic against abortion, for it clearly demonstrates God's personal involvement in the creation, formation, and development of the human baby within the womb. There is no question that the biblical authors viewed the unborn child as a living person.

Endnotes

1. William L. Holladay, *A Concise Hebrew and Aramaic Lexicon of the Old Testament* (Grand Rapids: Eerdmans, 1971), 353.
2. For further study, see my article, "A Fresh Look at the Imprecatory Psalms," *Bibliotheca Sacra* 138 (January–March 1981): 35–45.
3. Ronald B. Allen, "When the Psalmists Say, 'Praise the Lord!'" *Worship Leader* (October–November 1992), 8.

PROVERBS

Proverbs 1:1

Is Solomon the author of Proverbs?

Solomon is identified as the author or compiler of most of the book of Proverbs (1:1; 10:1; 25:1). According to 1 Kings 4:32, he spoke 3,000 proverbs. Only about 512 of them are found in the book of Proverbs. The book attributes to Solomon sections 1:1–9:18; 10:1–22:16; and 25:1–29:27. This third section was apparently published later by an editorial committee under the direction of King Hezekiah.

Two sections of Proverbs (22:17–23:14 and 24:23–34) are attributed to "the wise." Solomon was probably responsible for editing and compiling these proverbs. Proverbs 30:1–30 is attributed to Agur, the son of Jakeh, of whom nothing is known. Proverbs 31:1–9 (and possibly 31:10–31) is said to be the sayings of King Lemuel, a figure never named among the kings of Israel or Judah. Based on the statement in 1:1, some have understood "Lemuel" to be Bathsheba's name for Solomon.

Proverbs 1:7

What is the meaning of the expression "the fear of the LORD"?

The "fear of the LORD" is the fundamental lesson in our study of Hebrew wisdom literature (Job 28:28; Pss. 111:10; 115:13; Prov. 9:10; 31:30; Eccl. 12:13). Does the "fear of the LORD" involve a dreadful apprehension regarding God? While I would not deny a place for real fear in relationship to God's eternal judgment on unbelievers or His firm discipline of disobedient Christians, this is not the major thrust of the concept as presented in the Hebrew wisdom literature.

Fearing God is equated in Proverbs 2:5 with knowing Him. If you truly know God, you can't help having a healthy respect for His person. If you know that He is holy, just, sovereign, omnipotent, and eternal, you can't help but respect Him and want to please Him.

The wise teachers of antiquity reveal how the fear of the Lord is to be applied in the lives of God's people. Job 28:28 makes the concept of the "fear of the LORD" essentially synonymous with the expression, "to depart from evil." How do you fear the Lord? You turn from evil (Prov. 16:6) and obey His commandments (Ps. 111:10). Proverbs 8:13 indicates that the fear of the Lord involves more than action. The one who truly fears God shares God's attitude toward evil.

Based on our brief study of this concept, I define "the fear of the LORD" as an action-oriented response to God based on our knowledge of what is true about His character and His will for us. The one who truly fears God is not standing around with hands trembling and knees knocking but is responding with the whole heart to the person of God—seeking to obey Him and striving to do His will.

Proverbs 3:9–10

Does this text advance the prosperity equals success ethic?

It would be easy to mistake such statements as lending support to the prosperity equals success ethic. Basically, this philosophy states, Give to God from your material resources and He will give back to you more than you gave. This is often presented as a "guarantee" for the Christian's financial success and prosperity.

The problem with this philosophy is that it is based on old covenant promises that have been rendered obsolete by the new covenant. According to the old covenant, the people of Israel were promised physical blessings—prosperity and victory—for their obedience (Deut. 28:1–14). Disobedience would be followed by the curse of poverty, crop failure, enemy attack, captivity, and dispersion from the land (28:15–68). The principle of blessing for obedience, cursing for disobedience, provides the theological basis for the statement in Proverbs 3:9–10. Solomon is reminding the people that when they honor God with their tithes, He will bless them with plenty.

Under the new covenant, things are different. Under the new covenant believers are promised every *spiritual* blessing in and through Christ (Eph. 1:3). And God has promised to provide for the needs of His people (Phil. 4:19). But His provisions are based on grace, not on personal merit. We do not earn the blessing or provision of God through obedience.

Some proverbs, like 3:9–10, must be understood and appreciated with an old covenant perspective. Since we are under the new covenant, their direct application to us today is limited.

Proverbs 8:22–31

Should this passage be interpreted to refer to Christ?

This delightful poem personifies Wisdom as active and present with God from the beginning of Creation. Wisdom assisted in Creation as a "master workman" (8:30), rejoicing in God's work and delighting in humankind (v. 31). In Colossians 1:15–17, Paul seems to build from the concepts presented in Proverbs 8 to present the person of Christ. In Colossians 2:3 he declares that in Christ "are hidden all the treasures of wisdom and knowledge."

Should, then, Wisdom of Proverbs 8:22–31 be interpreted to refer to Christ? Obviously, there is a connection. But it is not a prophetic connection, for the language of Proverbs 8 is not prophetic. Nor is the link through typology, for a type has its fulfillment in an antitype that renders the type unnecessary. And this cannot be said about Wisdom.

Allen introduces the German word *Heilsgeschichte* as the key to resolving this issue. By this he refers to "the inner-connectedness of sacred history, where terms and concepts in the Old Testament that are not really types or prophecies still have an actual relationship to earlier or later issues, particularly culminating in the Person of the Savior Jesus."[1] He then suggests that in Proverbs 8, wisdom *"speaks of Christ* in the inner-connectedness of sacred history."[2]

In Proverbs 8:22–31, we see that wisdom is presented as an attribute of God that is singled out for particular display through His creation. This wisdom of God points ultimately to God's wisdom in Jesus Christ.

Proverbs 22:6

Does this verse promise that wayward children will one day return to the Lord?

Some have taken this verse as a promise that a child who goes to Sunday school may turn from the Lord and sow some wild oats, but will turn back to the Lord when he or she matures as an adult. This interpretation is not based on sound exposition nor does it match with reality.

Solomon was emphasizing that there are strategic opportunities for positive training and instruction during the childhood years. The lessons learned during these formative years will serve as guideposts for later adult life.

The phrase, "in the way he should go," literally reads, "according to his way" and points to a parental concern for the child's individuality, interests, and pursuits. A wise parent will recognize a child's inclinations and use these early years to confirm, correct, and encourage the building of a solid foundation.

Proverbs 31:6–7

Does this passage encourage alcoholic indulgence and drunkeness?

The Bible is very clear on the subject of the misuse of alcohol. Drunkenness is forbidden in both the Old and New Testaments (Prov. 20:1; Eph. 5:18). But the Bible recognizes the medicinal use of alcohol. Paul told Timothy to "use a little wine" for the sake of his stomach and frequent ailments (1 Tim. 5:23). The instructions in Proverbs 31:6–7 fall into this category.

Proverbs 31:1–9 contains the instructions King Lemuel received from his mother. She warned him to avoid wine and strong drink so that his mind could be alert to judge righteously and to exercise the duties of kingship. By way of contrast, she advises that wine and strong drink should be given to the one who is painfully perishing or needs some relief from mental anguish. There is no encouragement toward drunkenness here. The author simply recognizes the use of alcohol as a pain reliever or tranquilizer. Modern medicines, taken under a doctor's care, are more suited for such purposes today.

Proverbs 31:10–31

How should we interpret the woman presented in this passage?

Proverbs 31:10–31 is a poem that exalts the honor and dignity of womanhood. It presents a picture of the importance of a wife and mother in Israelite society. But how should we understand this remarkable woman? What woman, ancient or modern, can do all that she does? Surely, she creates feelings of inferiority among women who read of her many talents and abilities.

Some have concluded that this text describes a normal Israelite wife and that the poem presents God's standard for a wife and mother. Others, somewhat dismayed by this multigifted woman, have assumed that the poem presents an unattainable standard, but one for which women should strive. I suggest that this woman is a composite of womanhood. She is representative of the many opportunities a woman may pursue and talents she can develop.

Most women don't start off married life with the skills for which this woman is noted. This is reflected in the description she is given in verse 10. The word "excellent" speaks of one who has virtue, power, and capacity. She is a woman of potential. She will become a worthy woman, such as described here, through the encouragement and support of her loving husband. A godly woman grows more into the pattern of Proverbs 31 as she matures in a loving and supportive home.

Endnotes

1. Ronald B. Allen, *The Majesty of Man* (Portland, Oreg.: Multnomah Press, 1984), 164.
2. Ibid., 165.

ECCLESIASTES

Ecclesiastes 1:1

Who wrote the book of Ecclesiastes?

The author of Ecclesiastes identifies himself as the son of David, king in Jerusalem. While Solomon is not specified, he is the most likely author of this work. Many modern scholars, however, have argued that the language and vocabulary of Ecclesiastes differs significantly from other tenth-century B.C. works composed in Hebrew. They acknowledge that the purported author of Ecclesiastes is Solomon, but that was simply a literary device employed by some later unknown author.

In spite of these objections, the evidence for Solomonic authorship is strong and convincing. The author's references to his unrivaled wisdom (1:16), his unequaled wealth (2:7), his opportunities for pleasure (v. 3), and his extensive building activities (vv. 4–6) all suggest that Solomon wrote Ecclesiastes. No other descendant of David measures up to these qualifications. In addition, Jewish tradition recorded in the Talmud names Solomon as the author (*Megillah* 7a; *Shabbath* 30).

Ecclesiastes 1:2

What is the meaning of the expression, "vanity of vanities"?

The words, "vanity of vanities," express the thesis of the book. The Hebrew words constitute a superlative and could be rendered, "vapor of vapors, thinnest of vapors." Life with its activities is much like the morning mist or vapor that hangs over a mountain, river, or lake and then vanishes with the first rays of the sun. Like a thin vapor, life is here—and then gone. What was really accomplished? Is there any point to it all? All we leave behind is a picture album and some memories in the hearts of those that knew us. Solomon goes on in verses 3–11 to illustrate that life is futile because there is no guarantee of positive benefit for the work we do on this earth. Solomon's thesis accords well with the words of Paul in Romans 8:20–22 that all creation is subject to futility because of sin.

Ecclesiastes 1:3

What is the meaning of the expression, "under the sun?"

The expression "under the sun" is a metaphor where the place is identified by its location rather than its name. The place "under the sun" is simply the earth. The expression is used to describe the realities of life as it is on this earth. The expression serves to limit the range of Solomon's discussion. When he questions, "What advantages does man have in all his work which he does under the sun?" Solomon is not taking into consideration the eternal perspective on reward. He is simply saying that there is no guarantee on this earth of positive benefit from one's work.

Ecclesiastes 2:24

What does Solomon mean when he says, "there is nothing better than . . ."?

When Solomon says, "there is nothing better," he is not demeaning his own counsel. Rather, he is emphasizing it. Solomon is using a literary device that is the opposite of hyperbole, exaggeration for emphasis. Here and throughout the book, Solomon uses understatement for the sake of emphasis. Paul does a similar thing when he states, "I determined to know nothing except Christ crucified" (1 Cor. 2:2). Paul understates what he knows to highlight the significance of this one great truth. The phrase, "there is nothing better," means "the best thing, the most important thing, is this."

What kind of an approach to life is Solomon commending here?

Solomon points out in Ecclesiastes 2:24–26 that although God has not revealed the solution to all of life's frustration and futility, He has given believers the ability and opportunity to enjoy abundant lives. This solution is capsulized in the often-repeated refrain, Eat, drink, and be happy, for this is the gift of God! The words, "eat and drink" (2:24; 5:18; 9:7) are a Hebrew expression for enjoying life. Eating and drinking were an important part of any festive celebration. Solomon is saying, "Don't let the futilities of life take the joy out of living. Enjoy God's gift of life as a festival!" In spite of the futility of trying to put all of life together, we can live by faith and use this one opportunity to serve God and to enjoy life to the fullest.[1]

Is Solomon advocating an Epicurean philosophy of life?

Some have mistakenly identified Solomon's counsel with that of the Epicureans, "Let us eat, drink, and be merry, for tomorrow we die!" This philosophy originated with Epicurus (341–270 B.C.), a Greek philosopher at Athens. Epicurus condemned excess and commended a simple lifestyle. He viewed happiness and the avoidance of pain as the chief ends of life. This philosophy was later perverted by the hedonists (from Greek *hedon,* "delight"), who viewed pleasure and self-indulgence as the ultimate good. Epicurus said, avoid life and its pains by retiring from the world. The hedonists said, exploit life and its pleasures by indulgence in sensuality. Solomon rejects both extremes. As he develops his message throughout the book (3:12, 22; 5:18–20; 9:7–9; 11:9–10), he commends the enjoyment of life as a gift of God, living with an awareness that God will one day stand in judgment of your life and activities.

Ecclesiastes 3:19

Is the fate of people and animals the same?

When Solomon says that the fate of people and the fate of beasts is the same, he is referring to the fate of death. His discussion in this book is based on life "under the sun," here on this earth. He is not bringing into consideration the eternal perspective at this point. That will come later, in chapter 12. But on this earth, both people and animals die and go to the grave (3:20).

Ecclesiastes 7:16

What does Solomon mean, "Don't be excessively righteous"?

Solomon is not cautioning against possessing too much real righteousness or wisdom. Real righteousness and wisdom are highly valued and worthy of diligent pursuit (Ps. 15:1–2; Prov. 4:5). Instead, Solomon is cautioning against putting on a superficial display of righteousness or thinking oneself to be overly wise.

Ecclesiastes 9:2

How can the righteous and the wicked face the same fate? What about eternal reward and punishment?

In keeping with his perspective of life on this earth, "under the sun," Solomon acknowledges that death is no respecter of persons. He is not speaking here from the eternal perspective of heaven and hell. The key to verse 2 is found in verse 3, "Afterwards they go to the dead." All people—the righteous and the wicked—must face this fate.

Ecclesiastes 10:19

How can Solomon say, "money is the answer to everything"?

Various explanations have been offered for this verse. If connected with verse 18, it may be interpreted to draw a contrast between the effects of idleness and industry. While the lazy person's house leaks, the diligent earns the money necessary to provide a comfortable life.

Another possibility is to interpret verse 19 as giving expression to the philosophy of the foolish princes introduced in verse 16.[2] Verses 17–18 must then be considered parenthetical. It is the princes who "feast in the morning" (v. 16) who say, "money is the answer to everything" (v. 19).

Ecclesiastes 11:9

Is Solomon suggesting that we follow the evil impulses of our hearts?

In verse 9, Solomon once again exhorts us to enjoy life (compare 2:24). Specifically he says, "And follow the impulses of your heart and the desires of your eyes." Does this mean that we should feel free to follow any impulse or desire, whether good or evil? Obviously, such an interpretation would be out of step with the message of this book (12:13–14). There is accountability and judgment before the Lord.

The word "impulses" is better rendered "ways." The ways that Solomon refers to, I believe, are the hopes and desires God puts into our hearts as we delight ourselves with Him. As David exhorts, "Delight yourself in the LORD; and He will give you the desires of your heart" (Ps. 37:4). The hopes and desires God puts into our hearts are to be followed. This is sound advice. But the last line of Ecclesiastes 11:9 must also be considered: "Yet know that God will bring you to judgment for all these things." These words serve as a caution, curbing excess and indulgence.

Ecclesiastes 12:3–5

How should we understand Solomon's images of old age?

In these verses Solomon captures in a series of poetic images the physical decline of old age.

"watchmen of the house tremble"
> Arms and hands tremble with palsy or feebleness.

"mighty men stoop"
> Legs are bent and knees totter.

"grinding ones stand idle"
> Loss of teeth.

"those who look through the windows grow dim"
> Eyes begin to lose their sight.

"doors on the street are shut"
> Loss of hearing.

"sound of the grinding mill is low"
> Grinding of food in a toothless mouth.

"one will arise at the sound of a bird"
> Old people cannot sleep late; they rise early.

"daughters of song will sing softly"
> Again, the loss of hearing.

"afraid of a high place and of terrors on the road"
> A fear of stumbling.

"almond tree blossoms"
> Hair has turned white.

"grasshopper drags himself along"
> Crippled in old age.

"caperberry is ineffective"
> Loss of sexual potency.

Endnotes

1. This interpretive approach is developed by J. Stafford Wright in his classic article, "The Interpretation of Ecclesiastes" *Evangelical Quarterly* 18 (1946): 18–34.
2. A. Cohen, *The Five Megilloth* (London: Soncino, 1946), 179–80.

SONG OF SOLOMON

Song of Solomon 1:1

What is the meaning of the title, "Song of Songs"?

The title is a Hebrew superlative, like the expression, "the holy of holies." The holy of holies was the most holy place in the temple. Of the 1005 songs Solomon wrote (1 Kings 4:32), the title "Song of Songs" denotes this one as the most excellent song—Solomon's very best.

The term *song* is given to the title in recognition of the fact that it is poetry that was to be presented musically. In recognition of the fact that there are several different participants in the song, some Bibles have markings in the margins suggesting who might be presenting a particular section—the bride, groom, or chorus. These editorial comments are interpretive and do not appear in the original text.

Song of Solomon 1:2

How did such a romantic and sensual poem become a part of the Bible?

It has been said that if the Song of Solomon is merely a picture of earthly and sensual love, it would be "unworthy of a place in the canon."[1] This sort of thinking reflects a rather negative view of God's plan for marriage and the physical expression of love in marriage. Sexual union is a very significant aspect of married love. This union creates the one-flesh relationship of marriage and results in procreation of humanity according to God's design (Gen. 1:28; 2:24). Both the Hebrew Scriptures and the New Testament commend the joy and blessing of sexual union for married couples (Prov. 5:15–20; 1 Cor. 7:3–5). It should not be unexpected, then, that God's Word should provide instruction on the purity and beauty of wedded love as a divine gift.

Song of Solomon 1:5

The Shulammite refers to herself as "black." Was she African?

The Song of Solomon is a book of poetry where figures of speech flourish. In calling herself "black," the Shulammite is using hyperbole (exaggeration) for emphasis. She goes on in the next verse to explain that the sun had darkened her skin while she worked in the vineyards.

Song of Solomon 1:6

What is the family background of the Shulammite?

The Song of Solomon reflects a certain dramatic background featuring two major figures—Solomon and the Shulammite. In addition, the daughters of Jerusalem and the brothers of the Shulammite participate in the poetic narrative. Certain references in the song also suggest a historical setting. Any reconstruction of the historical setting of the song is based in some measure on hypothesis. With caution, I suggest the following reconstruction based on my study and interpretation of the song. King Solomon had a vineyard in the mountains of Lebanon (4:8; 8:11) that he entrusted to caretakers consisting of a mother, two sons (1:6), and two daughters—the Shulammite (6:13) and a little sister (8:8). The Shulammite was not appreciated by her brothers (1:6), and she was forced to work hard in the vineyard, leaving her little opportunity to care for her personal appearance (v. 6). Working in the vineyard and keeping the flocks (1:8) caused her skin to darken from the sun (v. 5).

One day while caring for her vineyard, a stranger approached. He showed interest in her, and she became embarrassed concerning her personal appearance (v. 6). The stranger turned out to be King Solomon, perhaps on a hunting trip. But the Shulammite maiden mistook him for a shepherd and asked about his flocks (v. 7). King Solomon spoke loving words to her (vv. 8–10) and won her affection (2:16). Eventually, Solomon took the Shulammite to Jerusalem as his bride (3:6–7).

The two were married and their love was consummated (4:16–5:1). But all was not well with the royal couple. The Shulammite often dreams of being separated from Solomon (3:1–2; 5:2–6; 6:1). She expresses her desire to spend more time with him (7:11–12; 8:1–2). At the Shulammite's request, they go together to the country (8:5), where they talk of love (vv. 6–7) and give themselves to each other (7:12; 8:12, 14).

Song of Solomon 1:7

Does a "shepherd-lover" appear in the story?

Following the lead of Jacobi (1771), Ewald (1826), Renan (1860), and Godet (1867), some interpreters have suggested that the Song of Solomon includes three major participants rather than two. The third is a shepherd-lover to whom the Shulammite remains faithful in spite of the romantic advances of Solomon.

This viewpoint is based on several references that include pastoral imagery (1:7; 2:16; 6:3). Actually, the word *shepherd* does not appear in the song in relationship to the Shulammite's lover. The word *shepherds* occurs just once (compare 1:8).

The shepherd imagery should not be unexpected in a poem that has a country or pastoral setting as its background, especially one that speaks of a king. It is well recognized that the term *shepherd* was used commonly in the ancient Near East with reference to the office of king (compare Ezekiel 34).

The major objections to the shepherd hypothesis include the following:
1. This song is presented as Solomon's best. What would motivate him to write such a song about a jilted relationship? If the shepherd-lover exists, then Solomon is a third-party intruder into a blissful relationship.
2. The nearest antecedent in 1:2 is Solomon.
3. The Shulammite looks for Solomon in the city, streets, and squares (3:2). She would not expect to find her shepherd-lover in these places.
4. The wedding described in the song is Solomon's (3:11).
5. Solomon describes the intimate kisses of the Shulammite (4:11).
6. The relationship between Solomon and the Shulammite is consummated sexually (4:16–5:1).
7. The descriptions of the Shulammite (4:1–5) and Solomon (5:10–16) suggest a mutual and reciprocal relationship. The imagery in 5:10–16 has an atmosphere of royalty that one would not expect to find in a description of a shepherd.
8. Solomon describes the intimate parts of the Shulammite (7:2–3).
9. The Shulammite gives herself to Solomon, an expression of submission (8:12).

Song of Solomon 2:7

Is someone asleep here? How should we interpret this verse?

In 2:6, the Shulammite expresses her legitimate desire as a married woman for sexual intimacies with her husband. The word translated "embrace" can better be translated "fondle" and speaks of sexual passion. Having expressed this desire, she turns aside in verse 7 to the "daughters of Jerusalem," the unmarried maidens of the court, offering them some wise counseling. This counsel is so significant that it is repeated three times in the book (2:7; 3:5; 8:4)! The Shulammite asks the unmarried maidens to take an oath that they will not "arouse or awaken love." Some translations fill in the text with *my* love. But she is referring here not to a lover but to a sexual desire. The words, "Until she pleases," are better rendered, "until it pleases," the *it* referring to sexual desire.

What the Shulammite is saying is this: Don't arouse or stir up sexual desire until it is appropriate in the marriage relationship. The physical expression of love in marriage is a mystical and beautiful experience.

Song of Solomon 6:8–9

How could Solomon speak of a loving and exclusive relationship with the Shulammite maiden when he had so many other women?

Solomon's excesses in acquiring seven hundred wives and three hundred concubines (1 Kings 11:3; compare Song 6:8–9) does not mean that he could not have spoken by divine inspiration regarding a mutually exclusive relationship (2:16; 7:10; 8:12). This poem may reflect the lesson of mutuality that Solomon learned the hard way through his own failings. By God's wisdom and divine inspiration, readers are warned to avoid his errors (2:7; 3:5; 8:4).

Interpretation of the Song of Solomon
What is the basis for the allegorical interpretation of this poem?

The erotic nature of the Song of Solomon raised concerns among many early readers and provoked opposition to its canonicity. Jerome, for example, insisted that because of its erotic content, the song should not be studied by anyone under thirty years of age! Bishop Theodore of Mopsuestia (360–429) ventured to interpret the song literally, but his work was banned by a church council. Unwilling to accept a literal view of the song and its message concerning marital love, many early interpreters opted for an allegorical interpretation.

The allegorical approach interprets Solomon and the Shulammite maiden as portraying the relationship between God and Israel or between Christ and the church. Accordingly, the rabbis interpreted "the pouch of myrrh which lies all night between my breasts" (Song 1:13) to refer to the Shekinah glory between the two cherubim that stood over the ark in the tabernacle. Christian allegorists understood the text to refer to Christ appearing between the Old and New Testaments.

The allegorical approach is not only questionable as a legitimate interpretive method, it is quite unlikely that sexual imagery would have been used in Israelite literature to depict the relationship between God and Israel. Baal worship, common among the Canaanites, made great use of sexual ritual (compare Num. 25:1–9). The Israelites were warned that ritual nakedness and sexual expression had no place in the worship of Yahweh (Exod. 19:15; 20:26). It would be completely out of keeping with the cultural background to have such imagery as found in the Song of Solomon used to express the love between God and Israel.

Endnotes
1. F. Godet, "The Interpretation of the Song of Songs" in *Studies in the Old Testament,* 9th ed.(New York: Hodder and Stoughton, 1894), 241.

ISAIAH

Isaiah 1:1

Who wrote Isaiah? Is there any evidence to suggest that someone else wrote the second half of the book?

The book purports to be the "vision" of the prophet Isaiah (1:1). Critical scholars have argued that an eighth-century prophet could not have foreseen the fall of Jerusalem in 586 B.C., the seventy-year captivity, or the return from Babylon decreed by Cyrus in 538 B.C. Denying the possibility of predictive prophecy, they have argued that the "Isaiah" who wrote chapters 1–39 could not have written chapters 40–66.

Johann C. Doederlein (1745–92), professor of theology at a university in Germany, was the first to publish a systematic argument for dating Isaiah 40–66 to the sixth century. He argued that since Cyrus is mentioned by name in 44:28 and 45:1, the author must have been a Jew living in Babylon between the rise of Cyrus (about 550 B.C.) and the fall of Babylon (539 B.C.). The sixth-century author of Isaiah 40–66 has become known as "Deutero-Isaiah."

Three lines of argument are used to advance the theory of the dual authorship of Isaiah.

1. *Historical Background.* While chapters 1–39 are written from a preexilic viewpoint, chapters 40–66 appear to be written from the standpoint of the Exile. How can the same author write from such different perspectives? The answer, of course, is that God enabled Isaiah to look into the future through the eyes of prophecy and write words of comfort to a people he envisioned in exile. Like other prophets of the Bible, he thinks, speaks, and writes as if the future has already happened.

2. *Literary Style.* While chapters 1–39 contain words of judgment written in a terse and sober style, chapters 40–66 are more flowing, warm, and compassionate. But I point out that a change in style may reflect a change in purpose, not necessarily a different author. Isaiah writes the first half of his book announcing words of judgment on disobedient Judah. In the second half of the book, he writes words of comfort for a people in captivity. His change in purpose requires him to modify his style.

3. *Theological Ideas.* While chapters 1–39 present Immanuel, the messianic King (7:14; 9:6–7; 11:1), chapters 40–66 describe Yahweh's Servant (42:1; 49:1; 50:4–9; 52:13–53:12). And yet both sections reflect a very elevated

view of a majestic, all-powerful God. The phrase, "the Holy One of Israel," occurs a dozen or more times in each section, but nowhere outside of Isaiah. The similarities between the two sections are greater than any differences.

The New Testament writers regarded Isaiah as a unified composition. The prophet is quoted twenty-one times by name in the New Testament—from both sections of the book. John 12:38–40 contains two quotations from Isaiah (53:1; 6:9). Documenting these quotes, the apostle John writes, "These things Isaiah said" (John 12:41). The earliest Hebrew manuscripts of Isaiah discovered in a cave near Qumran support the single authorship and unified composition of the book. In the Isaiah Scroll, chapter 40 begins on the last line of the column that contains Isaiah 38:8–40:2. There is no break in the manuscript to suggest that someone other than the eighth-century prophet Isaiah authored the second half of the book.

Isaiah 6:1

Why is the call of Isaiah placed here instead of at the beginning of the book?

While Jeremiah and Ezekiel place their calls at the beginning of their books, Isaiah places his in chapter 6, after the initial prophecies. The placement here rather than at the beginning of his book serves to accomplish two things. First, the vision of the thrice Holy One reinforces what Isaiah has already declared in the first five chapters—a holy God cannot tolerate sin! Second, it vindicates Isaiah's authority to deliver the messages of chapters 1–5. The readers might be wondering, "Why should we believe this prophet and respond to his message?" Chapter 6 demonstrates that Isaiah is called of God and that his message should not be ignored.

Isaiah 6:9–10

It appears that Isaiah's preaching was to have a negative effect on his hearers. What was his preaching intended to accomplish?

Isaiah was given a heartbreaking assignment—to warn the people of Judah with no prospect of a positive response. Some have interpreted these verses as merely predictive. God could foresee that the people would refuse the words of Isaiah and would lose their spiritual receptivity as a result. But this view does not seem to do justice to the text. These verses reveal that Isaiah's preaching had a sovereign and judicial purpose. His preaching was intended to harden the hearts of the people as Pharaoh's heart was hardened by the words of Moses (Exod. 4:21; 8:32). The hardening rests on God's sovereign decision to judge the disobedient and unresponsive nation.

Jesus used Isaiah 6:9–10 in Matthew 13:14–15 to explain that His teaching through parables would bring judgment by concealing truth from the unworthy. Paul quoted this text in Acts 28:26–27 to explain the unbelief of the Jews in his day. John used this text to show that the unbelief of the Jews and their rejection of Jesus actually fulfilled God's plan and purpose!

Some have wondered if this text removes people from responsibility for personal sin. The answer is, firmly, No! While God is sovereign over sin and belief, people are always responsible for their actions (Acts 2:33). The sovereignty of God never abrogates human responsibility.

Does this mean that the people of Isaiah's day had no choice but to disbelieve? No! God was offering the sinful nation forgiveness and blessing on the basis of repentance (1:16–19). But they had persistently refused. Now, as a generation under judgment, the words of Isaiah would serve only to harden their hearts and confirm their unbelief.

Isaiah 7:14–16

With whom is the prophecy of the virgin birth fulfilled?

Matthew's gospel makes it clear that the ultimate fulfillment of this prophecy is with Jesus Christ, whose mother conceived and bore Him while she was a virgin (Matt. 1:23). The problem we are confronted with as interpreters is that verses 14–16 form a single literary unit. And while Jesus quite adequately fulfills the prophecy of verse 14, verses 15–16 have nothing to do with Jesus and require fulfillment in the time of King Ahaz. Our challenge as interpreters is to recognize the ultimate fulfillment by Jesus without neglecting the historical fulfillment suggested by verses 15–16. There are three basic interpretations of the text.

1. *Single-Reference View*. According to the single-reference view, the text refers directly to the virgin birth of Jesus. The virgin is Mary, and the Immanuel is Jesus. This view is based on the view that the Hebrew word *almah* means "virgin," and Matthew records the only fulfillment of the prophecy. It is argued that the "sign" was promised not just to king Ahaz, but to the Davidic dynasty ("you," plural), and we should therefore look beyond the time of Ahaz for fulfillment. The major problem with this interpretation is that it ignores the historical significance of verses 15–16 and the possibility of a "near" fulfillment in Isaiah 8.

2. *Double-reference theory*. According to the double-reference view, there are two fulfillments of the prophecy. There was an immediate fulfillment in Isaiah's day when a woman (Isaiah's wife or the wife of Ahaz) had a child. The ultimate fulfillment is found in Mary's virgin birth of Jesus. This interpretation is built on the view that *almah* means "maiden," not "virgin." This view has the advantage of finding a fulfillment of verses 15–16 in Isaiah's day. The major problem is the interpretation of *almah*. The evidence that *almah* means "virgin," not "maiden" or "young woman" is strong and convincing.

3. *Full-Fulfillment View*. Like the double-reference theory, this interpretation acknowledges a historical fulfillment in Isaiah's day. Yet it maintains the correct rendering of *almah* as "virgin." The "virgin" in Isaiah's day was probably Isaiah's second wife. His first wife, mother of Shear-jashub (7:3) probably died. Apparently, Isaiah then married a "prophetess" (8:3) who was a virgin at the time the sign of Isaiah 7:14 was given. After Isaiah married her, the

prophetess conceived, and Maher-shalal-hash-baz was born in fulfillment of the prophecy. The birth of this boy was a sign to Ahaz. Before the child became a morally responsible person, the kings whom Ahaz feared would be judged. The devastation of Aram and Israel by Tiglath-pileser III from 734 to 732 B.C. fulfilled this prophecy.

But there is more. With the virgin birth of Jesus, the prophecy finds its *full* fulfillment. Whereas the near fulfillment involves a natural conception, the full fulfillment involves a supernatural conception. We conclude that there are actually two signs in Isaiah 7:14–16: the shadow and the substance. Verses 14–16 reveal a sign for Ahaz, fulfilled when the prophetess conceived and bore a son, Maher-shalal-hash-baz (Isa. 8:3–8). Verse 14 reveals a sign for David's dynasty, fulfilled when the Virgin Mary conceived and bore a Son, Jesus Christ (Matt. 1:23).

Isaiah 14:14–21

Who is the "King of Babylon" mentioned in this passage? Does this text teach anything about Satan's fall?

The tyrant of Isaiah 14 has been identified as either an Assyrian or a Babylonian king. Erlandsson points out the Assyrian background of the prophecies of Isaiah 1–37.[1] He observes that the Assyrian kings Tiglath-pileser, Sargon, and Sennacherib received the honorary title, "king of Babylon." This took place at the Babylonian New Year's Day festival when the ruler would grasp the hand of Marduk and be declared "king of Babylon."[2] This background would account for the title being applied to an Assyrian ruler.

Erlandsson identifies the wicked tyrant as Sennacherib (705–686 B.C.), who was king of Assyria when Babylon was completely overthrown and destroyed in 689 B.C. as a result of its continuous attempts to revolt against Assyria. Sennacherib describes the destruction of the city in terms similar to those found in Isaiah 14:23 and 21:9. Sennacherib died a humiliating death, as recorded in Isaiah 37:37–38.

The second question, Does this text teach anything about Satan's fall, is raised because of the King James Version's translation of the Hebrew *helel* as "Lucifer" in verse 12. Actually, the Latin term *lucifer* (light-bearing one) is a pretty good translation of the Hebrew term. Unfortunately, while this term was applied by Isaiah to the king of Babylon, many have followed the early church fathers (Tertullian, Origen, and Hippolitus) in applying this title to Satan.

It is argued that the similarity between the tyrant's sin and Satan's sin (Isa. 14:12–14; 1 Tim. 3:6) suggests the identification of the two. And since the tyrant fell (Isa. 14:14–15) and Satan fell (Gen. 3:14–15; 2 Peter 2:4; Jude 6; Rev. 12:4), they must be one and the same. There are convincing arguments against this view.

1. The historical context of Isaiah 14 concerns the overthrow of an arrogant king (a "man," v. 16)—the Assyrian tyrant Sennacherib. Nothing else is implied by the context.

2. While the tyrant of Isaiah 14 has been judged and no longer shakes kingdoms or threatens the earth (v. 16), Satan, "the god of this world" (2 Cor. 4:4), is alive and well (2 Cor. 2:11; 11:14; Eph. 2:2; 1 Peter 5:8).
3. There is adequate Scripture to substantiate Satan's pride and fall without using this passage to provide a Scriptural basis for this doctrine (Gen. 3:14–15; John 8:44; 1 Tim. 3:6; 2 Peter 2:4; Jude 6; Rev. 12:4).
4. The "fall from heaven" referred to by Christ in Luke 10:18 is His divine commentary upon what had just taken place as the disciples cast out demons in His name. This victory of the disciples foreshadows the ultimate banishment of Satan from heaven.
5. What is described in Isaiah 14:4–21 has not yet occurred in Satan's history of moral decay and judgment. While he was defeated at the Cross (John 12:31; 16:11; Col. 2:13–15), his banishment from heaven (Rev. 12:7–9), imprisonment (20:1–13), and final judgment (v. 20) are yet future.
6. Isaiah 14:20 is not in harmony with the fact that Satan will be united with his people in the lake of fire (Rev. 20:10, 15).

We conclude that Isaiah 14:14–21 concerns the fate of a historical king and that there is nothing to suggest that the passage teaches anything about Satan. The term *lucifer* is a Latin term that has migrated into our English Bibles and theological vocabulary. I have a box of matches that I picked up while traveling in Europe. The label reads, "lucifers" (light-bearers, or matches), a good and accurate use of the term.

Isaiah 36–39

What is the chronological order of the events recorded in these chapters?

The historical order of events in Isaiah 36–39 can be outlined as follows:
1. Hezekiah's illness (38:1)
    a. Hezekiah healed (38:5)
    b. Promised deliverance from Assyria (38:6)
2. Hezekiah's indiscretion (39)
    a. Visited by Babylonians (39:1)
    b. Displayed Judah's treasures (39:2)
    c. Warned of Babylonian captivity (39:6–7)
3. Sennacherib's attack (36–37)
    a. Jerusalem attacked (36)
    b. Jerusalem delivered (37; as promised in 38:6)

One wonders why Isaiah changed the order of events when composing his prophecy. It seems that he was more concerned with the thematic development of the book than with historical chronology when he wrote these chapters. Chapters 36–39 are intended to serve as the hinge of his book. Chapters 36–37 look back to the judgments announced in chapters 1–35 and show how they are fulfilled in 701 B.C. with Sennacherib's attack.

Chapters 38–39 look ahead to the Babylonian captivity and show how the historical situation of chapters 40–66 came about.

Isaiah 42:1

Who is the anonymous "Servant" mentioned by Isaiah?

The second half of Isaiah features a major figure repeatedly referred to as the "Servant of [Yahweh]." Some have interpreted the "Servant" to refer to an individual—Isaiah, Cyrus, or the Messiah. Others have taken the term to refer to the nation or remnant of Israel. The key to identifying the Servant of Yahweh is to see what the Bible says about Him. The following is a listing of ten characteristics of the Servant of Yahweh with New Testament references showing how Jesus fulfilled Isaiah's expectations for this Servant.

1. He will effect a proper ordering of all society (42:1; compare Matt. 25:31–46; Heb. 9:27–28; Jude 14–15).
2. He will mediate a new covenant for Israel effecting the salvation both of the people of Israel and the land of Israel (42:6–7; compare Acts 3:20–21, 25; Rom. 9:4; 11:26–27; Heb. 11:15).
3. He will not become discouraged or lose confidence in Yahweh during His rejection by Israel (49:4; 50:4–9; compare Matt. 11:25–27; John 16:33; Phil. 2:9–11; Heb. 12:2–3.)
4. He will learn submissively from Yahweh (Isa. 50:4–6; compare John 5:19).
5. While rejected by Israel, He will bring salvation to the Gentiles (42:6; 49:5–6; compare Matt. 23:37–39; John 10:16; Acts 13:37).
6. He will suffer vicariously for the sins of Israel and the Gentiles (compare 2 Cor. 5:21; Eph. 2:13–16; 1 Peter 2:24).
7. He will suffer innocently (53:9; compare John 8:46; Heb. 7:26).
8. He will suffer silently (53:7; compare Matt. 27:12, 14).
9. He will die during His sufferings and will be resurrected to an exalted position by Yahweh (52:13–14; 53:10; compare Matt. 27:50; Luke 24:36–39; Acts 1:3; 2:33–34).
10. He will die with criminals but will be buried with a rich man (53:9, 12); compare Matt. 27:4, 57, 60).

Isaiah 44:28; 45:1

How do we account for the mention of the name "Cyrus" when he lived 150 years after Isaiah's time?

Cyrus, king of Anshan, conquered Achmetha and inherited the kingdom of the Medes in 550 B.C. In 546 he defeated Croesus king of Lydia and captured his capital at Sardis. In 539 Cyrus captured Babylon and founded the Persian Empire. That Isaiah mentioned his coming 150 years before his arrival in history has led many to conclude that the second half of the book was written by someone other than the eighth-century prophet Isaiah. But there is really no problem with Isaiah announcing the coming of Cyrus if we believe in predictive prophecy. If God knows the future, then He can reveal it to His prophet. Through His prophets, God is able to announce the Virgin Birth (7:14), the coming of Cyrus (44:28; 45:1), and the sacrificial death of Christ (53:4–6) hundreds of years before the actual events.

Isaiah 52:13–53:12

What is the Jewish interpretation of this passage?

Evidence from rabbinic literature, including the prayers of the synagogue, indicate that early Jews applied this passage to the Messiah. The first-century *Targum Yonathan ben Uzziel*, a paraphrase of the prophets and generally acknowledged as an ancient authority, opens the prophecy of Isaiah 52:13–53:12 with the words, "Behold, my servant, the Messiah, prospers." Under the influence of the Jewish tragedies that occurred during the Crusades, Rabbi Sh'lomoh Yizhaqi (Rashi [about 1040–1105]) interpreted Isaiah 53 to refer to the suffering of Israel. Although rejected by the great Jewish scholar Rabbi Mosheh ben Maimon (Maimonides [1135–1204]), Rashi's opinion became authoritative in Jewish tradition.[3]

Endnotes

1. Seth Erlandsson, *The Burden of Babylon: A Study of Isaiah 13:2–14:23* (Sweden: CWK Gleerup Lund, 1970), 160–66.
2. Ibid., 88.
3. Frederick Alfred Aston, *The Challenge of the Ages* (New York: Research Press, 1971), 17.

JEREMIAH

Jeremiah 1:5

In what way did God know Jeremiah before he was in the womb?

This verse reveals that God predestined Jeremiah to be a prophet of the nations. The Hebrew word translated "know" *(yadah)* denotes an intimate relationship and selective affection. Before Jeremiah was born or even conceived in the womb, God knew him in an intimate and personal way and set him apart to the prophetic office. Jeremiah had done nothing to deserve this opportunity. He would simply minister by God's grace and His divine appointment.

Jeremiah 1:11

What is the significance of the sign of the almond tree?

The almond tree is the first tree to blossom in Israel in the spring. When the white blossoms of the almond appear, the people know that spring is near. The vision of the almond tree is interpreted by the Lord in verse 12 to signify the speedy and certain fulfillment of Jeremiah's prophecies. It is interesting that the Hebrew word translated "watching" comes from the same root as the word for "almond." As spring always follows the blossoming of the almond, so prophetic fulfillment would follow Jeremiah's predictions.

Jeremiah 7:18

Who is "the queen of heaven"?

The "queen of heaven" (also Jer. 44:17) is none other than the Assyro-Babylonian Astarte, also known as Ishtar. In Mesopotamia this god was known as the Queen, or Mistress, of Heaven.[1] Astarte was god of the evening star and principally concerned with sex and fertility. According to Philo, she was one of the wives of the Canaanite god El.[2] Small cakes bearing the image of Astarte were offered in her honor (v. 19).

Jeremiah 7:22

How can the denial of verse 22 be reconciled with the rest of Scripture attributing the sacrificial ordinances to God (Exod. 20:24)?

131

In Jeremiah 7:21–28, God calls His people to obedience rather than mere sacrifice. Rather than covering their wrongdoing with more elaborate ritual, God wants His people to love and obey Him from the heart. God reminds the people in verse 23 that when He entered into the covenant with them at Mount Sinai, He had called for their obedience—that's all (compare Exod. 19:3–8). The truth of verse 22 is confirmed in our study of Exodus 19–20. Even in the Decalogue, the basic stipulations of the covenant (20:1–17), there is no demand for sacrifice. Instruction concerning sacrificial ritual came later, after the people had accepted the covenant obligations (19:8).

Sacrificial ritual was important and was God's provision for dealing with inadvertent disobedience and human failure. But the ritual of sacrifice was never intended as an end in itself. God was never pleased when His people performed the rituals while neglecting the essential demand for worship and obedience from the heart (Isa. 1:10–17; Hos. 6:6; Amos 5:21–25; Mic. 6:1–8).

Jeremiah 20:7

Did God deceive Jeremiah?

God did not deceive Jeremiah, although the prophet boldly accuses Him of it. In a highly poetic and emotional prayer, the prophet vents his frustration over a ministry that is going none too well. He had been subjected to mockery, persecution, and physical abuse. But when he tried to quit preaching, the word of the Lord was like a "burning fire" in his bones that he cannot contain. His call compelled him to persist. It is in this context that he accuses the Lord, "Thou hast deceived me." Jeremiah seems to be saying that he had no idea of what was in store for him when he entered the prophetic ministry. Although God had alluded to the troubles coming his way (1:8, 18–19), he had not imagined that his ministry would be so difficult.

Jeremiah 22:28–30

If Jehoiachin (Coniah) was to die "childless," how can he be included in the messianic line (Matt. 1:12)?

Jeremiah 22 contains a prophecy concerning the kings of Judah. Most interpreters understand it to record prophecies concerning Shallum, Jehoiakim, and Coniah (Jehoiachin). Following this view, the line of Coniah was cursed (vv. 28–30). Jeremiah announces, "no man of his descendants will prosper sitting on the throne of David or ruling again in Judah" (v. 30). The problem is that Matthew includes Coniah (Jeconiah) in the genealogy of Jesus (Matt. 1:12). He does not seem to recognize a curse on Coniah. In support of the curse on Coniah, it is argued that Luke traces the genealogy of Jesus through Nathan rather than Solomon (Luke 3:31) and thus avoided the curse.

In his genealogy, Matthew is attempting to prove to Jewish readers that Jesus has a right to the throne as a legal heir of David. He did not see a curse on Coniah—because there is none. Rather than interpreting Jeremiah 22 as a prophecy concerning the last kings of Israel, I suggest that the prophecy announces God's judgment on Judah's last king, Zedekiah, illustrated by the divine judgment on his three predecessors.

In the first part of the chapter, God speaks to Zedekiah and warns him concerning the consequences of continued injustice and oppression (vv. 1–9). In the rest of the chapter, Zedekiah is reminded of God's judgment on his predecessors. This is intended to serve as an incentive to obedience and loyalty to Yahweh. Shallum (Jehoahaz) reigned only three months before being carried away to Egypt (vv. 10–12). Jehoiakim died and received a donkey's burial (vv. 13–23). Coniah (Jehoiachin) reigned only three months and then was taken captive to Babylon (vv. 24–28).

The prophecy concludes with application to Zedekiah (vv. 21–22). He is the man who would die childless and have no descendant on the throne of David. This is precisely what happened. With the capture of Jerusalem, Zedekiah's children were slain and the king was blinded and exiled to Babylon (2 Kings 25:6–7). None of Zedekiah's descendants sat on the throne of David.

We conclude that there is no curse on Coniah. The rhetorical question raised in verse 28, "Is this man Coniah a despised, shattered jar?" expects the answer, "no." Although exiled from the land due to disobedience to the covenant, Coniah was preserved in Babylon. He was later released from prison, given a living allowance, and set on a throne in Babylon (2 Kings 25:27–30). Coniah and his descendants are included in the messianic line (Matt. 1:12–16).

Jeremiah 31:31–34

What is the meaning and significance of the new covenant?

During the Passover meal on the night before His death, Jesus passed the cup and said, "This cup which is poured out for you is the new covenant in My blood" (Luke 22:20; compare 1 Cor. 11:25). The new covenant amplifies and confirms the promise of blessing made by God to Abraham in Genesis 12:1–3 (compare Ezek. 16:60). God said, "And I will bless you, . . . and so you shall be a blessing. . . . And in you all the families of the earth shall be blessed." This unconditional promise of God to Abraham and, through His descendants, to the world has its realization in the new covenant.

The major Old Testament text on the new covenant, Jeremiah 31:31–34, is expounded in Hebrews 8:6–13. There the writer of Hebrews declares that the new covenant "has been enacted" (perfect tense). It is in force and was inaugurated at Christ's death (Heb. 9:16–18).

The provisions of the new covenant are elaborated in Ezekiel 36:25–28 (see also Isa. 55:3; 61:8–9; Jer. 31:31–34). The death of Christ, inaugurating the new covenant, provides:
1. spiritual cleansing and forgiveness of sin. "I will sprinkle clean water on you" (Ezek. 36:25; see Jer. 31:34; 1 John 1:9).
2. spiritual rebirth regenerating the soul. "I will give you a new heart and put a new spirit within you" (Ezek. 36:26; Titus 3:5).
3. the indwelling ministry of the Holy Spirit. "I will put My Spirit within you" (Ezek. 36:27; John 14:17).

4. empowerment for godly living. "I will . . . cause you to walk in My statutes, and you will be careful to observe my ordinances" (Ezek. 36:27; see Jer. 31:33; Rom. 8:4–5).
5. a vital relationship with the living God. "So you will be My people, and I will be your God" (Ezek. 36:28; see Jer. 31:33–34; John 1:12).

The new covenant is said to be made "with the house of Israel and with the house of Judah" (Jer. 31:31). On this basis some have suggested that the new covenant is with the Jewish people only. Others have suggested that there are two new covenants—one for Israel and the other for the church. Yet others have implied that the new covenant is for Israel, but the blessings of the covenant may be appropriated by the church.

The New Testament reveals that God has future plans for ethnic Israel. The specificity of the promises in Genesis 12:1–3; Deuteronomy 30:1–10; and 2 Samuel 7:12–16 imply this. Yet in the body of Christ there is neither Jew nor Gentile (Gal. 3:28). Paul declares that believing Gentiles are heirs to the promises God made to Abraham (Rom. 4:16; Gal. 3:14, 29).

Participation in the new covenant by faith enables believing Gentiles to share in the rich spiritual heritage of the people of Israel (Gen. 12:3). Those who were once "separate from Christ, excluded from the commonwealth of Israel, and strangers to the covenants of promise, having no hope and without God in the world" have been "brought near by the blood of Christ" (Eph. 2:12–13). As a result, believing Gentiles "are no longer strangers and aliens," but "fellow citizens with the saints, and are of God's household" (v. 19). Together, believing Jews and believing Gentiles are one people of God.

So significant is the new covenant in relationship to Christian life and ministry that the apostle Paul by the Spirit of God is pleased to call believers ministers of a new covenant (2 Cor. 3:6). Unlike the old covenant with its passing glory (vv. 7, 11), the new covenant is characterized as "everlasting" (Isa. 55:3; Jer. 32:40; Ezek. 16:60; 37:26). This renewed covenant is based on God's unconditional promise and gracious provision in Christ. Unlike the old covenant under Moses, the new covenant mediated by One greater than Moses will never be broken (Jer. 33:20–21).

Jeremiah 36:30

How can this verse say that Jehoiakim would have no one to sit on his throne when 2 Kings 24:6 reports that Jehoiachin, his son, "became king in his place?"

Jeremiah 36 records Jehoiakim's contempt for the Word of God (vv. 20–26) and the judgment that came upon him (vv. 29–31). In verse 30 it is said, "He shall have no one to sit on the throne of David, and his body shall be cast out to the heat of the day and the frost of the night." Second Kings 24:6 records that his son, Jehoiachin (Coniah), became king at his death. But Jehoiachin ruled only three months before he was exiled, and Zedekiah, the son of Josiah, was placed on the throne (2 Kings 24:8–17). The key to this interpretive problem is to recognize that the expression, "to sit on the throne" (36:30) implies a measure of permanence. Jehoiachin's rule was short lived and ended in captivity. He did not sit with permanence or longevity on his father's throne.

Endnotes

1. J. A. Thompson, *The Book of Jeremiah* (Grand Rapids: Eerdmans, 1980), 284.
2. William Foxwell Albright, *Archaeology and the Religion of Israel* (Baltimore: John Hopkins Press, 1968), 73.

LAMENTATIONS

Why should we study Lamentations? What does this book contribute to our knowledge of God?

In Lamentations, Jeremiah poetically commemorates the destruction of Jerusalem by the Babylonians (586 B.C.) as God's judgment on His disobedient people. The book demonstrates that we should not take lightly the warnings of God. In Deuteronomy 28, God set forth the kinds of discipline the Israelites could expect if they broke the covenant. Jeremiah shows throughout Lamentations that the very curses that had been predicted nine hundred years earlier through Moses were precisely fulfilled.

1. Children will be taken into captivity (Deut. 28:32; Lam. 1:5).
2. People will scoff at Jerusalem (Deut. 28:37; Lam 2:15).
3. Parents will cannibalize their children (Deut. 28:53, 56–57; Lam. 2:20; 4:10).
4. Homes will be taken over by foreigners (Deut. 28:30; Lam. 5:2).
5. People will experience famine (Deut. 28:48; Lam. 5:10).
6. Women will be ravished (Deut. 28:30; Lam. 5:11).
7. The aged will be shown no respect (Deut. 28:26; Lam. 5:18).

In addition to setting forth the horror of divine judgment, Lamentations presents a powerful message of God's faithfulness and compassion toward those who seek Him (Lam. 3:19–39). Lamentations demonstrates that God is faithful in discharging every aspect of the covenant promise—the cursings as well as the blessings.

EZEKIEL

Ezekiel 1:4–28

How should we interpret such an unusual vision? What guidelines should we follow?

There are about as many differing interpretations as there are commentaries. This lack of consensus leads me to believe that perhaps we are all wrong in our approach to interpreting prophetic visions. We need some interpretive guidelines for apocalyptic literature.

The term *apocalyptic* is derived from the Greek word, *apokalypsis* (Rev. 1:1), which means "uncovering" or "revelation." According to Alexander, apocalyptic literature is "symbolic, visionary, prophetic literature, composed during oppressive conditions consisting of visions whose events are recorded exactly as they were seen by the author and explained through a divine interpreter, and whose theological content is primarily eschatological."[1] So defined, apocalyptic literature in Scripture includes Ezekiel 1:1–28; 37:1–14, 40–48; Daniel 2; 7–8; 10–12; Zechariah 1:7–6:8; and Revelation.

The literary form of apocalyptic literature arose out of the Mesopotamian dream visions that frequently appear in ancient Near Eastern documents dating from the seventh to sixth centuries B.C. God is the communicator par excellence and seems to have employed this culturally understood literary form to reveal His truth to His people in a creative and contemporary manner.

Apocalyptic, or dream vision, materials customarily include three major elements: (1) the description of the setting; (2) the record of the vision; and (3) the interpretation of the vision.

As careful students of Scripture, we must exercise caution to avoid freewheeling speculation in interpreting apocalyptic literature. The following guidelines are suggested:

1. Normal, grammatico-historical interpretation should be followed.
2. Look for the interpretation provided by the interpreting angel or the explanation provided in the text (Zech. 1:9, 13–14; 2:3; 4:1, 5; 5:5, 10; 6:4).
3. Do not *add* to the interpretation given by the divine interpreter.
4. Do not seek to interpret the minute details of the vision. The fact that the horse is red and the trees are myrtle (Zech. 1:8) does not appear to have any significance other than contributing to the reality and vividness of the vision.

5. The only exception to the latter two interpretive guidelines might be when one is confronted with a symbol that has interpretive significance due to previous revelation or insights gained from other Scripture texts on the same topic. When making such exceptions, caution and restraint must be diligently applied. Excess and speculation must be avoided.

So what is our interpretation of Ezekiel's vision? Applying these basic principles we see that Ezekiel's vision portrays "visions of God" (1:1) and "the appearance of the likeness of the glory of the LORD" (v. 28). This is, therefore, a vision of the glory of God.

Ezekiel 2:1

What is the meaning of the expression, "son of man," in the book of Ezekiel?

The designation "son of man" is used ninety-three times in Ezekiel to refer to the prophet himself. The meaning here is "mortal human being." The term expresses creaturely weakness in contrast with the majesty and power of almighty God. Some have suggested that Jesus may have drawn from Ezekiel's use of this term in referring to Himself as the "Son of Man." I suggest, instead, that Jesus drew from Daniel's use of this term in a messianic context (Dan. 7:13). Jesus used the expression to emphasize His messiahship, not His humanity.

Ezekiel 3:20–21

Does this text deny the eternal security of the believer?

Ezekiel refers here to a righteous individual who turns from righteousness, who sins, and who dies under God's judgment. Does this mean that this person has lost his or her salvation?

The key to the solution of this difficulty is to remember that Ezekiel was operating under the old covenant. Under the old covenant, the one who obeys the covenant enjoys life and blessing. The one who disobeys can expect disaster and death (Deut. 16:20; 30:19). Ezekiel is referring in this context to physical death—the loss of life—not the loss of salvation. Turning from the covenant would result in physical death, even for a righteous person.

Ezekiel 3:26–27

How could Ezekiel carry on his ministry as a prophet if he could not speak?

Ezekiel might best be remembered as the prophet of pantomime. For the first seven and one-half years of his ministry Ezekiel was mute (33:22). During this period his ministry as a prophet consisted of acting out little skits that had symbolic significance. The people of the community would gather around and wonder, "What is Ezekiel up to today?" They would no doubt question each other and debate the intended meaning. Finally, when the symbolic action was complete, Ezekiel would return home (3:24). Later, the city elders would come to consult him privately (8:1; 14:1; 20:1). Then Ezekiel would declare, "Thus says the Lord . . . ," and explain the symbolic action. When the report of Jerusalem's fall reached Ezekiel, his tongue was released (24:25–27) so that he could deliver a message of hope and encouragement to the Jews in exile.

Ezekiel 16:49

Was the sin of Sodom a lack of concern for the needs of the poor, rather than homosexuality?

In Ezekiel 16, the prophet presents an allegory that likens God's people to an adulteress wife. Through the imagery of adultery, the allegory graphically depicts the spiritual unfaithfulness of God's people. In 16:44–48, Ezekiel makes a comparison between three cities: Jerusalem, Samaria, and Sodom. Samaria was the capital of the northern kingdom of Israel. Sodom was a place renowned for its immoral practices and homosexuality (Gen. 19). In this text, Ezekiel points out that Jerusalem has become more corrupt than both her sisters who had established reputations for wickedness. Sodom's chief sin is here depicted as pride, luxurious living, and a neglect of the poor and needy. This material ease fostered the sexual perversion for which the city was well known (Gen. 13:13; 18:20; 19:4–5).[2] Sodom was guilty of both neglecting the needs of the poor and practicing homosexuality.

Ezekiel 28

Who is the "prince of Tyre"? Does this prince have anything to do with Satan?

Ezekiel 28 has often been interpreted to refer to Satan's sin and fall in the Garden of Eden. There are at least four different views regarding this problematic passage.

Mythological Version of the Paradise Story. Some interpreters see Ezekiel 28 as providing a mythological rendering of Genesis 2–3 or a variant of another paradise tradition that might have existed in Ezekiel's day. The references to "Eden" (28:13), "a cherub" (v. 14), and one who is "blameless" (v. 15) may lend support to this view. But more significant is the absence of any reference to the serpent, the woman, and the Tree of Knowledge of Good and Evil.

A Self-contained Mythological Tradition. According to some, Ezekiel 28 draws its background from ancient mythology (Mesopotamian, Phoenician, or Canaanite). According to this supposed myth, a glorious being grasped at yet higher honors and was driven from the garden on the sacred mountain. The king of Tyre, says Ezekiel, will meet a similar humiliating fate. The major objection to this view is that no such myth has ever been discovered in the literature of the ancient Near East.

A Description of Satan and His Sin of Pride. Many church fathers, including Jerome, have interpreted Ezekiel 28 to refer to Satan, the "blameless" and "anointed cherub" in "Eden, the garden of God." It is said that these verses fit only Satan, who in this case was indwelling a human, the king or "prince of Tyre."

The problem with this view is that while much of the passage could be applied to Satan, much could not. Certainly verses 18–19 could not apply to Satan unless they were viewed as prophetic. The interpreter must ask, Is there any good reason to depart from a literal, historical interpretation in this poetic text?

A Satirical Attack on a Proud Tyrian Ruler. The most natural way to interpret this poetic passage is to view it as a satirical attack on the king of Tyre using phraseology and imagery well known in Tyre at the time. Many of the images used in the passage are taken from the religious background of Tyre.

The patron deity of the city was Baal-melqart, "Baal, king of the city." Ithobaal II, who was king at Tyre in Ezekiel's time, apparently appropriated divine honors ("I am a god"). Sacral kingship was common in the ancient Near East. Ezekiel goes on to predict the king's humiliation and demise. In so doing, the prophet uses poetic language and terms that would be understood by the people of his day, who would be familiar with the religion of Tyre.

There are several interpretive keys that are helpful in considering this passage.

1. Recognize that this passage is poetic. Imagery and metaphor abound. "Blameless" need not refer to sinless perfection. The name "Eden" may mean a place of beauty, like Eden (compare 36:35).
2. The passage is addressed to "the prince of Tyre" (28:1) and concerns "the king of Tyre" (v. 12). Nothing else is implied by Ezekiel.
3. Chapters 27 and 28 are one literary unit. In chapter 27, Tyre is depicted as a great merchant vessel that is destroyed by an "east wind," probably Nebuchadnezzar (compare 17:10; 19:12). While chapter 27 focuses on the judgment on the city, chapter 28 describes the judgment on the *king* of that city. If Ezekiel is describing a literal city, he must also be describing a literal, earthly, human king.
4. The city and the king are described with similar terms—"perfect in beauty" (27:3; 28:12; compare 27:16–17 with 28:13; and 27:33 with 28:16).
5. If King Ithobaal actually occupied the Tyrian sanctuary of Baal-melqart, this would explain a great deal of the imagery—the cherub as a guardian of the sanctuary, the holy mountain as the temple site, and Eden, the garden of God (god) as the garden around the sanctuary.

Ezekiel 34:2

Who are the "shepherds" that are indicted here?

Ezekiel 34 contains an indictment against the wicked leaders of Israel who are referred to as "shepherds." The shepherd metaphor was used widely throughout the ancient Near East as a designation for both divine and human rulers. In an ancient Sumerian hymn, the god Enlil is addressed as the "faithful shepherd" of all living creatures. In the prologue of his famous law code, Babylonian king Hammurabi describes himself as a shepherd appointed by Enlil for his people. In the Hebrew Bible, the shepherd metaphor is applied both to Yahweh (Gen. 49:24; Ps. 23; Isa. 40:11) and to human leaders (Ps. 78:70–72; Zech. 11:4–14). In this chapter, the Lord condemns the wicked shepherds and presents Himself as the true shepherd of His people (see Ps. 23; John 10).

Ezekiel 38–39

When will the invasion and destruction of Gog take place?

Ezekiel 38–39 describes a future invasion of Israel by Gog and its allies at a time when the people of Israel are living securely in their land (38:8). Within the context of Ezekiel, the events of chapters 38 and 39 take place at the end of the age (38:8, 16) in connection with Israel's future restoration to the land and God's judgment on the nations. There is little agreement as to precisely when this battle takes place.

The views include: (1) before the Tribulation; (2) in the middle of the Tribulation; (3) at the end of the Tribulation; (4) between the Tribulation and the Millennium; (5) at the beginning of the Millennium; (6) after the Millennium; and (7) both at the end of the Tribulation and end of the Millennium (a double fulfillment).

None of these viewpoints are without difficulty. Within the context of Ezekiel, this invasion and the judgment that follows clears the way for the inauguration of worship and sacrifice during the messianic kingdom. With that in view, perhaps it is best to link this invasion with the events at the end of the Tribulation, culminating with the Second Advent. Additional arguments in favor of this viewpoint include the following:

1. The invasion of Gog will take place in the "last days" (38:16; compare v. 8). Israel has two ages, from an eschatological viewpoint: the present age (the age of promise) and the age to come (the age of fulfillment). The "last days" refer to the end of the present age, which includes the Tribulation.

2. The events associated with the invasion of Gog correspond to the events that will characterize the Tribulation. For example:

Event	Ezekiel	Revelation
earthquake	38:19	6:12
mountains thrown down	38:20	6:14
sword	38:21	6:4
pestilence	38:22	6:8
blood	38:22	8:8
hailstones, fire, and brimstone	38:22	8:7

3. The view harmonizes well with the chronology of eschatological events mentioned in Daniel and in Revelation.
    a. Israel makes a covenant with the beast (Antichrist) and occupies the land in false security (Ezek. 38:8, 11; Dan. 9:27).
    b. Because of a desire for spoils at the expense of easy prey, the "king of the north" (identified with Gog, compare Ezek. 38:15; 39:2) invades Israel (Ezek. 38:11; Dan. 11:40).
    c. The beast (Antichrist) breaks his covenant with Israel and moves into the land (Dan. 11:41–45).
    d. The king of the north (Gog) is destroyed on the mountains of Israel (Ezek. 39:1–4; Dan. 11:44).
    e. The land of Israel is occupied by the armies of the Antichrist (Dan. 11:45) until his destruction by the returning Messiah (Rev. 19:19–21).
4. The invasion and destruction of Gog is followed in Ezekiel's account by the restoration of Israel to the land as a cleansed, regenerate people (compare 38:22, 28–29). This must take place at the end of the Tribulation in connection with the establishment of Christ's millennial kingdom (compare Zech. 12:10–13:1; Matt. 24:31).

Whatever the exact timetable and chronology of the events of Ezekiel 38–39, the text illustrates how God will ultimately bring all wicked opposition under His hand of judgment in preparation for the establishment of Messiah's kingdom.

Ezekiel 40:5

How literally should we interpret Ezekiel's vision of the temple?

Ezekiel's vision of a temple, altar, and Levitical sacrifices appears to contradict the New Testament teaching concerning Christ's death as a final and complete work (Heb. 7:17; 9:12, 25–28). There are at least six interpretations of this vision.

1. *A Memorial of the Precaptivity Temple.* Some commentators have suggested that Ezekiel's description of the temple and altar is a literary memorial to the glorious temple of Solomon, which was destroyed by the Babylonians in 586 B.C. The major objection to this viewpoint is that such a memorial would be unnecessary since the books of Kings and Chronicles provide a very adequate description of Solomon's temple. In addition, Ezekiel's temple is quite different from that which Solomon built. This description lacks correspondence in many details.

2. *The Postexilic Temple.* Some scholars believe that Ezekiel 40–48 describes the temple that was to be built by the Jews after they returned from the Babylonian captivity. Accordingly, Ezekiel's vision was to serve as motivation for the returning exiles in rebuilding the temple. But there are many differences between this glorious temple and the one built by the Jews during the Restoration. In fact, it would have been physically impossible for the Jews of the Restoration to accomplish what is recorded in Ezekiel 40–48. Certain

topographical changes are necessary before Ezekiel's temple can be built in Jerusalem. And finally, there was no return of God's glory to the restoration temple as there will be with Ezekiel's temple (Ezek. 43:1–12).

3. *The Temple Depicts the Heavenly State.* Some students of the Bible interpret Ezekiel's vision to refer to the future consummation of the kingdom of God in its heavenly state. They equate the temple described in Ezekiel 40–48 with the eternal state described by John in Revelation 21–22. However, there are many differences between these passages. And Revelation 21:22 indicates that there shall be no temple in the eternal state.

4. *The Temple Depicts the Present Church Age.* Some theologians interpret Ezekiel's vision spiritually. They understand that the vision symbolizes the Christian church in its origin, development, influence, and consequent completion. However, this introduces unwarranted allegorization, which tends to read ideas into the passage rather than drawing out the truth. Furthermore, there is little that corresponds to the church in Ezekiel's vision.

5. *The Temple Will Be Built in the Millennial Kingdom.* In my opinion, there is no reason to depart from the normal (sometimes called "literal") interpretation of Scripture when we come to Ezekiel 40–48. When we encounter problems with a literal interpretation, we should seek to resolve the problems rather than quickly abandoning our interpretive approach. Taken literally, Ezekiel 40–48 describes a temple that will exist during the kingdom (millennial age). Other prophets confirm the view that there will be a literal temple in the future kingdom (Isa. 2:3; 60:13; Jer. 33:18; Joel 3:18; Mic. 4:2; Hag. 2:7–9; Zech. 6:12–15; 14:16, 20–21). The future temple will provide a place for Messiah's throne (Ezek. 43:7) and a place for sacrificial worship (v. 27).[3]

Ezekiel 43:27

How can burnt, peace, and sin offerings be offered on the temple altar when Christ is the final sacrifice?

Ezekiel 43:13–27 describes an altar for burnt offerings. The altar is over nineteen feet high, with steps going up the east side. It is to be cleansed and consecrated with sin offerings and burnt offerings. After the seven days of consecration, burnt offerings, peace offerings, and sin offerings (compare 45:17) are to be offered on the altar by the priests.

The major objection to a literal view of the temple is the problem of future sacrifices. Offering such sacrifices would seem to constitute a revival of the old covenant, contradict statements in the book of Hebrews, and discount the redemptive work of Christ. Is there a solution?

We should first point out that the similarities between the Mosaic regulations and these sacrifices do not constitute a revival of the Mosaic system. The differences indicate that Ezekiel's altar and sacrifices are entirely different than the Mosaic system. And even if there were no sacrifices mentioned by Ezekiel, the problem does not go away, for Jeremiah 33:15–18 refers to animal sacrifices in the kingdom.

It is significant, I believe, that Ezekiel calls the altar *ariel,* literally, "lion of God" (Ezek. 43:15–16). Who is the Lion that is from the tribe of Judah (compare Gen. 49:9; Rev. 5:5)? This is none other than Jesus Christ! The altar bears His designation because it represents His sacrifice.

I propose that the sacrifices in the kingdom are literal sacrifices that will serve as a continuous memorial that the Messiah has come, has shed His blood, and has made atonement for our sins.[4] The book of Hebrews clearly teaches that the sacrifices of the Old Testament never had redemptive efficacy (Heb. 10:4). Their value was in pointing to Christ, who would deal with sin once for all (Rom. 3:25). When God saw the sacrifices of Old Testament believers, it was as if He said, "That is good enough for now. I accept these tokens as a basis for your cleansing and forgiveness until the Lamb of God, the full and final sacrifice, can be offered." Just as the old covenant sacrifices pointed toward the death of Christ, so the kingdom sacrifices point back to His death. They will serve to commemorate the perfect sacrifice of Jesus Christ and the salvation provided through His blood.

Endnotes

1. Ralph Alexander, "Hermeneutics of Old Testament Apocalyptic Literature" (Th.D. diss., Dallas Theological Seminary, 1968), 45.
2. Ralph Alexander, "Ezekiel," in *The Expositor's Bible Commentary*, vol. 6 (Grand Rapids: Zondervan, 1986), 817.
3. For a complete study see *Messiah's Coming Temple* by John W. Schmitt and J. Carl Laney (Grand Rapids: Kregel Publications, 1997).
4. Ibid.

DANIEL

Authorship

Who wrote the book of Daniel and when was it written?

Internal indicators, such as the use of the first person (7:2; 8:1; 9:2; 10:2; 12:5), indicate that Daniel, the sixth-century prophet, is the author of and major contributor to the book. The work appears to contain some material not actually written by Daniel, like the testimony of Nebuchadnezzar (4). The Danielic authorship is confirmed by Jesus, who refers to the "abomination of desolation" (9:27) as that which was spoken of through Daniel (Matt. 24:15).

The detailed predictions about Persian, Greek, and Roman empires have led some scholars, following the lead of Porphyry, the third-century pagan philosopher, to suggest that the book was written much later by someone who simply used Daniel's name. If one cannot accept the possibility of predictive prophecy, one must conclude that the prophecies of Daniel were written as history sometime during the intertestamental period.

The date of writing is bound up with the question of authorship. If Daniel authored the book as has been suggested, then it was probably completed by around 530 B.C.

Daniel 1:1

Is Daniel mistaken about the year Nebuchadnezzar came to Jerusalem?

Daniel 1:1 records that Nebuchadnezzar came to Jerusalem in the third year of Jehoiakim (609–597 B.C.). But Jeremiah 46:2 records that Nebuchadnezzar defeated Jehoiakim in his fourth year, after the Battle of Carchemish. Since the Battle of Carchemish (605 B.C.) is a well-established date, we can conclude that Jerusalem was captured in 605 B.C. Daniel apparently reckoned the date according to the Babylonian practice of considering the first year of a king's reign as the accession year and the next year as his first official year. This means that Jehoiakim's third year, according to Babylonian reckoning, was his fourth year according to Jeremiah's nonaccession-year reckoning.

Daniel 1:4

How old was Daniel when he was taken to Babylon?

The Hebrew word translated "youths" *(yeladim)* is a rather broad term and is used of children as well as young men. The term is used of Joseph when he was sold into slavery by his brothers (Gen. 37:30). Jewish tradition suggests that Daniel was about fifteen years old at the time of his captivity.[1]

Daniel 2:4–7:28

Why does Daniel switch from Hebrew to Aramaic to write this section of the book?

Aramaic was the language used by the Jews in Babylon. In fact, they brought this language home with them when they returned from captivity (Ezra 4:7; Neh. 8:8). This section of Daniel presents prophecies about Gentile nations and would be of particular interest to them. Hence, Daniel 2:4–7:28 is recorded in the Gentile language.

Daniel 3:12

Where was Daniel when his friends where charged with refusing to bow before Nebuchadnezzar's golden image?

This is a question for which we do not have a biblical answer. Perhaps Daniel was away on special business or sick in bed. We can be sure that if Daniel had been present, he would have stood with his friends rather than bow before the image. This illustrates that the trials of some are not the trials of all. God appointed the three to experience the fiery furnace, and Daniel, the lions' den.

Daniel 4:33

What happened to Nebuchadnezzar that he began eating grass?

Nebuchadnezzar appears to have suffered a case of *zoanthropy,* the delusion that one has become an animal. This mental condition came upon him as divine judgment for his pride. In his *Introduction to the Old Testament,* Harrison reports his observations about a man in a British mental institution who suffered this condition. He reports that the man's daily routine consisted of wandering around the grounds of the institution plucking up and eating handfuls of grass as he went along. Harrison was told by the hospital attendant that the man never ate institutional food with the other inmates and that his diet consisted exclusively of grass from the hospital lawns. His only drink was water, which was served to him in a clean container so that he would not drink from muddy puddles. The only physical abnormality noted was the lengthening of his hair and a course, thickened condition of the fingernails. Harrison notes, "Without institutional care, the patient would have manifested precisely the same physical conditions as those mentioned in Daniel 4:33."[2]

Daniel 5:1

Who was "Belshazzar the king"?

Until 1854 when J. G. Taylor discovered the Nabonidus Chronicle, it was believed by many that Daniel was mistaken in referring to Belshazzar as "king." It was well established from lists of ancient kings that Nabonidus, successor to Nebuchadnezzar, was the last ruler of Babylon. Belshazzar was not even mentioned. Then, in 1854, a British consul named Taylor was exploring some ruins in southern Iraq on behalf of the British Museum. As he dug into a mud-brick tower that was part of a temple dedicated to the moon god, he found several clay cylinders inscribed in the cuneiform script. The inscriptions had been written at the command of Nabonidus, king of Babylon from 555 to 539 B.C. The Nabonidus Chronicle reveals that Belshazzar was the eldest son of Nabonidus and was the crown prince.[3] Another text reveals that Nabonidus entrusted the kingship to his eldest son.[4] These texts reveal that Belshazzar was coregent with his father, Nabonidus. Nabonidus was in charge of the military and Belshazzar was in charge of the administration of Babylon. This explains why Daniel was offered the position as "third ruler" (5:29) in the kingdom of Babylon.

Daniel 5:31

Who is Darius the Mede?

It is a well-established fact that Cyrus conquered Babylon and was the first king of Persia (539–530 B.C.). So why does Daniel mention "Darius the Mede"? There are at least three possible solutions.

1. *Historical Error.* According to this view, Daniel was mistaken. He confused Cyrus with Darius Hystaspes, who is associated with a later fall of Babylon in 520 B.C.

2. *Governor Gubaru.* John Whitcomb has argued that Darius was the royal title that Gubaru received from Cyrus when he was appointed governor of Babylon.[5] But Darius is repeatedly called "king" in chapter 6.

3. *Cyrus the Persian.* D. J. Wiseman of the British Museum identifies Darius the Mede with Cyrus the Persian.[6] He translates Daniel 6:28, "in the reign of Darius, even in the reign of Cyrus the Persian." In support of this view, Darius was made king (9:1–2), called king (6:8), and exercised the authority of a king (6:9). He is called king twenty-eight times in chapter 6. The evidence suggests that "Darius the Mede" was none other than the Persian king, Cyrus. It is not uncommon in ancient times for people to have two names. Cyrus [Darius] was of Median descent and ruled Persia.

Daniel 7:1

Why does Daniel step backward in his chronology to 553 B.C. after the fall in Babylon in 539 (chapter 5)?

In the first six chapters of Daniel, the author tells of his experiences in Babylon serving under Nebuchadnezzar, Nabonidus and Belshazzar, and Darius. Now in chapters 7–12 he records his four visions—chapter 7 (553 B.C.), chapter 8 (551 B.C.), chapter 9 (539 B.C.), and chapters 10–12 (536 B.C.).

Daniel 7:13

Is this text or Ezekiel 2:1 the background of the "Son of Man" concept in the Gospels?

The designation "Son of Man" is used by Jesus to refer to Himself about ninety-four times in the Gospels. The expression is used in Ezekiel to express Ezekiel's creaturely weakness in contrast with the majesty and power of almighty God. Some have suggested that Jesus may have drawn from Ezekiel's use of this term in referring to Himself as the "Son of Man." I suggest instead that Jesus drew from Daniel 7, as this term was used in a messianic context. In Daniel 7:13–14 the one "like a son of man" receives dominion, glory, and a kingdom. This corresponds with other Scriptures that speak of Christ's kingdom rule on the earth (2 Sam. 7:12–16; Luke 1:32–33). Jesus used the term "Son of Man" to emphasize His messiahship, not his humanity.

Daniel 7:9 and 8:9

Daniel 7:9 refers to a "little" horn and Daniel 8:9 refers to a "small horn." Are these the same?

In our study of Daniel 7, we discover that the "little" horn arises out of the "fourth beast," probably the reunified Roman Empire. The "small horn" of 8:9 arises out of the Greek Empire. The "small horn" is Antiochus IV Epiphanes (175–164 B.C.), who persecuted the Jewish people. The "little horn" of 7:8 is the Beast of Revelation, also known as the Antichrist (Dan. 9:26–27; 11:36–45; Rev. 13:1–8; 19:19–21).

Daniel 9:24–27

How should we interpret the prophecy of the "seventy weeks"?

There are four basic interpretations of the "seventy weeks" of Daniel 9:24–27.

Historical Interpretation. According to the historical interpretation, the prophecy is related to known history from the Babylonian period to the cleansing of the temple by the Maccabees in 164 B.C. The eschatological significance of the passage is denied. The main objection to this view is that Jesus and the New Testament writers witness to the future significance of this period (Matt. 24:15).

Jewish Interpretation. Josephus and other Jewish interpreters have viewed the prophecy as related to known history, specifically the suffering under Antiochus and Titus. It is suggested that the fall of Jerusalem brought about an end to the seventy weeks. But the chronology does not work. Adding the 444 years B.C. (the date of the decree to restore Jerusalem) to the 70 years A.D. yields 514 years instead of the 490 demanded by the prophecy.

Amillennial Interpretation. Amillennial interpreters understand that the seventy weeks terminates with the coming of Christ. Jesus is thought to be the "Prince who is to come." After three and one-half years of ministry (the middle of the Seventieth Week), He put an end to sacrifice by His death. But Jesus Himself did not teach this view. He interpreted the Seventieth Week as future (Matt. 24:15).

Premillennial Interpretation. According to the premillennial interpretation, the prophecy concerns the Jews and Jerusalem (Dan. 9:24) and reveals God's program for Israel. The church is not in view in any of these verses. The scope of the prophecy covers seventy "weeks" during which God will fulfill all His purposes regarding the nation of Israel. The "weeks" (literally, "sevens") constitute weeks of years. Nothing else—days or months—fits. Seventy weeks of years is the equivalent of 70 times 7, or 490 years. The Jewish year has 360 days (compare Gen. 7:11, 14; 8:3–4), so the sixty-nine weeks deals with a period of 173,880 days (69 times 7 times 360).

I suggest that Christ's ministry completed the first sixty-nine weeks of the prophecy. There appears to be a church-age gap between the sixty-ninth and seventieth weeks. The seventieth week of the prophecy corresponds with what Jeremiah calls "the time of Jacob's distress" (Jer. 30:7) and what the New Testament refers to as the Tribulation (Matt. 24:9, 21, 29; Rev. 7:14). The "prince who is to come" (Dan. 9:26) does not refer to Christ but to the Antichrist. He will make a covenant with the people of Israel during the Tribulation (v. 27) but will break it after three and one-half years. He is the one who will "put a stop to sacrifice and grain offering" in the temple (2 Thess. 2:4), claiming the worship that God alone deserves. But he will experience "complete destruction" when Christ returns at the Second Advent (2 Thess. 2:8; Rev. 19:19–21).

The prophecy of the seventy weeks concerns three great deliverances: the deliverance of the Jews from Babylon, the deliverance of God's people from bondage of sin, and the deliverance of the Jews from the oppression of the Antichrist by the returning Messiah (Dan. 9:25–27).

Daniel 12:11–12

What is the significance of the 1,290 days and the 1,335 days mentioned in the last chapter of Daniel?

These figures are given by an interpreting angel in response to Daniel's question, "My lord, what will be the outcome of these [tribulation] events?" (12:8). The angel explains that from a particular starting point, there will be 1,290 days. The starting point is the midpoint of the Tribulation when the "abomination of desolation" is set up (Matt. 24:15; 2 Thess. 2:4). The period from the midpoint of the Tribulation to the end is three and one-half years, or 1,260 days (Rev. 12:6). The angel tells Daniel there will be 1,290 days—30 days beyond the end of the Tribulation. The Bible does not reveal what will happen during these 30 days. I suggest that it may be during this period that Christ will judge the nations (Matt. 25) and regather the remnant of Israel to the Promised Land (Ezek. 20:34–38).

The angel then pronounces a blessing on the one who "keeps waiting and attains to the 1,335 days." This is a period that extends 75 days beyond the end of the Tribulation, 45 days beyond the previous period (1,290 days). I suggest that it is during these 45 days that the saints are resurrected and rewarded (Dan. 12:2–3), the borders of the kingdom are established (Gen. 15:18), and the chief officers appointed (Rev. 20:4). The blessings of the messianic kingdom will follow.

Endnotes

1. Judah J. Slotki, *Daniel, Ezra, Nehemiah* (London: Soncino, 1951), 2.
2. R. K. Harrison, *Introduction to the Old Testament* (Grand Rapids: Eerdmans, 1969), 1116.
3. James B. Pritchard, ed., *Ancient Near Eastern Texts* (Princeton: Princeton University Press, 1969), 309, footnote 5.
4. Ibid., 313 Col. b.
5. John C. Whitcomb, *Darius the Mede* (Presbyterian and Reformed Publishing Company, 1974), 1–18.
6. D. J. Wiseman, *Some Problems in the Book of Daniel* (London: Tyndale, 1965).

HOSEA

Hosea 1:2

Is the story of Hosea and Gomer historical, or is it a parable intended to teach a spiritual lesson?

Some scholars have viewed the account as a parable intended to illustrate the relationship between God and Israel. It is suggested that the names of the children suggest a symbolic story rather than historical reality, and that the events of chapters 1–3 would take too much time for God to use them to teach Israel a moral lesson.

There are no compelling reasons to regard Hosea as a fictitious story or parable. First, the literary form is that of simple narrative. There is no indication within the text that the author intends the reader to understand his book as a parable. Second, other prophets give their children symbolic names, though they are real children (Isa. 7:3; 8:3). Third, there is no inherent problem with the time period. Isaiah spent three years of his life acting out a sign (20:3). Fourth, the names of Gomer and her father have no symbolic significance. Fifth, the vividness of the account suggests that it records the personal experience of the prophet Hosea.

Hosea 1:2

Did Hosea actually marry a harlot, or did Gomer become a harlot after the marriage had taken place?

Many interpreters have seen a moral problem with God, who condemns adultery (Exod. 20:14; Heb. 13:5), commanding Hosea to marry a harlot. Would a holy God command a prophet to become associated with evil? There are many different answers offered to the question of what was Gomer?

An Idolater. It is suggested that Gomer was an idolater, not an adulterer. She rejected the true worship of Yahweh and committed spiritual adultery by pursuing other gods. But the reference to her having "children of harlotry" argues against this view.

A Concubine. At least one interpreter has suggested that Gomer was a concubine, not a true wife. But this doesn't really resolve the issue and only compounds the problem.

A Virtuous Woman. It has been suggested that Gomer was really virtuous, but Hosea ascribes harlotry to her in order to provide a basis for his prophetic ministry. But would a true prophet slander his wife to make a preaching point?

A *Temple Prostitute*. Some have regarded Gomer as a temple prostitute, deluded and misused. But the Hebrew has a word for the "temple prostitute" (Hos. 4:14) and it is not used here. And this interpretation does not resolve the moral issue.

A *Public Harlot*. It is argued strongly that Gomer was a public harlot when she married Hosea. But what does this teach about God's relationship with Israel? Did God "marry" Israel as a harlot? Some texts do suggest that the people of Israel were involved in idolatry (spiritual adultery) from the beginning (Josh. 24:14; Ezek. 23:8; Amos 5:25). But the phrase, "wife of harlotries," suggests that Gomer's wanton ways would be manifested while she was a wife. And the command in Hosea 3:1 suggests that the prophet once loved his wife. Would this have been likely if she had been a public harlot at the time of their wedding?

A *Woman Inclined Toward Harlotry*. I suggest that Hosea married Gomer, who had an inclination or tendency toward harlotry. After their marriage, she lapsed into harlotry and conceived children that were not Hosea's. There are several reasons why I favor this interpretation. First, this view gives recognition to Hosea's original love for Gomer (3:1). Second, this interpretation best parallels the relationship between God and His people Israel. They had a tendency toward unfaithfulness and eventually became apostate (Ezek. 16:8, 15). Third, this view explains how Hosea's children can be called "children of harlotry." They were conceived as a result of Gomer's adulterous relationships. Finally, this view lessens the moral difficulty of God commanding the prophet to associate himself with an evil woman since Gomer was not a harlot when she married Hosea.

God ordered Hosea to marry a woman who had an inclination toward harlotry and who eventually became a harlot. The marriage of Hosea and Gomer was a picture of the relationship between God and Israel. The physical unfaithfulness of Gomer illustrates the spiritual unfaithfulness of the people of Israel. But in spite of her adulteries, Hosea is commanded to love her (3:1) in demonstration of God's unceasing love for Israel.

Hosea 6:6

Does this verse reflect a prophetic rejection of the Mosaic sacrificial system?

It has been suggested that the prophet opposed the sacrificial system that was instituted through Moses at Mount Sinai. Hosea is not denying the validity of a sacrifice offered as an act of genuine worship. But he declares that mere sacrificial ritual means nothing apart from covenant loyalty and a knowledge of God (see Isa. 1:12–15; Mic. 6:6–8).

This has become a very significant verse in Jewish thinking regarding temple sacrifices. When Jerusalem was destroyed by the Romans in A.D. 70, Rabbi Yohanan ben Zakkai was leaving Jerusalem when someone cried out, "Woe unto us that this place, the place where the iniquities of Israel were atoned for, is laid waste." Rabbi Yohanan replied, "Be not grieved. We have another atonement as effective as this." "And what is it?" the other questioned. "It is acts of lovingkindness, as it is said, 'For I desire mercy, not sacrifice'"[1] (see Hos. 6:6).

Rabbi Yohanan ben Zakkai soon established a small school to teach that the sacrifices God now demanded of Jewish people were acts of love and mercy. His thinking and teaching became dominant in Judaism, enabling Jewish people to carry on their religion without a temple and sacrificial ritual.

Endnotes

1. Jacob Neusner, *Judaism in the Beginning of Christianity* (Philadelphia: Fortress, 1984), 96.

JOEL

Joel 1:4

Does Joel refer to literal locusts, or is he using the "locusts" as a symbol of judgment?

In verse 4, Joel uses four different terms for locusts. This variation has caused some controversy. Is Joel describing four different types of locusts, four stages of locust development, or merely using four poetic synonyms for locusts? The latter is probably correct. Joel uses the common word for locusts (*'arbeh*) and then gives three poetic equivalents.

The point is that the locusts came in successive, devastating swarms. Joel describes dramatically and poetically how swarm after swarm diminished the potential harvest to nothing.

While some would argue that these "locusts" are merely symbols of judgment, there is strong evidence to suggest that they should be interpreted literally.

1. Locust plagues were promised as a consequence of violating the Mosaic covenant (Deut. 28:38–39).
2. Joel's description matches reports of actual locust plagues.
3. The locusts are said to devour vines, bark, and vegetation. There is no reference to death, plunder, or the destruction of cities, as would be the case if they represented an invading army.
4. While the invaders are called "an army" (2:11), they are clearly identified as locusts in 2:25.

Few Westerners realize the tremendous damage caused by locust swarms. In some years the desert locust is just a solitary, stay-at-home grasshopper. But suddenly it may change its character, gather into a swarm, and begin a gluttonous migratory spree. The cause of swarming is not fully understood. Contributing factors include high temperatures, low humidity, and population crowding. These factors lead to anatomical changes that enable swarms to fly for thousands of miles.

Strong winds and double wings carry swarms from Africa to India, and some return. Breeding along the way repopulates and refreshes the swarms. A locust swarm can cover more than a square mile with fifty million insects—each two-inches long—capable of devastating a hundred ton of vegetation a day. Giant swarms of locusts have been known to blanket two thousand square miles (an estimated 2.5 billion insects), stripping the land, fouling the air with excrement, and triggering epidemics as the locusts die and decay. With serrated jaws rasping from side to side, adult locusts consume the equivalent of their body weight daily. Yet they are capable of living four days without feeding, surviving on stored fat. It has been estimated that a large swarm can devour in one day what forty thousand people eat in one year! In modern times, traps, poisons, and even flamethrowers have been used to fight the locusts, but the battle is becoming more difficult due to environmental objections to pesticides.[1]

Joel 1:15

What does Joel mean by the expression, "the day of the Lord"?

The Day of the Lord is a major theme of Old Testament prophetic thought. We discover this theme in the New Testament as well (1 Thess. 5:2; 2 Thess. 2:2). There are four major suggestions as to the origin of the concept: (1) holy war tradition; (2) an enthronement festival for Yahweh; (3) the execution of the covenant curses; and (4) the motif of theophany descriptions. It seems most probable that the concept of the Day of Yahweh originated with the conquest of Canaan—a conquest that was in fact Yahweh's war (Deut. 1:30; 3:22; Josh. 5:13–15; 6:2; compare Exod. 14:14; 15:3).

While most of the eighteen specific references to the Day of Yahweh in the Prophets speak of future historical or eschatological events, five texts describe and interpret the Day of Yahweh in terms of past historical events (Isa. 22:1–14; Jer. 46:2–12; Lam. 1–2; Ezek. 13:1–9). These texts reflect circumstances of military tragedy, defeat, and judgment. Such events may have provided the basis for the prophetic concept of a future historical or even eschatological "day" or period of divine judgment on the disobedient of Israel and the nations (Isa. 13:6, 9; Joel 1:15; Zeph. 1:14–18). Often there is a blending of the historical and eschatological as a historical judgment serves as a type or precursor of a greater future day of judgment.

The Day of Yahweh is not just a day of wrath and judgment on the disobedient. In eschatological contexts it is also seen to include deliverance and restoration for the righteous. The Day of Yahweh is a day of future hope, prosperity, and blessing (Isa. 4:2–6; Hos. 2:18–23; Joel 3:18–21; Amos 9:11–15; Mic. 4:6–8).

The eschatological Day of the Lord may be defined as that period of time during which God will deal with Israel and the nations through judgment and deliverance. While the Second Advent is preceded by signs (Matt. 24:29–30), the Day of the Lord is said to come unexpectedly (1 Thess. 5:2). Hence this period must begin shortly after the rapture of the church—an imminent and signless event.

According to Peter, the Day of the Lord will conclude with the purging of the heavens and of the earth in preparation for the creation of the new heavens and the new earth (2 Peter 3:10–13; compare Isa. 65:17; 66:22). Thus, the eschatological Day of Yahweh includes the prophesied events of the Tribulation period, the events of the Second Advent, the millennial kingdom, the final revolt of Satan, the Great White Throne judgment, and the purging of the earth in preparation for the new creation (compare Rev. 6–20). It is a day of both destruction and salvation, a day of wrath and a day of grace.

Endnotes

1. For further study and pictures, see the *National Geographic* articles, "Locust: The Teeth of the Wind" (August 1969) and "Report from the Locust Wars" (April 1953).

AMOS

Amos 1:3

On what basis does God judge the people of Damascus and other foreign peoples (1:3–2:3) who did not receive the law of God?

God's rule is not limited to the people of Israel. He rules the whole world, and the people of all nations are individually accountable to Him. The foreign nations, like Syria, are held accountable to God on the basis of natural revelation (Ps. 19:1–6; Rom. 1:18–20) and the law of conscience (Rom. 2:14–15). Amos demonstrates that if God holds the foreign peoples accountable for violations of social justice (1:3, 6, 11), certainly the people of Israel will not escape His judgment! Those who have received God's written revelation are even more accountable than the Gentile peoples who had no special revelation. Greater light means greater accountability.

Amos 2:1

Does this verse condemn cremation as a means of disposing of a corpse?

The transgression of Moab that the Lord condemns is not cremation but the dishonoring of the corpse of one's enemy. The burning of a body was usually reserved as a judgment for criminals (Lev. 20:14; 21:9; Josh. 7:15, 25). The Roman historian Tacitus indicates that the Jews were averse to cremation as was frequently practiced by the Greeks (*History* 5.5). A singular exception is the burning of the bodies of Saul and his sons (1 Sam. 31:11–13). This may have been done because the bodies were mutilated or were badly decomposed and the men of Jabesh wanted to transport the remains back home. Although not the custom of Jews or early Christians, there is nothing in Scripture that reveals a negative attitude toward cremation.

Amos 3:15

What does Amos mean when he refers to the "houses of ivory" that God will judge?

First Kings 22:39 refers to the "ivory house" that Ahab built. Many readers of the Bible assumed that this was merely exaggeration and without any historical basis. But the excavations at the royal city of Samaria proved otherwise. During the excavations of Samaria by George Reisner (1908–1910) and later by John Crowfoot (1931–1935), over five hundred ivory fragments were uncovered. Most of these fragments date to the ninth or eighth century B.C. The fragments are extraordinarily beautiful and portray both animal and religious motifs.[1] It appears from the archaeological discoveries that the walls and furniture of Ahab's palace were beautified with delicate ivory inlays. The expression "houses of ivory" is an exaggeration based on the extensive use of ivory in wood panels and furniture.

Amos 5:26

What are the idols that Amos is referring to here?

This verse has puzzled interpreters for years. The debate in verse 25 centers on the meaning of the two Hebrew words transliterated *sakkuth* and *kiyyun*. These words occur only once in the Hebrew Bible and so there is great debate about their meaning. Many modern scholars have suggested that the passage gives evidence of astral (star) worship. They have interpreted the words as divine names of the planet Saturn. The words, "the star of your gods" (or "your star gods") supports this interpretation. Gevirtz has emended the text to refer to "the shrine of your (god) Moloch, and to the abode of your images."[2] Isbell reconstructs the text following the Septuagint to read, "You will take up the tabernacle of Milcom, the star of your god [which is] Kiyyun, your images which you have made for yourselves."[3]

Within the context, Amos seems to be contrasting the faithful worship of God (v. 25) with Israel's idolatrous practices (v. 26). The question of verse 25 should be answered "yes." The people of Israel did present sacrifices and grain offerings in the wilderness (Exod. 21:4–6; Num. 7:10–88). But verse 25 reveals that the Israelites also succumbed to idolatry. Amos may be contrasting faithful worship in the wilderness (v. 25) with the idolatrous practices of his day (v. 26; 4:4–5). Or the prophet is demonstrating that Israel has been idolatrous from the beginning (compare Acts 7:42–43).

Amos 7:14

What kind of tree is the sycamore fig?

The sycamore fig *(Ficus sycomorus)* is a curious tree. The tree was grown mainly for its wood, which is light and very durable. It was used for chests and coffins in ancient times. The heavy foliage of the sycamore provides abundant shade. The green leaves are heart shaped, resembling those of a mulberry. The fruit of the sycamore smells like an ordinary fig but is inferior in taste. It was the fruit of the common people and the poor. In order to encourage ripening and make the fruit more palatable, the figs had to be slit. Land owners would often allow shepherds to graze their flocks among the sycamore trees in return for the shepherds' fulfilling this task. It has also been suggested that the sycamore fig may have provided fodder for the sheep.[4]

Endnotes

1. Some of the ivories are pictured in Philip King's *Amos, Hosea, Micah—An Archaeological Commentary* (Philadelphia: Westminster, 1988), 145–47.
2. Stanley Gevirtz, "A New Look At an Old Crux: Amos 5:26," *Journal of Biblical Literature* 87 (September 1968): 76.
3. Charles D. Isbell, "Another Look At Amos 5:26," *Journal of Biblical Literature* 97 (March 1978): 97.
4. T. J. Wright, "Amos and the 'Sycomore Fig,'" *Vetus Testamentum* 26 (July 1976): 368.

OBADIAH

Obadiah 1

Who were the Edomites?

The word *edom* means "red," and Edom is the name given to Esau when he sold his birthright for some red soup (Gen. 25:30). The Edomites were the descendants of Esau, Jacob's brother. The book of Obadiah records another chapter in the long story of enmity that existed between the descendants of Esau and the descendants of Jacob. Key events include:

1. Esau threatened to kill Jacob (Gen. 27:41).
2. Edom refused to allow Israel to pass through their land (Num. 20:14–21).
3. Saul fought against Edom (1 Sam. 14:47).
4. David subjugated Edom (2 Sam. 8:14).
5. Amaziah conquered Edom and captured Sela (2 Kings 14:7).
6. Edom rebelled against Judah (2 Chron. 21:8–10).
7. Edom celebrated Jerusalem's fall in 586 B.C. (Ps. 137:7; Lam. 4:21–22).
8. Judas Maccabeus conquered Idumaea, a later name for Edom (Josephus *Antiquities* 12.353).
9. John Hyrcanus forced the Idumaeans to adopt Judaism (Josephus *Antiquities* 13.257–58).
10. Herod, an Idumaean, sought to kill Jesus (Matt. 2:16–18).
11. Antipas, son of Herod, killed John the Baptist (Matt. 14:1–12).
12. During the Jewish War (A.D. 66–70), Idumaea was attacked and devastated by the Jewish military leader Simon ben Gioras (Josephus *War* 4.534–37).

Obadiah 10–14

What is the historical occasion of Edom's cruelty against Judah?

Many commentators believe that these crimes against Judah took place at the fall of Jerusalem in 586 B.C. However, Obadiah makes no mention of the Chaldeans, Nebuchadnezzar, the exile to Babylon, or the burning of the temple. The latter is especially significant since 1 Esdras 4:45 records that the Edomites burned the temple. Wouldn't Obadiah have mentioned this? I suggest that the historical background for this section is the reign of King Jehoram (853–841 B.C.) after Edom revolted against Judah and set up its own king (2 Chron. 21:8–10) and Judah was invaded by the Philistines and

160

the Arabs (vv. 16–17). Edom applauded this invasion, persecuting their Israelite relatives instead of protecting them.

Obadiah 20

Where is "Sephared"?

Knowing the location of this place would help date the book and show where the exiles were taken after the attack on Jerusalem (vv. 11–14). Unfortunately, the site has not been identified with certainty. Suggestions include Hesperides in North Africa, Sardis in Asia Minor, and Saparda, a district in southwest Media.

JONAH

Jonah 1:1

How should we interpret the book of Jonah? Is this history, fiction, or parable?

Jonah presents an opportunity for a wide range of interpretation. Five views have found support among biblical scholars. The first four views deny the historicity of the book.

1. *Fictional*. The book is not considered historical. It is interpreted as a fictional short story with a moral.

2. *Symbolic*. The author employs symbols to communicate a message. The three days and three nights in the fish is symbolic of Jonah's visit to Nineveh. His being vomited out is symbolic of his leaving the repentant city.

3. *Allegorical*. The events in Jonah are interpreted to correspond with important biblical concepts rather than as historical facts.

4. *Parabolic*. The book is interpreted as a story with a didactic aim. This is a prominent view today.

5. *Historical*. This view regards Jonah as an historical figure and the events of the book as historically accurate.

The are four major problems with the nonhistorical interpretations of Jonah. First, the Old Testament views Jonah as a historical person (2 Kings 14:25). Second, the New Testament views Jonah as a historical person (Matt. 12:39–40). Third, the New Testament views Nineveh's repentance as historical (Matt. 12:41). Fourth, while it would not be unexpected to have a parable within a historical narrative, it would be most unusual to have one that encompasses a whole canonical book!

I suggest that the account of Jonah is historical, but it is history with a satirical twist.[1] Jonah is the "unhero" of the book! He flees his commission, is eaten by a fish, his prophecy does not come true, and he is mad at God! In addition to recording a humorous historical experience in the life of the prophet Jonah, the account stands as a corrective against the narrow-minded and unforgiving attitude expressed by this reluctant prophet.

Jonah 1:17

What possibility is there that someone could survive being swallowed by a "great fish?"

Few people would question the historicity of Jonah apart from the fish story. It is the ultimate in a tall tale. What possibility is there that someone could survive being swallowed by a great fish?

Would it be possible to be swallowed by a large sea creature without being chewed up? In Sir Francis Fox's book, *Sixty-Three Years of Engineering*, it is reported that the sperm whale can swallow lumps of food eight feet in diameter.[2] In one of these whales was found the skeleton of a shark sixteen feet in length. Rimmer suggests that Jonah's "fish" may have been the rhinodon shark, which has no teeth and feeds by straining its food through great plates in its mouth. A large fish of this type would certainly be capable of swallowing a human being.[3]

What would be the chances of surviving inside the fish? Rimmer reports that whales, being air breathing mammals, have in their heads a large air storage chamber. The chamber is an enlargement of the nasal sinus and, in a large whale, can be as large as fourteen feet by seven feet, and seven feet high. This amounts to 686 cubic feet of space. It is possible that someone could survive for three days and three nights in such a chamber. Rimmer points out that if a whale takes into its mouth an object too big to swallow, it thrusts it up into the air chamber. If it finds that it has a large object in its head, it swims for the nearest land, lies in shallow water, and ejects it.[4] It is also reported that a sperm whale always ejects the contents of its stomach when dying.

Rimmer tells of an English sailor was once swallowed by a giant rhinodon shark in the English Channel. The sailor fell overboard attempting to harpoon the shark. Before he could be picked up, the man was swallowed. The entire trawler fleet sought to hunt the fish down so the sailor's body could be recovered and buried. Forty-eight hours after the accident occurred, the fish was sighted and killed. The carcass was towed to shore and the body cavity opened. Much to his friends' surprise, the sailor was unconscious but alive! He was rushed to the hospital where he was found to be suffering from shock alone. A few hours later he was discharged as being physically fit. Rimmer reports that he met the sailor in person and was able to corroborate the incident. The man's physical appearance had been effected by his experience. His body was entirely devoid of hair, and odd patches of yellowish-brown covered his skin.[5]

Fox reports an incident that took place in February 1891. A whale ship, *Star of the East,* was in the vicinity of the Falkland Islands when a large sperm whale was sighted three miles away. Drawing near for the kill, one of the two harpooning boats was upset. One man was drowned; the other, James Bartley, disappeared and was presumed dead. The whale was killed and the sailors worked all day and part of the night butchering it. As they began to work near the stomach, they were "startled by spasmodic signs of life." Inside they found the sailor, doubled up and unconscious. He was laid on the deck and revived by a bath of seawater. He was placed in the captain's quarters, where he raved as a lunatic for two weeks. But at the end of the third week he had entirely recovered and resumed his duties.

It is reported that Bartley's face, neck and hands were bleached to a deadly whiteness by the gastric juice in the stomach of the whale. He believes that he would have lived inside the stomach of the whale until he starved, for he lost his senses through fright and not from lack of air. After falling into the foaming waters, he was drawn into a dark place where the heat was intense. As he tried to find a way out and touched the slimy walls around him, he realized where he was and fell into an unconscience state as a result of the shock.

Other cases have been reported of people who survived the ordeal of being swallowed by a fish. A. J. Wilson reports two other incidents in which men were swallowed by whales and vomited up afterward with only minor injuries.[6]

It appears to be technically possible for a human to be swallowed by a whale or a great fish and survive. Actual incidents of such have been reported. Yet these reports must not be swallowed hook, line, and sinker! In response to an inquiry regarding the James Bartley incident, the widow of the ship's captain affirmed that no sailor fell overboard during the period that her husband commanded the vessel.[7] Was the incident a hoax? Believers must avoid propagating false rumors even when they seemingly support the Christian faith.

The validation of a modern Jonah story would serve as an encouragement to the faithful. But the lack of such validation ought not diminish a Christian's appreciation for the miracle in the Jonah story. All the miracles of Scripture lie in the shadow of the Great Miracle—the resurrection of Christ! The God who can raise the dead can appoint a fish to deliver Jonah! Faith in the Resurrection significantly diminishes the difficulty in believing Jonah's fish story.

Endnotes

1. Leland Ryken, *The Literature of the Bible* (Grand Rapids: Zondervan, 1974), 265–68.
2. Sir Francis Fox, *Sixty-Three Years of Engineering* cited by Ambrose John Wilson, *Princeton Theological Review* 25 (1927): 630–42.
3. Harry Rimmer, *The Harmony of Science and Scripture* (Berne: Berne Witness, 1940), 185.
4. Ibid., 183.
5. Ibid., 188–89.
6. *Princeton Theological Review* 25 (October 1927): 630–42.
7. *Expository Times* 17 (1905/1906): 521; 18 (1906/1907): 239.

MICAH

Micah 1:8

What was the point of Micah going barefoot and naked?

In Micah 1:2–7 the prophet announces the divine judgment that God will execute on His people through the Assyrians. Samaria would fall to the Assyrians in 722 B.C., and Jerusalem would be besieged in 701 B.C. It is in light of this coming judgment that Micah tells how he will express his grief. He will "lament like the jackals" and mourn "like the ostriches," animals known for their howling and screeching (Job 30:29). Going "barefoot and naked" were traditional expressions of mourning in the biblical period (2 Sam. 15:30; Isa. 20:2–4). The term *naked* probably means "without one's outer cloak" since public nudity would have been regarded as lewd. Micah probably wore a loincloth. By going without his clothes Micah depicted the conditions of slavery that many Israelites would face at the hands of the Assyrians.

Micah 3:4

Why will God refuse to answer those who "cry out" to Him? How does this fit with Jesus' teaching in Matthew 7:7?

In Micah 3:1–4, the prophet denounces the wicked rulers who hate good, love evil, and have used their public positions for personal gain. They have broken the covenant and must now face the consequences of their "evil deeds" (v. 4).

Micah is not referring here to those who "cry out" with repentant hearts, confessing their sins and seeking God's mercy. He is referring to those who have repeatedly refused God's call to repentance. They will "cry out" at the time of judgment in their attempt to avoid the consequences of their sins. But this will not save them from the cursings of the covenant due them for disobedience. This is quite a different situation than that spoken of by Jesus when He invites sinners to seek entrance into His kingdom. Those who truly seek God, with repentant hearts, will not fail to find Him (Heb. 11:6).

Micah 5:1

Who is the ruler who was smitten "on the cheek"?

Micah 5:1 takes us back to the thought of Micah 4:9–10, which describes the suffering that the Judeans will experience at the hands of the Babylonians. In 5:1, Micah addresses the people of Jerusalem and exhorts them to gather their troops to withstand the enemy that had laid siege to their city. He then announces that "they" (the Babylonians) "will smite the judge of Israel on the cheek." Within the historical context of the capture of Jerusalem, this must refer to the humiliation of Zedekiah when Babylon besieged and conquered the city. Zedekiah tried to escape but was captured, blinded, and taken to Babylon (2 Kings 25:6–7).

Micah 6:8

Why does God require these virtues and not salvation?

There is only one work that God requires of unbelievers. Jesus identified it in John 6:29: "This is the work of God, that you believe in Him whom He has sent."

The text of Micah 6:8 speaks to the issue of a believer's obligation, not of the unsaved's salvation. In verses 6–7 the questions are raised as to what sacrifice might be sufficient to fulfill one's obligation to God. The point is that no sacrifice, not even that of one's children, is sufficient to satisfy God. What God calls for among His people is justice, loyalty, and humility. These virtues are not a basis for salvation. But when practiced from the heart, they provide a basis for walking with God in a manner that pleases and honors Him.

NAHUM

Nahum 1:1

What is the relationship between the books of Jonah and Nahum regarding Nineveh?

Nahum contains a message of God's judgment and destruction of Nineveh. Someone has suggested that Nahum is Jonah's favorite book. It contains the message he wanted to preach!

About one hundred years before the ministry of Nahum, Jonah was sent to Nineveh to call the people to repentance. The people responded to the preaching of Jonah and God spared the city. Jonah's story reveals that God's mercy and compassion extend even to the most wicked people on the condition of repentance. Sadly, after time, the people of Nineveh fell back into their wicked ways. Although God is long-suffering and good (Nah. 1:3, 7), there comes a point where He must execute justice in a manner consistent with His holy character. Nahum announces the judgment and destruction of Nineveh, the proud capital of Assyria. The book of Nahum teaches that persistent wickedness will be judged by divine wrath.

Nahum 3:1

Why does Nahum refer to Nineveh as a "bloody city"?

The Assyrians were renowned for their cruel and bloodthirsty behavior. Not only is this evidenced in Scripture (2 Chron. 33:11; Isa. 33:1; 37:38; Jonah 1:2; Nah. 3:1), but their own kings boasted of the cruel treatment of their enemies and victims. The following quotations will demonstrate the truth of Nahum 3:1.[1]

> At Kinabu "600 of their warriors I put to the sword; 3,000 captives I burned with fire; I did not leave a single one among them alive to serve as a hostage. Hulai, their governor, I captured alive. . . . I flayed [him], his skin I spread upon the wall of the city of Damdamusa" (I, 146). At Petura "I formed a pillar . . . of heads over against his city gate and 700 men I impaled on stakes over against their city gate" (I, 156). King Assurnasirpal (883–859 B.C.)

> "Their warriors I slew with the sword . . . ; in the moat [of the city] I piled them up; with the corpses of their warriors I filled the wide

167

plain. With their blood I dyed the mountains like red wool" (I, 215). King Shalmaneser III (859–824 B.C.)

"13,000 of their warriors I cut down with the sword. Their blood like the waters of a stream I caused to run through the square of their city. The corpses of their fighters I piled in heaps" (I, 259). King Shamsi-Adad V (824–810 B.C.)

Of Dur-Illatai, "40,500 of its people, together with their possessions, their spoil, their property and goods, his wife, his sons, his daughters (and) his gods, I carried off" (I, 284). Tiglath-pileser III (745–727 B.C.)

Of Uaite, "I pierced his chin with my keen hand dagger. Through his jaw I passed a rope, put a dog chain upon him and made him occupy [guard] a kennel of the east gate of the inner [wall] of Nineveh" (II, 319). "In Arbela I tore out their tongues and flayed them. Dananu they laid upon a skinning-table in Nineveh and slaughtered him like a lamb. The others I slew. I cut off their members and had [them] carried about as an object lesson for all lands" (II, 335). Ashurbanipal (669–663 B.C.)

Nahum 3:8
Who or what is No-amon?

In the language of Egypt, the word *no* means "city." No-amon refers to the city of the god Amon, the imperial god of Egypt. Most biblical scholars identify No-amon with the city of Thebes, the capital of Upper Egypt during the New Kingdom (1580–1085 B.C.). The city was located on the Nile River about three hundred miles south of modern Cairo. On the east bank of the Nile are the ruins of the famous temples of Amon. West of the river is the Valley of the Kings where the tombs of many pharaohs have been discovered. When the Nile flooded, No-amon was surrounded by water. Like Nineveh with its moat, No-amon relied on the surrounding water for security. In spite of its natural strength, security, and alliances, No-amon was conquered in 663 B.C. Nahum warns that since God punished the sins of No-amon, Nineveh should not expect to escape His judgment.

Endnotes
1. Daniel D. Luckenbill, *Ancient Records of Assyria and Babylonia*, 2 vols. (Chicago: University of Chicago Press, 1926).

HABAKKUK

Habakkuk 1:6

Who are the "Chaldeans"?

The Chaldeans were originally a Semitic people of southern Babylonia. They were referred to as Kaldu in Assyrian writings. The Babylonians referred to these people as Kaldai. When Nabopolassar, a native Chaldean governor, ascended the throne of Babylon in 626 B.C., he inaugurated a dynasty that made the name famous. The Chaldean dynasty ruled Babylonia. The name "Chaldean" is used in this text as a virtual synonym for "Babylonian" (see Isa. 13:19).

The term is used somewhat differently in the book of Daniel (2:2; 4:7; 5:7–11). There the term is used of a priestly class of learned astrologers associated with the court magicians, enchanters, and soothsayers. This is consistent with Herodotus (464–424 B.C.), who distinguished between the ordinary Babylonians of his day and the Chaldeans, identified with the priests of Bel-Marduk (*Histories* 1.181, 183).

Habakkuk 2:4

Did Paul misinterpret Habakkuk 2:4 when he used it in Romans 1:17 and Galatians 3:11?

In Habakkuk 2:4, God sets forth an important principle. The upright person, living in reliance upon God, will be preserved, whereas the proud and wicked shall perish. By way of application, the wicked Chaldeans will be judged, but the upright people who live in reliance upon God will be preserved.

The phrase quoted by Paul is, "the righteous shall live by his faith." By "righteous," Habakkuk refers to the one standing in right relationship with God. The word "live" is used in a pregnant sense. It means more than "survives." It speaks of prosperity and blessing (Prov. 12:28; 11:19). "Faith" is a character quality and can refer to (1) faith, that is, trust in God; (2) faithfulness, that is, faithful actions; or (3) the *faithfulness* that springs from *faith.* I believe that the context favors the latter view. Habakkuk is referring to those with a deep-rooted reliance upon God marked by unswerving loyalty and steadfastness. Some have suggested that according to Habakkuk, the person justified by faith *lives,* while according to Paul, the justified person lives *by faith.* Actually, both statements are true and were a part of Habakkuk's message. The just shall live (be saved) by faith, and by faith (continual trust) shall the just live (walk through life).

Habakkuk 3:1

What is the meaning of the term shigionoth?

Chapter 3 of Habakkuk contains a prayer that was composed by Habakkuk (v. 1) and then given to the temple choir director who arranged musical accompaniment (v. 19). The term *shigionoth* appears in the superscription of the prayer as a melody indicator for those who would use the prayer with music. The Hebrew word *shigionoth* appears to be derived from *shagah,* "to wander," and may indicate an irregular or wandering melody.

ZEPHANIAH

Zephaniah 1:7 (see Joel 1:15)

Zephaniah 1:9

Why is God going to punish those who "leap on the temple threshold"?

The reference has nothing to do with disorderly conduct in a place of worship. The practice of leaping over the threshold probably refers back to what occurred in Ashdod when the Philistines placed the captured ark of the covenant in front of their idol Dagon (1 Sam. 5:2–4). The next morning, they found that Dagon had fallen on its face before the ark. They set Dagon up but discovered the next morning that the idol had fallen again and been destroyed! The head and hands of the idol were broken off on the threshold of the Philistine temple. First Samuel 5:5 explains a Philistine custom that resulted from this event. Neither the priests or visitors who enter Dagon's temple "tread on the threshold of Dagon" since it had been sanctified through contact with the broken idol's head and hands.

The reference to those who "leap on the threshold of the temple" appears to refer to the idolatry being practiced in Zephaniah's day. Those who "leap on the threshold" of the temple are worshiping foreign gods and following pagan customs.

Zephaniah 1:11

Who are the "people of Canaan"?

This is not a reference to the Canaanite people still living as a distinct community within Judah and Jerusalem. Most archaeologists and historians agree that the Canaanite threat was fully dealt with through the conquests of David. The "people of Canaan" mentioned here are the merchants of Judah who transacted their affairs like the Canaanites or Phoenicians. They were Judeans by ethnic background but Canaanites in terms of their business practices.

Zephaniah 3:9–13

How could Zephaniah offer such words of comfort to a people being warned of God's wrath and coming judgment?

It is not unusual that a prophet announces both judgment and blessing, condemnation and consolation. Isaiah, for example, devotes the first half of his book to judgment and the second half to consolation. In this passage, Zephaniah looks beyond the immediate circumstances of coming judgment to the days of future blessing when God's people repent. Verses 9–13 describe the spiritual deliverance of a converted "remnant" of Israel. These are those who will someday recognize Jesus as Messiah and receive the cleansing He provided at the Cross.

HAGGAI

Haggai 2:6–7

What does God refer to when He says, "I am going to shake" the heavens, the earth, and the nations?

Some commentators have interpreted the shaking of the heavens, the earth, and the nations historically, referring to the upheavals of the Persian Empire beginning in 522 B.C. Gaumata usurped the throne while Cambyses was on a campaign in Egypt. Then Cambyses took his own life and Darius claimed the throne. Rebellions broke out in Media, Elam, Parsa, and Armenia. According to the historical view, Haggai believed that the upheavals within Persia would lead to the liberation of the Jews and the establishment of God's rule over His people.

Evidence from Haggai and other texts suggests that the shaking of the nations is eschatological. Haggai 2:22–23 makes it clear that the shaking is preparatory for the inauguration of the messianic kingdom. There is abundant evidence from Scripture that Christ's second coming will be accompanied by great shaking (Isa. 2:19; 13:13; 24:18–20; Matt. 24:29–30), as will the events of the Day of the Lord (Ezek. 38:20; Joel 3:15; 2 Peter 3:10). The shaking of the heavens, the earth, and the nations refers to God's intervention into the affairs of this world whereby He will shake the material universe and overthrow earthly kingdoms in preparation for the establishment of the messianic kingdom (Heb. 12:26–27).

Haggai 2:7

Does the "desire" of the nations refer to Christ?

From the earliest times, this passage has been interpreted to refer to the Messiah. This was the view of Jerome, translator of the Latin Vulgate, who received his interpretation from Jewish rabbis. The idea is that the nations have longed for the coming of the Messiah. At Christmas we sing Charles Wesley's "Hark! The Herald Angels Sing." The fourth verse begins, "Come, Desire of Nations, come," based on Wesley's messianic interpretation of Haggai 2:7.

Most modern commentators take the view that the Hebrew word refers not to the Desired One (Messiah) but to desirable things (that is, wealth or treasure). By the figure of metonymy, the "desire of all the nations" signifies the object of their desire. Haggai 2:8 specifies that object as gold and silver. The context lends support to this interpretation. The purpose of the passage is to console the people regarding their second temple, which was nothing in comparison with the first (vv. 2–3). Yet this was not a cause for discouragement. God would manifest his power and beautify His house with precious things (v. 8). Isaiah 60:7, 13 confirms that God will glorify His house and beautify His sanctuary in Messiah's kingdom.

Haggai 2:9

What is the Lord referring to when he mentions the "latter glory of this house"?

God encourages the builders of the second temple not to despair over its humble beginnings. The "latter glory" will exceed "the former" declares the Lord. The "former" refers clearly to Solomon's temple (1 Kings 6). The "latter glory" may refer either to the second temple or the millennial temple. The temple rebuilt by the restoration community was later refurbished by Herod. The temple mount was expanded to about thirty-five acres to accommodate the fabulous remodeling that was eventually completed shortly before its destruction by the Romans (A.D. 70). But as great as was Herod's temple, it will be no match for the beauty of the future temple described by Ezekiel (Ezek. 40–43). The promise of "peace" (Hag. 2:9) points to a time when the Prince of Peace (Isa. 9:6–7) will bring about peace and security in the Millennium.

Haggai 2:23

What is the significance of the promise to Zerubbabel, "I will make you like a signet ring, for I have chosen you"?

God promised to make Zerubbabel, the grandson of king Jehoiachin (2 Kings 24:14), who was taken into captivity in 597 B.C. (1 Chron. 3:19), "like a signet [ring]." A signet, engraved with the king's seal, was used to endorse official documents. To guard against misuse, the signet was usually worn on the king's person, as a ring or on a necklace. The reason for this promise is found in the words, "for I have chosen you." God had chosen Zerubbabel and would keep him safe, like a signet, to fulfill his appointed purpose.

The promise to Zerubbabel relates both to him personally and to the Davidic line, which he represents. Certainly verse 23 contains a personal promise to Zerubbabel. He would have his place in God's plan and purposes. As an elect believer, he would have his place in the kingdom (compare Dan. 12:2–3, 12).

The fact that the events predicted by Haggai in verses 21–22 did not transpire in Zerubbabel's lifetime suggests that the prophecy extends beyond Zerubbabel's personal experience. As a descendant of David, Zerubbabel represents the Davidic line. God was speaking to Zerubbabel as a Davidic descendant: "Your line is like a signet that will be preserved for the fulfillment of the promises made to David" (2 Sam. 7:12–16; compare Luke 1:32–33). The line of Zerubbabel was preserved. The Gospel genealogies reveal that Jesus the Messiah is Zerubbabel's greatest descendant (Matt. 1:12; Luke 3:27).

ZECHARIAH

Zechariah 9:1–17

Does Zechariah predict the conquest by Alexander the Great or by some other warrior?

Commentators have engaged in a great deal of discussion regarding the historical setting of the passage based on the allusions in the military campaign (vv. 1–7) and the reference to the sons of Greece (v. 13). Most conservative commentators have followed the view that verses 1–7 predict the conquest by Alexander the Great. The difficulty is that no one historical setting really answers the situation described in the passage. The text must be forced to serve one historical hypothesis or another.

Recent research suggests that Zechariah 9 describes a cosmic war and reflects a particular genre of literature found in the ancient Near East. This literary form, found in such texts as *Enuma Elish,* the Ugaritic Baal Cycle, and Isaiah 52:7–12 has been designated a "Divine Warrior Hymn."[1] At the heart of such a poem is the reenactment of the warrior-god's battle against the enemy, resulting in the reestablishment of peace.

This approach has merit in that (1) it recognizes that Zechariah 9 is a distinctive form of ancient Near Eastern literature, (2) it avoids the numerous hypotheses and endless debate over which historical situation is allegedly being described, and (3) the approach focuses on the general meaning of the text rather than speculating about particular historical details.

Zechariah 9, then, can be viewed as a Divine Warrior Hymn that prophetically depicts God's intervention among the nations with a view to the establishment of the ideal (that is, messianic) kingdom that Yahweh has promised Israel as their inheritance. Although virtually all ancient conquerors followed this basic route from north to south, the military campaign and city list of 9:1–8 does not find its place in ancient history. Rather, it reflects the future subjugation of all the territories surrounding Israel under Yahweh's authority.[2] The text could be outlined as follows:

I. The Conflict and Victory (v. 8)
II. The Victory Shout and Procession (v. 9)
III. The Inauguration of Messiah's Reign (v. 10)
IV. The Release of Captives (vv. 11–13)
V. The Theophany of the Divine Warrior (v. 14)
VI. The Victory Banquet (v. 15)
VII. The Restoration of Prosperity (vv. 16–17)

Zechariah 9:9

What does Zechariah predict about the first coming of Jesus the Messiah?

Zechariah's predictions about Messiah's first coming include the following:
1. Messiah will enter Jerusalem riding on the colt of a donkey (9:9; compare Matt. 21:1–8).
2. Messiah will be rejected by Israel (11:4–11; compare Matt. 12:22–32; 21:33–43; 23:37).
3. Messiah will be betrayed for thirty pieces of silver (11:12–13; compare Matt. 26:14–16).
4. Messiah's hands and feet will be pierced (12:10; compare Matt. 27:31–33; John 20:24–27).
5. Messiah will provide cleansing at the Cross (13:1; compare Titus 3:5; Heb. 9:13–14).

Zechariah 11:17

Who is the "worthless shepherd"?

The worthless shepherd who abandons his flock is to be judged. The Lord declares that "a sword will be on his arm and on his right eye." As a result, the arm that should have protected the sheep will be withered, and the eye that should have watched over the flock will be blinded. The worthless shepherd is not identified in the text. Most Jewish commentators see a fulfillment in King Herod (63–4 B.C.), noted for his harsh dealings with the Jews. Others suggest Alcimus (163–159 B.C.), the high priest who treacherously betrayed the Maccabees (1 Macc. 7:1–25). A comparison of his person and work with the sinister figure in Daniel 7:25–27 and 11:36–39 suggests the view that he represents the Antichrist (compare 2 Thess. 2:1–12; Rev. 13:1–10).

Zechariah 12:10–13:1

What does Zechariah predict about Messiah's second coming?

Zechariah makes several significant predictions about Messiah's second coming. These include the following:
1. Messiah will be accepted by Israel (12:10–13:1).
2. Messiah will judge and destroy Israel's enemies (14:3, 12–15).
3. Messiah will return to the Mount of Olives (14:4).
4. Messiah will reign from Jerusalem (14:9).

Endnotes
1. Paul D. Hanson, "Zechariah 9 and the Recapitulation of an Ancient Ritual Pattern," *Journal of Biblical Literature* 92 (March 1973): 37–59.
2. See my book, *Zechariah* (Chicago: Moody Press, 1984), 95–101.

MALACHI

Setting

When and under what circumstances did Malachi minister?

While the book is not dated, scholars are in agreement that internal evidence suggests that Malachi ministered during the postexilic period. A date of around 432 B.C. has much to commend it. In the thirty-second year of Artaxerxes (464–424 B.C.), or 432 B.C., Nehemiah left Jerusalem to visit the king in Babylon (Neh. 13:6). Some time after the visit he returned to Jerusalem and initiated temple, Sabbath, and marriage reforms (vv. 4–29). A Persian governor was apparently in authority during Nehemiah's absence (Mal. 1:8). Such a ruler would not have been in office during Nehemiah's governorship of 444–432 B.C. or during his governorship after his return from Babylon.

There is close agreement between the sins that Malachi denounced and those that Nehemiah sought to correct. Both books have reference to the problem of priestly laxity (Mal. 1:6 and the following verses; Neh. 13:4–9, 29), the neglect of tithes (Mal. 3:7–12; compare Neh. 13:10–13), and intermarriage with foreign women (Mal. 2:10–16; compare Neh. 13:23–28).

It was probably during Nehemiah's absence between his first and second governorships that the corruption and abuses developed. It is reasonable to assume that Malachi protested these abuses during Nehemiah's absence. When Nehemiah returned, he dealt with these abuses and instituted reform.

Malachi 1:3

How can God, who is love, say that He "hated" Esau?

In Malachi 1:2–5, the prophet emphasizes God's love for Israel. In response to God's assertion, "I have loved you," the people raised the question, "How hast Thou loved us?" In verses 2–4, God's love for His people is demonstrated by His choice of Jacob over Esau. The story of God's choice of Jacob is found in Genesis 25. Before Rebekah's sons were even born, God said that the older (Esau) would serve the younger (Jacob). This was an undeserved, electing love.

While God's electing love for Jacob may be troubling, it is not nearly so troubling as His hatred for Esau. How can God hate someone? One way to deal with this issue is to understand the Hebrew word translated "hated" *(saneh)* in a milder sense than is commonly understood. The word can be used in a comparison to refer to one who is not preferred, as in the case of Leah (see Gen. 29:30–31). Understood in this way, God chose Jacob and merely passed by Esau. The problem with this view is that the Lord goes on in Malachi 1:3–4 to tell of His treatment of Edom. God's words to the Edomites seem to reflect their deserved judgment for continued opposition to God.

Within the context of verses 2–4, God is not speaking about the person of Esau but about the Edomite nation that descended from him. God does not hate Esau, the individual, but Edom, the nation that demonstrated such hostility against their Israelite kin (Obad. 10–14). As a nation that actively opposed God's purposes for His people Israel, the Edomites became the subjects of God's extreme indignation or hatred.

Malachi 2:16

Does God hate divorce, or only treacherous divorce?

Nowhere in the Bible is there a more definitive statement regarding God's attitude toward divorce. And yet some have argued that God is not condemning divorce, but only divorce that involves treachery. When no treachery is involved, then divorce should be regarded as acceptable and permitted.

The problem in the context is that Jewish men were divorcing their wives to marry idolatrous women (2:10–12). Consequently, God was rejecting their worship (v. 13). In verse 14, Malachi condemns the people who have "dealt treacherously" by violating their marriage covenant. Although the exact meaning of verse 15 is debated,[1] the exhortation is clear, "let no one deal treacherously against the wife of your youth." Verse 16 concludes the discussion by presenting two arguments against divorce. First, God hates it. Second, God hates the one who wrongs a spouse in this way. "So take heed to your spirit," says the Lord, "that you do not deal treacherously."

As I read this text, I find that God repeatedly declares that divorce entails dealing "treacherously." In no place does Malachi distinguish divorce that is treacherous from divorce that is not. Only by reading a New Testament "exception" (see Matt. 19:9) into this passage could someone conclude that Malachi condemns only treacherous divorce. According to Malachi, divorce breaks a covenant, constitutes treachery, and God hates it.

Malachi 4:5–6

Malachi predicts the coming of "Elijah." Who fulfills this prophecy?

At the close of the Old Testament canon, Malachi prophesied the coming of "Elijah the prophet" who "will restore the hearts of the fathers to their children, and the hearts of the children to their fathers." Biblical scholars debate the question of who fulfills this prophecy. The following are four major views on this subject:

Elijah will come again. Some scholars believe that Elijah will personally come again and minister as one of the two witnesses (Rev. 11:3–6) during the Tribulation. The major difficulty with this view is that there is no mention of

Elijah in Revelation 11:3–6. And the ministry of the two witnesses differs from that described in Malachi 4:6. They minister judgment, not restoration, and come *in* the day, not *before* the Day of the Lord.

Elijah may not come again. Others believe that the prophecy will be fulfilled by one who will come in the "spirit and power of Elijah" (Luke 1:17). Pentecost writes, "The prophecy is not fulfilled completely in John the Baptist, but Elijah himself is not required to fulfill it."[2] It is believed that John the Baptist partially fulfilled the prophecy and there may yet be another fulfillment but not necessarily by Elijah the Tishbite.

Elijahs are coming. According to Kaiser, Malachi was predicting a succession of announcers who will continue their ministry up to the second advent of Messiah when the "first and last Elijah" will step forth. Such "forthtellers" include John the Baptist, Augustine, Calvin, Meno Simons, Luther, Zwingli, Moody, and Graham. Kaiser believes that Elijah will return during the Tribulation as one of the two witnesses (Rev. 11:3–6). He views this as "generic" or "successive fulfillment."[3]

Elijah will not come again. Many scholars believe that John the Baptist fulfilled the prophecy completely and Elijah will not come again. While not without problems, this view seems to be the position taken by the New Testament authors. Matthew indicates that John the Baptist fulfills Malachi 3:1 and 4:5 (Matt. 11:10–14). Jesus said, "And if you care to accept it, he himself [John the Baptist] is Elijah, who is to come" (v. 14). In His answer to the disciples' question in Matthew 17:10–13, Jesus affirms the Jewish view with respect to the sequence—first Elijah, then Messiah (v. 11). However, He refutes the claim that it was the physical Elijah the Tishbite that had to come first (v. 12). The disciples understood that Jesus was speaking about John (v. 13). Basically, Jesus was saying:

Elijah must come (v. 11)—Yes, you are right!

Elijah has come (v. 12)—It is past!

Elijah is John (v. 13)—He had the same kind of ministry. Additional support is found in Luke's gospel where the angel Gabriel quotes from Malachi 4:6 in announcing John's birth, indicating that he would fulfill the prophecy (Luke 1:17). Filled with the Holy Spirit, Zecharias quotes Malachi 3:1 with reference to John's ministry (Luke 1:76).

The major objection to this viewpoint is that John denied being Elijah (John 1:21). How is this denial consistent with the view that he fulfilled the prophecy? Perhaps John was responding to the Jewish expectation that Elijah the *Tishbite* would come again. He was saying, "I am not Elijah the Tishbite." Yet he was fulfilling the prophecy.

A second objection relates to the success of John's ministry. Did he "restore the hearts of the fathers to their children, and the hearts of the children to their fathers" (Mal. 4:6)? Was John really that successful in bringing about repentance in the day in which he lived? According to the biblical record people from "all Judea and all the district around the Jordan" came to receive John's baptism, in keeping with their repentance (Matt. 3:5–6; compare 14:5; 21:32; Acts 19:3). He appears to have had a successful ministry.

In the fulfillment of this prophecy it is evident that the term "Elijah" focuses more on the *office* of Elijah than on the *person* of Elijah. John the Baptist fulfilled Malachi 3:1 and 4:5–6 in an unexpected way. He came "in the spirit and power of Elijah."

Endnotes

1. For expanded comment on this text, see my book, *The Divorce Myth* (Minneapolis: Bethany House, 1981), 47–48.
2. J. Dwight Pentecost, *Things To Come* (Grand Rapids: Zondervan, 1958), 312.
3. Walter C. Kaiser Jr., "The Promise of the Arrival of Elijah in Malachi and the Gospels," *Grace Theological Journal* Vol. 3, no. 2 (1982): 221–33.

NEW TESTAMENT

MATTHEW

Matthew 1:1

What is the genealogy of Jesus intended to prove?

The genealogy presents Jesus as a descendant of two key figures with whom major covenants were enacted. Matthew wants to show that the One being introduced as Messiah comes in fulfillment of the covenants made with Abraham and with David. As a descendant of Abraham and of David, Jesus has a legal right to the throne of Israel. While the genealogy establishes Jesus' legal sonship to Joseph, it denies that He was Joseph's physical son. The feminine pronoun translated "whom" in verse 16 indicates that Jesus was from Mary, not Joseph. This fact is confirmed in verse 18.

Matthew 1:21

What is the meaning of the name Jesus?

Jesus is the Greek rendering of the Hebrew name *Yeshua,* or "Joshua" as it appears in the Bible. The Hebrew name is based on the noun *yesha'* (salvation) combined with the name of God, *Yahweh. Yeshua* means in Hebrew, "Yahweh is salvation." The name given to God's Son communicates the message of who He is and what He will accomplish. He is the promised Savior and will save His people from their sins.

Matthew 1:23

Was Jesus ever called "Immanuel"? How was the prophecy of Isaiah 7:14 fulfilled?

Matthew 1:23 records the first of a long list of fulfilled prophecies designed to show that Jesus of Nazareth is really the long-expected Messiah of Israel. The viewpoints regarding the fulfillment of the prophecy of the Virgin Birth are presented in this text in answering the question at Isaiah 7:14–16. But we are left with a perplexing issue. Was Jesus ever called Immanuel? If not, how could He fulfill the prophecy?

There is no place in the New Testament where Jesus is directly called *Immanuel.* The name in Hebrew means "God with us." And although Jesus is never called Immanuel, He certainly fulfills the significance of the name as God dwells among His people in Christ. We see this in Matthew 18:20, when

Jesus told the disciples, "For where two or three have gathered together in My name, there I am in their midst." And, in 28:20, Jesus declares, "I am with you always, even to the end of the age." As God incarnate, Jesus is "God with us" *(Immanuel).*

Matthew 1:25

When was Jesus born?

We know that Jesus was born before the death of King Herod. According to Josephus, Herod died in the spring of 4 B.C. before Passover (*Antiquities* 27.190, 213), which was celebrated on April 11 in that year. Jesus could not have been born after this date. Hoehner argues persuasively that Jesus was born in either 5 B.C. or in the winter or spring of 4 B.C.[1]

It is usually objected that this date would make Christ too old. Luke says that at his baptism Jesus was "about thirty" (Luke 3:23). But Hoehner points out that Luke's term "about" *(hosei)* provides some flexibility.[2] If Jesus was baptized in the summer or autumn of A.D. 29, He would have been thirty-two or perhaps thirty-three years of age.

It is surprising to discover that Jesus was born B.C. (before Christ)! This is due to a mistake made centuries ago. The present Christian Era is a dating system invented by Dionysius Exiguus (about A.D. 496–540), a monk living in Italy, at the request of Pope John in A.D. 525. Dionysius modified the Alexandrian system of dating, which was based on the reign of Diocletian, a persecutor of the church, and prepared a numbering system from the "incarnation of our Lord Jesus." Dionysius placed Christ's birth 753 years from the foundation of the city of Rome, failing to note that Jesus was born under King Herod, who died 750 years from the foundation of Rome. The dating system was questioned in the eighth century and was rejected in the ninth century but has continued to the present day.

Matthew 2:2, 10

Was the "star" that led the magi a natural or supernatural phenomena?

Astronomers have noted that there was a conjunction of planets in 7 B.C. on May 29, September 29, and December 4. Also, in February, 6 B.C., Mars moved into the configuration, forming a triangle with the other two planets. It is thought that the three planets may have appeared as a very bright "star."[3] However, the planets were probably not close enough together to present the appearance of a single star. And the Greek word translated "star" is singular, not plural.

It has also been suggested that the star that appeared to the magi was a comet. In March of 5 B.C., a "sweeping star," or comet, is noted in Chinese astronomical sources. A "comet without a tail," probably a nova, appeared in April of 4 B.C. These unusual events, together with the conjunctions of planets, could have attracted the attention of the magi.

The Greek word translated "star" *(aster)* may be literally rendered "light," "flame," or "fire." Since a star would not have moved or stood still, it is quite possible that the "star" of Bethlehem was not a star, but a manifestation of God's *shekinah* glory. The magi may have learned of the Jewish messianic expectation from Numbers 24:17, "a star shall come forth from Jacob." They linked the appearance of a new "star" with the birth of Israel's king.

Matthew 2:15

How does Matthew see Jesus' sojourn in Egypt as a fulfillment of Hosea 11:1, "Out of Egypt I called My son"?

There are many different ways New Testament writers use the Old Testament. Sometimes there is direct fulfillment of prophecy (Matt. 2:6). At times, the Old Testament quotation may be used to introduce a new thought (Gal. 3:16) or explain a concept (1 Peter 1:24–25). In this case, the citation is used to show a correspondence between an Old Testament and a New Testament event. In Matthew 2:15, the author is building on the correspondence between Israel and Christ. Both were persecuted by kings. Both were protected by God. Both descended into Egypt. And the return of both was providential in the history of Israel. Hosea's designation of Israel as Yahweh's son suggested to Matthew God's greater Son, Jesus. Longenecker comments, "That which was vital in Israel's corporate and redemptive experience finds its ultimate and intended focus in the person of Jesus the Messiah."[4]

Matthew 2:23

What Scripture did Matthew have in mind when he wrote that Jesus' return to Nazareth fulfilled prophecy?

It appears that Matthew has noted the phonetic similarity between the name "Nazareth" and the messianic title *netzer* (branch, or shoot) in Isaiah 11:1. The term is used to describe the lowliness and obscurity of Jesus' background. Because of its proximity to Sepphoris, the Roman capital of Galilee, the city of Nazareth was regarded as a despised and insignificant town. Matthew builds his citation upon the *netzer* lowliness motif, as well as upon the phonetic similarity.

Matthew 3:7

Who were the Pharisees and the Sadducees?

The Pharisees and the Sadducees were two Jewish groups who were active in the time of Jesus. The Pharisees took matters of Jewish ceremony quite strictly and separated themselves from those who were not so diligent. Josephus describes them as "a body of Jews with the reputation of excelling the rest of their nation in the observances of religion, and as exact exponents of the laws" (*War* 1.110). Josephus refers to them as the "leading sect" and regards them as "the most accurate interpreters of the law" (*War* 2.162). In terms of doctrine, they believed in the sovereignty of God, the eternal nature of the soul, and the resurrection.

While the Pharisees were middle-class Jews who were associated with the synagogue, the Sadducees were of the priestly aristocracy and were associated with the temple. They were the leaders with power, money, and influence in the time of Jesus. Josephus records that while "the Pharisees are affectionate to each other and cultivate harmonious relations with the community, the Sadducees, on the contrary, are . . . rather boorish in their behavior, and in their conversation with their peers are as rude as to aliens" (*War* 2.166). The Sadducees believed in human freedom to choose good or evil and did not believe in the persistence of the soul after death or in the resurrection (Matt. 22:23). They held these views not because they were liberal but because they were quite conservative and accepted only those doctrines that they believed were taught by Moses in the Pentateuch.

Matthew 3:11

What did John mean when he said that Jesus would baptize "with the Holy Spirit and fire"?

The baptism "with the Holy Spirit" is a clear reference to the Pentecost event (Acts 2) when the believers were "filled with the Holy Spirit" (v. 4). Some have also linked the words "and fire" to the day of Pentecost because of the "tongues as of fire" that appeared (v. 3). But Luke does not actually say that fire appeared on Pentecost. Something appeared that Luke describes as "tongues as of fire." The word "as" (*hosei*) indicates a comparison with fire, but does not necessarily say that fire was present.

John explains the words "and fire" in the following verse (Matt. 3:12). There he refers to the winnowing process, which separates the wheat from the chaff. What is to be done with the chaff—the broken bits of straw? It is to be burned up—a clear reference to eternal judgment on unbelievers (compare Matt. 13:24–30). In Matthew 3:11, John is simply announcing the twofold dimension of the Messiah's ministry—sending of the Holy Spirit and future judgment.

Matthew 4:1–11

In comparing Matthew with Luke 4:5–12, how do we account for the different order of events in the Temptation?

Both Matthew and Luke record three temptations, but Luke reverses the order of the last two temptations. The adverbs "then" *(tote)* in Matthew 4:5 and the "again" *(palin)* in verse 8 indicates that Matthew is recording the event chronologically. Luke, on the other hand, uses the conjunction "and" *(kai),* which does not suggest a sequential order for the temptations. While Matthew records the event chronologically, Luke may be listing the temptations topically. For Luke, the temptation at the pinnacle of the temple served as the climax of the event.

Matthew 4:17

What did Jesus mean when He announced, "the kingdom of heaven is at hand"?

Since the time when His dominion over this earth was first challenged by Satan, God has been working to reassert His sovereign rule. This may be called God's "kingdom program." The kingdom of God involves a king who rules, a people who are ruled, and a place where this rule is recognized. Quite simply, we may define the kingdom of God as "God's people, in God's place, under God's rule."[5]

The kingdom of God was promised in the Abrahamic covenant (Gen. 12:1–3), foreshadowed in God's promise to David (2 Sam. 7:12–16), and anticipated by the Old Testament prophets. As the people of Israel anticipated the future kingdom, the prophets announced what it would be like.

1. Peace will prevail. There will be no war in God's kingdom (Isa. 2:4).
2. God will reign in Jerusalem. People will come from the surrounding nations to worship Him there (Isa. 2:3; Joel 3:1).
3. Justice and righteousness will prevail in government and throughout the land (Isa. 9:7).
4. Agriculture will flourish. There will be no lack of food in God's kingdom (Amos 9:13).
5. There will be no physical infirmity or handicaps. No one will be blind, deaf, lame, or mentally handicapped (Isa. 35:5–6).
6. The people of Israel will be safe and secure in Israel, their promised land (Amos 9:14–15; Obad. 19–21).

Before Jesus was born, the angel Gabriel told Mary that her son, Jesus, was destined to receive the throne of His ancestor David and to rule God's kingdom forever (Luke 1:31–33). John the Baptizer had announced the coming of Israel's Messiah King. Finally, Jesus arrived on the scene saying, "The prophesied kingdom is yours to take! Repent of your works religion and accept Me as your true King!"

Matthew 4:23

Why did Jesus heal people and do miracles?

Miracles are seen throughout biblical history, but their greatest display appears during the ministry of Christ. These miracles serve six strategic purposes.[6]

1. *to introduce a new era.* The first purpose of Jesus' miracles is to introduce the prophesied Messiah who in turn announced "the kingdom is at hand" (Matt. 4:14; 10:7). The miracles accompanied the kingdom offer and substantiated that offer (Matt. 12:28).

2. *to authenticate Christ.* The second major purpose is to authenticate the messiahship of Christ. His works are a witness to His person as Messiah and Son of God (John 20:30–31). They are the insignia of His deity and messiahship.

3. *to authenticate Christ's message.* As miracles were used to authenticate Christ's person, so they served to authenticate His message. Christ appeals to His miracles in John 10:38 to substantiate His message concerning His oneness with the Father. His message was certified authentic by the miracles He performed.

4. *to instruct disciples.* After the rejection of Christ by the Jewish leaders (Matt. 12), His miracles were less public and became agents of instruction for the benefit of His disciples. The miracles instructed them concerning Christ's power (Mark 4:4; 5:1–20), trust in Christ's provision (John 6:3–6), prayer (Mark 6:48; 7:24–30), and an outreach to Gentiles (Matt. 15:21–28; Mark 7:3).

5. *to reveal conditions in the future kingdom.* A special purpose for which Christ used His miracles was to reveal the conditions of the future kingdom, the messianic (millennial) age. The miracles foreshadow in a brief display the removal of sickness (John 5:1–18), death (John 11:17–44), disease (Luke 14:1–6), and hunger (Matt. 15:32–38) in the kingdom. The miracles also point to the joy and prosperity that will characterize the kingdom (John 2:1–11) and that in the kingdom Satan will be restricted (Matt. 8:28–34).

6. *to display mercy.* One final purpose of Christ's miracles was to display mercy on suffering humanity. His mercy and compassion often moved Him to act (Matt. 14:14; 15:32; Mark 1:41; Luke 7:13). He often healed in response to pleas for mercy (Matt. 15:25; 17:15; Mark 10:47–48; Luke 17:13). Christ's healing miracles outnumber all the other miracles.

The miracles of Christ had varying results: belief (John 2:11; 4:50), conviction (Luke 5:8), following Jesus (Mark 10:52), emotion (Matt. 8:27; 12:23; Mark 7:37), worship (Mark 2:12; John 9:38), recognition of Christ's uniqueness (Luke 7:16; John 6:14), and rejection (Matt. 12:24; John 5:16; 11:53).

Matthew 5–7

How should we interpret Jesus' Sermon on the Mount?

The greatest problem with the Sermon on the Mount is its interpretation. Several theories have been set forth by theologians and expositors.

1. *Pattern for Christian Life.* Augustine (354–430) believed that the sermon was "a perfect pattern for the Christian life." This view is held by amillennial theologians who equate the church with the kingdom and by premillennialists who believe that the passage is not primarily for the future age.

2. *Impossible Ideal.* Gerhard Kittel believed that the precepts of the sermon could not be fulfilled and that Jesus recognized this fact. Like the law, it was designed "to bring His hearers to the consciousness that they cannot in their own strength fulfill the demands of God."

3. *Interim Ethic.* According to Johannes Weiss and Albert Schweitzer, the sermon presents "an emergency ethic for His disciples' use during the brief interval between His preaching and the cataclysmic coming of the Kingdom of God." As such, it has no application to the twentieth century.

4. *Way of Salvation*. A. Tholuck views the sermon as the purest type of Christian doctrine. If the sermon presents a way of salvation, it is a pretty rigid plan to follow.

5. *Kingdom Ethic*. Barthians view the sermon as presenting an ethic not to be fulfilled in this world but possible to live when God concludes history and ushers in His supernatural kingdom. Dispensationalists have usually interpreted the sermon as setting forth the principles applicable in the future millennial kingdom.

6. *Historical Approach*. The Sermon on the Mount is set in the historical context of Jesus' offer of the kingdom (Matt. 4:17). Entrance into the kingdom was the key issue confronting the Jews following Jesus (5:20). Rather than describing the characteristics of the future millennial kingdom, the sermon sets forth the high requirements that must be met in order to enter that kingdom. Was the righteousness that the Jews had by keeping their religious traditions sufficient for entrance into the kingdom? Jesus says, "No! You must find righteousness in Me!" The theme verse is Matthew 5:20, "For I say to you, that unless your righteousness surpasses that of the scribes and Pharisees, you shall not enter the kingdom of heaven" (also 7:13, 21).

Although designed to deal with a particular historical issue, we find the principles of the sermon applicable to believers of every age. The sermon reveals the holiness of God and serves as a guide for Christian conduct in this present age.

Matthew 5:1–12

What is the point of the Beatitudes?

The Beatitudes are designed to show that the kingdom spoken of by Christ is the one prophesied in the Old Testament. They also emphasize the righteous character of those who will be citizens of God's kingdom. The Beatitudes follow a pattern that includes three parts: (1) pronouncement of blessing; (2) description of a virtue; and (3) promise of reward in the kingdom.

The Beatitudes are essentially God's promises that those who manifest certain virtues will enter the kingdom of God. This section serves to introduce the sermon and prepares the way for the major message in 5:20: "Unless your righteousness surpasses that of the scribes and Pharisees, you shall not enter the kingdom of heaven."

Verse 3. Those who recognize their own lack of merit and who trust in the righteousness of Christ alone will find their reward in the kingdom (Ps. 51:17; Isa. 57:15; 66:2;).

Verse 4. Those who mourn (their own sinfulness and spiritual poverty) will be comforted in the kingdom (Isa. 61:2–3; Zech. 12:1–13:9).

Verse 5. The gentle who recognize the strength in Christ will inherit the earth (Ps. 37:11; 76:9; Isa. 11:1–4).

Verse 6. Those who hunger and thirst for true righteousness, as that found in Christ, will be satisfied (Isa. 55:1).

Verse 7. Those who show mercy will experience it themselves (Ps. 18:25).

Verse 8. Those who have pure hearts, a characteristic of true righteousness, will see God (Ps. 24:3–5).

Verse 9. The peacemakers shall enjoy the peace of the kingdom (Isa. 11:9; 32:17–18).

Verse 10–12. The persecuted will receive their reward from God in the kingdom (Dan. 12:1–2; Rev. 20:4).

Matthew 5:32

How does a man who divorces his wife make her commit adultery?

Jesus is saying that a man who divorces his wife exposes her to the temptation to remarry, thus committing adultery. Jesus makes it very clear from the next line that legal divorce does not necessarily end a marriage relationship as far as God is concerned. Since the marriage union actually ends with the death of the spouse (1 Cor. 7:39), marriage to a divorced person violates an existing relationship, resulting in adultery. For further discussion, see answers at Matthew 19:6–7 and 19:9.

Matthew 5:39

What did Jesus mean when He said, "Do not resist him who is evil"? Did He endorse pacifism?

In Matthew 5:39–42 Jesus gives three illustrations of what he means by not resisting evil. In each case there is a voluntary doubling of the deed to emphasize the disciple's willingness to accept injustice and respond to hostility with kindness, courtesy, and love. Jesus is using hyperbole (exaggeration) to emphasize the attitude His followers should have toward those who threaten them. Jesus exemplified his own teaching on this when He refused to strike back at those mistreating Him (John 18:22–23). Instead of taking matters into their own hands, God's people should leave vengeance to the Lord (Rom. 12:19–21).

Is Jesus calling disciples to a wholesale acceptance of physical abuse, injustice, and criminal wrongs? To answer yes is to misunderstand and misapply the illustrations. The command to turn the other cheek calls for an attitude that refuses to return an insult or a wrong done. Offering your coat to one who demands your shirt reflects a willingness to settle a dispute in a way that brings peace and reconciliation. Going the extra mile reflects a willingness to cheerfully do more than what is required.

Is Jesus teaching that Christians should not resist criminal actions? No. Both Jesus and Paul raised objections to unjust and unlawful treatment (John 18:22–23; Acts 16:37). Other Scriptures call for believers to protect life and uphold justice (Prov. 24:11–12; Amos 5:15, 24).

Matthew 5:43

Where in the Bible does it teach "hate your enemy"?

Love for one's enemies is clearly taught in Leviticus 19:18, but there is no teaching in the Bible that we should hate our enemies. This is a Pharisaic addition, something taught by the religious leaders of the first century but not found in the Bible.

Matthew 6:13

If God does not tempt us, why should we pray that He not "lead us into temptation"?

James 1:13 makes it clear that God cannot be tempted by evil and "He Himself does not tempt anyone." Jesus suggests that we pray for deliverance from situations in which we might be enticed and overcome by sin. Paul directs us to "make no provision for the flesh" (Rom. 13:14). Jesus is simply asking that we request God's help in accomplishing this.

Matthew 6:16

Should Christians practice fasting?

There was only one fast required by Mosaic Law—the Day of Atonement (Lev. 16:29–34), but many other fast days were added (Zech. 8:19). Those fasting would put ashes on their heads, dress in old clothes, and not shave or wash. This was all for show! Jesus rebuked the Pharisees for their wrong motives. Fasting should be with a view to God's approval, not to human praise.

Although there is no New Testament command that instructs believers to practice fasting, there we do have the example of Jesus (Matt. 4:2) and the church at Antioch (Acts 13:3). Fasting involves setting aside the preparation and eating of food to give oneself to God and to devote time to prayer. This may demonstrate the seriousness of the believer about a certain matter of prayer. Fasting is an expression of dependence upon God rather than upon daily nourishment. When fasting, a believer should avoid calling attention to the practice and should spend additional time with the Lord in prayer, meditation, worship, and Bible reading. Drink plenty of water, but avoid fluids containing sugar or caffeine.

Matthew 8:16–17

Does Matthew's quote from Isaiah 53:4 suggest that there is physical healing in the Atonement?

Matthew refers to Jesus' healing ministry as a fulfillment of Isaiah 53:4, as quoted by Matthew, "He Himself took our infirmities, and carried away our diseases." According to Genesis 2:17 and 3:19, sickness and death are the result of sin. Hence, through His healing ministry, the effects of sin were being removed. By dealing with the effects, Jesus demonstrates His competence to deal with the ultimate issue—sin itself. Matthew presents Jesus' healings as illustrations of His redemptive work, visible pledges of His plan to remove sin. Gundry comments, "The healings anticipate the passion in that they begin to roll back the effects of sin for which Jesus came to die."[7]

Is there healing in the Atonement? Although some have interpreted Isaiah 53:4 as a reference to physical sickness, the allusion in 53:9 to Christ's burial suggests that Matthew understood Isaiah 53 to refer to Messiah's vicarious suffering and death. Isaiah simply used sickness as a poetic picture of the effects of sin. There is no promise in Scripture that sickness will be fully removed in this lifetime. God may heal today, but this is evidence of His power and sovereignty—it is not demanded by the Atonement.

And yet, we learn in Isaiah 35:5–6 that there will be no sickness in the kingdom. Christ's atonement provides for our complete redemption. When fully redeemed, the effects of sin will be removed—from this earth and from our bodies!

Matthew 8:20

What does Jesus mean when He refers to Himself as "Son of Man"?

There is debate as to whether Jesus drew upon Ezekiel's use of the term (Ezek. 2:1) to emphasize His humanity or whether He drew upon Daniel's use of the term to emphasize His messiahship. The issue of Jesus' humanity was never really a concern for the disciples. The issue before the nation was His messiahship. Daniel 7:13 uses the term with reference to the Messiah receiving dominion, glory, and a kingdom from God. Jesus probably used the expression *Son of Man* to avoid the political connotations of the term *Messiah*.

Matthew 10:5–6

Why did Jesus tell His disciples not to go to the Gentiles or Samaritans but only to the people of Israel?

Jesus came as the "Savior of the world" (John 4:42) and offered the gift of salvation to Jews, Samaritans, and Gentiles. But at this early point in His ministry, the disciples were to focus their witness on the Jewish people. They were the ones who had been prepared by the Prophets and by the ministry of John the Baptizer to receive Israel's Messiah. Jesus wanted to make sure that the Jewish people had full opportunity to respond to His claims and accept Him as Messiah. Later, after His rejection by Israel, Jesus began to broaden the disciples' horizons by ministering to non-Jews (Matt. 15:21–28). Before leaving the earth, Jesus commanded His disciples to make disciples of "all the nations" (28:19).

Matthew 10:23

Did Jesus teach His disciples that He would return during their lifetime?

Matthew 10:22 anticipates a situation of persecution that will be realized during the Tribulation (24:9–13). The one who endures this persecution will be delivered physically at Messiah's return and will enter the kingdom. The words "to the end" is a clue that Jesus is speaking eschatologically. Verse 23 looks prophetically, anticipating the ministry of the disciples from the first century to the Lord's return. The word "whenever" (hotan) suggests that the situation being described is not limited to the first century.

Jesus is not saying that He will return during the lifetime of the Twelve. Rather, by means of His followers Jesus will have a ministry throughout the present age and even during the future Tribulation. They will be preaching the good news of Messiah's (second) coming right up to the end!

Matthew 11:3

Did John the Baptizer have a lapse of faith?

After his imprisonment by Herod Antipas, John sent a delegation of his disciples to Jesus with the question, "Are you the Expected One, or shall we look for someone else?" It has been suggested that John was having second thoughts about whether or not Jesus was the Messiah. Others suggest that John needed some clarification regarding Jesus' ministry. "Why is the Messiah being rejected? If the Messiah came to establish His kingdom, what am I doing in prison? In view of Jesus' rejection by the religious leaders, do we look for another Messiah?" While these questions are not unreasonable in light of John's situation, there is another possible explanation for his inquiry.

I suggest that John sent his disciples to Jesus not because of his doubts but because of theirs! It was John the Baptizer who leaped in the womb when his mother, Elizabeth, heard Mary's greeting (Luke 1:41). It was John who baptized Jesus and saw the Holy Spirit descend upon Him as a dove (Matt. 3:16). It was John who identified Jesus as "the Lamb of God" (John 1:29) and "the Son of God" (v. 34). John was not in doubt regarding Jesus' messiahship or deity, but his disciples certainly were. John sent them to Jesus to have their doubts answered. They returned fully assured of the truth of Christ's person (Matt. 11:4–6).

Matthew 11:12

In what way did the kingdom of heaven "suffer violence"?

There is great difficulty in understanding what Jesus intended in this verse. The difficulty is with the Greek word *baizetai,* which means "to force" or "to constrain." This present-tense verb can be understood in either the middle or the passive voice.

Understood in the middle voice, the verse would be rendered, "the kingdom of heaven is pressing forward and vigorous people are eagerly taking possession of it." In other words, the kingdom is advancing and people of great faith and courage are embracing it.

Understood in the passive voice, the verse would be rendered, "the kingdom of heaven is suffering violence, and violent people [that is, leaders of Israel] are arresting it from coming," or "trying to force their way into it [that is, without repentance]."

The latter view is suggested by the circumstances described in Matthew 3:7–10. The religious leaders wanted to participate in John's baptism but were unwilling to repent. Such an attitude did violence to principles of the kingdom.

Matthew 12:31–32

What is the sin, "blasphemy against the Spirit," that shall not be forgiven?

Many believers have been troubled by the question, "Have I committed the unpardonable sin?" A proper understanding of the historical circumstances can help clarify this issue and provide much-needed relief for troubled saints.

The Context

In Matthew 12:22–23, Jesus miraculously liberated a man from demon possession. The evidence of His miracles pointed to the fact that Jesus was the Messiah and that the kingdom was at hand (v. 28). The Pharisees could not deny the fact of the miracle. In a desperate attempt to turn the multitudes from following Jesus, the religious leaders declared that He did the miracle by the power of *Beelzebul,* an expression used in biblical times to refer to Satan (compare 2 Kings 1:1–6). They were saying, "These credentials are of hell, not of heaven!"

The Sin

After refuting the Pharisaic interpretation of His miracles (Matt. 12:25–30), Jesus warned these religious leaders of blasphemy that "shall not be forgiven" (v. 31). *Blasphemia* (blasphemy) may be defined as "slander" or "defamation." To "blaspheme" *(blasphemo)* is to "speak lightly or profanely of sacred things." *Blasphemy* may be defined as impious and irreverent speech against God. Speaking in an impious and irreverent manner against Christ may be forgiven. But speaking in an impious and irreverent manner against the Holy Spirit will never be forgiven (12:32). This is designated an "eternal sin" (Mark 3:29).

The Pharisees had attributed Christ's miracles to the work of Satan (Matt. 12:24). They were saying that Jesus was in league with the Devil, doing Messiah's work by Satan's power.

The Views

1. The *Sin of Unbelief.* Some have identified this sin as the sin of unbelief, which cannot be repented of after death. In this sense, to die in unbelief is "eternal sin." No one would disagree with the fact that unbelief at death has eternal consequences. But is this what the Pharisees were doing?

2. *Sin Leading to Death.* Some have linked this sin with 1 John 5:16 where the apostle writes of a "sin leading to death." But Stott argues that this cannot refer to a sin punishable by death (Acts 5; 1 Cor. 11), since the life with which it is contrasted is clearly spiritual or eternal life.[8] Those who were committing "sin leading to death" were the false teachers who had rejected the Son and thus forfeited spiritual life.

3. *Incorrigible Unbelief.* Others have linked this sin with that of Pharaoh's, whose heart was hardened by his deliberate, open-eyed rejection of the known truth. The key question is whether there is scriptural evidence for the view that an unbeliever can come to a point, or cross the line, after which forgiveness is impossible. Note that the unpardonable sin makes *forgiveness* impossible— not repentance. Can an unbeliever come to a point where repentance is possible but forgiveness is not? This would certainly limit the "whosoever" of the Gospel.

4. *Attributing Modern Miracles to Satan.* It has been said that those who call the recent sign-and-wonders movement a work of Satan are committing the unpardonable sin. The problem with this analysis is that the unpardonable sin, as described in the biblical text, involves more than calling miracles the work of Satan. The sin involves the rejection of Christ and of His proclamation of the kingdom.

5. *A Unique, First-Century Sin.* Following the lead of Chafer, many hold the view that the historical circumstances of the unpardonable sin cannot be reproduced today. Jesus was in Israel offering the kingdom and doing miracles to authenticate that offer. The Pharisees saw the evidence of Jesus' miracles but attributed this to the work of Satan. They spoke in an irreverent and impious way regarding the ministry of the Holy Spirit. This sin could not be forgiven them. It was in light of these unique circumstances that the teaching on the unpardonable sin is given. The sin of these Jewish leaders is seen to have serious consequences for the nation (compare Matt. 23:37–38, 45; Luke 19:11–27).

This view that limits the "unpardonable sin" to the first century appears to be most consistent with the historical context and the textual information. The admonition should not be divorced from this historical context and should not be applied generally.

Many believers have wondered if they have committed the unpardonable sin. To those who worry that they have committed this sin, their very spiritual concern reflects the fact that they have not. Further, the circumstances necessary to reproduce this sin are not possible today.

Matthew 12:40

If Jesus was buried on Friday and raised on Sunday, how could He fulfill the "sign of Jonah" requiring "three days and three nights"?

The expression "three days and three nights" has led some people to believe that Jesus needed to be in the grave a full seventy-two hours in order to fulfill the prophecy. This thinking is based on a western rather than Oriental understanding of time. In ancient Israel the Jewish people wondered, "If a baby boy is born just before sunset, does the partial day count for the purpose of numbering the eight days until circumcision? Or does the numbering begin with the first full day?" The rabbis debated this and concluded that any part of the day would be regarded as the whole for the purposes of reckoning time (Jerusalem Talmud, *Shabbath* 9.3).

It is also clear from Hebrew Scripture that the phrase *three days* does not demand a seventy-two-hour period. This is seen in the book of Esther where it is recorded that Esther and the Jews determined to fast "three days," night and day (Est. 4:16). Then she appeared before the king "on the third day" (5:1). Jesus used a similar phrase, "on the third day" (Matt. 16:21; 17:23) to describe the time of His resurrection. The expression clearly indicates a time period shorter than seventy-two hours. Jesus was in the grave during part of Friday, all of Saturday, and part of Sunday. Since the partial days count for the whole in Hebrew reckoning, He fulfilled the requirements of Jonah's prophecy. Both in the case of Jonah and Jesus, the time period ends with a surprise. Jonah was delivered and Jesus was resurrected.

Matthew 13:10

Why did Jesus speak in parables that often tended to obscure His message?

Jesus used the parables in addressing mixed crowds made up of friends and enemies, those responding to His messianic claims and those rejecting them. Jesus explains His use of parables in Matthew 13:10–17. The parables served to *reveal* truth to the responsive yet at the same time to *conceal* truth from those rejecting Him. Quoting Isaiah 6:9–10, Jesus said that people who reject Him will be ever hearing but will never understand. Because of their refusal to receive the truth, in judgment on them, the parables would obscure the truth.

Matthew 13:31

Was Jesus mistaken when He referred to the mustard seed as the smallest of all seeds?

It has been argued that Jesus erred in identifying the mustard seed as the smallest seed. Scientifically we know that there are smaller seeds. However, Jesus was not referring to all seeds but to the garden seeds, the seeds a farmer would plant in the field. The black mustard seed is smaller than a grain seed, a grape seed, or a cucumber seed. It is smaller than the period at the end of this sentence. Of all the garden seeds, it is the smallest, with the greatest growth potential! In the time of Jesus, the mustard seed was a standard Jewish illustration of something small (Mishnah *Tohoroth* 8.8; *Niddah* 5.2).

Matthew 14:4

Why did John the Baptizer condemn Herod's marriage?

Herod Antipas, tetrarch of Galilee, married the daughter of Aretas IV, a Nabatean king. On a journey to Rome, Antipas visited his half-brother Herod Philip (not Philip the Tetrarch) and fell in love with Philip's wife, Herodias. Herodias was the daughter of Philip's brother Aristobulus, making her Philip's niece. She agreed to become Antipas's wife under the stipulation that Aretas's daughter be ousted. The two were married in violation of Mosaic laws against incestuous marriage (Lev. 18:16; 20:21).

Matthew 15:22–28

Why did Jesus seem reluctant to respond to the Canaanite woman's appeal for help?

Jesus' initial response to the woman must be understood in light of the instructions He gave the disciples (Matt. 10:5–6). The priority at this time was proclaiming the kingdom to the Jews, who had been prepared by the prophets to receive it. Jesus makes it clear to the Canaanite woman that He was sent as Messiah to Israel (v. 24). When she persists, Jesus responds, "It is not good to take the children's bread and throw it to the dogs" (v. 25). The word "dogs" *(kunariois)* is a diminutive form that refers to little puppies, not to unclean scavengers. The woman is totally undeterred by what might be taken as a harsh reply. She responds, "Yes, Lord; but even the dogs feed on the crumbs which fall from their master's table" (v. 27). She is saying, "The loss of a scrap won't upset anyone. Give me the blessing Israel is neglecting."

Jesus then responded to the woman and healed her child. Because of their rejection, Christ would not set up His kingdom for the people of Israel. But those who approached by faith received personal blessing. Jesus commends the woman saying, "Your faith is great." She persisted in believing that God is good and responds to those who request. Jesus' initial answer may have led a lesser person to curse God, but she honors Him with radical trust in His goodness.

Matthew 16:18

What did Jesus mean when He said, "Upon this rock [petra] I will build my church"? Is Peter the rock?

This text is the first of two teachings by Jesus on the church (compare Matt. 18:15–18). Here Jesus promises to "build" His church. The difficulty in this passage is determining what or who is the *petra* upon which the church is built. There is an obvious play on words going on in this verse. Jesus said, "You are *Petros* and upon this *petra* I will build My church." The Greek word *petros* refers to a movable rock or stone. The word *petra* refers to an immovable rock formation or rock mass. There are three main interpretations of this passage.

1. The *petra* is Peter, the first pope. This is the traditional viewpoint presented by the Roman Catholic Church. However, Jesus could have said, "upon *you*," if He was referring to Peter. And the demonstrative pronoun "this" is feminine and would not refer to Peter. Peter is not the only "rock" in Scripture (Deut. 32:4, 31; Eph. 2:19–21; 1 Peter 2:5). How do we know Jesus was referring to him? Finally, the majority of the church fathers say Peter was not the rock (Chrysostom, Ambrose, Augustine, Jerome).

2. The *petra* is Christ. This viewpoint fits well with other Scripture (1 Cor.

10:4; Eph. 2:20; 1 Peter 2:6–8). But Christ could have said, "upon Me." And the feminine demonstrative pronoun "this" would not be used to refer to Jesus.

3. The *petra* is Peter's confession. This view fits better with the feminine demonstrative pronoun "this." But is the church built on the confession of a fallible human?

I would like to suggest another alternative. I believe that Jesus was referring not to Peter's confession, but to the *truth* of his statement that Jesus is the Messiah, the Son of God. The church rests on no more fundamental fact than this. This viewpoint, I believe, fits the context, the Greek syntax, and is consistent with Scripture and Christian theology. The church is founded on the divinely revealed truth that Jesus is the Messiah, the divine Son of God.

Matthew 16:18; 18:18

Did Peter and the apostles receive God's authority to forgive sins?

Peter, and later the other apostles (Matt. 18:18), are granted the authority to "bind" and to "loose." These terms were used by the rabbis to refer to activities that they required to be fulfilled or did not require to be fulfilled. By judicial pronouncement, they would "bind" or "loose" a person with regard to the law. That is, they were bound to the obligation or freed from the obligation. Peter and the apostles are granted the authority to make similar announcements based on what God has done.

Based on one's response to the Gospel, the apostles could declare, "Because you have rejected Christ, you are bound to the law and to its penalty." Or, "Because you have received Christ, you are free from the law and its penalty."

It is important to understand that the apostles did not determine an individual's destiny. They simply made judicial pronouncements based on what God had already done. This is evident from the use of the periphrastic future perfect, best rendered "shall have been bound" and "shall have been loosed." Authority to grant forgiveness is God's alone. Jesus simply gave the apostles the privilege of announcing what God had already accomplished in heaven.

Matthew 16:28

Did Jesus mistakenly think that some of His disciples would be alive when He came to establish the kingdom?

Verse 28 is a hinge verse linking chapters 16 and 17. In chapter 16, Peter had confessed Jesus to be the Messiah, the Son of God. Yet Jesus had predicted His suffering and death (v. 21). Peter's response (v. 22) indicates that he feared that the Messiah's death would prevent the establishment of His coming kingdom. What a discouraging thought!

In order to encourage the disciples and to strengthen their faith, Jesus promises that some of them will have a foretaste of His kingdom glory (v. 28). That promise was fulfilled six days later when Jesus took Peter, James, and John up on a high mountain—probably Mount Hermon (ninety-two hundred feet). There He was transfigured, displaying His inner glory, which had been veiled when He took on humanity. Moses, the great lawgiver, and Elijah, the great prophet, appeared with Jesus. Moses had died. Elijah had been taken to heaven in a whirlwind. Their presence there demonstrated that neither Jesus' death nor ascension would prevent the coming of His kingdom.

The Transfiguration was intended to dispel the idea that Christ's death meant an end to the kingdom home. It was a premature revelation of the essential glory that belongs to Christ and that will be revealed when He comes to establish His kingdom. Jesus was not mistaken in thinking that some of the disciples would witness the inauguration of His kingdom. He simply encouraged them with the promise that some would experience a foretaste of His kingdom glory!

Matthew 18:17

What did Jesus mean when He said, "Let him be to you as a Gentile and a tax-gatherer"?

In Matthew 18:15–17, Jesus presents four steps for spiritual accountability in dealing with a Christian who is involved in sin: (1) private reproof; (2) private conference; (3) public announcement; (4) public dismissal.[9] The fourth step involves the dismissal of the unrepentant sinner from congregational fellowship. In Jesus' day, a "Gentile" or a "tax-gatherer" was regarded as an outsider in relationship to the believing community of Israel. Jesus is saying that the person who refuses to repent of known sin should be regarded by the church as an unbeliever rather than as a believer. Ultimately, God alone knows the individual's spiritual condition. But on the basis of conduct, the person's deeds demonstrate that he or she is unsaved and should be removed from the assembly. In ecclesiastical terminology, this is referred to as "excommunication."

The purpose of excommunication is not to punish the sinner but to demonstrate that on the basis of the person's conduct, he or she cannot be regarded as a brother or a sister in Christ. There is no need to treat disfellowshiped church members poorly. We should treat them as we would any other unbelievers. Don't share Christian fellowship with them, but seek to present the message of Christ with the hope that they will repent and enter into the family of God. Excommunication is with a view to evangelism and winning the lost for the Lord.

Matthew 19:6–7

Were Jesus and Moses in disagreement on the matter of divorce?

When questioned on the subject of divorce, Jesus told the religious leaders, "What therefore God has joined together, let no man separate" (Matt. 19:6). The Pharisees responded that Moses had "commanded" divorce (v. 7). The problem is not a contradiction between Jesus and Moses but a misinterpretation of Moses by the Pharisees. The Pharisees interpreted Deuteronomy 24:1–4 to require divorce for some kinds of sexual sin or impurity. But a careful exegesis of the text reveals that it simply demonstrates otherwise.

In Deuteronomy 24:1–3, Moses describes the case, specifying the conditions for which the command in verse 4 applies. In this case Moses describes a man who divorces his wife and she remarries. Then her second marriage ends either by death or by divorce. The command that applies is given in verse 4. A man may not remarry his former wife if she has in the meantime been married to another man. Even though her second husband divorces her or dies, she may not be reunited in marriage to her first husband.

There is no *command* in Deuteronomy 24:1–4 or anywhere in the Bible requiring a man to divorce his wife for sexual impurity. The Mosaic "command" to divorce one's wife is based on Jewish tradition rather than careful exegesis of the Hebrew text. There is no contradiction between Jesus and Moses in affirming the permanence of marriage (compare Gen. 2:24; Matt. 19:4–9).

Matthew 19:9
What is the meaning of the expression, "except for immorality"?

In Matthew 19:9, Jesus declares that divorce and remarriage constitute adultery. This means that a merely formal or legal divorce does not necessarily dissolve the actual marriage that was made permanent by God. The only exception, according to Jesus, is the case of *porneia* (translated "immorality" in the NASB). A proper understanding of this word is crucial to determining the teaching of Jesus on divorce and remarriage.

Many evangelicals have equated *porneia* with "adultery." There is, however, another word *(moicheia)* that Jesus would have used had He intended to side with the school of Shammai in allowing divorce and remarriage in the case of adultery.

One viewpoint is that *porneia* refers to any kind of sexual misconduct. This would place Jesus somewhere between the views of Shammai and Hillel, two famous rabbis who lived and taught in the time of Jesus. But the disciples' response to the teaching ("it is better not to marry," Matt. 19:10) indicates that Jesus was teaching a much more conservative view. A second viewpoint is that *porneia* refers to unfaithfulness during betrothal. While supported by a consideration of the Jewish context of the gospel, this view appears to be excluded by the fact that Jesus is speaking about marriage rather than about betrothal.

A third viewpoint fits well with the historical, geographical, and cultural context of Matthew's gospel—a book clearly designed to benefit Jewish readers (compare Matt. 1:23; 2:5–6, 15, 18, 23, etc.). This view is that *porneia* refers to incestuous marriage. Leviticus 18:6–18 forbids marriages between near relatives. Such illicit unions were not regarded as legal marriages. According to this viewpoint, the exception clause in Matthew 19:9 simply states that Christ's prohibition against divorce does not apply in the case of an illegal, incestuous marriage. Since one lexical meaning of *porneia* is "incest" or "incestuous marriage" (Acts 15:20, 29; 1 Cor. 5:1), this must be considered as a possible interpretation of the exception.

This viewpoint is supported by first-century Palestinian texts and would account for the inclusion of the exception in Matthew and its absence in Mark and Luke. The Jewish readers of Matthew's gospel were well aware of the incest of the Herods—Archelaus, Antipas, and Agrippa II—as reported by the historian Josephus. Since Jesus was in the jurisdiction of Herod Antipas when confronted by the Pharisees, it is reasonable to assume that He might refer to Herod's incestuous marriage.

In Matthew 19:1–8, Jesus declared that divorce was inconsistent with the teaching of Moses and should not be practiced. But the "exception" indicates that His strong prohibition against divorce did not apply in the case of an illegal, incestuous marriage (v. 9).

Matthew 19:21

Must Christians give away their money and possessions to become followers of Christ?

This statement is set in the context of a discussion with a young man who asked Jesus, "What good thing shall I do that I may obtain eternal life?" (19:16). The rich young man wanted to gain eternal life by doing. Jesus responded to the young man in such a way as to show him that he could not do enough to gain eternal life. When confronted with the commandments, the man professed to keep them all. Then Jesus added the words of verse 21, "Sell your possessions and give to the poor, . . . and come, follow Me."

The rich young man found this requirement was impossible to fulfill, for he was more in love with his money than with God. The point of the story is that it is impossible to gain eternal life by doing. But what is impossible for people is made possible with God (v. 26). Through faith, even a rich man like Zacchaeus can receive what is impossible to gain through self-effort.

Christians are not called upon to give all their possessions away. But we should never let money or things take God's place in our lives. And we must remember that the only treasure we will enjoy forever is that which is laid up in heaven.

Matthew 20:29–34

How is Matthew's account of the healing of the two blind men consistent with Mark and Luke?

All three of the Synoptic Gospels record Jesus' miraculous healing of the blind somewhere in the vicinity of Jericho (Matt. 20:29–34; Mark 10:46–52; Luke 18:35–43). But the accounts appear to be contradictory. Mark and Luke mention only one blind man, while Matthew mentions two. And Luke records that the miracle took place as Jesus was entering Jericho, while Matthew and Mark record that it took place as they were leaving the city.

The accounts are not contradictory but contribute different details. Matthew mentions two blind men, while Mark and Luke refer to the more prominent of the two, whom Mark actually identifies as Bartimaeus. As for the relationship of the miracle to Jericho, in the time of Jesus there were two Jerichos, located about one-half mile apart. The Old Testament site of Jericho was located near

Elisha's spring, while the New Testament site, built by Herod, was situated on the Wadi Qilt. Apparently the miracle took place as Jesus was traveling between the two sites—"going out" of one Jericho and "approaching" the other. It is easy to say there's a contradiction. It takes a little more work and research to discover there are reasonable explanations for these synoptic differences.

Matthew 21:7

Did Jesus ride on one or two animals during his royal entry into Jerusalem?

Jesus instructed two of His disciples to bring "a donkey" and "a colt with her" for Him to ride into Jerusalem (21:2). Some have mocked the accuracy of Scripture by suggesting that Matthew has Jesus riding into Jerusalem on two animals! The words in the Greek text of Matthew 21:7, "upon them He sat," are used in support of this hypothesis. But the text of Matthew is clear. Jesus rode into Jerusalem on the young colt of the donkey in fulfillment of Zechariah 9:9. Garments were laid on the back of the young animal to form a makeshift saddle. The words, "upon them He sat," refer to the garments, not to the two animals.

Matthew 21:12–19

Did Jesus curse the fig tree before or after He cleansed the temple?

Matthew appears to place the cursing of the fig tree the day after the cleansing of the temple. But Mark 11:11–14 places the event in the morning of the same day as the cleansing of the temple. How can these two accounts be reconciled?

We should first note that the similarities are greater than the differences. Both accounts include the cursing of the fig tree, Jesus' comment to the disciples about the cursing, and the cleansing of the temple.

The difference between the two accounts is that Mark places the cleansing of the temple between the cursing and the comment that Jesus makes to His disciples on the following day. Matthew, for the sake of thematic development, places the cursing with the comment, which was made the day after the cleansing. Mark, true to his style, has given us the more detailed account, recording the chronological order of events. Matthew, more interested in thematic development, has telescoped the two events into one. Putting the two accounts together, we see that Jesus cursed the fig tree before cleansing the temple and commented on the withered tree the next day in response to His disciples' question.

Matthew 22:15

Who were the Herodians?

The Herodians are usually thought to be the political supporters of the Herodian dynasty. But the dynasty of Herod had not been ruling in Judea since the expulsion of Archelaus in A.D. 6. There is a better alternative.[10]

When Herod became king in 37 B.C., he adopted the policy of selecting his own high priest. Between 23 B.C. and A.D. 6, the house of Boethus was the ruling family of high priests. The descendants of the house of Boethus are probably the Herodians of the New Testament.

Matthew 23:5

What are "phylacteries"?

Phylacteries are small black boxes containing portions of Scripture, which Jewish men strap to their foreheads and arms during prayer. The custom is based on the exhortation of Deuteronomy 6:8, "And you shall bind them as a sign on your hand and they shall be as frontals on your forehead." Jesus rebuked the practice of the first-century religious leaders who enlarged their phylacteries to make a public display of their spirituality.

Matthew 23:8–10

Is it wrong to call religious leaders by exalted or honorific titles?

In Matthew 23, Jesus denounces the scribes and the Pharisees for their religious hypocrisy. They were motivated by a desire to be noticed rather than by their love for God.

In verses 8–10, Jesus warns His followers against seeking and using exalted titles. The term *rabbi* in Hebrew means "my great one" and was used as a reverential form of address or title of respect for Jewish teachers. Prominent rabbis were also addressed by the fatherly term *abba,* "father" or "papa." The term translated "leader" refers to one who is a "guide" or "teacher," like the Latin *doctor.*

The titles, rabbi, father, and doctor, all serve to place one believer above the others and undermines the doctrine of the priesthood of all believers (1 Peter 2:9). Jesus warns us against seeking and using honorific titles, which create unbiblical distinctions between God's people. Christ alone is deserving of such honor. It is possible to recognize leaders and to follow their leadership without using exalted titles.

Matthew 24:1–3

To whom is the Olivet Discourse addressed?

The Olivet Discourse is addressed to Jesus' disciples as representatives of the Jewish nation, which had fallen under God's judgment due to their rejection of the Messiah (compare Matt. 23:37–39). As believers in Christ, the disciples were part of the Jewish remnant with whom God would fulfill His prophetic program. They needed to know something about this program and how God's covenanted program would be realized.

The Olivet Discourse is not addressed to the church, since the church was not inaugurated until Pentecost (Acts 2). The reference to the Jewish practice of Sabbath worship would also suggest that the discourse is not for the church. Pentecost points out, "Consistency of interpretation would seem to eliminate any application of this portion of Scripture to the church or church age, inasmuch as the Lord is dealing with the prophetic program for Israel."[11]

Matthew 24:3

What question is the Olivet Discourse intended to answer?

Jesus had just announced the destruction of Jerusalem (24:2) due to the rejection of the Messiah. The disciples responded with two questions—one of history and the other of eschatology. First, "Tell us, when will these things be?" This question relates to the destruction by Titus in A.D. 70. The answer to this question is recorded in Luke 21:20–24. Second, "And what will be the sign of Your coming, and of the end of the age?" This is actually one question, not two. The single definite article encompasses the twofold reference as one. Zechariah 14:1–8 indicates that the "end of the age" coincides with the "coming" of the Messiah. What we have here, then, is a question of eschatology. The disciples were asking Jesus to reveal the "sign" of His coming, an event that would bring this present age to an end.

The Olivet Discourse records the signs that will occur during the Tribulation that will indicate to the believing Jewish remnant that the end of the age and Messiah's (second) coming is near.

Matthew 24:32–34

Does the blossoming of the fig tree represent the birth of the State of Israel?

Many have interpreted the fig tree as representing Israel and have identified 1948, when Israel became a state, as the year the tree blossomed. It is argued that the generation that saw Israel become a nation would witness Messiah's return. Since forty years has been regarded as a biblical generation, it was expected that Jesus would return in 1988. Obviously, this did not happen and illustrates the danger in setting dates for Christ's return.

Jesus is not saying, watch Israel. He is simply saying that those who witness the signs of the Tribulation should recognize that a process has begun that will lead to the consummation of a program. As the new leaves of the fig tree indicate that summer is near, so the signs of the Tribulation indicate that the Second Coming is near.

The word translated "generation" *(genea)* in verses 34 would better be rendered "race." The race or people of Israel will not be destroyed but will be preserved until the consummation of the program. This remark is intended as an encouragement in light of the intensive persecution of believers during the Tribulation.

Matthew 24:40–41

Is Jesus referring here to the rapture of the church?

In light of the uncertainty concerning the exact day and hour of the Messiah's second coming, Jesus gives an exhortation to watchfulness and preparedness (Matt. 24:37–44). He exhorts people not to go through this period ignoring God's warning. In verses 40–41, Jesus teaches that at His coming there will be a separation of those who are prepared (believers) from those who are not (unbelievers). Two people will be busy at work. When Messiah comes, one will be taken into judgment and the other will be left to enjoy Christ's kingdom.

The parallel in Luke 17:34–37 makes it clear that the one "taken" is removed for judgment, like the tares in the parable of Matthew 13:40–41. Those who are taken are not believers who are raptured, since the Rapture will occur before the Tribulation (compare 1 Thess 5:9; 2 Thess. 2:1–3).

Matthew 25:31–46

This passage seems to teach that salvation is the result of good deeds. How does this reconcile with the Bible's emphasis on salvation by faith (Eph. 2:8–9)?

The Olivet Discourse closes with a description of the judgment on the nations to determine who among the Gentile people will be permitted to enter Messiah's kingdom. The judgment described here is for living Gentiles who survive the Tribulation and meet Christ as He returns. This judgment is distinguished from the Great White Throne judgment on the wicked, which will follow the Millennium (Rev. 20:10–15).

In this judgment, the Son of Man, King Jesus, will separate the sheep (believers) from the goats (unbelievers). The sheep will be invited to enter Messiah's kingdom (v. 34) while the goats will be dismissed to "eternal fire" (v. 41). The distinction between the sheep and the goats is made on the basis of how they treated certain "brothers of Mine" (v. 40). These brothers are apparently Jewish believers who come to faith during the Tribulation and will suffer terrible persecution because of their commitment to Christ. Because of the Antichrist's economic policies (Rev. 13:16–17), they will have no means of support and will be dependent on Gentile believers for their survival.

Those who come to the aid of these suffering Jewish believers demonstrate by their deeds that they are followers of Christ. This is not salvation *by* works, but salvation *that* works (Eph. 2:9–10). Those who don't respond to the obvious needs of the Jewish believers demonstrate by their neglect that they are not believers in Christ (Titus 1:16). Throughout Scripture salvation is always by God's grace through personal faith. Matthew 25:31–46 in no way contradicts this foundational teaching.

Matthew 25:41

Do wicked unbelievers experience everlasting torment in a fiery hell, or are they annihilated and merely pass out of existence?

Traditionally, Christians have held to the view that those who have rejected Christ suffer the pains of an everlasting, fiery hell. But there have arisen some among evangelical Christians who argue that these traditional views are founded on early Greek philosophy and that the biblical texts are capable of an alternative interpretation.

There are two texts of Scripture that suggest to me that hell involves everlasting punishment. Matthew 25:46 sums up the judgment on the sheep and goats with the words, "And these will go away into eternal punishment, but the righteous into eternal life." The same word *aionion* (eternal) is used to describe the punishment of the wicked and the blessing of the righteous. Whatever we say about the duration of "eternal" life for believers must be said about "eternal" punishment for unbelievers. Since "life" for believers is everlasting (John 10:28), so must be the punishment for unbelievers.

In a second text, Revelation 20:10, John describes those in the "lake of fire" being "tormented day and night forever and ever." The expression *day and night* is used in Revelation to express the concept of "forever." The lake of fire is described in Revelation 19:20 as a place that "burns with brimstone." In the saddest verse in the Bible, John declares that anyone whose name is not written in the book of life is "thrown into the lake of fire" (Rev. 20:15).

The doctrine of eternal punishment for those who have rejected Christ appears to be thoroughly biblical. This is not an easy teaching or one that brings us joy. But the unpleasantness of a doctrine should not cause us to deny biblical truth. Teaching on eternal damnation may serve as a motivation for evangelism and an encouragement toward repentance and belief.

Matthew 26:6–13

Did the anointing of Jesus at Bethany take place two days or six days before Passover?

Matthew, Mark, and John record Jesus' anointing in Bethany at a meal during the week before Passover. Matthew 26:2 and Mark 14:1 mention that Passover was "two days" off. John 12:1, however, mentions that Jesus came to Bethany "six" days before Passover. How can the variant accounts be reconciled?

One possibility is that these are two events and that the anointing took place twice. But a close comparison of the accounts yields numerous similarities. All mention Bethany, the valuable ointment, the concern for waste, the poor, the preparation for burial.

If they are the same account, which chronology is preferred? It seems that the fourth gospel gives the chronological sequence. Jesus arrived at Bethany six days before Passover. Mary and Martha prepared supper and the anointing took place at that time. But what of Matthew and Mark's "two days"? A closer look reveals that the "two days" are mentioned in connection with Jesus' fourth and last announcement of His impending death (Matt. 26:2). This notice is followed by an account of the plot of the religious leaders (vv. 3–5) and then the story of the anointing (vv. 6–13). Matthew does not use the "two days" in connection with the anointing. He simply says, "Now when Jesus was in Bethany." Matthew and Mark are not providing a chronological link between the "two days" and the account of the anointing. They actually place the anointing out of sequence here. But for what purpose?

Matthew and Mark set the anointing by Mary in contrast with the animosity of the religious leaders (Matt. 26:3–5; Mark 14:1–2) and to highlight Judas's interest in financial gain (Matt. 26:15; Mark 14:11). There is no contradiction between the Synoptics and John. Only John provides us with the time of the anointing, "six days before the Passover."

The three gospel accounts of this incident actually compliment one another, filling in details for each other. Mary and Martha were preparing a meal in the home of Simon the leper six days before Passover. John names Mary and says she anointed Jesus' feet (John 12:3). Matthew and Mark don't identify Mary and record that a woman anointed Jesus' head (Matt. 26:7; Mark 14:3). Apparently Mary anointed both Jesus' head and feet.

Matthew 26:30

What hymn did Jesus sing with His disciples as they left the Upper Room for the Mount of Olives?

According to well-established Jewish tradition, the Hallel psalms (Pss. 113–118) were sung during the Passover meal. The last psalm to be sung would be Psalm 118. The last verses of the psalm (vv. 22–29) provide significant insight into the experience of Christ as He headed for Gethsemane.

Matthew 26:34

Did Peter deny Christ three times or six?

Each of the Gospels records just three denials of Christ by Peter, but because of the differing details it has been argued that Peter received two different warnings about denying Christ and in each warning was told that he would deny Christ three times.[12] Did Peter deny Christ before the cock crowed and another three times before the cock crowed a second time?

Only in Mark's gospel is there any indication that the cock crowed a second time before Peter completed his denials of Christ (Mark 14:30, 72). Both the warning recorded in Matthew 26:34 and the warning in Mark 14:30 were given after the group left the Upper Room. The chronology of the passages is identical. The only difference in the accounts is that Mark indicates that the cock will crow twice before the third denial.

The major problem with the six-denials theory is that Peter would have confronted his failure after the first cock crowed (Matt. 26:75; Mark 14:72; Luke 22:62). Having been reminded of Jesus' prediction, it is doubtful that he would have denied Christ three more times. A second problem is that this theory ignores the principle of preference for the clearest interpretation. Since all four gospels record Jesus' prediction of three denials by Peter, it would be better to affirm what is clear—the three denials—and seek to explain the second cock crow in that light.

Those who have had experience with chickens can tell you that a cock never crows just once! Perhaps Matthew, Luke, and John record the general warning to Peter, and Mark provides the detail that the cock crowed twice.

The accounts are complimentary, not contradictory. There were three denials by Peter and then the cock crowed—twice!

Matthew 26:39–44

What did Jesus mean when He prayed, "Let this cup pass from Me"?

It is clear from the context that Jesus is using the word "cup" in a metaphorical sense. What did He mean by the cup? Some have suggested that Jesus was asking God to deliver Him from death. And yet He had announced His impending death again and again to the disciples (compare Matt. 16:21). Others suggest that in His holiness, Jesus is repulsed at the thought of becoming sin for humankind (2 Cor. 5:21). It is also possible that Jesus was agonizing over the prospect of spiritual separation from God the Father during His death.

Perhaps a combination approach is reasonable in dealing with this question since there is nothing in the immediate context that identifies the cup. During His prayer in the garden, Jesus was dealing with the issue of becoming sin bearer (John 1:29) and being forsaken by the Father (Matt. 27:46). In His prayer, Jesus asked to be delivered from the cup of physical and spiritual suffering. But He submitted to the Father's will (Matt. 26:42).

Matthew 26:51

What was Peter doing with a sword?

The word translated "sword" *(machairan)* is used in the Septuagint to refer to the large knife Abraham used for sacrificial purposes (Gen. 22:6, 10). Peter may have used this instrument in the preparations for Passover (Matt. 26:17) and may still have had it with him.

Luke 22:36–38 provides another insight into the matter of Peter's sword. Before leaving the Upper Room, Jesus told His disciples, "Let him who has no sword sell his robe and buy one" (Luke 22:36). Exactly what Jesus meant by this statement is subject to debate, but the disciples responded, "Lord, look, here are two swords." Jesus may have referred to the sword as a figure of the dangerous struggle ahead. Apparently the disciples took Him literally and produced two swords as evidence that they were ready. The presence of these weapons at Jesus' arrest would place Him among criminals and serve to fulfill the prophecy of Isaiah 53:12.

Matthew 26:59

What was the "Council" or Sanhedrin that was involved in the trial of Christ?

The Greek term *sunhedrion* means "assembly" or "council." According to rabbinic tradition, the Sanhedrin had its origin with the council of seventy elders appointed to assist Moses (Mishnah *Sanhedrin* 1.6). In the Roman period, the Sanhedrin became the court of justice in the land. Although answerable to the Roman government, it had almost exclusive control of the internal government and affairs of the people.

There were seventy-one members, including scribes, elders, and priestly aristocracy (both Sadducees and Pharisees). According to Josephus, the Sanhedrin met on the temple mount on the western side of the enclosing wall (*Wars* 5.144; 6.354). The Mishnah describes the Sanhedrin as exercising authority in the following areas: idolatry, false prophets, sins of the high priest, declaring war, enlarging Jerusalem. In the period of Roman rule, the Sanhedrin had authority to punish but not to execute. Since the Jewish leaders wanted Jesus to be executed (Matt. 27:1), this necessitated a Roman trial.

Matthew 27:1

Did the Jewish leaders abide by their own law in the trial of Christ?

The evidence indicates that there were at least five violations of Jewish law by the Sanhedrin in the trial of Jesus.

1. The Sanhedrin convened in the house of Caiphas rather than in its regular meeting place (*Sanhedrin* 11a; *Middoth* 5.4).

2. The Sanhedrin met at night rather than at the prescribed time during the day (Tosephta *Sanhedrin* 7.1).

3. The Sanhedrin convened on the eve of a Sabbath and festival day (Passover), which was illegal procedure (*Sanhedrin* 4.1; Josephus *Antiquities* 16.163).

4. The sentence of condemnation was pronounced the same day as the morning trial. According to Jewish law, before any verdict of guilty could be declared and sentence imposed, the court was required to recess until the following day, when it would reexamine the evidence (*Sanhedrin* 4.1; 5.5).

5. The special formalities required in capital cases providing for the possibility of acquittal were not followed (*Sanhedrin* 4.1).

Matthew 27:5

Did Judas die by hanging or by some other means?

Matthew records that after attempting to return the money he had received for betraying Jesus, Judas went away and "hanged himself." Yet Luke's account in Acts 1:18–19 records that he plummeted into a ravine and died. Some suggest that Judas attempted to hang himself, but the rope broke and he fell to his death.

There is another possible interpretation of Judas's death. The Greek word translated "hanged" *(apagcho)* may be translated "strangled," as in the Greek translation of 2 Samuel 17:23. There we read that Ahithophel committed suicide by strangling himself. Strangulation was a form of execution and of suicide in ancient times. Perhaps Judas strangled himself at the edge of a ravine and then fell to his death as Luke records (Acts 1:18).

Matthew 27:9–10

Why does Matthew cite Jeremiah when Zechariah 11:12–13 seems to be the correct source of the quotation?

Having described the return of the thirty pieces of silver by Judas and the purchase of the potter's field, Matthew introduces a Scripture quotation from Zechariah 11:12–13 with the words, "Then that which was spoken through Jeremiah the prophet was fulfilled." Some have simply acknowledged that Matthew was mistaken or that a later scribe made the error. It has also been suggested that Matthew used the name Jeremiah to refer to the Prophets, since Jeremiah is the first prophetic book in the Talmudic passage *Baba Bathra* 14b.

Some have suggested that Zechariah received the quotation from Jeremiah, and that Matthew is referring to the original source. Longenecker believes that Matthew was drawing from a "testimonia" collection where quotations from several sources were assigned to the more prominent author.[13]

Careful study of the quotation indicates that Matthew quoted Zechariah 11:12–13 (the thirty pieces of silver) and alludes to Jeremiah. 18:1–4 and 32:6–9 (the purchase of the field). I suggest that Jeremiah is named because he is the major prophet and mentions what Matthew wanted to stress—the purchase of the field.

Matthew 27:25

Are the Jewish people responsible for the death of Jesus?

During the trial of Jesus, the religious leaders persuaded the crowd to demand that Jesus be crucified. Although Pilate recognized that Jesus was innocent, he yielded to the demands of the people who said, "His blood be on us and on our children!" This statement has led many people to blame Jewish people for the death of Christ. In the eyes of some people, this text means that all Jewish people for all time are to blame and deserve punishment for Jesus' death.

Several points are worthy of note.[14] First, the mob that said, "His blood be upon us and on our children," spoke only for themselves and not the other Jews of Jesus' day or Jews of later generations. Second, these Jews had no authority to bring guilt on their descendants. The Prophets clearly teach that the son will not share the guilt of the father (Deut. 24:16; Ezek. 18:20). Third, the New Testament does not blame the Jewish people for the death of Jesus. Peter acknowledges that they acted in ignorance (Acts 3:17).

The Bible indicates that both Gentiles and Jews shared responsibility for the trial, condemnation, and crucifixion of Christ (4:27). Rather than blaming the Jewish people, we should marvel at God's sovereign plan for our redemption!

Matthew 27:52–53

How should we understand Matthew's reference to the saints who came out of the tombs and appeared in Jerusalem?

Some have suggested that these were Old Testament saints because of what Christ accomplished through His death. But Acts 2:29, 34 indicates that the Old Testament saint David was still in his tomb. Others have suggested that these were saints raised at the moment of Christ's death and point to the significance of His death. But Paul indicates that Jesus is the "first fruits" of the resurrection (1 Cor. 15:20–23). The text indicates that these saints were raised "after" (v. 53) Christ's resurrection and as a result of it. Most likely, they were raised with mortal bodies. Like Lazarus, they died again.

Matthew 28:1–10

To whom did Christ appear on the day of His resurrection?

There were five appearances of Jesus on the day of His resurrection:
1. to Mary Magdalene (Matt. 28:1; Mark 16:9–11; John 20:11–18)
2. to Mary and other women (Matt. 28:1, 9–10)
3. to Simon Peter (Luke 24:33–35; 1 Cor. 15:5)
4. to the two disciples (Luke 24:13–32)
5. to the ten apostles (Mark 16:14; Luke 24:36–43; John 20:19–25)

Matthew 28:19–20

What is the imperative in the Great Commission?

The imperative in the Great Commission is the command, "make disciples" (*matheteuo*). Making disciples requires evangelism and includes follow-up. Accompanying activities include (1) immersing those who believe, and (2) instructing them in the teachings of Jesus.

Endnotes

1. Harold W. Hoehner, *Chronological Aspects of the Life of Christ* (Grand Rapids: Zondervan, 1977), 11–27.
2. Ibid., 38.
3. Jack Finegan, *Handbook of Biblical Chronology* (Princeton: Princeton University Press, 1964), 245–46.
4. Richard N. Longenecker, *Biblical Exegesis in the Apostolic Period* (Grand Rapids: Eerdmans, 1975), 145.
5. Graeme Goldsworthy, *Gospel and Kingdom* (Exeter: Paternoster Press, 1981), 53.
6. J. L. Booth, "The Purpose of Miracles" (Th.D. diss., Dallas Theological Seminary, 1965).
7. Robert H. Gundry, *Matthew* (Grand Rapids: Eerdmans, 1982), 150.
8. John R. W. Stott, *The Epistles of John* (Grand Rapids: Eerdmans, 1964), 187–90.
9. For further study, see my book *A Guide to Church Discipline* (Minneapolis: Bethany House Publishers, 1985), 48–58.
10. Harold H. Hoehner, *Herod Antipas* (Cambridge: Cambridge University Press, 1972), 331–42.
11. J. Dwight Pentecost, *Things to Come* (Grand Rapids: Zondervan, 1958), 278.
12. Johnson M. Cheney, *The Life of Christ in Stereo* (Portland, Ore.: Western Baptist Seminary Press, 1969), 218–19.
13. Longenecker, *Biblical Exegesis,* 150.
14. Galen Peterson, *The Everlasting Tradition* (Grand Rapids: Kregel Publications, 1995), 100–101.

MARK

Synoptic Problem

Was Mark the first gospel written, and did Matthew and Luke draw from Mark's material?

Many scholars have argued that Mark was the first gospel written. In order to solve the problem of the relationship of the Synoptic Gospels to each other, B. H. Streeter (*The Four Gospels*, 1924) presented a four-source hypothesis that, though modified, has been regarded by many scholars as the most workable explanation of gospel origins. The four sources include:

Q	(Quelle): material used by Matthew and Luke but not by Mark
M	(Matthew): material found uniquely in Matthew based on a "Jerusalem sayings" document
L	(Luke): material found uniquely in Luke based on Caesarean oral tradition
Mark:	the Roman gospel upon which Matthew and Luke are based

The priority of Mark is key to the whole four-source hypothesis. According to the view, Mark wrote first and the other synoptic writers depended upon this original work. Matthew used Mark, Q, and his Jerusalem sayings document as his main sources. Luke used Mark, Q, and his Caesarean tradition, which was probably oral in character rather than written.

The crux of the issue is whether the similarities observable in the Synoptic Gospels can be accounted for *only* on the basis of literary dependence. To those who adopt this view, it seems inconceivable that the similarities and differences could be accounted for in some other way.

One of the major difficulties with the concept of literary dependence is why Matthew, an apostle, would need to gather material from Mark and Luke, neither of whom were apostles. This hypothesis is also contradicted by the view of the early church that the gospels with the genealogies (Matthew and Luke) were written first (Eusebius *Historia Ecclesiastica* 6:14).

There are several alternatives to the hypothesis that the gospel writers depended upon each other and other literary sources for their material.

1. Oral Tradition

Oral tradition may account for the similarities of the Gospels. The early teaching of Jesus was passed on by His disciples according to a fixed pattern that the gospel writers were acquainted with.

2. Audience and Purpose

The purpose of the writer and particular needs or interests of his readers may have led each of the gospel writers to emphasize different things—to include some material and to omit other data that was deemed nonessential to his aim.

3. Divine Inspiration

The Holy Spirit may have, and in fact did, lead the gospel writers to record the same teachings and narratives, often in the same words (John 14:26; 16:12–14; 2 Tim. 3:16–17; 2 Peter 1:20–21).

We cannot be dogmatic in suggesting a solution to the synoptic problem, but the alternatives suggested here must be given careful consideration before accepting the tentative hypothesis of the literary dependence of the Gospels.

Mark 2:26

Was Jesus mistaken when He identified Abiathar as high priest when the account in 1 Samuel 21:1–6 names Ahimelech?

As 1 Samuel 21 records, David had his dealings at Nob with Abiathar's father, Ahimelech. But there are several reasons why it was not wrong or inaccurate to name Abiathar in connection with this incident.

First of all, shortly after David met with Ahimelech, Saul had the priests at Nob slaughtered, including Ahimelech (22:18–19). Only Abiathar escaped! He fled to David and served as priest until David's death. He was the high priest during David's day, even though he was not high priest at the time of the incident.

Second, Jesus did not say that Abiathar was high priest at the time but that it was literally "in the time of Abiathar." Abiathar was alive when the incident took place and served as high priest after his father's death. The event Jesus referred to took place in the *time* of Abiathar, although not during his *tenure* in office.

Mark 3:6 (see Matthew 22:15)

Mark 3:28–30 (see Matthew 12:31–32)

Mark 4:2 (see Matthew 13:10)

Mark 4:30–32 (see Matthew 13:31)

Mark 5:1–2

How many demoniacs were healed by Jesus, and where did the miracle occur?

Matthew 8:28 mentions two demoniacs, while Mark 5:2 and Luke 8:27 mention only one. There is no contradiction between these accounts. While Matthew records that there were two demoniacs present, Mark and Luke report concerning the more prominent one—the demoniac who spoke with Jesus.

The location of the incident is a bit more difficult. Matthew records "the country of the Gadarenes" (Matt. 8:28). Mark mentions the "country of the Gerasenes" (Mark 5:1; Luke 8:26). The name "Gergesenes," found in some textual variants, was introduced into the Bible by Origen, who had geographical objections to the other readings and preferred the allegorical significance he found in the name.

That leaves us with two locations for the miracle—the territory of the Gadara (Matthew) or the territory of the Gerasa (Mark and Luke). How can the miracle be represented as taking place in two different territories? The solution is found in an understanding of Decapolis and its city-states Gadara and Gerasa.

Decapolis was not a definitely bounded political unit. It was made up of the territories of a number of independent cities. Each controlled the territory and villages of its immediate vicinity, and some even controlled separate enclaves of land. Gadara, for example, was five miles from the Sea of Galilee but possessed territory on the lakeshore. Since the city was home to a sizable Jewish population, it is reasonable that Matthew would describe the miracle as taking place in the territory of Gadara. This would have been familiar to his Jewish readers.

Mark and Luke, on the other hand, wrote to Roman and Greek readers, respectively. Undoubtedly, these readers would have heard of the splendor of Gerasa with its temples, theaters, hippodrome, and public buildings. Although thirty-five miles from the sea, the historical and biblical data suggests that Gerasa shared the jurisdiction over the southeast lakeshore with Gadara. It is likely that Mark and Luke identified the vicinity of the miracle in relationship to this famous city, which would be more well known among the readers unfamiliar with Palestine.

In describing the location of the miracle of healing the demoniac, the geography and history allowed for either name—Gadara or Gerasa. The authors chose the one that would communicate most effectively to their respective readers.

Mark 7:24–30 (see Matthew 15:22–28)

Mark 8:11–13

Does Mark 8:12–13 contradict Matthew 12:38–39 in saying that there would be no sign given to the Jews who were rejecting Christ?

Mark 8:11–13 records an incident where Jewish leaders demanded a "sign from heaven" that would prove Jesus' claims and answer their objections. They were saying in essence, "Your miracles are merely deception and fraud. Show us a sign 'from heaven,' like causing the sun to stand still [Josh. 10:12–14] or calling down fire [1 Kings 18:30–40]."

The problem was not, of course, with the miracles Jesus had performed but with the Pharisees' interpretation of them. To these leaders who were rejecting Him, Jesus promised no more signs. And none were given. Yes, Jesus performed other miracles, but none were for the purpose of displaying His power or proving His messiahship to those who persisted in rejecting Him.

But to this account Matthew 16:4 adds, a sign will not be given, "except the sign of Jonah." By the "sign of Jonah," Jesus is referring to His own resurrection. This statement is not in contradiction with Mark's account. Matthew's record simply clarifies the fact the resurrection of Christ was the final sign to the nation of Israel that Jesus was whom He claimed to be—the Messiah and the Son of God. Matthew included the reference to Jonah because his Jewish readers would see the connection between Jesus and Jonah. Mark left this out because the reference to Jonah would mean little to Roman readers unfamiliar with the Old Testament.

Mark 10:46–52 (see Matthew 20:29–34)

Mark 11:11–14 (see Matthew 21:12–19)

Mark 13:1–3 (see Matthew 24:1–3)

Mark 13:4 (see Matthew 24:3)

Mark 13:28–30 (see Matthew 24:32–34)

Mark 14:1 (see Matthew 26:6–13)

Mark 14:30 (see Matthew 26:34)

Mark 14:36 (see Matthew 26:39–44)

Mark 14:47 (see Matthew 26:51)

Mark 15:1 (see Matthew 26:59)

Mark 15:25

Was Jesus crucified at the "third hour" or at the "sixth hour" (John 19:14)?

Mark 15:25 records that it was the "third hour" when Jesus was crucified. But John 19:14 records that it was "about the sixth hour."

The difference between the two accounts can be attributed in part to different ways of calculating time. John, it appears, followed the Roman time system, which counted the hours from midnight to midnight. Accordingly, the "sixth hour" would be 6:00 A.M. Mark, on the other hand, was following the Jewish custom of counting the hours from daybreak. Mark's "third hour" would be 9:00 A.M.

Close examination of the text indicates that Jesus' trial concluded about 6:00 A.M. (John) and that Jesus was crucified at 9:00 A.M. (Mark). During the intervening period Jesus was taken from the court of Pilate, mocked by the Roman soldiers, led to Golgotha, and prepared for crucifixion.

Mark 16:9–20

Are the last twelve verses of Mark part of the original text?

There are actually four possible endings to the gospel of Mark. Which ending represents the original text? The problem is significant, for if an ending is not authentic, then it is not divinely inspired. The four endings are as follows:

The Codex Washingtonianus. In the fourth century A.D., the traditional ending of Mark was circulated in an expanded form (beginning after verse 14). This text is preserved by Jerome and the Codex Washingtonianus.

Two verses after Mark 16:8. An abbreviated ending of Mark is attested by four Greek manuscripts from the seventh, eighth, and ninth centuries. It reads:

> And they promptly reported all these instructions to Peter and his companions. And after that, Jesus Himself sent out through them from east to west the sacred and imperishable proclamation of eternal salvation.

The last twelve verses absent. The last twelve verses of Mark are absent from the two oldest complete manuscripts of the Greek New Testament— Codex Vaticanus and Codex Sinaiticus. Eusebius and Jerome write that the passage in question was absent from almost all Greek manuscripts known to them. It is argued that the last twelve verses of Mark differ in style and vocabulary from Mark 16:1–8. It is also pointed out that the connection between 16:8 and 16:9 is awkward. Most of those who take this position believe that the last page of Mark's manuscript was lost and the last twelve verses were added by someone who wanted to supply a more appropriate conclusion.

The Traditional Ending. The traditional ending, found in the KJV and other translations of the Textus Receptus, is supported by a vast number of Greek manuscripts and two very early witnesses—Irenaeus (A.D. 202) and the Diatessaron (second century A.D.). In his review of W. R. Farmer's *The Last Twelve Verses of Mark* (Cambridge University Press, 1974), Hodges warns:

> The reviewer recommends that all teachers and students of the Greek text read this volume carefully before they make any public utterance which could cast doubt on the validity of an ending to Mark which is

found in the overwhelming majority of the surviving Greek manuscripts and which is attested by supporting evidence earlier than any manuscript which omits it.[1]

Mark 16:16

Is baptismal regeneration being taught in this verse?

The words of Jesus, "He who has believed and has been baptized shall be saved," may lead someone to think that baptism is necessary for salvation. However, the very next phrase reveals clearly that this is not the case. Jesus goes on to say, "but he who has disbelieved shall be condemned." The only basis for condemnation is a refusal to believe. There is no condemnation for failure to be baptized. It may be concluded that the only basis for salvation is belief in Christ—not belief and baptism.

While baptism does not save, it is not unimportant. The New Testament knows of no believer that is not baptized. Those who believed were identified with Christ and His local body of believers by baptism (compare Acts 2:41; 8:36–38; 16:31–33).

Mark 16:17–18

Should Christians be miracle workers?

Christ promised that certain signs or miracles would characterize the apostolic age. Paul referred to these miracles as the "signs of a true apostle" (2 Cor. 12:12). Miracles did follow the proclamation of the Gospel from Jerusalem to Samaria and throughout the Roman world. God used these miracles to introduce the church age and to authenticate the message and messengers of that new era.

Is Jesus commanding that we do these things? Some say yes. "I handle serpents because it's in the Bible, like a commandment," explains a church leader from an Appalachian mining town. "And I drink poison like strychnine because the Bible says it won't hurt me. Now, either every word in that Bible is right or it's wrong."

This is not a matter of whether the Bible is right or wrong. It is the issue of whether this text applies to us. I suggest that the promise of immunity to snakebites and poison was given in the context of persecution during the apostolic age. Jesus is referring to situations where persecutors would force believers to do certain life-threatening things. Grassmick points out that in the Greek, the first two clauses in verse 18 may be understood as conditional clauses with the third clause as the conclusion.[2] Accordingly, Jesus is saying, "If they are compelled to pick up snakes, and if they are compelled to drink deadly poison, it shall not harm them."

A thorough study of apostolic miracles indicates that they fulfilled their function in the apostolic era and ceased around A.D. 70. This is evidenced by the decline in miracles following Pentecost, with none being recorded in the last decade of the apostolic age. The early church fathers Chrysostom and

Augustine confirm the fact that there was an absence of miracles after the apostolic age.

While there may be miracles today, there is no biblical basis for us to expect them. And events people often claim to be miracles do not match the biblical pattern of apostolic miracles. Jesus told His generation that there would be no more miracles presented them except one—the sign of Jonah—the Resurrection (Matt. 12:39). I suggest that we focus on the one great miracle—Christ's resurrection—rather than seeking miraculous ministries.

Endnotes

1. Z. C. Hodges, review of *The Last Twelve Verses of Mark,* by W. R. Farmer, *Bibliotheca Sacra* 133 (April–June 1976): 178.
2. John D. Grassmick, "Mark" in *The Bible Knowledge Commentary* (Wheaton: Victor Books, 1983), 196.

LUKE

Luke 2:2

Was Luke mistaken in linking the census with the governorship of Quirinius?

Quirinius was actually governor of Syria twice (3–2 B.C. and A.D. 6–7). But neither of these periods fit what we know to be the date of Christ's birth (5–4 B.C.), before the death of Herod (see on Matt. 1:25). Many solutions have been offered to resolve this problem, but the most reasonable one was presented by Higgins, who translates Luke 2:2, "This census took place *before* Quirinius was governor of Syria."[1] In this context, *prote* (first) is virtually equivalent to *pro* (before), as in John 15:18. Luke is merely stating that the census at the time of the Nativity took place some time *before* Quirinius held office. Hoehner suggests that the census would have occurred after Herod fell into disfavor with Augustus in 8–7 B.C. and was probably after Herod's execution of Alexander and Aristobulus in 7 B.C. As Herod's illness became more intense it is likely that Augustus would have wanted to have a census and to estimate the condition of the state before Herod's death. "Therefore, a census within the last year or two of Herod's reign would have been reasonable, and in fact, most probable."[2]

Luke 3:23–38

Why does Luke present a different genealogy for Jesus than the one in Matthew?

Matthew's genealogy *descends* from Abraham to Jesus. Luke's *ascends* from Jesus, past Abraham, to Adam. Matthew gives the genealogy of Joseph, proving Jesus' legal right to the throne of Israel. Luke gives the genealogy of Mary, linking Jesus not only with Israel, but with the whole human race. Matthew traces the Davidic line through Solomon (Matt. 1:7), while Luke traces the line through Nathan (Luke 3:31). Both genealogies demonstrate Jesus' right to the throne as an heir of David.

Luke 4:5–12 (see Matthew 4:1–11)

Luke 6:17–49

How do we account for the differences between Luke's and Matthew's versions of the Sermon on the Mount?

It is clear that Matthew and Luke record two similar but distinctly different discourses. Luke places the discourse after the call of the Twelve, while Matthew places it after the call of the first four disciples (Matt. 4:18–22), about a year earlier. Matthew records a sermon on a "mount," while Luke records a sermon Christ preached on a "level place" (Luke 6:17). Matthew records that Jesus sat down (Matt. 5:1), while Luke records that Jesus stood (Luke 6:17). The sermon recorded by Luke contains only 30 verses while the sermon recorded by Matthew contains 107 verses. Not a single truth in Luke is in the same phraseology and language as the corresponding truth found in Matthew. It is most likely that Jesus repeated the essential message of the "sermon on the mount" on at least two different occasions during His ministry.

Luke 8:26 (see Mark 5:1–2)

Luke 9:51–19:18

How should we understand and interpret Luke's travel narrative in Luke 9:51–19:18?

Luke clearly indicates that Jesus was traveling to Jerusalem (9:51; 13:22; 17:11). The difficulty arises in trying to trace the course of His journey. Jesus began by going through Samaria (9:52), but later He was at Bethany (10:38–42). Luke then placed Him "between Samaria and Galilee" (17:11), and still later Luke said He was at Jericho (19:1). The apparent disarray of the topographical notices has led many to question the geographical accuracy of Luke.

Many scholars have concluded that Luke's account does not record a literal journey but is a collection of detached episodes arranged around a travel motif. It is believed that Luke had a great deal of miscellaneous teaching by Jesus that he needed to set in some historical context. So he invented a travel story as a place to deposit this material. But it has been noted that Luke's three references to Jesus making His way to Jerusalem correspond closely to John's mention of three journeys to Jerusalem during the last six months of His ministry (John 7:2, 10; 10:22; 12:1).[3] This suggests that Luke's central section is substantially more geographically accurate than some have supposed. Apparently Luke records three journeys that Jesus made to Jerusalem during the last six months of His ministry. These journeys to Jerusalem correspond quite well to the account given by John.

Luke 9:60

What did Jesus mean, "Allow the dead to bury their own dead"?

In Luke 9:59–61, Jesus is teaching that the kingdom of God takes priority over other temporal issues. When calling a follower, someone responded, "Permit me first to go and bury my father" (v. 59). Burial was a very important duty in Jewish society. According to the Talmud, it took precedence over the study of the law, temple service, killing the Passover lamb, and the observance of circumcision (*Megillah* 3b). But Jesus taught that the demands of the kingdom are the highest priority. He said, "Allow the dead to bury their own dead" (v. 60). By this He meant that the *spiritually* dead could care for those who are *physically* dead.

It is probable that the man's father was not dead at the time he spoke to Jesus. His words were more of an excuse. He was saying, "Let me take care of my father until his death, and then I'll follow You." Jesus was teaching that those who are alive to Christ should make His kingdom their highest priority.

Luke 11:29–30 (see Mark 8:11–13)

Luke 12:10 (see Matthew 12:31–32)

Luke 16:1–8

Why did the master commend his servant who dealt fraudulently with his master's accounts? The story seems to present this scoundrel as a praiseworthy example.

This account follows Luke 15, which emphasizes that God is seeking to save the lost. The parable of the unjust servant is designed to show the disciples and those listening their need of responding to the graciousness of God. The servant who is being dismissed from his position masterminds a plan to guarantee a secure future. He introduces a plan of debt reduction to his master's debtors, reducing each debt. In the ancient world, relationships were built on the principle of reciprocity—a favor is returned. By decreasing the obligations of those indebted to his master, the wise servant secured his own future. Those who had benefited from his kindness, though fraudulent, would be obligated to demonstrate an appropriate good turn.

The master commends the servant's shrewdness in recognizing his need and seizing upon the opportunity available to him. He had the authority to abrogate the servant's arrangement with the debtors. But he responded graciously. The parable does not commend the servant for dishonesty but for responding wisely to the opportunity before him. The ministry of Jesus confronted people with the opportunity to do something about their future. The wise person will respond to such opportunity, receiving God's grace and commendation. God is even more gracious than the master was to the unjust servant. No matter what you have done, He will graciously forgive and receive you.

Luke 16:19–31

What does the story of the rich man and Lazarus teach about eternal punishment?

The parable of the rich man and Lazarus was intended to teach those who love money (Luke 16:14) that riches do not guarantee one's entrance into God's kingdom. When the poor man died, he went to be with Abraham in a place of blessing. But when the rich man died, he went to "Hades," a term used here to refer to the place of the (wicked) dead. It is important to understand that his riches did not send him to Hades. The parable is designed to show that his riches did not keep him from Hades! Many Jews in Christ's day thought that riches were a sign of God's approval and meant deliverance from judgment. Jesus taught that deliverance from judgment comes only through belief in His person (John 3:18).

The parable of the rich man and Lazarus teaches several important lessons about eternal punishment: First, there is conscious torment (vv. 24, 28). Second, there are flames (v. 24). Third, there is no escape (v. 26). Fourth, riches won't keep you from going there (vv. 22–23).

Luke 17:21

Did Jesus teach that the kingdom of God was internal and spiritual rather than physical and literal?

Jesus statement, "the kingdom of God is in your midst" (Luke 17:21), has been interpreted to mean that He did not anticipate a physical, literal kingdom for Israel. A careful study of the biblical teaching on the kingdom of God shows that it is both spiritual and literal, both present and future. There is abundant evidence that Christ and His disciples anticipated a future kingdom (Matt. 25:34; 26:29; Luke 19:11; 22:30; Acts 1:6; 1 Cor. 15:50; 2 Tim. 4:18; Rev. 20:1–6)). While a future, literal kingdom cannot be denied, Scripture also teaches that the kingdom of God is developing as a spiritual reality in this present age (Matt. 5:20; 13:11; Luke 18:16; John 3:3, 5; Col. 1:13; 4:11).

The kingdom of God involves God's people, in God's place, under God's rule. This kingdom was inaugurated through the coming of the promised Messiah. God's kingdom is a present, developing reality, to be fully realized at the return of the King. Then all that which was promised David (2 Sam. 7:12–16) will be consummated—the throne, the dynasty, and the kingdom. And Christ, the King, will reign throughout eternity (Luke 1:32–33).

Luke 23:43

If Jesus died and was buried for three days, how could He tell the thief on the cross, "Today you shall be with Me in Paradise"?

Although Jesus' physical body was buried for three days, the immaterial part of His body (His "spirit") was immediately reunited with God the Father. This is suggested by His words on the cross, "Father, into Thy hands I commit My spirit" (Luke 23:46; see also 2 Cor. 5:8). The teaching that Christ first descended to hell is based on a misinterpretation of Ephesians 4:8–9 (see on Eph. 4:9) and is not included in the earliest editions of the Apostle's Creed.

Luke 24:50–51

Did Jesus ascend from Bethany, or from the Mount of Olives as recorded in Acts 1:9–12?

The village of Bethany is located on the east slope of the Mount of Olives, about a mile and a half from Jerusalem. Luke records that Jesus walked with the disciples "as far as Bethany" (Luke 24:50). There He blessed the disciples and ascended. The disciples then returned to Jerusalem "from the mount called Olivet" (Acts 1:12). Luke wrote both accounts and saw no contradiction between the statements. Contrary to popular tradition, Jesus ascended from the eastern slope of the Mount of Olives near Bethany rather than from the summit.

Endnotes

1. A. B. J. Higgins, "Sidelights on Christian Beginnings in the Graeco-Roman World," *The Evangelical Quarterly* 41 (October 1969): 197–206.
2. Harold H. Hoehner, *Chronological Aspects of the Life of Christ* (Grand Rapids: Zondervan, 1977), 23.
3. H. E. Gilleband, "The Travel Narrative in St. Luke," *Bibliotheca Sacra* 80 (1923): 237–45.

JOHN

John 1:1

What is the meaning of the Greek word translated "Word" (logos) used in John 1:1–18?

In the first century, the *logos* was an established philosophical concept that John drew upon, added to, and enriched to communicate truth about the Person of Christ. In Greek thought, the *logos* was a bridge between the transcendent (holy) God and the material (evil) universe. Philo (about 20 B.C.–A.D. 54), an Alexandrian Jew, used the term to denote the intermediate agency by which God created material things and communicated with them. In Jewish thought, the "word" (*memra* in Aramaic) was sometimes substituted for God's name. The "word" was understood as the instrument for the execution of His will or the personification of His revelation.

There are various shades of meaning to the term *logos* that were familiar to both Jews and Greeks of the first century. John draws from this concept but enriches the meaning. The divine *Logos*, Jesus, is more than a mediating principle. He is a divine person! He is more than the personification of God's revelation. He is the incarnation of God! In the prologue of his gospel (1:1–18), John emphasizes the personal existence and incarnation of the divine *Logos*.

*Does this verse teach that the Word (*logos*) is divine?*

The statement, "the Word was God," means that Jesus, the *Logos,* is divine. The Jehovah's Witness *New World Translation* translates this phrase, "the Word was *a* god," denying the Trinity and the deity of Christ. According to this view, Jesus was a semideity. But John has expressed the view in the very best way possible. By avoiding the use of the definite article (the), he has emphasized the divine *character* of the *Logos*. The *Logos* participates in the very essence of divine nature! Had John used the article, he would have expressed the error of Sabellius, who held that the Father and Son were one person. This would have contradicted John's previous statement, which distinguishes the Father and Son.

John 1:12

What does it mean to "believe" in Jesus?

The word *pisteuo* (believe) is used ninety-eight times in John's gospel and essentially means to "trust." It never refers merely to intellectual agreement with a proposition. Belief involves a personal response of reliance upon and commitment to a truth. John uses several words as near synonyms to the word *believe*. Belief involves receiving Christ (John 1:12), obeying Christ (John 3:36), and abiding in Christ (John 15:1–10; 1 John 4:15).

A twenty-four-year-old Portland, Oregon, resident demonstrated the biblical concept of belief when she placed her life in the hands of high-wire artist Philippe Petit. At the dedication of the new concert hall, Petit *carried* Ann Seward across a wire strung eighty feet above a Portland street. Afterward, Seward commented, "I think that one of the most beautiful things about the performance was that it took a lot of trust—absolute trust." And that is what it means to believe in Jesus—to trust Him and His redemptive work to carry us safely to heaven.

John 1:14

Was Jesus, the divine Logos, "begotten" by God?

The word translated "only begotten" here and in John 3:16 is the Greek word *monogenes*. The word *mono* clearly means "one" or "only." But there is debate as to whether *genes* is derived from *genos* (kind) or *gennao* (to beget). It is helpful to note that the term is used in Hebrews 11:17 of Isaac, who was not Abraham's only-begotten son. Abraham was also the father of Ishmael. This suggests that "only begotten" may not be the best translation. Recently, scholars and translators propose that *monogenes* might best be rendered "unique" or "one-of-a-kind."

John 1:21

In light of the statements in Luke 1:17; Matthew 11:11–14; 17:10–13, why did John the Baptizer deny that he was "Elijah"?

Based on the prophecy of Malachi 4:5, the Jewish people of the first century expected that Elijah would personally return before the Day of the Lord. The religious leaders questioning John were wondering if he was Elijah the Tishbite, who had returned in the flesh. John answered no! He was not Elijah himself, but he came "in the spirit and power of Elijah" (Luke 1:17), thus fulfilling Malachi's prophecy.

John 2:1–11

Since Jesus made wine, is it wrong for Christians to drink it?

The Bible quite clearly condemns drunkenness—an improper use of an alcoholic beverage (Eph. 5:18). God's judgment on an improper use of wine appears to be reflected in His judgment on Nadab and Abihu (Lev. 10:1–7). This incident is followed by God's instruction to Aaron, "Do not drink wine or strong drink, neither you nor your sons with you, when you come into the tent of meeting, so that you may not die" (v. 9). The Bible also provides cautions regarding the misuse of alcoholic beverages (Prov. 23:29–35). Proverbs 20:1 declares, "Wine is a mocker, strong drink a brawler, and whoever is intoxicated by it is not wise." In keeping with such warnings, Paul says that elders and deacons are not to be "addicted to wine" (1 Tim. 3:3, 8).

In spite of these warnings, the Scriptures recognize that wine is one of God's gifts to His people (Ps. 104:15). Wine is associated with joy and blessing (Deut. 7:13; Eccl. 9:7–10; Amos 9:13–14; Joel 3:18). This perspective is reflected by Paul's words in Colossians 2:20–23 and 1 Timothy 4:1–5 where he condemns asceticism.

It is quite clear on the basis of historical research that in antiquity wine was diluted with water. The ratio would vary from place to place, but generally it was one part wine to three parts water. Only barbarians would drink unmixed wine. This cultural issue has bearing on the modern use of wine. Quite obviously, the wine purchased in stores today is unmixed. Its alcoholic content is considerably greater than that of the wine of the first century.

The high alcohol content of today's undiluted wine has led to much abuse and addiction. Alcoholism is the third-largest health problem in the United States today and is said to damage directly the lives of one out of every four or five Americans. Alcohol-related deaths run as high as two hundred thousand per year. Half of all traffic fatalities and one-third of all traffic injuries are alcohol-related. It has been estimated that ten million Americans are alcoholics, with more than three million of them teenagers.

Every Christian must make a decision whether to use or avoid the use of alcoholic beverages. There is no proof text for total abstinence, nor is there any text advocating social drinking. One must be guided by one's conscience and by the principles of the Word. This is an issue where consciences may differ (Rom. 14:1–5) and the application of the scriptural principles may vary, depending upon the situation at hand.

The principle of love-limited liberty must be kept in view when making a decision on this matter. The use of wine is an area of liberty—yet Paul suggests that Christian liberty should always be exercised with love and self-restraint (1 Cor. 8:9–13). He specifically declares, "It is good not to eat meat or to drink wine, or to do anything by which your brother stumbles" (Rom. 14:21).

John 3:3

What does Jesus mean by the phrase "born again"?

Jesus explains what He means by "born again" (literally, "born from above," Greek, *gennao anothen*) in the verses that follow (John 3:4–6). It is clear that Jesus is not talking about another physical birth. Physical birth happens only once. The new birth Jesus refers to is a spiritual rebirth. This involves entering into the new covenant through personal faith in Jesus Christ. The person who is born from above experiences a heavenly birth, wrought by the Holy Spirit, resulting in a regenerated life. The only way to enter God's kingdom, becoming one of His people, is through being "born again."

John 3:13

How do Jesus' words, "no one has ascended into heaven," reconcile
with the fact of Elijah's ascension (2 Kings 2:11)?

In this context, Jesus is referring to His authority to bring a message from
heaven. The point here is that no one has ascended to heaven to bring an
authoritative message back from God. So we are totally dependent upon Jesus.
He has authority to speak concerning heavenly things since He came from
heaven.

John 4:9

What was the stigma associated with being a "Samaritan"?

When the northern kingdom of Israel was conquered and exiled by Assyria
(722 B.C.), vast numbers of Israelites were forced from their homeland, and
foreigners were brought in from Mesopotamia to occupy the land (2 Kings
17:24). These newcomers brought with them their foreign gods and customs.
Yet they also recognized the importance of worshiping "the god of the land"
(v. 27). They soon developed a syncretistic religious system of idolatry and
the worship of Yahweh that was incorporated into the daily lives of the Israelites
remaining in the land. The Samaritan community of the first century had its
roots in this mixture of true and idolatrous worship.

Hostilities between the Jews and Samaritans increased when the returning
Judean exiles refused to allow the Samaritans to participate in the rebuilding
of the Jerusalem temple (Ezra 4:1–3). The temple that the Samaritans then
built on Mount Gerizim to compete with the Jerusalem sanctuary was
destroyed by a Jewish leader, John Hyrcanus, in 128 B.C. (Josephus
Antiquities 13.253–56). By New Testament times, the Samaritans were
regarded as apostate, unclean half-breeds. According to the Mishnah,
Samaritan women were deemed "unclean as menstruants from their cradle"
(*Niddah* 4.1).

John 5:3–4

Should these verses, explaining why the sick were gathered at the
pool of Bethesda, be regarded as authentic Scripture?

Many scholars do not regard these verses as authentic since they do not
appear in the oldest and best Greek manuscripts. For this reason, many
translations put the verses in the margin. New Testament scholar Zane Hodges
has offered six arguments for the originality of this material.[1] (1) Most Greek
manuscripts include the text. (2) The antiquity of the text is affirmed by
Tertullian in the third century. (3) The reading was widely diffused as evidenced
by the versions and church fathers. (4) In view of its content and connections
with the traditions of Bethesda, the text is unobjectionable on stylistic grounds.
(5) The deliberate omission from some manuscripts can be explained as
motivated by a falsely perceived "pagan tinge." (6) The statement about the

assembled sick in verse 3 and the response of the invalid in verse 7 demand the presence of verse 4 to make the text comprehensible.

In agreement with Hodges, I suggest that evidence for the authenticity of this text remains strong and compelling.

John 5:28–29

Does judgment according to one's deeds mean that salvation is based on works?

The Bible teaches very clearly that salvation is by grace, through faith, apart from meritorious works (Eph. 2:8–9). Yet there is a relationship between faith and works (James 2:14–26). While good works do not save, they may serve as the distinguishing marks of belief. Evil deeds, on the other hand, may reflect an attitude of unbelief (see John 3:36). While salvation is always a grace gift, the life one lives either validates or refutes the faith professed (compare Matt. 7:16–18; Titus 1:16). Those who commit "evil deeds" (John 5:29) are unbelievers who will be resurrected and judged.

John 5:31

What did Jesus mean by His words, "My testimony is not true"?

Jewish tradition held that self-testimony without supporting witnesses (Deut. 19:15) could not be regarded as legally valid. The Mishnah records the teaching of the rabbis that "none may be believed when he testifies of himself" (*Ketuboth* 2.9). Jesus' statement should be understood in the context of a Jewish court. His testimony would not be legally admissible if it stood alone.

John 6:15

Why did Jesus reject the attempt of the multitude to make Him king?

The Jews of Jesus' day longed for a dynamic and powerful figure who could lead them in their political struggle against Rome. Suffering so long under Roman rule, they were eager for an anointed king from among their own ranks. Jesus had the qualities and credentials that commended Him to leadership, and the people decided to make Him king by force. By popular demand, they intended to force kingship upon Him, enlisting Him to lead them in their opposition against Rome.

As sincere as this effort may have appeared to the disciples, Jesus knew that the crowds were more interested in being fed (6:26–27). He rejected this superficial offer of kingship and immediately sent His disciples away by boat and withdrew to a mountain to pray (Matt. 14:22; Mark 6:45). Before He rules them as their king, His people must accept Him by personal faith.

John 6:53–54

What did Jesus mean when He told the disciples that they must "eat" His flesh and "drink" His blood?

In these verses Jesus uses the very strong metaphor of eating and drinking to illustrate the necessity of assimilating His person. The words "eat" and "drink," denote the operation of the mind in receiving, understanding, and digesting the truth. A similar use of this metaphor appears in the apocryphal Ecclesiasticus where wisdom speaks, "Those who eat me will hunger for more, they who drink me will thirst for more" (24:21).

The cause-and-result formula for eternal life is illuminated by the parallel in John 6:40: "Everyone who looks to the Son and believes in him shall have eternal life" (NIV). If the results are the same (eternal life), then the actions leading to this result must be theologically equivalent. Eating and drinking Christ is another way of saying "looking to and believing in Christ."

John 7:8

Was Jesus lying to His brothers when He said, "I do not go up to this feast"?

Jesus' brothers recognized the eschatological implications of the Feast of Tabernacles (Zech. 14:6) and suggested that if Jesus wanted to present Himself to the world (John 7:4), this would be an excellent opportunity to do so. Although Jesus replied, "I do not go up to this feast" (v. 8), He later went "in secret" (v. 10). Various answers have been offered for this difficulty. A few manuscripts add the word "yet" in verse 8, thus smoothing the text and eliminating the problem. Some commentators suggest that Jesus simply changed His mind. I suggest that while Jesus negated His brothers' request to present Himself publicly in Jerusalem at the Feast of Tabernacles, He was not denying the possibility of attending the feast in a different manner later on. John 7:10 makes it clear that He would attend the feast but not in a public manner or for the purpose that His brothers had suggested.

John 7:38

What Scripture is Jesus referring to here?

Although some have linked Jesus' words with Ezekiel 47:1–11, I suggest the Scripture He had in mind was Isaiah 44:3, "I will pour out water on the thirsty land . . . ; I will pour out My Spirit on your offspring."

John 7:53–8:11

Should the story of the adulterous woman be considered part of the original text?

Serious questions are raised as to the authenticity of the passage about Jesus and the adulterous woman. It has been argued that this passage is (1) absent in the oldest and best manuscripts, versions, and patristic citations; (2) foreign to the context; and (3) linguistically incompatible with the vocabulary and style of the fourth gospel. The objections have led some to conclude that while the account is historical, it was not original to John's gospel.

In spite of the questions, doubts, and denials regarding John 7:53–8:11, several insightful arguments have been set forth in favor of its authenticity.

The Stylistic Trait. Johnson has observed a stylistic trait in the fourth gospel of introducing short explanatory phrases to interpret the significance of words just spoken.[2] Note the following:

6:6	And this He was saying to test him.
6:71	Now He meant Judas.
11:13	Now Jesus had spoken of His death.
11:51	Now this he did not say on his own initiative.
13:11	For He knew the one who was betraying him.
13:28	Now no one of those reclining . . . knew for what purpose He had said this to him.

This very stylistic trait is observable within the questioned passage. "And they were saying this, testing Him" (John 8:6). Since this interjectory statement is a part of the whole narrative, it can be argued that the passage is an integral and authentic part of the whole gospel.

The Controversy Pattern. Trites works along different lines but comes to the same conclusion as Johnson. He has demonstrated that the same type of controversy language, imagery, and terminology that is observed in John 1–12 is also evident in 7:53–8:11.[3]

Tracing this controversy pattern through chapters 1–12, Johnson points out that the forensic language used in John depicts a cosmic lawsuit between God and the world. The Jews appeal to their law, and Jesus appeals to His witnesses (John the Baptist, Scripture, His works, and the Father). All this is presented to achieve the purpose that the author has stated in John 20:30–31. It is quite significant that this controversy pattern, evidenced throughout the book, is displayed in 7:53–8:11. Note the forensic language and imagery.

8:3	Judicial examination
8:4	Accusers involved
8:6	Challenge presented
8:6, 10	Legal words
8:9	Case collapses
8:10–11	Verdict pronounced

Whatever textual problems may be associated with the passage, Trites argues that there is no overriding contextual problem.[4] The case of the adulterous woman fits admirably into the controversy developed in John 1–12.

The Textual Evidence for Inclusion. Hodges presents textual evidence in favor of the pericope.[5] He points out that evidence for the inclusion of this story is very early and that the passage is found in a very large majority of the surviving Greek manuscripts. There are about 450 Greek texts that include the pericope.

Hodges also appeals to evidence from the church fathers to argue for the authenticity of the text. He cites Jerome (about 420), who writes, "in the Gospel according to John in many manuscripts, both Greek and Latin, is found the story of the adulterous woman who was accused before the Lord."[6] He also quotes the explanation of Augustine (about 430) for the absence of the passage in some manuscripts: "certain persons of little faith, or rather enemies of the true faith, fearing, I suppose, lest their wives should be given impunity in sinning, removed from their manuscripts the Lord's act of forgiveness toward the adulteress, as if He who had said, 'sin no more' had granted permission to sin."[7]

Hodges presents convincing evidence from Greek manuscripts, early translations, and the church fathers for regarding the text as authentic. The vast majority of the surviving Greek manuscripts of John's gospel contain the story, and it is likely to have always been found in the majority of the extant Greek texts of every period.

It is quite clear that the evidence against the inclusion of this passage is not as overwhelming as it is sometimes made out to be. We should exercise considerable caution before suggesting that John 7:53–8:11 is not part of Scripture.

John 8:11

Did Jesus do away with the death penalty for adultery?

The law clearly required the death penalty for one found guilty of adultery (Lev. 20:10; Deut. 22:22–27). The fact that a man was not brought with her suggests that the incident was "set up" to catch the woman so as to confront Jesus with a difficult dilemma—to adhere to Jewish law (calling for an execution) or to support Roman law (which prohibited Jews from exercising the death penalty in most cases). Whose law was Jesus going to support? The law of the Jews also required that those who testified at a trial could not be "malicious" witnesses (Deut. 19:16), promoting violence and perverting justice. Since the woman was clearly guilty, Jesus called for her to be stoned (John 8:7). But in keeping with the law (Deut. 19:16–19, 21), He demanded that the execution be initiated by qualified (nonmalicious) witnesses. Those present recognized that they were not qualified and so the woman was set free. Jesus neither condemned her nor condoned her adultery. He simply said, "from now on sin no more" (John 8:11).

John 9:39

How do we reconcile Jesus' statement, "For judgment I came into this world," with the words in John 3:17, "God did not send the Son into the world to judge the world"?

Although these statements may appear contradictory, they are saying different things. The difference is between purpose and result. Jesus did not come for the *purpose* of condemnatory judgment (John 3:17), but His coming *results* in sifting or separation as people are divided according to their responses to Him. The inevitable result of Christ's coming is that people must make a decision for or against Him—and this decision determines their destiny.

John 10:28–29

Although no one is able to "snatch" the sheep out of God's hand, can they remove themselves from His protection and care? Can believers become lost, or are they eternally secure?

Jesus uses a double negative in verse 28 to emphasize that His sheep "shall never perish." To emphasize further the security of His sheep, He declares, "No one shall snatch them out of My hand." The word "snatch" *(arpazo)* is used in 10:12 of the wolf's attack and suggests an act of aggression or violence. Eternal security rests not on believers' ability to cling but on Christ's infinite power to keep His own in His hand. The sheep (true believers) may feel secure because they are secure. Since salvation is God's work, it is not something that people can undo. Other Scripture verses offer further evidence of the believer's security in Christ.

1. The Holy Spirit places believers in the body of Christ (1 Cor. 12:13). There is no evidence in Scripture that believers are ever removed from the universal body of Christ.
2. The Holy Spirit seals believers until the day of redemption (Eph. 1:13; 4:30). Loosing one's salvation would involve breaking God's seal before the day of final redemption.
3. God has begun a process that leads from predestination to glorification without any possibility for loss (Rom. 8:28–30).
4. No one can charge God's elect with anything that could cause them to lose their salvation (Rom. 8:33).
5. The Lord Jesus continually intercedes for believers (Heb. 7:25; 1 John 2:1), and that is sufficient to keep us saved.
6. Nothing can separate a believer from the love of God that is in Christ Jesus (Rom. 8:39).

John 10:30

Do Jesus' words, "I and the Father are one," contradict the concept of the Trinity?

Here Jesus claims to share an essential unity with God the Father, but He does not deny the concept of the Trinity—three divine persons in a single godhead. The word "one" *(hen)* is neuter and speaks of one essence, not one person. To speak of one person would contradict what John said about the "face-to-face" *(pros ton theon)* relationship between God and the divine Logos (1:1). The Father and Son share a oneness of divine essence yet remain two distinct persons within the godhead.

John 10:34

What did Jesus mean by the words, "I have said you are gods"?

In John 10:34–36, Jesus is defending His claim to be God (v. 33). He does so by using the kind of biblical argument typically used by the rabbis. The words, "I have said you are gods," is a direct quote from Psalm 82:6 as translated by the Septuagint. The psalmist refers to the judges of Israel as "gods" *(elohim)* because they were to be God's representatives and administrators of His justice. From this historical situation, Jesus argues the principle that a divine commission may allow individuals to bear a divine title. Jesus is saying, "If the Bible calls 'gods' those who are no more than merely human, how much more would this title apply to Me, the one the Father has sanctified and sent!"

John 11:4

Was Jesus mistaken when He said that Lazarus's sickness was "not unto death"?

Jesus did not mean by these words that Lazarus would not die (compare 11:14, 21). Rather, He was saying that physical death would not be the final outcome of this sickness. Instead, Lazarus's death and miraculous resurrection would bring glory to God!

John 12:1–11 (see Matthew 26:6–13)

John 12:39–40

How is it that the Jews who were rejecting Jesus "could not believe"?

Verses 39–40 provide John's explanation for the unbelief so prevalent among the Jewish people who had witnessed Jesus' miracles. The words "they could not believe" express in the strongest possible terms the sovereignty of God over the Jews' rejection of Christ. John then offers a rather free rendering of Isaiah 6:10 to show that God sovereignly intended to blind the Jewish people to the truth of Jesus' message. These verses demonstrate that God's sovereign purposes have not been frustrated through the unbelief and opposition of evil people. Rather, His purposes have been accomplished.

This raises all sorts of theological objections such as, "How can God hold people responsible for their unbelief when it has been sovereignly determined by divine election?" There are mysteries for which God has not provided complete answers. But believers can be assured that God is good, loving, and just. And His sovereignty never does away with the principle of personal responsibility. God is sovereign over belief and unbelief, but each person must make a personal decision to trust in Christ. And apart from personal faith in Him, there is no salvation.

John 13:10

Does this verse teach the need for confession and cleansing from sin?

This text is often interpreted to teach the believer's need for confession and cleansing from occasional sin. The word "bathed" *(louo)* is interpreted to refer to the washing of regeneration (Titus 3:5), and the word "washed" *(nipto)* would point to the cleansing of 1 John 1:9. Accordingly, Jesus would be teaching, "If you have 'bathed' [been regenerated], then you need only to be 'washed' [cleansed from sin through confession]."

While those who teach this interpretation are emphasizing an important truth, there is no compelling reason from the context to interpret the text in this way. Although the bathing and washing imagery could well illustrate the teaching of Titus 3:5 and 1 John 1:9, spiritual cleansing from sin is not the point of this passage. First, Jesus was dealing with the problem of the disciples' lack of humility (Luke 22:24–27), not an issue of sin. Second, in His explanation (John 13:12–17), Jesus makes no reference to the washing of regeneration or the cleansing from sin. Third, Jesus commanded His disciples to follow His example (12:14–15, 17), and they have no authority to cleanse others from sin. Fourth, Judas's feet were washed, yet he was unsaved. There was no cleansing from the defilement of sin in his case. Jesus makes the lesson of this text clear in His explanation of the footwashing. The disciples are to manifest the attitude of humble servants in their relationships with one another.

John 14:13

What does it mean to pray "in Jesus' name"?

In ancient times a man's name was almost synonymous with his reputation. Children were often named or renamed to commemorate a significant event or to call attention to a character trait. The name of the prophet Samuel, "name of God," commemorates the fact that his birth was God's answer to Hannah's prayer. Moses changed the name of his successor, Hosea ("salvation"), to Joshua in order to remind him and the Israelites that "Yahweh is Salvation" (Num. 13:16).

Praying in Jesus' name means that a believer's requests are presented to the Father on the basis of Christ's person and work—all that He is and has done. Specifically, this means

1. to pray in accordance with all that Jesus' name stands for as divine Son of God who died for our sins;

2. to appeal to the Father on the basis of Jesus' merits and influence as the believers' High Priest (Heb. 4:14–16; 7:25);

3. to pray a prayer consistent with Jesus' holy and righteous character;

4. to request the Father for what Jesus would want;

5. to seek that which would glorify the Father (John 14:13; 17:4);

6. to pray believing that God will grant the request for Jesus sake (Matt. 21:22).

To pray in Jesus' name is like signing His name to our prayer. This is the kind of prayer God delights to answer!

John 14:28

In what way is God the Father "greater" than Jesus?

Jesus' words, "for the Father is greater than I" (compare 10:29), has given rise to the theological error that Christ is a created being and thus inferior to God the Father. The words in 14:28 must be understood in light of 10:30, "I and the Father are one." Jesus is clearly presented in John as the divine Son of God (20:30–31). Yet in relationship to His incarnation and messianic office, the Father is in a position of authority over Christ. While coequal with the Father in the godhead, in His incarnation Jesus became the submissive, obedient, subordinate Son (compare John 13:16; 1 Cor. 11:3; Phil. 2:6–8). Equality and hierarchy are not mutually exclusive concepts. The Father and the Son are equally divine, but the Father is "greater" by way of His position of authority.

John 15:2

What happens to the fruitless branches?

In John 15:1–2, Jesus teaches that fruitbearing results from abiding in Christ. In expounding the analogy of the vine and branches, Jesus explains that the fruitful branches are pruned in order to increase productivity. The fruitless branches, on the other hand, "He [God] takes away" *(airo)*. The word *airo* is used twenty-three times in John's gospel. In eight places it could be translated "take or lift up" (5:8–10, 12; 8:59; 10:18, 24). In thirteen places it must be translated "take away" or "remove" (11:39, 41, 48; 16:22; 17:15; 19:15, 31, 38; 10:1–2, 13, 15). How is Jesus using the word in this context?

Some commentators have argued that the fruitless branches are "lifted up" so they can receive exposure to the sun and thus produce abundant fruit. It has been suggested that the grapevine stalks, which usually lay on the ground, were raised during the growing season. There is no evidence that this was the practice in ancient Israel. The Mishnah speaks of two kinds of vines in Israel, the trellised and the ground-trained vine *(Peah* 7.8). Schultz points out that "most of the vines in Palestine trail on the ground, because it is believed that the grapes ripen more slowly under the shadow of the leaves."[8] Verse 6, describing the destruction of the fruitless vines, appears to contradict the view that the branches are "lifted" with a view to greater fruitfulness.

Most commentators interpret *airo* to refer to the removal of the unproductive branches.[9] This view fits best within the context of verse 6. The question remains, however, What is the ultimate fate of the fruitless branches?

Arminians have consistently interpreted the fruitless branches as Christians who lose their salvation. This viewpoint, however, is quite inconsistent with the words of Jesus in John 10:28–29. Others have argued that the fruitless branches represent true Christians who are removed to heaven by physical death, as God's final step in divine discipline. The major difficulty with this view is that verse 6 indicates that the removal of the fruitless branch is a prelude to judgment, not to blessed fellowship with Christ in heaven. Such a fiery destiny awaits only unbelievers (Matt. 3:12; 5:22; 18:8–9; 25:41; 2 Thess. 1:7–8; Rev. 20:15).

The view that best answers to the immediate context and to the theological themes of John's gospel is that the fruitless branches represent disciples who have had an external association with Christ that is not matched by an internal, spiritual union, entered by personal faith and regeneration. The fruitless branches are lifeless branches—branches without Christ. This view has the advantage of consistency with the immediate context and with John's theology of belief. John recognizes that *profession* of faith is not the same as *possession* (1:50; 2:11, 22; 6:69; 11:15; 16:30; 17:8; 20:8). The profession of some, like Judas, is false or superficial and does not result in salvation. This view is also consistent with first-century agriculture. The Mishnah speaks of a "defective grape-cluster" that is "cut off" (*Peah* 7.4) and "dead branches" (of trees) that are pruned or lopped off (*Shebiith* 2.3).

The major objection against interpreting the fruitless branches as unbelievers is the presence of the phrase "in Me" *(en emoi)*. How could a fruitless, unbelieving branch be "in Christ"? Godet has suggested that the words "in Me" may modify either the "branch" (adjectival) or the participle "bearing" (adverbial).[10] If interpreted adverbially, the verse would read, "He cuts off every branch that bears no fruit in Me." The bearing of fruit takes place "in the sphere of" *(en)* Christ—by His influence and enablement. The words "in Me" refer not to the place of the branch but to the process of fruit-bearing.

John 16:16

Was Jesus referring to His death followed by His postresurrection appearances or to His ascension followed by His second coming?

Among the commentators there are three major views as to the meaning of Jesus' announcement in 16:16. Some have suggested that spiritual insight regarding the person of Christ will follow His physical departure. According to this view a distinction is made between the two verbs translated "see." The first "see" *(theoreo)* is interpreted to mean physical sight, and the second "see" *(orao)* is taken to refer to spiritual sight or understanding. There is, however, no clear distinction between these two verbs in John's usage (compare 1:39; 14:19; 20:18). They appear to be used as synonyms in verses 16–17.

A second interpretation takes Jesus' announcement to refer to His second coming, which will follow His ascension to heaven. But then the "little while" must be extended to nearly two thousand years!

It seems best to understand Jesus to be referring, in verse 16, to the short time between His death and His resurrection. This view fits well with Jesus' similar remarks in John 14:18–19. Christ's resurrection appearances would follow shortly after His death. Three days after His death, Jesus appeared to His disciples in His resurrection body.

John 17:3

Is eternal life something believers get in heaven, or do we have it now?

In John 17:3, Jesus provides His definition of the eternal life that He has authority to confer. While we usually think of eternal life as something to be enjoyed in heaven after death, Jesus indicates that eternal life is a present possession. It is something we enjoy as believers here on earth and throughout eternity. Jesus equates eternal life with an intimate and personal knowledge of God the Father and Christ His Son. The word "know" *(ginosko)* speaks of an intimate relationship, not just an awareness of certain facts. This knowledge of God comes through Jesus Christ (1:18). Since "know" is in the present tense, Jesus must be referring to a growing and vital personal relationship with God. Eternal life may be defined as an ever-increasing knowledge of God the Father mediated through Christ the Son. Eternal life means an abundant, spiritual life with God—a life that will never end.

John 18:28

If Jesus ate the Passover with His disciples in the Upper Room on Thursday night, why had the Jews at the trial of Christ (Friday A.M.) not yet eaten their Passover?

The Synoptic Gospels indicate beyond reasonable doubt that Jesus ate the Passover (Matt. 26:17–20; Mark 14:16–17; Luke 22:13–14) with His disciples in the Upper Room the Thursday evening, Nisan 14, and was crucified on the next day, Friday, Nisan 15. However, John 18:28 (also 19:14) indicates that on the day of Jesus' trial and crucifixion the Jews had not yet eaten the Passover. How could the Jews anticipate Passover on the evening of Jesus' death while Jesus and the disciples had already observed the feast? How does John's account and the synoptics fit together?

Harold Hoehner's insightful study seems to offer the best theory for reconciling the data.[11] Hoehner suggests that two Passovers were observed by the Jews of Jesus' day on the basis of two different methods of reckoning a day. Earlier Israelites reckoned a day from sunrise to sunrise (compare Gen. 19:34; Josephus *Antiquities* 3.248). Accordingly, the day begins in the morning after the preceding night. This method of reckoning was employed by Jesus and the synoptics and was perhaps the custom followed in Galilee.

In later Israelite reckoning it was the practice to count the day beginning with the evening at sunset (compare Lev. 23:27; Deut. 16:4). This sunset-to-sunset reckoning appears to have been the official Jewish method of reckoning a day and was followed by the Judeans and used by John in his gospel.

According to this hypothesis, Jesus and His disciples observed Passover on Thursday, Nisan 14, with the Galileans. The Judeans sacrificed their Passover lambs Friday afternoon, Nisan 14 according to their reckoning, and observed the feast that evening. Other than the evidence for the two Jewish ways of reckoning, there is no explicit support for the theory in the New Testament or in the Mishnah, although it is interesting to note that the section of the Mishnah devoted to the Passover is titled, *Pesachim,* "Passovers." Numbers 9:1–14 does allow for a second Passover one month after Nisan 14 in the case of one who is unclean or on a distant journey. Perhaps this text served as the basis for what became a first-century tradition.

This hypothesis not only accounts for the data both in John 18:28 and in the synoptics, but also provides a precise fulfillment of Old Testament typology. According to this view, Jesus died on Friday afternoon at the time the Passover lambs of the Judeans were being sacrificed (John 19:36; compare 1 Cor. 5:7).

John 18:36

When Jesus said, "My kingdom is not of this world," was He denying the existence of a future, earthly kingdom?

In response to Pilate's question, Jesus admitted that He has a kingdom, but not as the world commonly understands kingdoms. Jesus' kingdom is a different sort of kingdom than Pilate would be thinking of. The words, "not of this world," mean that Jesus' kingdom does not take its origin or draw its power from the unbelieving world. Although Jesus' kingdom will eventually involve an earthly domain (compare 2 Sam. 7:12–16; Rev. 20:4–6), it will not depend on people for its establishment and support. Jesus never denied the fact that He had the right to a future, earthly kingdom. The point of His response to Pilate was that His kingdom would involve the exercise of heavenly, rather than earthly, power and dominion.

John 20:17

Why was Mary commanded by Jesus, "Stop clinging to Me, for I have not yet ascended to the Father"?

At His resurrection appearance to Mary Magdalene, Jesus gave her the command, "Stop clinging to Me, for I have not yet ascended to the Father." The negative particle *me* with the present imperative commands the cessation of an act in progress. The explanatory clause introduced by "for" *(gar)* follows. Complicated explanations have been offered as to why Mary could not touch Jesus before the ascension, especially since Thomas was invited to touch Him (20:27). Perhaps Jesus knew Mary's thoughts and did not want her to conclude that He had returned to stay.

The best solution for the explanatory clause is offered by McGhee, who suggests that the *gar* should be taken as the anticipatory conjunction "since" rather than the causal conjunction "for."[12] McGhee punctuates the text differently than traditional readings and renders verse 17, "Don't cling to Me. Since I have not yet ascended to the Father, go to My brothers and tell them I am ascending to My Father and your Father and My God and your God." Accordingly, Jesus is simply stating a matter of fact, that is, He has not yet ascended to the Father, not explaining why Mary should not cling to Him.

John 20:22

Did the disciples receive the Holy Spirit before Pentecost?

This verse has presented some difficulty in regard to the giving of the Holy Spirit. It seems clear from Acts 2:1–17 that the Spirit came upon the disciples at Pentecost. Was there some bestowal of the Spirit at this time? Those who take John 20:22 as a promise of the Spirit's coming at Pentecost fail to appreciate the full significance of the symbolic gesture associated with Jesus' words. He breathed on them and said, "Receive the Holy Spirit." He did not say, You will receive the Holy Spirit. The expression seems to imply that some gift was offered and bestowed then and there. It seems likely that this bestowal of the gift of the Spirit was a preliminary provision for the disciples during the fifty days until Pentecost. Although not wanting to detract from the significance of Pentecost for the church, John apparently thought it was necessary to mention in his gospel the provision of the Holy Spirit, which Jesus had promised His disciples (1:33; 7:37–39; 14:16–17, 26; 15:26–27; 16:13–15). The significance of this promise demanded an account of its fulfillment within John's gospel.

John 20:23

Were the disciples given authority to grant forgiveness of sins?

This verse has been used by the Roman Catholic Church as the biblical basis for the priest's authority to forgive sins. It is quite clear from the Bible that God is the One who has the power and authority to forgive sins (Isa. 43:25). Jesus, of course, had this authority and demonstrated it during His ministry (Mark 2:5–10). Is Jesus now granting the disciples divine authority to forgive sins?

A proper interpretation of this verse can be determined only on the basis of a careful study of the Greek grammar. The verbs "have been forgiven" and "have been retained" are both in the perfect tense. The perfect tense portrays past action and affirms an existing result. This means that God's action of forgiveness took place prior to the offering of forgiveness by Jesus' disciples. Mantey argues convincingly that both in Matthew 16:19 and in John 20:23 the grammar used by Jesus did not provide the disciples with personal authority to forgive sin.[13] He offers the disciples the privilege of giving assurance of the forgiveness of sins by correctly announcing the terms of forgiveness. In presenting the Gospel, the terms of salvation are presented. Acceptance by faith brings God's forgiveness. Unbelief means that guilt remains.

Endnotes

1. Zane Hodges, "The Angel at Bethesda—John 5:4," *Bibliotheca Sacra* (January–March 1979): 39.
2. Alan F. Johnson, "A Stylistic Trait of the Fourth Gospel in the Pericope Adulterae," *Bulletin of the Evangelical Theological Society* 9 (spring 1966): 91–96.
3. Allison A. Trites, "The Woman Taken in Adultery," *Bibliotheca Sacra* 131 (April–June, 1974): 137–46.
4. Ibid., 146.
5. Hodges, "The Woman Taken in Adultery (John 7:53–8:11): The Text," *Bibliotheca Sacra* 136 (October–December 1979): 318–32.
6. Jerome, "The Dialogue against the Pelagians" 2.27, quoted in Hodges, "The Woman Taken in Adultery," 330.
7. Augustine, "Adulterous Marriages" 2.7, quoted in Hodges, "The Woman Taken in Adultery," 330.

8. Merril C. Tenney, ed., *Zondervan Pictorial Encyclopedia of the Bible*, (Grand Rapids: Zondervan, 1975), s.v. "Vine, Vineyard."

9. For further study, see my article, "Abiding is Believing: The Analogy of the Vine in John 15:1–6," *Bibliotheca Sacra* 146 (January–March 1989): 55–66.

10. F. Godet, *Commentary on the Gospel of John,* 3d ed., 3 vols. (Edinburgh: T. & T. Clark, 1893), 162.

11. Harold Hoehner, *Chronological Aspects of the Life of Christ* (Grand Rapids: Zondervan, 1977), 76–90.

12. Michael McGhee, "A Less Theological Reading of John 20:17," *Journal of Biblical Literature* 105 (June 1986): 299–302.

13. James R. Mantey, "Evidence That the Perfect Tense in John 20:23 and Matthew 16:19 Is Mistranslated," *JETS* 16 (1973): 129–38.

ACTS

Acts 1:3

What is the meaning of the phrase, "the kingdom of God"?

The kingdom of God involves a King who rules, a people who are ruled, and a sphere in which this rule takes place. A key text that elaborates this subject is 2 Samuel 7:12–16, where God promised that one of David's descendants would reign over a kingdom forever. Throughout the Old Testament, the prophets and the people of Israel anticipated the coming of their Messiah King and the fulfillment of this kingdom promise.

The ultimate fulfillment of God's kingdom will be realized when Jesus Christ, descendant of David, takes the throne of Israel and rules over God's people forever. The fulfillment of the kingdom program with Jesus is clear from the words of Gabriel to Mary in Luke 1:31–33. Gabriel reports that Jesus is destined to receive the throne of David, to reign over the house of Jacob forever, and to rule a kingdom that has no end—all in fulfillment of 2 Samuel 7:12–16. Jesus presented the prophesied kingdom to Israel when He announced, "Repent, for the kingdom of heaven is at hand." Because Jesus was rejected, the culmination of His kingdom was delayed. Revelation 11:15 indicates that the kingdom promises will be realized following the Tribulation period, at the Second Advent, when the Jews accept Jesus as their Messiah (Zech. 12:10–13:1).

While a future, literal kingdom cannot be denied, Scripture indicates that the kingdom of God exists in the present age. While the kingdom is not the church, one might say that the church is the most visible and significant aspect of God's kingdom as it is developing today. The kingdom of God has been inaugurated by Christ's first coming, but it has not yet been culminated. The kingdom of God is a present, spiritual reality to be fully realized at the return of Christ. Then, the literal throne, dynasty, and kingdom (Luke 1:32–33) of God will be consummated and will continue throughout all eternity.

Acts 1:4

What was it that "the Father had promised"?

Jesus told the apostles to wait in Jerusalem until they received "what the Father had promised." God had promised His people the indwelling Spirit as divine enablement for kingdom living (Ezek. 36:27; Joel 2:28). Jesus

241

reaffirmed this promise in the Upper Room (John 14:16–17, 26; 16:7, 13) and before His ascension (Luke 24:49). After Pentecost, Peter acknowledged that the church had received "from the Father the promise of the Holy Spirit" (Acts 2:33).

Acts 1:12

How far is a "Sabbath day's journey"?

A Sabbath day's journey was calculated in biblical times as about two thousand cubits, or a half-mile. The distance limitation determined by Exodus 16:29, "let no man go out of his place on the seventh day," as interpreted by Numbers 35:5, which indicates that the city extends two thousand cubits outward from the walls.

Acts 1:18 (see Matthew 27:5)

Acts 1:26

Was the church wrong in choosing Matthias?

Some have argued that the church was wrong in replacing Judas with Matthias and that they should have waited for Paul to fill the vacancy. However, Paul would not have met the qualifications stipulated by the church. His apostleship was unique—an apostleship of a different order (1 Cor. 15:8–9; 2 Cor. 11:15). While the appointment of Matthias was recognized by the church (Acts 2:14; 6:2), it is clear that this was God's choice (1:24), not merely that of the church. There is nothing in the text that suggests God's disapproval of the selection of Matthias.

Acts 2:16–21

In what way was Joel 2:28–32 fulfilled in the events of Pentecost?

In Acts 2, Peter explains the tongues phenomenon by appealing to Joel's prophecy. There are five major viewpoints regarding how Joel is being used.

Complete Fulfillment. Amillennial interpreters see a complete fulfillment of Joel's prophecy. The outpouring of the Spirit ushered in the kingdom—the church age. They explain that the wonders in the skies were fulfilled at the Crucifixion, when darkness covered the land. But this view does not adequately explain how the wonders were fulfilled.

Nonfulfillment. Some premillennial interpreters believe that Peter was simply using Joel's prophecy as an illustration of what was transpiring in his day—not as a fulfillment of it. Peter was saying: "This is that Holy Spirit which was spoken of by Joel. You should recognize tongues as the work of God's Spirit." It is believed that Joel's prophecy will be fulfilled in a future day when the remnant of Israel believes. Problem: This view does not adequately explain the fulfillment formula, "This is what was spoken" (Acts 2:16).

Continuous Fulfillment. According to this view, Joel's prophecy began to be fulfilled at Pentecost and continues to be fulfilled in every age. The Holy Spirit is given to those of every age who ask for Him (Luke 11:13). Problem: No believer is commanded to ask for the Holy Spirit. Every believer receives the Spirit at conversion (Rom. 8:9, 14; 1 Cor. 12:13).

Partial Fulfillment. According to this view, Joel 2:28–29 was fulfilled at Pentecost, and verses 30–32 will be fulfilled at the end of the Tribulation in connection with the second coming of Christ. What has been made available at Pentecost will be appropriated and realized by Israel at the end of the Tribulation when the remnant of Israel receives Jesus as their Messiah (Isa. 32:15; 44:3; Zech. 12:10–13:1). Problem: Why did Peter quote verses 30–31 if they were not being immediately fulfilled?

Full Fulfillment. One objection to the partial view is that there are clear indications in Scripture that there will be some manifestation of the Holy Spirit in connection with the second advent of Christ (Isa. 32:15; 44:3; Zech. 12:10–13:1). This view involves a slight modification of the partial view and allows for the "filling up" of the prophecy at the Second Advent. The prophecy has been fulfilled and will be fulfilled *in full* at the Second Coming, when the physical wonders in the sky will also be realized.

Acts 2:38

Did Peter teach that baptism was necessary for salvation?

Baptism was viewed in ancient times as a public sign of faith, identifying a new believer with the Christian community. This meant severing ties with Judaism and becoming a follower of Jesus. The Bible teaches clearly that salvation and the forgiveness of sins is always through faith in Christ (Eph. 2:8–9), not the result of baptism. The phrase, *"for* the forgiveness of your sins," should be rendered *"because of* the forgiveness of your sins." This is an example of the causal use of the preposition *eis*.[1]

Acts 2:41

Were there enough pools and reservoirs to baptize three thousand people in Jerusalem during one day?

There were eight large pools in Jerusalem during the first-century period. In addition, there were hundreds of Jewish ritual pools *(mikva'ot)*. Forty-eight of these ritual pools have been excavated just south of the temple area. There were plenty of pools available to baptize new believers in Jerusalem.

Acts 3:19–20

Would Jesus have returned and set up His kingdom if the Jewish people had repented?

It seems likely that if the Jewish people had repented at Peter's preaching, there might have been a very short church age! But Peter was not locking himself into a time schedule for prophetic events. His point is simply that there can be no blessing until the Jewish nation changes its mind about Jesus. Jesus will not come bringing the blessings of the kingdom apart from Israel's repentance.

Acts 4:19–20

Are there times when a Christian may choose to disobey civil authority?

While Paul and Peter commanded believers to "be in subjection to the governing authorities" (Rom. 13:1–7; 1 Peter 2:13–17), there appear to be times when Christians may disobey governing authorities. "Civil disobedience" may be defined as any action taken by an individual citizen who, out of regard for personal conscience, violates the laws of government that are in conflict with the higher law of God.

We find numerous examples of civil disobedience in Scripture: the Hebrew midwives (Exod. 1:15–17), Moses' parents (vv. 22–2:3), Rahab (Josh. 2), Obadiah (1 Kings 18), Daniel's friends (Dan. 3), Daniel (Dan. 6), Peter and the apostles (Acts 4:19–20; 5:9), Paul (16:37–40). It seems clear from these examples that when civil law and the commands of Scripture are in opposition, we must recognize and obey the higher law—God's law. God's commands take precedence over all human authority (5:29).

Biblical examples of civil disobedience are seen in the following areas: (1) protection of innocent human life; (2) protection of God's people—the Hebrews and the prophets; (3) refusing to bow down to a false god; (4) refusing to cease personal worship of God; and (5) refusing to cease proclamation of the Gospel.

The following issues should be considered by anyone contemplating civil disobedience:

1. Civil disobedience is a last resort effort after other legislative measures have been tried and have repeatedly failed.
2. Civil disobedience should focus on priority issues—worship of God and issues of personhood (life, abortion, euthanasia, infanticide).
3. Make sure you know the consequences of your actions and are prepared to accept them.
4. Destruction of life or property violates other clear teachings of Scripture and is not warranted.
5. Those involved should not participate for the purpose of attracting attention to themselves or to gain a sense of superiority.
6. Believers are ambassadors for Jesus Christ and their attitudes and actions must be above reproach at all times.
7. One must come with a conviction of personal conscience that this is the right thing and the only thing to do. As for the consequences of civil disobedience, William Booth, founder of the Salvation Army, said, "No great cause ever achieved triumph before it devoted a certain quota to the prison population."

Acts 4:32–34

Did the early church practice communism?

The voluntary sharing of property to meet needs is not communism. Communism says, What is yours is mine. Christianity says, What is mine, is yours. The early Christians voluntarily shared from their own resources to help meet the physical needs of others. This was the logical extension of their practice of Christian fellowship (*koinonia,* Acts 2:42).

Acts 5:1–11

What was the sin of Ananias and Sapphira?

The sin of Ananias and Sapphira was not keeping back part of the proceeds from the sale of their property. It was pretending to give all when they gave only part. They pretended a greater sacrifice than they were willing to make. Their actions constituted a lie not just to people but to God (Acts 5:4).

Acts 5:36–37

Did Luke make a mistake in placing Theudas before Judas of Galilee?

Josephus tells us about a "prophet" called Theudas who led a large crowd of rebels to the Jordan, promising them that the river would be divided (*Antiquities* 20.97–99). His promise failed, and Theudas was executed (A.D. 44–46). Judas of Galilee led a religious and nationalist revolt in A.D. 6, but the movement was crushed by Rome (*Antiquities* 28.4–10). Some have suggested that Luke made a historical mistake in placing Theudas before Judas. But this view rests on the assumption that the "Theudas" referred to by Luke is the same "Theudas" mentioned by Josephus. Theudas was a sufficiently common name in the first century. It appears quite evident that Luke and Josephus were referring to two different individuals.

Acts 7:2

Was Stephen mistaken in saying that Abraham received God's call when he was living in Mesopotamia?

Genesis 11:31–32 records no divine call of Abraham at Ur in Mesopotamia. However, 12:1–4 records God's call from Haran. I suggest that Abraham received two calls. First, while living in Mesopotamia, he was called to leave Ur (compare Gen. 15:7; Neh. 9:7; Acts 7:2). Later, while living in Haran, he was called to go to Canaan (Gen. 11:31; 12:1–4).

Acts 7:6

Was Stephen mistaken when he referred to the period of Egyptian bondage as "four hundred years"?

Exodus 12:40 and Galatians 3:17 indicate that the Israelites lived in the land of Egypt for 430 years. This period began with Jacob's descent into Egypt (1876 B.C.) and ended with the Exodus (1440 B.C.). Genesis 15:13 and Acts 7:6 give this period as 400 years. Since there is not a textual problem here, I suggest that the 400 years represents a rounding down of the 430 figure.

Acts 7:15

Was Stephen wrong in saying that "seventy-five" of Joseph's relatives migrated to Egypt?

Exodus 1:5 records the number as "seventy." But Exodus 1:5 in the Septuagint, Acts 7:14, and one Hebrew manuscript from Qumran give the number as "seventy-five." This higher figure is apparently based on the Septuagint's listing of Joseph's three grandsons and two great-grandsons in Genesis 46:20.

Acts 7:16

Did Abraham purchase the tomb in Hebron or in Shechem?

The problem here is that Stephen names Abraham when the transaction at Shechem involved Jacob. Stephen appears to confuse Jacob's purchase of property at Shechem (Gen. 33:18–19; Josh. 24:32) and Abraham's purchase of the cave of Machpelah at Hebron (Gen. 23:16). This is a tough one!

It has been suggested that the two purchases of land are telescoped here in the same way the two separate calls of Abraham may have been telescoped in Acts 7:2.[2] Another possibility is that Abraham may have purchased property in Shechem (compare Gen. 12:6) long before Jacob arrived there. Later this property was reoccupied by Jacob, who negotiated the repurchase of Abraham's original tract.[3]

Acts 7:54–60

Did the Jews have the legal authority to stone Stephen?

In the New Testament period in Palestine, only Rome had the authority to carry out an execution (compare John 18:31). There was just one exception. The Jews could execute anyone who violated the sanctity of the temple. Josephus records the words of General Titus to the Jewish rebels, "And did we not permit you to put to death anyone who passed it [the barrier], even were he a Roman" (*Antiquities* 6.126). Stephen was charged with speaking against "this holy place," that is, the temple. His words may have been construed to constitute a violation of temple sanctity. If so, then the Jews may have justified a legal execution on this basis. On the other hand, the stoning of Stephen may have simply been an act of mob violence without any legal basis.

Acts 8:9–24

Was Simon the magician genuinely converted when he "believed."

Although Simon "believed" and was "baptized," the evidence indicates that he did not experience personal regeneration. Peter rebuked him, saying, "your heart is not right before God" (Acts 8:21). He viewed Simon as "in the bondage of iniquity" (v. 23) and urged him to "repent of this wickedness" and seek God's forgiveness (v. 22). It may be that Simon was like the Cretans who professed a relationship with God but were devoid of the reality (Titus 1:16). Jesus said, "You will know them by their fruits" (Matt. 7:20). What do you think? Does Simon give evidence of the fruit of faith?

Acts 8:37

Is this verse part of the original text?

Acts 8:37 is not found in the three major Greek manuscripts—Codex Sinaiticus (fourth century A.D.), Codex Alexandrinus (fifth century A.D.), Codex Vaticanus (fourth century A.D.). This suggests that the verse is not original to Acts but was added later, reflecting the early practice of a new believer making a public confession at baptism.

Acts 12:1

Who was this "Herod" who executed James and imprisoned Peter?

Acts 12:1 refers to Herod Agrippa (A.D. 37–44), the grandson of Herod the Great. He ruled practically the same territory as his grandfather.

Acts 13:14

Was Luke mistaken in using the designation "Pisidian Antioch"?

Historians point out that Antioch was actually in the province of Phrygia. This has been confirmed by two inscriptions. But Antioch was located very near Pisidia. Since Pisidia was the more prominent and well-known region, it was common to distinguish this Antioch as "Pisidian Antioch."

Acts 15:20

Does this verse prohibit a Christian from receiving a blood transfusion?

The prohibitions in Acts 15:20 are all based upon the laws and regulations given to Israel under the old covenant. Of concern to some is the command regarding blood. While the sacrificial system was functioning at the temple, the blood of animals had a special purpose. It was to be used only for atonement. It was not to be eaten or to be used in some secular way. The prohibition in Acts 15:20 regarding blood was a reminder to Gentile Christians not to offend the Jewish Christians by eating meat that had not been properly drained of blood. This was a cultural issue for first-century Jewish and Gentile believers. The prohibition has nothing to do with the medical practice of giving a blood transfusion.

Acts 16:3

Why did Paul circumcise Timothy after insisting in Galatians that this was unnecessary (Gal. 5:6; 6:12–15)?

The Jerusalem Council had declared that circumcision was not necessary for Gentiles (Acts 15:19). But because of Timothy's mixed family background (16:1), Paul thought it expedient to regularize and clearly identify his ethnic situation. Being circumcised would enlarge Timothy's usefulness for ministry, enabling him to go with Paul among Jewish populations. As Bruce remarks, in Timothy's case, circumcision was "nothing but a minor surgical operation performed for a practical purpose,"[4] not a religious rite.

Acts 16:22

Why didn't Paul appeal to his Roman citizenship to avoid this beating?

Roman law exempted Roman citizens from degrading forms of punishment. A Roman citizen would claim his legal rights by declaring, "I am a Roman citizen!" We wonder why Paul didn't appeal to his legal rights during this beating instead of the next day (Acts 16:37). We don't have a biblical answer to this question. Perhaps Paul did voice his Roman citizenship, but his words were either not heard or ignored.

Acts 18:23

Why did the Athenians have an altar to "the unknown God"?

The background of this altar is recorded for us by an ancient Greek writer, Diogenes Laertius, in his *Lives of Philosophers* (1.100). According to his account, around 600 B.C. a terrible plague broke out in Athens. It was believed by the city leaders that one of their many gods had been offended and had brought on the plague. Sacrifices were offered to the gods, but to no avail. Then Epimenides suggested that the Athenians had possibly offended an unknown god. He ordered that a number of sheep be released in Athens and that wherever they lay down, a sacrifice would be offered to an unknown god. Altars were built and sacrifices were offered. Soon the plague ended. When Paul visited Athens, one of these altars was still standing. He used the altar as a point of reference in preaching before the Areopagus.

Acts 19:1–7

What was the spiritual status of the disciples of John who had not yet received the Holy Spirit?

When Paul arrived at Ephesus he discovered twelve disciples of John the Baptizer. These men had responded to the message of John and had received his baptism. They were believing Jews who loved God and were looking for the coming of His Messiah. But they had not yet entered into the new covenant, receiving the indwelling ministry of the Holy Spirit. After Paul told them about Jesus, they were baptized and spoke with tongues. This served as a mini-Pentecost for this pocket of Jewish believers who had not yet heard that Jesus, the Messiah, had come. The historical situation makes this a unique experience during the transitional period of Acts.

Acts 19:10

Did Paul minister in Ephesus for two years or three?

Luke notes in Acts 19:9–10 that Paul taught at the school of Tyrannus for two years during his stay in Ephesus. Yet when addressing the elders of Ephesus, Paul comments that he ministered to them for three years. There is no real discrepancy between these two accounts. Paul arrived in Ephesus in the spring of A.D. 53 and remained there until the spring of A.D. 56, a period of three years. The "two years" in Acts 19:10 refers to the period of his teaching ministry at the school of Tyrannus.

Acts 21:4

Was Paul disobedient to the Spirit of God when he insisted on going to Jerusalem?

Some have argued that Paul's return to Jerusalem after his third missionary trip was an act of disobedience for which he was imprisoned for two years. It is argued that not only was Paul warned by the Holy Spirit (Acts 21:4), the prophet Agabus warned him of the consequences (vv. 10–11) and the believers at Caesarea asked him not to go (v. 12).

On the other hand, it is possible to view these warnings as a test of Paul's obedience. There is no clear command, "Don't go!" issued by God to Paul. Only his sufferings were predicted. Paul is never rebuked for going to Jerusalem, and he never refers to his imprisonment as the consequence of disobedience. God had told Paul from the beginning that his witness before "Gentiles and kings and the sons of Israel" would cost him much suffering (9:15–16). I suggest that Paul was willing to go to Jerusalem in spite of the personal suffering anticipated (20:24).

Acts 21:23–26

How could Paul agree to participate in Jewish temple ritual?

To correct a false interpretation of Paul's ministry (Acts 21:21), the Jerusalem elders proposed that Paul join four Jewish believers in a purification rite and pay the expenses of their temple offering. Some have wondered how Paul, who so strongly opposed the "works of the law" (Gal. 2:16), would submit to this requirement.

Paul saw no problem in observing Jewish ritual as long as it was viewed Christologically and not as a basis for justification. For Paul, there was no problem in being Jewish. He felt free to participate in Jewish worship and ritual as long as it was considered nonessential for salvation and sanctification (compare 1 Cor. 9:20).

Acts 22:9

Did his companions hear God speak to Paul on the Damascus road?

Acts 9:7 records that Paul's traveling companions "stood speechless, hearing the voice, but seeing no one." However, in Acts 22:9 Paul says that his companions "did not understand the voice of the One who was speaking to me." The apparent contradiction is clarified by examining the Greek text. The Greek language makes a distinction between hearing a sound as a noise or as a message. It appears that Paul's companions heard God's voice as a sound but not as distinct words so as to understand the message. For a similar example, see John 12:28.

Acts 23:2–5

Why didn't Paul recognize the high priest?

Some have wondered why Paul did not recognize the high priest during his examination before the Sanhedrin. The high priest would have been dressed in his distinctive robes. Why did Paul say, "I was not aware, brethren, that he was high priest"?

It has been suggested that Paul's eyesight had deteriorated to such a point that he could not see clearly. This may have been due to the blinding vision on the Damascus road. Paul refers to his vision difficulty in Galatians 4:15. Another possible interpretation of Paul's remark is that he was simply saying, "I didn't think the High Priest would speak like that." Either way, Paul ceased his verbal protest when informed that he was reviling the high priest.

Acts 25:11

What was involved in Paul's "appeal to Caesar"?

The right of appeal was one of the most ancient and cherished rights of a Roman citizen. This right was usually asserted to appeal the verdict of a lower court but could be exercised at any stage in the proceedings. The case would then be transferred to Rome and judged by the emperor. The appeal to Caesar was possible only in cases not defined by statute laws. Only extraordinary charges had the possibility of appeal to Caesar.[5]

Acts 28:30–31

What happened to Paul after the "two years" mentioned by Luke?

Some think that Paul was killed after his two years in Rome. A more likely scenario is that he was released and ministered for another five or six years before his death. Paul refers to the possibility of his release in several of his prison letters (Phil. 1:25; 2:24; Philem. 22). The Pastoral Epistles make many references to Paul's travels and ministry after his first Roman imprisonment. Eventually, Paul was arrested and brought again to Rome. During this imprisonment, he was treated more harshly (2 Tim. 2:9) and anticipated his death (4:6–8). Paul's martyrdom probably took place in the spring of A.D. 68. According to early tradition, the apostle was beheaded with a sword, on the Ostian Way, just outside the city gate.

Endnotes

1. H. E. Dana and J. R. Mantey, *A Manual Grammar of the Greek New Testament* (Toronto: Macmillan, 1927), 104.
2. F. F. Bruce, *The Book of Acts* (Grand Rapids: Eerdmans, 1954), 149.
3. Gleason L. Archer, *Encyclopedia of Bible Difficulties*, 379–80.
4. Bruce, *Paul: Apostle of the Heart Set Free* (Grand Rapids: Eerdmans, 1977), 215.
5. A. N. Sherwin-White, *Roman Society and Roman Law in the New Testament* (Grand Rapids: Baker Book House, 1963), 60–64.

ROMANS

Romans 1:17

What does Paul mean by the words, "the righteousness of God"?

In Romans 1:17 Paul reveals the essence of the Gospel. The good news is that a right relationship between humans and God is available through faith in Christ. The words, "righteousness of God," may refer to (1) the righteousness that God gives, (2) the righteousness that God approves, or (3) both. It is clear from Scripture that God grants through His justifying grace the very righteousness that He approves. God is righteous in dealing with sin. He does not pretend it isn't there. He judges it in Christ and then accepts the believing sinner as righteous. The righteousness of God imparted to undeserving sinners is strictly a faith process from start to finish, "from faith to faith."

Romans 2:5

Are unbelievers really lost apart from faith in Christ?

The main point of Romans 1:18–3:20 is that unbelievers are lost and face God's righteous judgment apart from saving faith in Christ. Paul emphasizes that this is true of Gentiles (1:18–32), morally good people (2:1–6), Jewish people (2:17–3:8), and all humankind (3:9–20). Paul sums up his main point of this first section of Romans in 3:23, "For all have sinned and fall short of the glory of God."

Paul makes it clear that God is not unfair in judging unbelievers (1:18–19). God has revealed Himself through His creation so that the truth of His existence and divine attributes is clearly "evident" (v. 19). On the basis of this general revelation, the world is "without excuse" in its rejection of God (v. 20). God promises that there will be a "day of wrath and revelation" of His "righteous judgment" (2:5). Paul insists that this judgment will be without partiality (v. 11). Paul's teaching concerning the way of salvation corresponds to the words of Christ, "I am the way, and the truth, and the life; no one comes to the Father, but through Me" (John 14:6).

The encouraging thing for us to remember is that Jesus died for the sins of the world and His provision of salvation extends to all who will believe. No one is eternally lost apart from his or her personal decision to reject God and His self-revelation. Those who respond to this general revelation will receive further light (Heb. 11:6) and have the opportunity to receive salvation in Christ (John 6:37).

Romans 3:31

What did Paul mean when he said, "we establish the Law."

Paul has insisted that people are justified by faith apart from the works of the Law (Rom. 3:28). This may lead some to conclude that the Law is worthless and has no vital function. Paul answers that in verse 31. The Law fulfills a vital role in confronting people with sin. This role is confirmed, or established, by everyone who turns to Christ. Verse 31 teaches that the Law is vital and operative, but not as a means of salvation.

Romans 5:1

Does being "justified" mean "just as if I'd never sinned"?

The Greek word *dikaioo* (justify) means "to declare righteous." It is a judicial term that means that a verdict of acquittal has been pronounced. But there is more. The term does not mean "just as if I'd never sinned." That would leave Christians in a state of spiritual and moral neutrality. In addition to God forgiving and removing our sin, the believing sinner has been imputed with the righteousness of Christ (compare Zech. 3:1–5).

An illustration may help communicate the meaning of justification. If my son in college writes a check for two hundred dollars not realizing that he has only one hundred dollars in his account, he is in debt one hundred dollars. If I send him one hundred dollars to cover the overdraw, then he is debt free but penniless. But if I send him two hundred dollars, then not only is his debt paid, but he has a positive balance of one hundred dollars. This is something like what God has done for us. He has not only paid our debt of sin, but He has added Christ's righteousness to our account. We are not morally neutral. We possess the very righteousness of Christ!

Should the verse be rendered, "We have peace" (indicative), or "Let us have peace" (subjunctive)?

There are two possible readings of this text. The subjunctive form of the verb ("Let us have") appears in such formidable manuscripts as the fourth-century Codex Sinaiticus, the fifth-century Codex Alexandrinus, the fourth-century Codex Vaticanus, and the fifth-century Ephraemi Rescriptus. Metzger acknowledges that the subjunctive has far better external support than the indicative.[1] Murray writes that the evidence for the subjunctive cannot be summarily rejected. He comments, "May not the exhortation here . . . presuppose the indicative? The thought would be, 'Since we have peace with God, let us take full advantage of this status.'"[2] Murray is suggesting that the exhortation is relevant and necessary to the cultivation of the privilege. Robertson translates Romans 5:1, "Let us enjoy (or retain) peace with God."[3] Although the indicative is the more *expected* reading, the subjunctive ("Let us have peace") has the strongest support.

Romans 5:12

How is the human race related to Adam and his sin?

Romans 5:12 declares that sin and death entered the world through one man—Adam. Paul concludes, "and so death spread to all men, because all sinned."

There are two possible interpretations of Paul's statement. Many theologians believe that God *contemplates* all people as one with Adam and his sin. Since Adam represented the human race, God regards all people as sinners because of his acts. Others believe that the entire human race was *seminally* present in Adam. This perspective is based on the concept of the corporate solidarity of the human race in Adam (compare Heb. 7:9–10). According to this second view, when Adam sinned, the entire human race actually *participated* in the sin. People are not just designated sinners, they *are* sinners by virtue of their participation in Adam's act. Although debated, the second view best corresponds with Paul's words, "all sinned."

Romans 6:19

What does it mean to be sanctified and how is this accomplished?

The word *hagiazo* (sanctify) means "to set apart." Christians are set apart from the unbelieving world through regenerating faith in Christ. There are three aspects to sanctification. *Positional* sanctification occurs for all believers at the time of their salvation. They become "saints" positionally through faith in Christ (1 Cor. 1:2, 30). *Final* sanctification will take place when they see Jesus and are made like Him (1 John 3:2). *Experiential* sanctification is that process of conforming their personal experience to their position as saints in Christ (Rom. 6:19, 22). It is this aspect of sanctification that is the subject of Paul's exhortations in Romans 6–8.

Paul explains that sanctification is based on identification with Christ and His death (v. 3). Believers must count on their being "dead to sin" (v. 11). The process of sanctification involves conforming to Christ by refusing to yield to sin and yielding instead to God (vv. 12–13). Such yielding cannot be accomplished by the strength of the human will but only by the power of the Holy Spirit (8:3–4). In summary, the believer is sanctified as he or she yields to God's will and conforms to God's Word by the power of the Holy Spirit.

From a practical point of view, here are some steps believers may take to help bring their daily lives in line with their position as saints in Christ.

1. Apprehend every evil thought (2 Cor. 10:5).
2. Evaluate your thoughts by Philippians 4:8.
3. Remember who you are (Eph. 1–2; compare 2 Peter 1:5–9).
4. Recognize God's will (1 Thess. 4:3).
5. Present yourself to God (Rom. 6:13).
6. Yield to God's will (Rom. 12:1–2).
7. Resist the Devil (James 4:7).
8. Take the "way of escape" (1 Cor. 10:13; 2 Tim. 2:22).
9. Draw near to God (James 4:8).

10. Be filled with the Word of God (John 17:17).
11. Continue in an attitude of prayer (Col. 4:2).
12. Share in Christian community (Acts 4:42).
13. Sing Christian hymns; listen to Christian music (Eph 5:19).
14. Think wholesome thoughts (Phil. 4:8).
15. Guard your eyes from evil (Ps. 119:37).
16. Avoid enticing opportunities (Prov. 7:25).
17. Be accountable to a spiritual friend (James 5:16).

Romans 7:14–25

Who is this person who struggles so much with sin? Is it Paul? If so,
is he describing his experience before or after his conversion?

Romans 7:14–25 is without question the most debated and controversial section of the epistle. Who is this person who struggles so much with sin? The answer given has serious implications. Our interpretation of the passage will determine in large measure our understanding of the doctrine of sanctification, the subject under consideration in Romans 6–8.

The views are as follows:

1. *Preconversion life of Paul* (Greek fathers, John Wesley, F. L. Godet, L. C. Allen, L. Goppelt). According to this view, Paul is reflecting on his preconversion struggle to avoid sin and please God. But this view seems to conflict with Paul's own description of his life under Judaism (Gal. 1:14; Phil. 3:5–6).

2. *Postconversion life of Paul* (Latin fathers, Augustine, Luther, Calvin, F. F. Bruce, W. Hendriksen, J. Murray). According to this view, Paul is reflecting on his present struggle as either an immature or mature Christian. This kind of struggle with sin is understood to be normative for believers in light of the principle of sin and their own flesh. But how does this struggle harmonize with the triumphant Paul of Romans 8?

3. *Nonautobiographical account of humanity* (W. G. Kummel, K. Stendahl, P. J. Achtemeier, J. A. Fitzmyer). According to this view, the passage does not describe Paul but rather humanity in general, humanity in Adam. But Paul consistently uses the first person in this account. Would the original readers have understood that Paul was not referring to himself?

4. *Personal identification with Adam and the Fall* (Longenecker). According to Longenecker, the Adam of Romans 5 finds his voice in Romans 7.[4] But not just Adam. By virtue of our identification with Adam and our sharing in a corporate community, this is all humanity in Adam. Paul is not speaking historically of himself, but theologically of what happened to Adam and all humanity. Paul is in Adam and Adam is in him. There is an abiding realization of the futility of human effort (7:25). Estrangement, perversity, and inability characterized Adam and humanity in him. Yet the name "Adam" is never mentioned here, as it is in Romans 5. Would the original readers have linked this struggle to Adam and to the corporate Adamic community?

5. *Life of legalism* (C. Ryrie, Griffith Thomas, J. A. Stifler). According to

this approach, Paul represents the struggle of people, before or after conversion, who rely on the law and their own efforts for sanctification. The experiences described by Paul are not those of the Christian life as it ought to be and can be by the power of the Holy Spirit (8:3–4). This view has the advantage of consistency with the major context of chapters 6–8, which develop the theme of sanctification. Yet Paul's discussion in these verses has only positive things to say about the law (7:14, 22, 25). And the fact that Paul doesn't seem to have had a personal struggle over the issue of sanctification by the law would be out of keeping with the first-person account.

6. *Conflict of the flesh with the true self* (J. Carl Laney, Neil Anderson). According to this perspective, Paul is dealing with the problem of the flesh— the physical desires of the human body, which are found to be in conflict with his new, regenerate person—his deepest and truest self. Putting all the commentaries and interpretive viewpoints aside, it seems that the real problem for Paul in Romans 7:14–25 is his "flesh" (vv. 14, 18, 25), which is waging mortal conflict with his spiritual desires of his "inner man" (v. 22). The "inner man" is that renewed person Paul is by virtue of his identification with Christ (6:1–7). In Christ, Paul has been set free from the dominion of sin (v. 14), but he still experiences life on earth with a physical body, "flesh." The body is not intrinsically bad but can be used for evil purposes. Believers are called upon to present their "members as instruments of righteousness to God" (v. 13). This decision is an act of the will based on a recognition of one's new identity in Christ. The believer who forgets this identity may respond to temptation by presenting the members of his or her body as "instruments of unrighteousness" (v. 13). In so doing, the believer is responding to the flesh in a manner out of keeping with the new identity. The process of sanctification can be summarized as follows:

a. Identify with Christ (6:1–5).
b. Reckon the old (unregenerate) man as dead (6:6).
c. Fulfill God's will by the power of the Holy Spirit (8:3–4).
    i. Present the members of your body as instruments of righteousness to God (6:13).
    ii. Refuse the mastery of sin (6:16–19).

How does Romans 7:14–25 fit into this scheme? Paul is recognizing here the same conflict mentioned in Galatians 5:17: "For the flesh sets its desire against the Spirit, and the Spirit against the flesh; for these are in opposition to one another, so that you may not do the things that you please." There, too, Paul provides the solution, "Walk by the Spirit, and you will not carry out the desire of the flesh" (v. 16).

Similarly, in Romans 7:14–25, Paul reflects in a very personal way the struggle of the flesh against his true self as a new creature in Christ. Paul's deep desire, based on his new identity, is to please God. Yet his flesh, his physical body, wages war against his mind, tempting him to do things contrary to the will of God. The struggle will always be there. Relying on his own resources means defeat. But through the new covenant provision of the indwelling ministry of the Holy Spirit (Rom. 8:1–4), there is victory.

Romans 9:11–13

Isn't God's election of Jacob and rejection of Esau unjust?

God's dealings with Esau and Jacob have been challenged as arbitrary and unjust. Paul responds to this charge in Romans 9:14–29 by demonstrating the error in such thinking. First Paul appeals to history (vv. 15–18), reminding his readers of Israel's experience with Pharaoh. Paul demonstrates in history that the sovereign God grants mercy according to His will and hardens whom He will. Paul's second appeal is to logic (vv. 19–24). He argues that as the potter has sovereignty over his clay, so God has sovereign authority over His creatures. Paul's third appeal is to the Old Testament prophets (vv. 25–29). He cites several passages from the prophets (Hos. 2:23; 1:10; Isa. 10:22–23; 1:9) to demonstrate that election is consistent with the Old Testament prophets.

Paul's main point is that no one should complain that God's elective purposes are unjust. Election is consistent with God's work in history, with His sovereignty, and with the teaching of the Old Testament. Election may seem to be unjust from a limited, human perspective. When we have questions about the justice of God, we must remember that God is holy, righteous, and just. He will do nothing contrary to these basic attributes.

Romans 9:22

Is "double predestination" a biblical concept?

Those who hold to the doctrine of election generally agree that as an exercise of His sovereignty God chose certain individuals to believe and be saved (compare Eph. 1:4). The question is whether in choosing some to believe God also chose others to disbelieve and be condemned. The concept of God choosing some people to disbelieve and be condemned seems rather objectionable to many Christians. It certainly seems to be unfair and contrary to the mercy of God. The ultimate question for students of Scripture is whether or not this doctrine is biblical.

In Romans 9:19–24, Paul points out that as the potter has sovereignty over the clay, so God has sovereign authority over His creatures. From the same lump He has authority to make a vessel "for honor" *(eis timen)* and another "for dishonor" *(eis atimian)*. Paul uses the actions of the potter to provide a direct analogy for God's dealings with people. There are "vessels of wrath prepared for destruction" (v. 22) and "vessels of mercy, which He prepared beforehand for glory" (v. 23). The word "prepared" is a perfect middle or passive participle of *katartizo,* "to prepare, make, create." The middle voice would be translated, "prepared themselves," indicating personal involvement and accountability. The passive voice would be rendered, "prepared," indicating God's act of preparing certain people for destruction. In the analogy, the pot does not determine its own destiny. The parallels within the analogy suggest that the participle should be translated in the passive voice, "prepared."

A number of biblical passages seem to support this interpretation of Romans 9:22 (Exod. 4:21; Prov. 16:4; Isa. 6:9–10; 1 Peter 2:8; Jude 4). But we must be careful here. The Bible clearly teaches that God is ultimately behind every action (Eph. 1:11). But while God stands behind the destiny of both the elect and the nonelect, He may not do so in exactly the same way. It may be significant that when Paul uses the verb *katartizo* to speak of the nonelect in Romans 9:22, he does not specifically state God as the subject, as he does when he speaks of the elect's destiny in 9:23. The difference is subtle but significant. While God is sovereign over the destinies of both the elect and the nonelect, He is not behind the destiny of the nonelect in the same way He is behind the destiny of the elect. The problem with "double predestination" is that it gives the idea that the two predestinations are of equal character when they are not. This crucial difference is supported in Romans 6:23, where punishment is considered as "wages" earned while eternal life is considered as a "free gift."

Romans 10:4

If Christ is the "end" of the law, do the laws of the Old Testament have a place in the believer's life?

Romans 10:4 reveals that "Christ is the end *[telos]* of the law for righteousness to everyone who believes." The Greek word *telos* combines the idea of aim (goal) and termination. Christ is the one to whom the law points (Luke 24:44; Gal. 3:19, 24–25), thus He is its aim, or goal. The law directs people to Christ. But Christ is also the end of the law.

First, Christ fulfilled the law in His person. He came under the law to redeem those under the law (Gal. 4:4–5). He became a curse for us (3:13), canceling the debt against us (Col. 2:14). His work not only wipes out the curse of the law, but fulfills the demands of the old covenant for us (Matt. 5:17), presenting before the Father a positive righteousness for all those who are in Him.

Second, the law is abrogated as a contractual obligation. Christ's death inaugurated the new covenant, which abolishes the commandments and ordinances (Eph. 2:15) and ends the distinction between Israel and the Gentiles in Christ (vv. 11–18).

New covenant believers are not under a contractual obligation to obey the old covenant (Mosaic) laws. And yet Paul is not ready to throw out the principles of personal holiness reflected in many of the Old Testament laws. Paul appeals to several of the Ten Commandments as expressing the will of God for the believer (Rom. 13:9). He teaches that the requirement of personal righteousness, which is reflected in the law, will be fulfilled not by the power of the flesh but by the power of the Spirit (Rom. 8:3–4). Paul recognizes that under the new covenant, the moral principles of the law have been internalized for the believer. By the power of the Holy Spirit, new-covenant believers will walk in God's statutes and observe His ordinances (Ezek. 36:27).

In discussing the application of the principles of holiness reflected in the law, it is well to distinguish between the abiding and temporary aspects of the law. The law as a contractual obligation—the agreement between God and

Israel mediated by Moses at Mt. Sinai—has ended. This means that certain requirements concerning circumcision, foods, feasts, and Sabbath-keeping have ended (Col. 2:16). But the law as the righteous standard that reflects God's holiness is abiding. God's will that men and women live holy lives has not changed (Lev. 19:2; 1 Peter 1:16). Yet the contractual obligation of the law as set forth in the Mosaic covenant has been terminated by Christ's death and inauguration of the new covenant.

Should Christians today live by the moral teachings reflected in God's law? Yes, but not for the purpose of attaining righteousness (Rom. 8:2–3). Christ has fulfilled that requirement for us (Rom. 10:4). Yet the moral code reflected in the law of God ought to be obeyed in that it is founded on principles that are timeless. Christians enabled by the Holy Spirit will obey the law wherein it reflects God's holiness (Rom. 8:4). The Christian will live a holy and moral life, not because of the law, but out of love for Christ (John 14:15).

Romans 10:9–10

Is confession of one's faith necessary for salvation?

New believers have sometimes been instructed that they must confess their faith publicly. Frequently, this act of confession is thought of as a work which must be performed in order to guarantee one's salvation. Romans 10:9–10 has often been cited as a basis for this position. Paul makes it clear throughout Romans that belief in Christ is the total basis for a believer's justification (5:1; 9:33; 10:13). But faith in Christ is not merely an intellectual experience. Those who believe become regenerated and enter into the process of being sanctified. Those who believe do so with sincerity and are anxious to acknowledge Christ as their Lord. Christians are a confessing people—confessing Christ as a result of their new-found faith.

I suggest that in Romans 10:9–10 Paul is using the terms "confess" and "believe" as two ways of referring to the same basic thing. As "righteousness" and "salvation" are united concepts, so are confession and belief. A belief that is genuine is marked by confession. A confession that is true reflects saving faith. If there is any doubt about Paul's meaning in verses 9–10, he clarifies the issue in verse 11: "For the Scripture says, 'Whoever *believes* in Him will not be disappointed'" (*emphasis added*). Faith and faith alone is the essential requisite for salvation.

Romans 11:21

Is Paul saying that God might cut believers off as He did unbelieving Jewish people?

In the analogy of the olive tree (Rom. 11:17–24), Paul shows that unbelieving Israel (the branches) have been broken off from God's blessing (the rich root) in order that believing Gentiles (a wild olive) might be grafted in. Then in verse 21, Paul gives the warning, "For if God did not spare the natural branches, neither will He spare you."

This is not a warning that believers will lose their salvation. Paul insists that God moves people from being foreknown to being glorified without any loss along the way (8:29–30). Paul is addressing Gentiles in general and warning them against pride in view of Israel's loss. God will not spare the Gentile unbeliever any more than He will a Jewish unbeliever. Believers, whether Jew or Gentile, will never be "cut off" (vv. 38–39).

Endnotes

1. Bruce M. Metzger, *A Textual Commentary on the Greek New Testament* (London: United Bible Societies, 1971), 511.
2. John Murray, *The Epistle to the Romans* (Grand Rapids: Eerdmans, 1968), 159, n. 1.
3. A. T. Robertson, *Word Pictures In The New Testament,* vol. 4 (Nashville: Broadman Press, 1931), 355.
4. Richard N. Longenecker, *Paul, Apostle of Liberty* (Grand Rapids: Baker Book House, 1976), 92–97.

1 CORINTHIANS

1 Corinthians 3:15

Is Paul suggesting that believers will experience the fires of purgatory before going to heaven?

In 1 Corinthians 3:13–15, Paul teaches that God will evaluate and reward the quality of each Christian's work. The results will entail both reward and loss, but Paul is quick to say that the loss will not endanger one's salvation. But what is the meaning of Paul's phrase, "as through fire"? Is he referring to the fires of purgatory?

Fire is used in Scripture as an image of judgment (compare 2 Thess. 1:8). Passing through fire is indicative of a narrow escape (Amos 4:11; Zech. 3:2). Paul uses the image of burning to refer to the testing of the believer's works. Worthless works will be burned up, to the believer's loss. But no harm will come to the believer, although the experience is likened to a narrow escape. Note Paul's use of the word "as" *(hos)*. Paul is not saying that the believer passes through fire. His warning is hypothetical. It is merely as if this were the case.

The doctrine of purgatory is based on the apocryphal book of 2 Maccabees, which was never accepted by Judaism or by the New Testament writers as inspired. Second Maccabees 12:44–45 commends prayers and sacrifices for the dead so that they might be released from their sins. But Christ has paid the full and final sacrifice for sins (Heb. 1:3; 10:14). There is no biblical basis for purgatorial suffering for sins before entering heaven.

1 Corinthians 5:5

What does it mean to deliver someone to Satan "for the destruction of his flesh"?

In dealing with the case of an unrepentant sinner in the church at Corinth, Paul took steps to deliver the offender over to the domain of Satan. The apostle is referring to the process of *excommunication,* whereby a sinner is put out of the church (compare Matt. 18:15–17). Paul makes this clear in verse 13, where he writes, "Remove the wicked man from among yourselves."

Scholars debate the meaning of the phrase, "for the destruction of his flesh." It has been suggested that Paul is referring to the ruin of the physical body through sickness or even death. This view may be supported by 1 Corinthians

11:30, where we see that persistent sin may lead to bodily sickness or death. Another possibility is that the "flesh" *(sarx)* to which Paul refers is the offender's attitude of sinful self-satisfaction. This view coincides with Paul's use of the word "flesh" in 1 Corinthians 3:1–3 and is suggested by the immediate context. Paul is simply leading the church through the process of excommunication so that the offender may repent, return to God, and be saved to full conformity to Christ at His return, "in the day of the Lord Jesus."[1]

1 Corinthians 5:9

To what letter is Paul referring?

Some have argued that Paul is referring to the letter he is writing— 1 Corinthians. Accordingly, Paul is using the "epistolary aorist" not to refer to a past event but to a present, decisive action. Others believe that the letter being referred to is part of 2 Corinthians, perhaps chapters 10–13. The third possibility is that Paul wrote a letter to the Corinthians prior to 1 Corinthians. In the sovereign providence of God, this letter was not preserved as part of God's inerrant and inspired Word.

1 Corinthians 6:9–10

Is Paul saying that people who are guilty of such sins cannot be saved?

In dealing with the problem of lawsuits among believers, Paul tells the Corinthians that they should take their disputes before the church rather than to the courts of "unrighteous" judges (6:1). In verses 9–10, Paul cites various kinds of unrighteous behaviors that demonstrate why the unbelieving world is not qualified to judge the church. These people, by their very conduct, show that they have no place in God's kingdom. Why, then, should they stand in judgment over the disputes of believers? People guilty of such sins can be saved by grace, through personal faith, on the basis of Jesus' cleansing blood. Paul reminds the Corinthians that they were just like these sinners before they were justified in Christ.

1 Corinthians 7:10–11

What options are available to the person who is divorced?

Jesus taught that marriage is designed by God to be a permanent relationship (Matt. 19:6). Here, Paul appeals to the authoritative command of Jesus, "not I, but the Lord," that marriages not be violated by divorce. The wife "should not leave her husband," and "the husband should not send his wife away." Paul, a first-century apostle and student of the teachings of Jesus, clearly understood that Jesus upheld the permanence of marriage. But Paul recognized that in a sinful world divorce would occur. What are the options available for a person who suffers the tragedy of a divorce?

Paul presents two options for the divorced person. The first option is to "remain unmarried." The present tense of the verb "remain" *(meno)* indicates that this is to be an ongoing or permanent state. The second option is to "be reconciled" to one's spouse. The aorist tense of the verb "reconciled" *(katallasso)* emphasizes the attainment of the reconciliation process. Paul does not consider any other options, because neither did Jesus.[2]

1 Corinthians 7:15

Is Paul suggesting that a person who is deserted by an unbelieving spouse has the right to remarry?

Many interpreters of verse 15 have understood Paul to be modifying the teaching of Jesus by allowing divorce and remarriage in cases of desertion. After calling for Christians to live with their unbelieving partners, Paul writes, "Yet if the unbelieving one leaves, let him leave; the brother or the sister is not under bondage in such cases." It is argued that the words, "not under bondage," grant permission to divorce the unbeliever and remarry. But would Paul permit in verse 15 what he forbids in verses 10–13? Under the command of Jesus, remarriage after divorce is not allowed (vv. 10–11).

In verses 12–16, Paul has been arguing his case for the permanence of marriage. In verses 12–13, he clearly prohibits the believer from separating from the unbelieving spouse. Verse 14 provides a reason for maintaining the union. Through the continuation of the relationship, the unbelieving spouse and children are sanctified, "set apart," to receive a Gospel witness, which would be unlikely in the case of a divorce. Now in verse 15, Paul responds to the practical question, "Does the biblical teaching require me to preserve the marriage at the cost of becoming a 'slave' to a deserting, unbelieving spouse?" Paul's answer is "no." If the unbeliever insists on leaving the relationship, the believer is "not under bondage." The word translated "under bondage" *(douloo)* literally means "to be a slave." The abandoned spouse need not act like a slave, following the deserting spouse all over the empire trying to preserve the union. Instead, the abandoned spouse may find "peace" in this difficult situation. Nothing in verse 15 suggests the possibility of a new marriage for the abandoned spouse. To argue for remarriage based on this verse is to read something into the text that is neither stated nor implied.

While there is nothing in this text providing grounds for the remarriage of a deserted spouse, one wonders if there is any other passage that sheds further light on this question. The teaching of Jesus and Paul are consistent. Divorce and remarriage constitute an act of adultery (compare Matt. 5:32; 19:1–12; Mark 10:1–12; Luke 16:18; Rom. 7:2–3). The exception for *porneia* is discussed in the question on Matthew 19:9. For an in-depth study of these divorce and remarriage texts, see my book, *The Divorce Myth* (Minneapolis: Bethany, 1981).

1 Corinthians 7:36–38

Who is the "man" and "his virgin"? What is the situation Paul is referring to?

There are three main interpretations of the situation referred to in verses 36–38. (1) The "man" is the virgin's husband. According to this view, the couple had entered into a "spiritual marriage" and were living in sexual abstinence. (2) The "man" is betrothed to the virgin. According to this view, the couple had agreed to remain single and celibate but now have had a change of heart. (3) The "man" is the virgin's father or guardian. According to this view, the father had wanted to keep his daughter a virgin. But Paul says that he should let her marry if she shows no inclination toward living a life of celibacy. Whatever the precise situation being referred to, Paul grants permission for the virgin to marry (7:36) but affirms his own preference for celibacy (vv. 37–38).

1 Corinthians 10:8

Was Paul in error when he said that "twenty-three thousand" people died (compare Num. 25:9)?

Some have linked Paul's "twenty-three thousand" with the "three thousand" who died in Exodus 32:28. But a study of 1 Corinthians 10:5–10 indicates that Paul drew all his illustrations for this text from the book of Numbers. There is a text in Numbers 25:9 that records how "24,000" people died as a result of God's judgment. This figure, I suggest, records the total of those who died, including the leaders (apparently numbering one thousand) who were executed (Num. 25:4). Paul's figure of "twenty-three thousand" refers only to those who perished in the plague.

1 Corinthians 11:5

Did Paul teach that women should wear head coverings when they pray?

According to Jewish custom, a bride went bareheaded until her marriage, as a symbol of her freedom. When she married, she wore a veil as a sign that she was under the authority of her husband. It is quite probable that both Jewish women and respectable Greek women of the first century wore such head coverings in public. But there were women at Corinth who were not wearing the traditional covering (1 Cor. 11:5–6). Paul responds by explaining the need for the woman's head to be covered when she participates in a public ministry of "praying or prophesying" (v. 5). Building his case on certain facts from creation (vv. 7–9), the presence of angels (v. 10), and the pattern in nature (vv. 14–15), Paul concludes that the woman "ought" (v. 10) to cover her head in situations of ministry where role relationships appear to be confused or reversed. Paul concludes by affirming that this practice is universal among the churches of God (v. 16).

Paul clearly supports the practice of women covering their heads when participating in the public ministry of praying or prophesying. The question most people have is whether or not this first-century custom is binding on believers today. While the answer to this question is debated, it is significant that Paul argues his case not from culture but from theological and biblical truths. Whatever you conclude regarding this debated subject, it is important to remember that God gives priority to the attitude of the heart over external ritual. It is possible for a woman to wear a head covering while not having an attitude of submission. This would violate the spirit of Paul's teaching while keeping it to the letter.

1 Corinthians 13:8

Have tongues ceased?

In upholding the permanence of love over temporal and partial gifts (1 Cor. 13:8–10), Paul declares that tongues "will cease." Paul associates this cessation of tongues with the coming of "the perfect" *(to teleion)*. The key question for us is, "What is the 'perfect'?"

Some have argued that the "perfect" refers to the completed canon of Scripture. It then logically follows that since we have a completed Scripture, tongues have ceased. Others have suggested that the "perfect" refers to the second coming of Christ. This view would allow for the continuation of tongues through this present age. A third view suggests that the "perfect" refers to the maturity of the body of Christ.[3] This third approach seems broad enough to embrace the relative maturity implied in Paul's illustration (v. 11) as well as the absolute maturity depicted in verse 12. The word *teleios* (mature) pictures the church growing collectively as a body, beginning with its birth and progressing through different stages during the present age. The church will reach complete maturity at the return of Christ.

The question, "When will tongues cease?" is bound with the question, "When will the church be mature?" Certainly, the church will be mature at the return of Christ (v. 11). It may also be considered mature when a time of continuing revelation is no longer necessary. At such a time, the gifts of knowledge, tongues, and prophecy will no longer be needed to provide or to verify special revelation.

1 Corinthians 14:34

Was Paul in error in his appeal to "the Law"? Where in the law is this principle taught?

In discussing the matter of women using their speaking gifts in the meeting of the church, Paul appeals to "the Law" as a basis for silence and submission. He writes, "but let them subject themselves, just as the Law also says" (1 Cor. 14:34). Some scholars have rejected this teaching since they find no basis for it in the law. Others suggest that this is Paul "the rabbi" writing here, appealing to the teachings of rabbinic Judaism. Is there any place in the law where Paul might have found a biblical basis for his appeal for female submission?

In Numbers 30:1–8 Moses discussed the matter of keeping vows. The principle is set forth, in verse 2, that people shall keep their promises, doing all that they say. But there are two exceptions. When a wife or an unmarried daughter makes a vow, the fulfillment of the obligation is dependent upon the approval of the husband or the father. This clearly indicates that the wife and the daughter are subject to the husband and the father. The principle of female subjection to proper authority within the home is taught in the law.

1 Corinthians 15:29

What does it mean to be "baptized for the dead"?

In 1 Corinthians 15:29–34, Paul argues the logic of the believer's resurrection from the viewpoint of Christian experience. Within this context he refers to "baptism for the dead." What was Paul referring to? The difficulty of the question is evidenced by the fact that there are at least thirty-six interpretations of this phrase!

The key word in the phrase is the Greek word *huper,* which can be rendered "in behalf of" (Rom. 10:1) or "in place of" (2 Cor. 5:14). Morris takes the first option.[4] He understands that Paul is referring to an abnormal baptismal rite that was peculiar to the Corinthians. Believers were using proxy baptism to immerse those who had died before they had been baptized. This practice did not meet with Paul's approval, but he simply refers to it in his attempt to show the logic of believing in the resurrection. The major difficulty with this view is that in the first century Christian baptism was administered without delay (compare Matt. 28:19; Acts 8:35–38; 10:47–48). It is not at all likely that there would have been a significant number of people in Corinth who had believed but had not been baptized.

The other option for *huper* is to understand that Paul is referring to those who are baptized "in place of" dead believers. Accordingly, Paul may refer to adding new converts to take the place of those who have died. "Baptized" would be understood to refer to all that baptism signifies—evangelism, conversion, and church growth. According to this view, Paul is saying, "Your efforts at evangelism and church growth are to no avail if the dead are not raised. Since you are doing these things, you should believe the resurrection!"

Although the Corinthians knew exactly what Paul was referring to, it remains unclear to modern interpreters. But while we have lost touch with this cultural element, Paul's message remains clear. Baptism *huper* the dead is to no avail apart from the resurrection.

1 Corinthians 15:50

How is Paul's doctrine of the physical resurrection consistent with his statement that "flesh and blood cannot inherit the kingdom of God"?

Paul concludes his defense of the doctrine of the resurrection by explaining the process by which the resurrection body is obtained—by the Rapture (15:52) or through death (vv. 54–57). The importance of this is stressed in verse 50 where Paul declares that "flesh and blood cannot inherit the kingdom of God."

Paul's point is that you cannot go to heaven in your present, mortal body. The perishable body must be changed and modified in order to enter into the heavenly sphere. The resurrection body will not be made of flesh and blood, but it will be a very real, glorified, human body.

Endnotes

1. For further study, see my book *A Guide to Church Discipline* (Minneapolis: Bethany House, 1985).
2. For further study on the question of divorce and remarriage, see my book, *The Divorce Myth* (Minneapolis: Bethany House, 1981).
3. Robert L. Thomas, "Tongues . . . Will Cease" *Journal of the Evangelical Theological Society,* Vol. 17, no. 2 (spring 1974): 81–89.
4. Leon Morris, *The First Epistle of Paul to the Corinthians* (Grand Rapids: Eerdmans, 1958), 218–19.

2 CORINTHIANS

2 Corinthians 2:14

What seems to be the historical background for the imagery used in verse 14?

The imagery Paul uses in this verse is taken from the Roman triumph. Polybius says that the Senate could add glory to the successes of Roman generals by bringing their achievements before the eyes of the citizens through a "triumph." This was the highest honor that could be conferred on a Roman. The best known triumph is the one commemorated by the Arch of Titus, which depicts the Roman victory over the Jews in A.D. 70.

In a Roman triumph, the victorious general entered the city on his chariot and rode through the streets among throngs of cheering Romans to Capitoline Hill, where he would make a solemn offering to Jupiter. As he drove through the streets filled with the aroma of burning incense, a man held a laurel wreath over his head and whispered in his ear, "Remember, you are only a man."

Paul draws from this rich background in verse 14. God is the victorious General who leads us, His followers, in His triumph in Christ. As believers, we share in His victory, manifesting the sweet incense of His person everywhere we go.

2 Corinthians 5:10

If our sins were judged at the Cross, why must believers stand before the judgment seat of Christ?

The issue at the judgment seat *(bema)* of Christ is not the punishment of sin but the reward of service. After the church is taken to heaven, individual believers will be judged for their works. Each believer's life will be examined with regard to his or her faithfulness as a steward of the abilities and opportunities entrusted to each by God. Paul reveals in 1 Corinthians 3:14–15 that faithfulness will be graciously rewarded and unfaithfulness will result in the loss of reward. The judgment seat of Christ should serve as a motivation for godly living and for faithful service for Christ.

2 Corinthians 6:15

Who or what is "Belial"?

In 2 Corinthians 6:14–16, Paul asks five rhetorical questions, each of which expects a negative answer. The stress in this section is on the incompatibility of Christianity with heathenism. In verse 15, Paul asks, "Or what harmony has Christ with Belial?" The term *belial* is actually a Hebrew word that has been transliterated into Greek and means "worthless." In the Old Testament this term was often joined with another word like *son* or *daughter*. In later Jewish writings, the term was used as a proper name for Satan (Book of Jubilees i.20). Paul is using the term in this way. To his question, "What harmony has Christ with Satan?" we answer, "None!"

2 Corinthians 10:10

Do we know anything about the personal appearance of Paul?

In an early manuscript called the Acts of Paul and Thekla (par. 3), Paul is described as follows: "Baldheaded, bowlegged, strongly built, a man small in size, with meeting eyebrows, with a rather large nose, full of grace, for at times he looked like a man and at times he had the face of an angel." Many scholars believe that this rather plain and unflattering account may embody a very early tradition.

2 Corinthians 12:2–4

Who is the man that was "caught up into Paradise"? What was this all about?

Most commentators agree that Paul is relating his own experience of receiving a vision of heaven. Paul's vagueness about the incident and his use of the third person seems to reflect his genuine humility and uncertainty regarding details of the experience. He recounts that the vision took place fourteen years earlier. Since he was writing 2 Corinthians in A.D. 56, we can date the vision about A.D. 42, while he was still in Tarsus before Barnabas brought him to Antioch (Acts 11:25–26). Paul reports that he was taken to the "third heaven," which is beyond the earth's atmosphere (first heaven) and the stars (second heaven). Paul is not sure whether he was physically present in heaven or whether his spirit partook of this experience. There in Paradise, Paul saw and heard some wonderful things. Paul explains in the verses that follow that God gave him a "thorn in the flesh" to keep him from becoming proud as a result of his great privilege (2 Cor. 12:5–9).

GALATIANS

Galatians 1:2

Was Galatians written to the churches in north or south Galatia?

The major introductory problem in Galatians is the identity of the readers. The name "Galatia" (1:2) applies not only to the original territory possessed by the Gauls located in the north-central part of Asia Minor, but also to the entire Roman province extending southward to the borders of Lycia, Pamphylia, and the kingdom of Antiochus. To which of these regions did Paul refer when he wrote Galatians? This is not merely a question of geography. It is also a question of chronology. If Paul wrote to the churches of south Galatia, then the letter is early, written shortly after his first missionary journey. If the epistle is addressed to the churches of north Galatia, then the letter was written on Paul's third journey, perhaps about the time he wrote Romans.

Paul's contacts with Galatia. Two references to Galatia are found in Acts. Luke records in 16:6 that Paul, on his second missionary journey, passed through "the Phrygian and Galatian region." The missionary team was forbidden by the Holy Spirit to continue west to Asia, and neither were they permitted to go north to Bithynia. Traveling northwest, Paul came to Troas (Acts 16:18). Another reference to Galatia is found in Acts 18:23. There the terms "Galatia" and "Phrygia" are used in connection with Paul's journey through the "upper country" (19:1) on his way to Ephesus, where he spent three years of his third missionary journey.

Was Galatians written to the churches in the south of the province, which Paul and Barnabas evangelized on their first journey (Acts 13–14)? Or was the letter written to a group of churches in north Galatia, which were founded on the second and third journeys (16:6; 19:1)?

North Galatian theory. According to the north Galatian theory (defended by J. B. Lightfoot), Paul addressed the epistle to Galatia proper, which he did not visit until his second journey on his way to Troas (Acts 16:1–8). A similar trip is mentioned in Acts 18:23. Paul's first visit to this region would be after the Jerusalem Council of Acts 15, and his epistle would have been written after his second missionary journey, any time from A.D. 53 to 56. The similarity of Galatians and Romans, a letter clearly written at a later date (A.D. 56–57), favors this view.

South Galatian theory. According to the south Galatian theory (defended by Sir William Ramsey), Paul addressed the epistle to the churches of south Galatia

(Pisidian Antioch, Iconium, Lystra, Derbe), which he established on his first missionary journey. His epistle would have been written before the Jerusalem Council, and the visit to Jerusalem mentioned in Galatians 2:1 would refer to the famine relief visit mentioned in Acts 11:27–30. Paul later revisited these Galatian churches on his subsequent missionary journeys (Acts 16:1–6; 18:23).

The strongest argument in favor of the south Galatian view is that if Paul had written the letter after the Jerusalem Council, he certainly would have made reference to the council's decision in favor of Gentile Christian freedom from the Mosaic Law. This omission indicates that the letter was written before the council met, when Paul had visited only the churches of South Galatia.

The vacillation of Peter (Gal. 2:11 and the following verses) would have been most unlikely after the council's decision. And the references to Barnabas as though well known to the readers (vv. 1, 9, 13) would also favor the south Galatian theory. Evidence suggests that Paul completed his first missionary journey in the autumn of A.D. 49 and probably wrote Galatians from Antioch that same year.

Galatians 1:19

Does this verse indicate that James, the half brother of Jesus, was an apostle?

It is difficult to see how Paul would include James within the circle of the apostles. Although the term *apostle* appears to be used of those other than the Twelve (Acts 14:4, 14), James would not have qualified as an apostle based on the criteria of Acts 1:21–22. He had not been a follower of Jesus since the ministry of John the Baptizer (compare John 7:5). Another problem with this verse is that it suggests that Paul did not see any of the apostles, except James. This is contrary to the evidence in Acts 9:27 that he visited with the apostles and recounted his experience on the Damascus road.

There is another rendering of this verse that is more suitable to our understanding regarding James and to the statement of Luke in Acts 9:27. Trudinger translates Galatians 1:19, "Other than the apostles, I saw no one *except*, James the Lord's brother."[1] Paul is emphasizing in this text that his contact with the churches in Judea and Jerusalem was very limited. He certainly did not receive his Gospel from these churches where he had such little contact.

Galatians 2:1–10

To which of Paul's Jerusalem visits is he referring, the famine relief visit (Acts 11:27–30) or the Jerusalem Council (Acts 15:1–29)?

Those who adhere to the south Galatian viewpoint understand that Paul is referring to the famine relief visit. According to the north Galatian theory, this text refers to the Jerusalem Council. The reference to the "revelation" (Gal. 2:2) supports the famine-relief visit, which was initiated by Agabus's prophecy of a world famine. The mention of Barnabas (1:1), who accompanied Paul on the first journey (Acts 13:2), also lends support to this view.

272 ANSWERS TO TOUGH QUESTIONS

Galatians 2:11–14

What was the problem with Peter that Paul was compelled to oppose him?

Peter was guilty of failing to practice the Gospel of grace consistently. It had been his custom to eat with uncircumcised, that is, Gentile believers at Antioch. But he broke fellowship with them when visitors from Jerusalem arrived. When Paul saw that the conduct of Peter was not straightforward, Paul rebuked him publicly. Peter's hypocrisy had public consequences and required public clarification. Peter had not been teaching that Gentiles should adopt Jewish customs, but his actions suggested that they should. Paul took strong steps to rebuke and correct this inconsistency for the sake of Peter and for the sake of the church.

Galatians 3:17

Was Paul correct in saying that the Law was given 430 years after the promise was made to Abraham?

Paul's point in Galatians 3:17 is that the law that came later could not set aside the promises that were made earlier. The 430 years to which Paul refers is the period of time the Israelites spent in Egypt (Exod. 12:40) from the descent of Jacob (1876 B.C.) until the exodus under Moses (1446 B.C.). It seems that Paul is referring in Galatians 3:17 not to the initial giving of the promise to Abraham (Gen. 12:1–3) around 2100 B.C. but to the later confirmation of the covenant to Jacob (46:1–4) before he took his family to Egypt (1876 B.C.). Paul is not mistaken. The law was given 430 years after God's promise to Abraham was confirmed to Jacob.

Galatians 4:21–31

How should we understand Paul's appeal to allegory? Does this validate allegorical interpretation?

In Galatians 3–4, Paul presents evidence of the sufficiency of the Gospel of grace apart from works of the law. As his final appeal, Paul recounts the birth of Isaac to Sarah and of Ishmael to Hagar. Then he writes in 4:24, "This is allegorically speaking." What did Paul mean by this?

Allegory is a "description of something under the image of another." An allegory makes an analogy between the details of a fictitious story and spiritual truth. Some would suggest that Paul is saying that Genesis is allegory, not history. But Paul clearly recognizes the historicity of the Old Testament, appealing to the stories as a basis for his theology (compare Rom. 5:12–14; 1 Tim. 2:13–14). Others believe that Paul is suggesting that we interpret the Old Testament allegorically, as did the rabbis, Philo, and Origen. But Paul clearly believed in a literal interpretation of Scripture (compare 3:16).

Paul's discussion in Galatians 4:21–31 is more in line with biblical typology than with the excesses of Alexandrian allegory as practiced by the rabbis.

Paul uses the historical situation of Isaac and Ishmael to make a point that applies to the Galatian crisis. The point is this: The Judaizers do not have the authority or the blessing of God.

Paul draws on a historical incident in the Old Testament that provides a picture of the sonship of Isaac in contrast to the slave status of Ishmael (Gen. 16–17, 21). Paul reminds the Galatians that Abraham had two sons, but only one inherited the promises. He contrasts the law of Sinai, issued in slavery, with the covenant of promise, issued in liberty. The point Paul is making is summarized in Galatians 4:31. The believers are sons of the freewoman, not of the slave. So they must repudiate their bondage to the law and live in the freedom of the Spirit.

The value of the allegory is twofold. First, it enforces the principle of grace by a citation from the law (v. 21), which was the Judaizer's chief authority. Second, it utilizes a method of interpretation that the Jewish and rabbinical school employed. If these Judaizers relied upon allegorical interpretation, Paul answers them by their own method! Paul was not averse to using methods from his Jewish training if they could serve his purpose.

Galatians 6:16

To whom does Paul refer when he writes, "Peace and mercy be upon them, and upon the Israel of God"?

Many commentators suggest that Paul is referring to believing Gentiles ("them") and believing Jews ("the Israel of God"). By adding the phrase, "and upon the Israel of God," Paul singles out Jewish Christians for special mention. But one wonders why Paul would argue, "neither is circumcision anything, nor uncircumcision" (6:15), and then distinguish the two believing peoples in the very next verse.

A better solution is to understand that Paul is identifying believing Gentiles with "the Israel of God." The conjunction "and" *(kai)* between "them" and "the Israel of God" is *epexegetical,* identifying the two as one. The *kai* might be better translated, "even." In verse 16 Paul brings the argument of this epistle to a pinnacle. Gentile believers don't need Jewish ritual because no one can be justified by the works of the law (2:16). There is no difference spiritually between Jewish and Gentile believers (3:28; 6:15). The whole Christian community—believing Jews and believing Gentiles—constitute the sons and daughters of Abraham through faith (Rom. 4:11–12, 16). This affirmation does not undermine the distinctiveness of the Jewish people in biblical prophecy nor detract from the specific promises made by God to ethnic Israel.

Endnotes

1. L. Paul Trudinger, "A Note on Galatians 1:19," *Novum Testamentum* 17 (1975): 200–202.

EPHESIANS

Ephesians 1:1

Was this letter written to the church at Ephesus or to some other group of believers?

The words "at Ephesus" are absent from several important documents, including fourth-century Codex Sinaiticus and fifth-century Codex Vaticanus. The second-century heretic Marcion designated this epistle as "to the Laodiceans." This has led many scholars to suggest that the letter was an encyclical, intended to be read by a larger circle of Christian communities among which Ephesus was most prominent. The letter has traditionally been associated with the Ephesians, but we cannot be 100 percent sure that the letter was written with only the church at Ephesus in mind.

Ephesians 1:4–5

What is the difference between the terms "chose" (that is, elected) and "predestined"?

The biblical truth of divine election is expressed by Paul in the words of verse 4: "just as He chose us in Him before the foundation of the world." The Greek word translated "chose" *(eklego)* means "picked out" or "selected." Used here in the middle voice, the word means "to choose someone for oneself." *Election* may be defined as God's act of choosing those who, through personal faith, will be saved and will become members of the body of Christ.

The word translated "predestined" *(proorizo)* means "marked out by boundaries beforehand." Used in verse 5, the word places special emphasis on God's will and His active involvement in the life and destiny of the believer. God has determined beforehand that those who believe in Christ will be adopted into His spiritual family and conformed to the image of His Son (Rom. 8:29–30).

The doctrine of election teaches that believers are chosen to become God's children through faith in Christ. God's choosing never cancels out or eliminates the necessity of personal faith. Those who are chosen are also predestined. God has marked out the boundaries of their lives from beginning to end. While there is freedom of movement within those boundaries, the destiny that God has purposed will be accomplished. The doctrines of election and predestination are among the more mysterious workings in God's economy.

We don't understand them completely, yet they are biblical teachings and we embrace them by faith.

Ephesians 2:8–10

What is the relationship between a believer's salvation and good works?

Throughout the Bible it is clearly taught that salvation is always by God's grace, through personal faith, based on blood—ultimately the blood of Christ. Paul highlights this great redemptive truth in Ephesians 2:8–10. Paul emphasizes, in verse 8, that salvation is a "grace" gift (that is, free), which is appropriated through personal "faith." Grace is the source of salvation, while faith is the channel through which it is effected. Yet even the faith to believe, insists Paul, is a gift of God.

What is the relationship of this free gift to works? Paul makes it very clear, in verse 9, that our salvation is "not as a result of works." Nothing sinners could possibly do has the capacity to move them out of darkness into the light, out of death into life. Why did God provide salvation in this way? Verse 9 indicates that it prevents boasting. Since salvation is not earned or deserved, no one can boast that he or she has achieved it.

Although we are saved completely by grace, "works" do show up in verse 10. While good works cannot save (v. 9), they do accompany salvation (James 2:17). According to Paul, believers are God's workmanship, "created in Christ Jesus for good works." Paul further explains that God has prepared for believers opportunities for good works in which to participate. Good works may be thought of as the fruit of genuine faith. When people become saved, they are also regenerated and begin the process of sanctification. This change in life produces a change in behavior that marks them, by God's grace, as part of the redeemed community.

Ephesians 3:3–6

What does Paul mean by the phrase, the "mystery of Christ"?

In Ephesians 3:3 Paul begins to elaborate on the "mystery" that he introduced in 1:9. A divine *musterion* (mystery) is a sacred secret that has not been previously revealed, and when it is revealed, it is understood only by the initiated (that is, believers). Paul makes no claim to be the sole recipient of this revelation (3:5). While the "mystery" was unknown by Old Testament revelation, it has been made known through the New Testament apostles and prophets.

Paul identifies the mystery as the fact that "Gentiles are fellow heirs and fellow members of the body, and fellow partakers of the promise in Christ Jesus through the gospel" (3:6). The mystery is not that Gentiles would be blessed by God. That is clearly revealed in the Old Testament (Gen. 12:3; Joel 2:28; Amos 9:12). The mystery is that Jews and Gentiles are united on an equal basis in one spiritual body! Together they share an inheritance—a body and the promises of God!

Ephesians 4:8

How is Paul using Psalm 68:18, and to what does the psalmist refer?

Ephesians 4:7 indicates that believers are the recipients of God's grace measured by the Gift, which is Christ (appositional genitive). Paul goes on to explain how Christ's work provides the basis for the bestowal of other gifts (that is, gifted persons) to the church (vv. 8–10).

There are four basic views regarding this historical background of Psalm 68:18. These include (1) an eschatological vision of hope for humanity's future, (2) a song of triumph after some great military victory, (3) a song to celebrate the kingship of God at the so-called enthronement festival of Yahweh, or (4) a direct prophecy of Christ and His coming kingdom. In addition to these suggestions, Smith proposes the possibility that Paul is appealing to the principle of analogy with the Levites based on Psalm 68:18.[1]

In Psalm 68:18, God's stay at His sanctuary is preceded by His ascension and the taking captive of certain persons. The gifts received made it possible for God to remain in His sanctuary among His people. Who are the "captives"? Smith proposes that the psalmist was thinking of the Levites, who were separated from among the sons of Israel (Num. 8:6, 14) for the purpose of performing the service of the Lord (vv. 11, 19) so that the Lord might dwell among them. The Levites are referred to as "gifts" (8:19; 18:6). They are also said to have been "taken" and "given." The Levites were "taken" or received from among the sons of Israel as captives for His service and given as gifts to Aaron. According to Smith, "The captives are the gifts. Captives are taken and gifts are given, but both the captives and the gifts are the Levites."[2]

Paul, then, is appealing to the principle of analogy in his use of Psalm 68:18. He wants his readers to understand that God has, throughout history, chosen special men as leaders of the spiritual community. The grace given to fill such leadership positions is directly proportional to the need. Those responsible for teaching, preaching, and other spiritual duties receive the necessary gifts from God to meet the needs of those served. These servants were "gifts" of God given to bring people into a relationship with God and to build up the body of Christ.

As the Levites were taken captive by God as a special group and "given" to minister to the needs of Israelites, so God ordained New Testament apostles, prophets, pastors, and teachers to win the lost and to minister to the body of Christ (Eph. 4:12).

Ephesians 4:9

Did Jesus descend into hell?

The Apostles' Creed affirms that Jesus "suffered under Pontius Pilate, was crucified, dead and buried; he descended into hell, rose again the third day." Is there biblical support for the familiar but mysterious statement, "He descended into hell"?

It is important to realize that the Apostles' Creed was not written or approved by a single church council at one specific time. It gradually took shape from about A.D. 200 to 750. The phrase, "He descended into hell," was not found in any of the early versions of the creed. Moreover, Rufinus, the only person who includes the phrase before A.D. 650, did not think that it meant that Christ descended into hell. He understood the phrase simply to mean that Christ "descended into the grave," that is, was buried. Later this phrase was incorporated into versions of the creed that already had the phrase "and buried," so some other explanation had to be given. This led to various attempts to explain the phrase in some way that did not contradict Scripture.

Some have taken the phrase to mean that Christ suffered the pains of hell while on the cross. Others have understood it to mean that Christ continued in the "state of death" until His resurrection. Others have argued that Christ did descend into hell after His death on the cross.

Support for Christ's descent into hell has been drawn from Ephesians 4:9. Paul writes: "Now this expression, 'He ascended,' what does it mean except that He also had descended into the lower parts of the earth?" Paul is saying in this context that the Christ who went up to heaven (in His ascension) is the same one who had come down from heaven (v. 10). That descent from heaven occurred when Christ came to earth and was born as a human. This text refers to the incarnation of Jesus not to a descent into hell! The expression, "the lower parts of the earth," is an appositional genitive. This means that the "lower parts" refers to "the earth." For example, "the city of Portland" refers to the city, which is Portland. The "city" and "Portland" are one in the same. The words of Jesus to the thief on the cross, "Today you shall be with Me in Paradise" (Luke 23:43) imply that Jesus went immediately into the presence of the Father in heaven after His death.

There appears, then, to be little biblical or historical support for the inclusion of a descent into hell in the Apostles' Creed. It would probably be best to drop this from a creed that is supposed to summarize the basic and vital tenets of the Christian faith.[3]

Ephesians 4:11

Is there one office or two in the phrase "pastors and teachers"?

Many scholars have appealed to the "Grandville Sharp" rule to argue that the phrase "pastors and teachers" refers to one office, not two. The Grandville Sharp rule states: "When two words in the same case are preceded by the definite article, are joined by *kai,* and the second term does not have the article before it, then the two terms have reference to one and the same thing." At first glance, the rule seems to fit this situation. There are two words joined by *kai* and preceded by the definite article. However, the words are in the plural, and the Grandville Sharp rule was never intended to apply to plurals. If it did, the apostles and prophets in Ephesians 2:20 would be one and the same.

Without the application of the Grandville Sharp rule we are left with five offices or gifted leaders given to the church—apostles, prophets, evangelists, pastors, and teachers. I believe there is a natural and logical relationship between the last two offices. Pastors should be able to teach (1 Tim. 3:2; 5:17) and teachers should give spiritual watch care over their students (1 Peter 5:1–4). But the offices or gifts of pastor and teacher are biblically distinct.

Ephesians 5:21

Does this verse command the mutual submission of husbands and wives?

We hear much these days about the mutual submission of husbands and wives to each other in marriage. This means that the husband must, at times, place himself under the authority of his wife, acknowledging her leadership in the marriage. Is this what Paul had in mind when he wrote, "And be subject to one another in the fear of Christ"?

We must first consider the word translated "be subject." The Greek word *hupotasso* means "to rank under," "to obey a high authority." The present tense indicates that you are to keep on doing this, not just occasionally, but always. The imperative mood indicates that this is a command, a direct appeal to the will. The middle voice reveals that this is something you are to do yourself rather than having it imposed upon you.

Looking within the context of Ephesians we discover that the command, "be subject," is given at the beginning of a section dealing with how believers relate to those in positions of authority. Verse 21 serves as the introduction to this section, calling Christians to obedience to rightful authorities. Paul proceeds in 5:22–6:9 to give some specific examples that ought not to be reversed—wives to husbands, children to parents, slaves to masters. The concept of mutual submission is not based on careful exegesis and brings a great deal of confusion to the role relationships of marriage. God's directions are clear. The wife is called upon to place herself under the authority and leadership of her husband (v. 22), and the husband is to love his wife as Christ loved the church (v. 23). This does not mean that the husband should be a dictator or that the wife should be a doormat. The husband is to lead through sacrifice and love, and the wife is to submit with sincerity and respect.

Ephesians 6:5

Does the Bible support the institution of slavery?

Slavery was universally taken for granted in the first century. It was practiced in Jewish, Roman, and Greek cultures, although the institution varied in some degree from culture to culture. Jewish slaves had certain privileges and were under legal protection. Their term of forced service was limited to six years (Exod. 21:2), and they were not to be sent away empty-handed (Deut. 15:13–15). As commanded by biblical law, the Jews were careful to avoid treating slaves with cruelty (compare Exod. 21:7–11; Deut. 21:10–14). Slaves among non-Jewish peoples did not receive such consideration.

The Bible has been wrongly used to support the institution of slavery. What it does call for is Christian consideration for the well-being of slaves in situations where this institution may exist. Neither the teachings of Jesus nor the teachings of Paul condemn slavery as such. Rather than trying to overthrow the cultural institution of slavery, Paul sought to work within the system, requiring that slaves obey their masters (Eph. 6:5; Col. 3:22–24) and that masters not mistreat their slaves (Col. 4:1; 1 Peter 2:18–20).

It is helpful for us to recognize the distinction between the institution of slavery and the abuses to which the institution was subject. Kidner comments, "By accepting the system, even while humanizing it, it allowed that society was not ready to do without it." He suggests that God's way "was the long process of spiritual nurture, education and sharpening the conscience rather than one of premature social engineering."[4]

Although Paul seems to have been supportive of emancipation (compare 1 Cor. 7:21; Philem. 21) he was definitely more concerned for spiritual freedom than for release for slaves. He remarks, in 1 Corinthians 7:22, that a believing slave is "the Lord's freedman" and that a free believer is "Christ's slave."

Endnotes

1. Gary V. Smith, "Paul's Use of Psalm 68:18 in Ephesians 4:8," *Journal of the Evangelical Theological Society* (summer 1975): 181–89.
2. Ibid., 187.
3. For further study, see Wayne Grudem, "He Did Not Descend Into Hell," *Journal of the Evangelical Theological Society* 34:1 (March 1991): 103–13.
4. Derek Kidner, *Hard Sayings: The Challenge of Old Testament Morals* (London: Inter-Varsity Press, 1972), 33.

PHILIPPIANS

Philippians 1:13

What was the "praetorian guard"?

The praetorian guard was an elite group of soldiers in the Roman army that was designated to guard the emperor, his family, and those under his charge. They had higher pay, higher status, better conditions, and a shorter length of service than ordinary legionaries. The barracks for the praetorian guard were located on the outskirts of the city of Rome.

The praetorian guard became a very powerful force in Roman politics. Their commander, if not completely loyal, could exert considerable pressure on the emperor. After the assassination of Caligula, Claudius (A.D. 41–54) was placed on the throne by the praetorian guard. Since Paul had appealed to Caesar, he was under the care and protection of the praetorian guard. This situation provided him with a very strategic witnessing opportunity. Near the catacombs south of Rome is a chapel dedicated to the memory of Saint Sebastian, a member of the praetorian guard who was shot with arrows by his commander when he professed Christ.

Philippians 2:6–7

What does Paul mean when he writes that Christ "emptied Himself"?

Theologians have debated and wrestled with this question for centuries. Within the context of Philippians, Paul is exhorting the Philippians to exemplify an attitude humility, showing concern for the needs of others, not just themselves (Phil. 2:3–4). He then provides the Philippians with an illustration (vv. 5–8). The Philippians are to manifest in their own lives the attitude of humility displayed by Christ.

In verse 6 Paul explains that in His preincarnate state, Jesus possessed the essential qualities of God. The expression, "form of God" (*morphe theou*), refers not to an empty shell but to appearance backed up by reality. Jesus shares the nature and essence of God. But He did not exploit His equality with God to His own advantage. Instead, He "emptied himself" (*kenoo*). Of what did Christ empty Himself? Some suggest that He gave up some aspect or attribute of deity. But James 1:17 reveals that God does not change. Others suggest that in His incarnation, Jesus veiled His glory. While this is true (John 17:5), it is not what Paul is saying in Philippians 2:6. Many argue that Paul is referring to the fact that in His incarnation, Jesus laid aside the independent exercise of some of His attributes. While this appears to be true (compare Matt. 24:36), it is not a truth revealed here.

Usually the answer to an exegetical question is revealed within the context itself. I believe that is the case here. The word *kenoo* can literally mean "emptied," as it is usually translated. But *kenoo* is also used by Paul in a metaphorical sense. We see this in 1 Corinthians 1:17 where Paul expresses his concern that the cross of Christ not be "made void" *(kenoo)*. It is clear that the meaning of any word is dependent upon its relationship to other words and sentences that form its context. Greek lexicons support the translation of *kenoo* in the metaphorical sense, "to make of no account." This fits perfectly in verse 6 where the emptying is explained by the two modal participles that follow. Jesus "emptied Himself" *by* "taking the form of a bond-servant, and being made in the likeness of men."

In His incarnation, Jesus made Himself of no account by receiving the essential nature of a servant and becoming human. He lost nothing in this process. Rather, He took on a new role (servanthood) and entered a new ministry dimension (humanity).

Philippians 2:12–13

Does verse 12 advocate salvation by works, in contradiction with Paul's teaching elsewhere?

Years ago I met someone on an airplane who sought to refute the idea that salvation is completely by grace by citing Philippians 2:12, "Work out your salvation with fear and trembling." It is too bad this person had not read the *next* verse. Paul writes, "For it is God who is at work in you, both to will and to work for His good pleasure."

The biblical teaching on salvation is very clear. People are saved by God's grace as His provision for redemption in Christ is appropriated by personal faith (Eph. 2:8–9). But the term *salvation* does not always refer to the same thing in Scripture. There are three aspects of the believer's salvation— justification, glorification, and sanctification. In justification, believers have been declared righteous positionally (Rom. 5:1). Glorification relates to their future destiny when God's work in their lives is complete (Rom. 8:30; 1 John 3:2). Sanctification is the present process of bringing their personal conduct into conformity with their position in Christ (1 Thess. 4:3).

Paul's command to "work out your salvation" is set in the context of a call to obedience (v. 12). He is clearly writing about the believer's sanctification rather than justification or glorification. Yet even sanctification is not a human work. Paul insists that "it is God who is at work in you," empowering committed believers by the Holy Spirit to live God-honoring lives (compare Rom. 8:3–4).

Philippians 3:2

What did Paul mean by the warning, "Beware of the dogs"?

In Philippians 3:1–3, Paul warns the Philippians about some Judaizers who had reached Macedonia and were seeking to convince the believers to adopt Jewish practices. He refers to these false teachers in verse 2 and describes them by their creed, their conduct, and their character. As to their creed, they advocate "circumcision." As to their conduct, they are "evil workers." As to their character, they are "dogs."

In Paul's day, the term translated "dogs" *(kunas)* was a term of reproach used by Jews to describe Gentiles as ceremonially impure. This usage of the term is evidenced throughout Scripture (Deut. 23:19; Matt. 15:26–27; Rev. 22:15). In ancient times dogs were not the lovable pets that we enjoy in our culture. They were wild animals without homes, feeding on the refuse and filth of the street and fighting among themselves. They jeopardized the health and well-being of those in the communities where they wandered. Taking a term used by Jews to describe Gentiles, Paul applies it to the Judaizers, who seek to undermine the cleansing of the Cross by promoting legalism.

Philippians 4:5

Was Paul mistaken when he wrote, "The Lord is near"?

Some have thought that Paul must have been mistaken when he wrote the words, "The Lord is near." Two thousand years have passed since he wrote to the Philippians, and Jesus has not yet come. How could he have viewed Christ's coming as near?

The answer to this question is found in the biblical teaching on the doctrine of *imminence*. This doctrine means that the church has been given no signs that must precede Christ's coming. Rather, believers are to live with the prospect that Christ could come for His church at any moment. That's why believers are encouraged to be "looking for the blessed hope" (Titus 2:13) and living pure lives (1 John 3:3). From the point of view of Bible prophecy, there is nothing that must take place before Jesus returns. So His return is "near" or "at hand." It could take place before you finish reading this page!

COLOSSIANS

Colossians 1:15

If Jesus is "the first-born" of creation, how can He be eternally existent?

In Colossians 1:15 and 1:18, Jesus is declared to be the "first-born of all creation" and the "first-born from the dead." The Greek word *prototokos* (firstborn) literally means "first child." The word can be used in a temporal sense, referring to the first child among many. But the word is also used when referring to one who has the rank or position of heir. In the biblical period, the firstborn son received the birthright, including the right of a double inheritance, the privilege of becoming head of the family, and the right of parental blessing (Gen. 27:19; Deut. 21:17). The birthright gave the firstborn the most prominent position among the siblings.

In using this term of Christ, Paul is not saying that He had a temporal beginning. As God, He exists from eternal past and throughout eternity future (John 1:1). Paul is emphasizing in the word *prototokos* the position or rank of Christ as chief over all creation and most prominent among those to be raised from the dead.

Colossians 1:20

Does this verse teach that all people will be saved?

It would be a serious mistake to conclude that Paul's statement in Colossians 1:20 means that all people, including unbelievers, are saved through Christ's work of reconciliation. Paul understood and taught that apart from personal faith in Jesus Christ, there is no salvation (Rom. 10:1; 1 Tim. 2:15; compare Acts 4:12). What, then, did Paul mean when he wrote that it was God's good pleasure "through Him to reconcile all things to Himself"?

The word, "reconcile" *(katallasso)* means "to change." Christ's work of reconciliation means that by His death humankind's state of alienation is changed so that now people are able to be saved (Rom. 5:11). The provision of reconciliation is for the entire world (2 Cor. 5:19), just as Christ is the propitiation for the sins of the whole world (1 John 2:2). But people appropriate this provision in a saving sense only when they exercise justifying faith (Rom. 5:1). Nowhere does the Bible teach that all people will be saved. Both Jesus and Paul speak clearly of the punishment of the wicked and unbelieving (Matt. 25:41; 2 Thess. 1:7–9).

Colossians 1:24

What does Paul mean when he refers to "filling up that which is lacking in Christ's afflictions"?

It is clear that Paul's sufferings could not add anything to the vicarious sufferings of Christ as atonement for our sins. This work was completed at the cross (John 19:30; Heb. 1:3; 9:28). But Scripture reveals that Christ suffers when His people suffer (Acts 9:5). And so Paul's sufferings for the sake of the church can be called Christ's afflictions as well. That which Christ did not suffer on earth He suffers now because of the persecutions and tribulations experienced by Paul. Christ's suffering was for the salvation of the body. Paul's was in service to the body.

Colossians 3:22 (see Ephesians 6:5)

1 THESSALONIANS

1 Thessalonians 1:10
What did Paul mean by the phrase, "the wrath to come"?

In 1 Thessalonians 1:10, the believers are encouraged to anticipate the coming of Jesus from heaven, "who delivers us from the wrath to come." The phrase, "wrath to come" (*tes orges tes erchomenes*) recalls a very similar phrase used by John the Baptizer (Matt. 3:7; Luke 3:7) to describe an eschatological judgment on the wicked. John the Apostle appears to refer to this day in Revelation 6:16–17 when he writes of the "wrath of the Lamb," which comes upon wicked unbelievers during the Tribulation. These references would indicate that the "wrath" to which Paul refers is none other than the judgments of the future Tribulation. Paul anticipated the coming of Jesus, who will deliver believers from the coming wrath of the Tribulation (compare 1 Thess. 5:9).

1 Thessalonians 4:4
Does the "vessel" refer to one's own body or to one's spouse?

The Greek word *skeuos,* translated "vessel," can refer to a physical vessel, like a jar or a container. But the word is also used metaphorically to refer to one's own body (2 Cor. 4:7; 2 Tim. 2:21) or to one's own wife (1 Peter 3:7). Either of the metaphorical usages are exegetically possible in 1 Thessalonians 4:4. But the word translated "possess" *(ktaomai)* may provide a clue. This word may be rendered "procure for oneself" or "acquire." What Paul seems to be referring to is the process of taking a wife in marriage. He insists that this process be done "in sanctification and honor." Christian courtship and premarriage relationships should be characterized by purity and chastity, not the "lustful passion" of unbelieving Gentiles (v. 5).

1 Thessalonians 4:13
Did Paul believe in the doctrine of "soul-sleep"?

In 1 Thessalonians 4:13–18, Paul corrects a misconception held by the believers that the Rapture was for living saints only and that those who had died in Christ would miss out. He points out that the living shall not precede the dead (v. 15). The Rapture begins with the dead rather than the living but includes both (v. 17).

Within this context, Paul refers to those who have "fallen asleep in Jesus" (v. 13). This very common New Testament metaphor appears to be drawn from Jesus' words, in John 11:11, where He uses the word "sleep" *(koimao)* to refer to Lazarus's death. Later this metaphor is used by Luke (Acts 7:60), Paul (1 Cor. 7:39), and Peter (2 Peter 3:4). Sleep is a very appropriate metaphor for death since believers will awake from death in the resurrection.

It is clear that the metaphor of sleep refers to the situation of the body, not the soul. Biblical evidence makes it clear that the immaterial part of a person, "soul" and or "spirit," is present with Christ at death. Recall that Jesus promised the repentant thief that he would be with Him in Paradise the very day he died (Luke 23:43). And Paul declared that when we are "absent from the body" we are "at home with the Lord" (2 Cor. 5:8). The story of the rich man and Lazarus (Luke 16:19–31) makes it clear that the soul is conscious after death.

1 Thessalonians 4:16

If the dead are resurrected to meet Christ at the Rapture, how can Paul say that being "absent from the body" is to be "at home with the Lord" (2 Cor. 5:8)?

The Bible does not provide us with a simple chapter-and-verse answer to this question. We do believe that both of these statements are true. It is possible that believers in heaven are given temporary bodies with which to enjoy heaven's glories until the resurrection. It is also possible that they simply enjoy heaven through an immaterial body (made of soul and spirit) until the resurrection. When Christ returns for His church, He will bring with Him the believers who have died and gone to heaven (1 Thess. 4:14). At that time their physical bodies will be raised and made imperishable (1 Cor. 15:42; 1 Thess. 4:16). Then in their glorified bodies believers will enjoy the presence of God throughout eternity.

1 Thessalonians 5:2

What does Paul mean by the expression, "the day of the Lord"?

The Day of the Lord is one of the great themes of the Old Testament prophets (compare answer on Joel 1:15). As seen in the Prophets, this is a day of wrath on the wicked and of restoration for the righteous. The eschatological Day of the Lord may be defined as that period during which God will deal with Israel and the nations through judgment and deliverance. While the Second Advent is preceded by signs (Matt. 24:19–30), the Day of the Lord is said to come unexpectedly (1 Thess. 5:2). Hence this period must begin shortly after the rapture of the church—an imminent and signless event.

According to Peter, the Day of the Lord will conclude with the purging of the heavens and the earth in preparation for the creation of the new heavens and the new earth (2 Peter 3:10–13; compare Isa. 65:17; 66:22).

Thus, the eschatological Day of Yahweh includes the prophesied events of the Tribulation period, the events of the Second Advent, the millennial kingdom, the final revolt of Satan, the Great White Throne judgment, and the purging of the earth in preparation of the new creation (compare Rev. 6–20). It is both a day of destruction and of salvation, a day of wrath and of grace.

1 Thessalonians 5:19

How might a believer "quench the Spirit"?

The word translated "quench" *(sbennumi)* was used literally in ancient times of putting out a fire (Eph. 6:16). The word is also used figuratively of quenching, stifling, or suppressing something. To quench the Spirit would be the equivalent of "resisting" the Spirit or "grieving" the Spirit (4:30). A believer could quench the Spirit by (1) refusing the Spirit's leading, (2) pursuing a known sin, or (3) failing to depend upon the Spirit. Within the immediate context, Paul may have in mind the particular sin of regarding a prophetic utterance, given by the Spirit, with contempt (1 Thess. 5:20).

2 THESSALONIANS

2 Thessalonians 1:9

Will the wicked be destroyed, or will they suffer eternal punishment?

In 2 Thessalonians 1:9, Paul refers to those who do not know God as paying "the penalty of eternal destruction." Some have concluded that Paul is referring here to the annihilation of the wicked by which their existence is terminated in an instant. Paul's phrase, "away from the presence of the Lord," recalls the words of Jesus in describing eternal judgment, "Depart from Me, accursed ones, into the eternal fire which has been prepared for the devil and his angels" (Matt. 25:41). This is a clear allusion to the lake of fire (compare Rev. 19:20; 20:10, 14), the place of continual, eternal, punishment (see answer on Matt. 25:41).

The word translated "destruction" *(olethros)* can be rendered "ruin" or "death." The descriptive phrase that follows, "away from the presence of the Lord," indicates that Paul is referring to separation from God rather than to annihilation. As troubling as this may be, the biblical concept of eternal judgment includes conscious, unceasing torment (compare Luke 16:22–28).

2 Thessalonians 2:3

What did Paul mean by the "apostasy"?

The church at Thessalonica was going through such severe trials that some believers actually thought they were living in the midst of "the day of the Lord," the Tribulation period. Paul argues against such a view, pointing out that two events must precede the Day of the Lord. He writes, "Let no one in any way deceive you, for it [the Day of the Lord, v. 2] will not come unless the apostasy comes first, and the man of lawlessness is revealed, the son of destruction" (v. 3). The "man of lawlessness" is an obvious reference to the "little horn" of Daniel 7:8, the Antichrist of the end time. His appearance marks the beginning of the seventieth "week," the Tribulation (compare Dan. 9:27).

The second event that must precede the Day of the Lord is the "apostasy" *(apostasia)*. It is doubtful that the "apostasy" mentioned in 2:3 refers to doctrinal defection. Doctrinal defection was already going on in Paul's day (1 Tim. 1:3; 6:3–5) and would not have been a sufficiently specific event to warrant Paul's mentioning it as something that must precede the Day of the Lord.

The Greek word *apostasia* is derived from a verb meaning "depart from" *(aphistemi)*. The most basic root meaning of *apostasia* is "departure." While the word can be used metaphorically of departure from doctrine (Acts 21:21), the context of the passage must ultimately determine its meaning. It is significant that in 2:1 Paul is writing about "the coming of our Lord Jesus" and particularly about that aspect of the event which relates to "our gathering together to Him." A comparison with 1 Thessalonians 4:17 suggests that this is a clear reference to the Rapture. Two events, then, must precede the Day of the Lord—the rapture of the church and the revelation of the Antichrist. Believers who have not experienced these events can be assured that they are not suffering Tribulation judgments.

2 Thessalonians 2:6–7

Who or what is the restrainer?

Paul argues in 2 Thessalonians 2 that the Day of the Lord cannot begin until the Antichrist is revealed, and the Antichrist cannot be revealed until the restrainer is removed. Since the restrainer has not been removed, the Thessalonians are not in the Day of the Lord.

There are six major views as to the identity of the restrainer: (1) the Roman Empire; (2) human government; (3) the Jewish state; (4) Satan or another evil power; (5) the archangel Michael; and (6) the Holy Spirit. Each of these possibilities must be evaluated in light of three criteria: (1) the gender shift from neuter *(to katechon)* to masculine *(ho katechon),* (2) the ability to hold back Satan, and (3) the reason for wanting to hold back Satan.

The Holy Spirit best answers to these criteria. First, the neuter of verse 6 relates to the Spirit (neuter) doing the restraining, while the masculine of verse 7 relates to the person of the Holy Spirit doing the restraining. Second, the Spirit of God is actively involved in restraining evil. Third, no one would be better suited or more interested in restraining the work of Satan.

The word translated "restrains" (v. 6) means "to hold back" (compare Rom. 1:18). The full manifestation of the evil of the Antichrist is held back to the end that (*eis to,* with infinitive of purpose) he can be revealed at the time set by God. The purposes of Satan are already at work, but there is a present restraining ministry that deters the culmination of Satan's purposes for the Antichrist.

The removal of the restraining ministry of the Spirit will take place at the rapture of the church. This does not mean that the ministry of the Holy Spirit in the life of individual believers will be dramatically changed in the Tribulation. The Holy Spirit will still be involved in conviction of sin, regeneration, indwelling, and sanctification. While the restraining work of the Spirit ceases at the beginning of the Tribulation, other works of the Spirit continue as essential elements of the new covenant.

2 Thessalonians 2:11

Why would God send upon people a deluding influence "so that they might believe what is false"?

Second Thessalonians 2:11–12 reveals the consequences of unbelief on those who have chosen to reject God rather than to accept His provision of salvation in Christ. The key is in verse 12, where Paul refers to these people as those "who did not believe the truth, but took pleasure in wickedness." The "deluding influence" is both a punishment and the result of their rejection of the truth. Because they have chosen a lie rather than the truth, they are divinely confirmed in their delusion.

1 TIMOTHY

1 Timothy 2:4

If God "desires" all people to be saved, why doesn't he simply save them?

This verse reveals the heart of God. The word translated "desires" (*thelo*) refers to God's moral will, not His deliberate decree. In this sense, God's will is for all people to come to a saving knowledge of His Son Jesus Christ (2 Peter 3:9). But there are other aspects of God's person that must be considered. His holiness and justice demand that the sins of unbelievers be atoned for before they stand in His presence. And so while God "desires" all people to be saved, this cannot happen apart from their being declared righteous through faith (Rom. 5:1). As Paul declares in Romans 3:26, through the sacrifice the Savior made at the Cross, God can be "just and the justifier of the one who has faith in Jesus."

1 Timothy 2:11–12

Did Paul have something against women? Why did he not give them authority equal to that of men?

Contrary to the opinions of some, Paul had a very high view of women. The Jews of Paul's day did not believe that women should be taught the Scripture. To teach a woman the law, they held, would be to defile it! Rabbi Eliezer said, "If a man gives his daughter a knowledge of the Law it is as though he taught her lechery" (Mishnah *Sotah* 4.3). Paul breaks out of his cultural background and rabbinic training when he writes, "Let a woman quietly receive instruction" (1 Tim. 2:11). The words translated "receive instruction" *(manthano)* mean "be discipled." Paul wanted women to be taught God's Word!

While Paul wanted women to learn, verse 12 reveals that he did not authorize them to assume the role of authoritative teachers in the church. This does not mean that they should never teach. They have a responsibility to teach younger women (Titus 2:3) and children (2 Tim. 3:14). There may be occasions where they may teach men, even as Priscilla with Aquila instructed Apollos (compare Acts 18:26). However, Paul's concern in his instruction to Timothy is what goes on in the meeting of the church (compare 1 Tim. 3:15).

Some scholars have argued that Paul's instruction has limited application and was only meant for the first-century situation at Ephesus. But the present tense, "I am continually not permitting," suggests that the action is continuous. And Paul's words in 1 Corinthians 14:33–35 indicate that this rule applied in all the churches.

Verse 12 goes on to explain that a woman should not assume a position of leadership in which she would exercise authority over men. The word translated "exercise authority" (*authenteo*) means "govern," "have mastery over." This indicates clearly that leadership in the church should be the responsibility of men rather than of women. This is consistent with Paul's list of qualifications for the elder in 1 Timothy 3:1–7. This does not mean that women cannot function as leaders. They can function as leaders over women's groups and various organizations. But in the church, any exercise of female leadership needs to be under the authority of elders and pastors. Paul argues, in verses 13–15, that the created order establishes roles for men and women, which, if ignored leads to disaster.

This is a difficult teaching for some women to accept. In spite of Paul's affirming words, "Let a woman be taught," it may seem like he is putting women down. This is not the case at all. Paul simply recognizes that the church is going to operate more effectively and according to God's design if authoritative teaching and leadership is a male function. Women should be encouraged to exercise their teaching and leadership gifts in appropriate contexts.

1 Timothy 2:15

What did Paul mean by the phrase, "preserved [literally, saved] through the bearing of children"?

After discussing the conduct of women in the context of the meeting of the church (2:9–14; compare 3:15), Paul affirms that women will be "saved through the bearing of children." How is this expression to be understood?

Physical Salvation in Childbirth. Some believe that Paul offers encouragement to women that they will be physically delivered through the sufferings of childbirth if they continue in the faith. A major problem with this viewpoint is that it doesn't match with reality. Many godly women have died in childbirth.

Spiritual Salvation Through Childbirth. Roman Catholic tradition affirms that the soul is saved through the bearing of children. If a woman dies in childbirth, she will be saved spiritually. But the end of the verse refutes this viewpoint, if and it is contrary to the doctrine of salvation by faith (Eph. 2:8–9).

Spiritual Salvation Through the Incarnation of Christ. Many take the view that Paul is referring to salvation through *the* childbearing—the Incarnation of Christ as promised to Eve (Gen. 3:15). But the concept of the incarnation seems to be somewhat removed from the context. If Paul wanted to convey this truth, he would be hard-pressed to find a more obscure way to do it. This viewpoint does not offer an adequate explanation for the conditional clause, "if they continue in faith." It must also be noted that the work of redemption focuses more on Christ's resurrection than on His birth.

Spiritual Fulfillment Through Motherhood. Looking to the context for their interpretation, some expositors have suggested that women will be saved from a life of meaninglessness and will find their spiritual fulfillment through being good mothers and wives. This view has the advantage of dealing with the context and focuses on the key exegetical question, "Saved from what?" But Paul points out in 1 Corinthians 7:32–35 that the unmarried woman without a family is able to give herself with wholehearted devotion to the Lord's work. Paul does not view marriage as necessary for meaning and fulfillment in life.

Personal Deliverance from the Temptation to Usurp Authority. The problem Paul is dealing with in 1 Timothy 2:8–15 is the issue of women who want to teach or exercise authority over men in the church. Paul appears to be saying that by assuming the role of a mother and homemaker, a strong and aggressive woman may be delivered from the sin of usurping authority in the church. This view not only answers the question, "saved from what?" but also explains the conditional clause, "if they continue in faith." They are delivered only if they continue in the sphere of faith, love, and holiness, exercising self-restraint.

Taking this viewpoint, "saved" would refer to physical rather than spiritual deliverance (compare Luke 1:71; Acts 7:25; 27:34; Heb. 11:7). The "childbearing" *(teknogonias)* would be taken to refer to the bearing and raising of a family. The definite article would be generic, referring to the whole process and related activities. Paul certainly has that idea in mind in 1 Timothy 5:14, where he uses the verbal form of the noun *(teknogoneo).*

Crucial to an understanding of this viewpoint is a proper interpretation of Genesis 3:16 where, as part of the curse, God told the woman, "Yet your desire shall be for your husband, and he shall rule over you" (see on Gen. 3:16). The woman's desire is to control her husband—to usurp his divinely appointed headship. As a consequence, the man must now actively seek to maintain his headship in the face of opposition. As a result of the Fall, men no longer rule easily.

We see from Genesis 3:16 that as part of the curse, there is a tendency for women to usurp men's authority. For some women this tendency is stronger than for others. For those who struggle, 1 Timothy 2:15 presents a means of deliverance. Those that recognize a strong tendency in this direction should make their families the focus of their ministries and thus be delivered from opportunities to usurp authority in the church.

1 Timothy 3:2

What did Paul mean by the qualification, "husband of one wife"?

The qualification, "husband of one wife" *(mias gunaikos andra)* is listed among a series of qualifications for the office of elder (1 Tim. 3:1–7). Some have suggested that Paul is prohibiting polygamy. But there was no need for such a requirement since polygamy was forbidden by Roman law and was not practiced by the Greeks or Romans of Paul's day. Others have suggested that the phrase excludes remarried widowers. But Paul saw nothing wrong with the remarriage after the death of a spouse (1 Cor. 7:39). Still others have argued that the qualification requires faithfulness to one's present wife, whether or not this is the second or third marriage. It is argued that the absence of the definite article *(the)* indicates that the emphasis is on quality, not character, not past history.

Taken within the context, I suggest that the qualification "husband of one wife" (literally, *one woman's man*) refers to a man who has one wife—that is, one marriage. A man who is divorced and remarried would not meet the qualification. The other qualifications tend to support this view. How could he be above reproach, manage his household well, and have a good reputation if he has divorced and remarried?

The word translated "one" is in the place of emphasis and is so regarded as the most significant part of the qualification. "One" *(eis)* is used in Scripture in contrast to more than one, as in Mark 12:6, "only one son," and Matthew 23:8, "one is your teacher." Never in the New Testament does *one* suggest more than one. It is always used quite literally.

A comparable phrase occurs in 1 Timothy 5:9 where Paul presents qualifications for women being placed on the widows' list. To qualify, a widow must have been the "wife of one man" *(henos andros gune)*. The phrase literally reads "one man's wife." The context indicates clearly that this refers to one marriage. Whatever the phrase means in 1 Timothy 5:9, it must share a similar meaning in 1 Timothy 3:2.

The phrase, "husband of one wife," suggests three related character qualifications. First, no divorce and remarriage (divorce by itself may not be disqualifying). The man has one wife, not two women with whom he has a one-flesh marriage relationship. Second, no infidelity. The man is completely faithful to his one wife (1 Tim. 5:2; 2 Tim. 2:22). Third, no wandering eyes. Jesus condemned the Pharisees for keeping the letter but not the spirit of the law. According to Jesus, the one who covets immoral relationships in his heart is as guilty as the one who does the physical act (Matt. 5:27–28).

The qualification "husband of one wife," may exclude some very godly and mature Christians from the office of elder. But there are many other opportunities of ministry for which they may be suited—evangelism, youth ministry, visitation, counseling, Sunday school teaching, church secretary, treasurer, chair of the C. E. committee. When God, in His sovereign wisdom, closes one door, He usually opens another one.

1 Timothy 3:11

Do the "women" mentioned here refer to deaconesses or to the wives of the deacons?

In 1 Timothy 3:8–13, Paul lists the qualifications for the office of deacon. Within that listing Paul writes, "Women must likewise be dignified, not malicious gossips, but temperate, faithful in all things." Is Paul referring here to a separate office, the office of deaconess? Some have concluded that this is indeed the case and that Phoebe (Rom. 16:1) is an example of such a deaconess.

The context is always a clue as to the meaning of a debated phrase. And the place of this verse in the middle of a paragraph about deacons suggests that Paul is referring here to the *wives* of deacons rather than introducing another separate office. And while Phoebe is called a *deacone*, this is probably a general rather than technical use of the word, as in 1 Corinthians 16:15. Paul is saying in 1 Timothy 3:11 that the wives of church leaders must be exemplary. Marital or domestic problems may disqualify a capable church leader.

1 Timothy 5:20

Is the "rebuke" required when an elder sins or only in the case of persistent sin?

Although Paul set high standards for elders (1 Tim. 3:1–7), he knew that they would not be immune to sin. In 1 Timothy 5:19–21, he provides directions for dealing with elders who sin. In verse 20, he directs the church to "rebuke" those elders who sin. Is the rebuke necessary for a single sin or only in the case of repeated sin?[1]

The present active tense of the participle *(hamartanoutas)* has been taken to mean that the rebuke is necessary only in the case of those who "continue in sin." A genuinely repentant elder need not be publicly rebuked. Others suggest that the present participle is merely descriptive, suggesting that the occasion of any well-attested sin would call for public rebuke. No distinction would be made between those who have repented and those who continue sinning.

Within the context of this passage, Paul sets in contrast the "elders who rule well" (v. 17) with "those who are sinning" (v. 20). Those who rule well are to be doubly honored. Those who default in their duties are to be publicly rebuked. The *Jerusalem Bible* gives a clear rendering of the text of verses 19–20, "Never accept any accusation brought against an elder unless it is supported by two or three witnesses. If any of them are at fault, reprimand them publicly, as a warning to the rest." The present tense of the participle suggests that one slipup would not necessitate a public rebuke. But circumstances that reflect a regular failing or character deficiency demand that public discipline be administered.

1 Timothy 5:23

Was Paul an advocate of social drinking?

Timothy, who was experiencing ill health at Ephesus, was apparently avoiding the use of alcohol. He was doing this at the expense of his health. So Paul instructed him to "use a little wine for the sake of your stomach and your frequent ailments." This advice is given in relationship to a medical problem not social relationships. This text does not support the concept of social drinking (compare Prov. 20:1; 23:31). For further discussion on the use of wine, see my comments on John 2:1–11.

1 Timothy 6:10

Is money an intrinsic evil to be avoided?

In 1 Timothy 6:6–10, Paul warns of the perils of pursuing riches instead of finding contentment in God's basic provisions. In verse 10, he declares that "the love of money is a root of all sorts of evil." Notice that Paul did not say that money was evil. Rather, the love of money is a source of evil.

Jesus said, "You cannot serve God and mammon" (Matt. 6:24). Double allegiance is impossible. Giving oneself to the pursuit of riches will displace one's love for God and will result in self-destruction.

Endnotes

1. For a complete study of the discipline of Christian leaders, see chapter 10 in my book, *A Guide to Church Discipline* (Minneapolis: Bethany House, 1985).

2 TIMOTHY

2 Timothy 2:12

What did Paul mean, "If we deny Him, He also will deny us"? Does this mean that Christ will turn His back on a believer who fails to witness?

In 2 Timothy 2:11–13, Paul explains the need for earthly suffering as grounded in the believer's unity with Christ (compare John 15:18–21). The first two statements (vv. 11–12) show that present suffering has future consequences. But the third statement concerns us. Jesus made a similar statement in Matthew 10:33, "But whoever shall deny Me before men, I will also deny him before My Father who is in heaven." Will Christ deny us if we fail Him? This question was of great significance to Christians experiencing persecution.

In dealing with a difficulty like this one, it is helpful to be reminded of what is clearly revealed elsewhere. Jesus declared in John 10:28, "And I give eternal life to them, and they shall never perish; and no one shall snatch them out of My hand." In Romans 8:29–30, Paul shows that God sovereignly moves us from being "predestined" to being "glorified" without any loss. These passages teach clearly that true believers do not loose their salvation. So how do we understand this text?

It is possible to interpret 2 Timothy 2:12 as referring to something that is *hypothetical*. Kent points out that the verb "will deny" is future tense, indicating that Paul is not stating what is presently the case.[1] In other words, Paul wasn't thinking of his readers as denying Christ, although the consequence of any future denial is clear. Another possibility is that Paul is referring to something that is *actual*. Such a denial would constitute a disowning of Christ, not a temporary denial such as Peter's. An actual denial of Christ would evidence that one's profession of faith is a fallacy. Such a denial would be not merely from weakness but from unbelief, for no true believer would deny Christ in this way.

During times of Christian persecution, many were forced to repudiate their faith and sacrifice to the emperor. Many of those who refused died as martyrs. Other true believers may have lapsed, due to the suffering or the threat of death. For those of us who sometimes fail, 2 Timothy 2:13 provides an encouragement, "If we are faithless, He remains faithful; for He cannot deny Himself." Our failure to be true to Christ does not alter His abiding faithfulness.

2 Timothy 3:16
Should Christians believe in the inspiration of the Bible?

Some people believe that the Bible is a book of myths and stories that reflect humanity's attempt to explain human existence. Others believe that the Bible is a good book that teaches moral lessons for living. But for Christians, the Bible is a very special and unique book. Second Timothy 3:16 reveals that "all Scripture is inspired by God."

Notice that Paul refers here to all Scripture, not to just some parts or books. This means that all sixty-six books of the Bible share in this special quality. The word "Scripture" is a general term for the Bible, including both the Old and New Testaments. The words, "inspired by God," are the translation of one word in the Greek text, *theopneustos*. This word might best be rendered, "God-breathed." All Scripture shares the quality of being breathed out as the breath of God. This means that God guided and directed the human authors of Scripture so that His revelation to humanity was recorded without error in the words of the original manuscripts.

There are two more things we can conclude about Scripture from this passage. If all Scripture is "God-breathed," then the Bible is inerrant (John 17:17). It will not be proven false or mistaken. And it is also infallible. That is, it is not capable of teaching deception. *Inerrancy* speaks of the accuracy of the record. *Infallibility* refers to the reliability of Scripture as a guide.

These statements about the Bible are not just sound theology. They have very practical implications. Since we have an inspired, inerrant, and infallible Bible, it is "profitable for teaching, for reproof, for correction, for training in righteousness." All this is designed to make God's people proficient for ministry and equipped to serve God (v. 17).

Endnotes
1. Homer Kent, *The Pastoral Epistles* (Chicago: Moody Press, 1958), 272.

TITUS

Titus 1:16

Is it possible for someone to make a false profession of Christ?

The problem with the Cretans was that they professed a knowledge of God, but that profession did not match with reality. Their detestable deeds and disobedience proved their profession false. The principle emphasized here is that one's conduct ought to be consistent with one's confession. The life we live provides a test of the faith we profess.

It is indeed possible for someone to believe something about Christ, profess faith, and be baptized without experiencing personal regeneration, new birth, and justification. This may happen in the case of a child who professes Christ without a basic understanding of the Gospel. Sometimes people respond to an emotional appeal, raising a hand or walking an aisle, without actually believing in Jesus. In some cases, people may profess faith in Christ, but the one they embrace is someone other than the Christ of the Bible. It usually becomes apparent, either to the individual or to their associates, that the profession of faith is faulty. No wonder Paul charged the Corinthians, "Test yourselves to see if you are in the faith; examine yourselves! Or do you not recognize this about yourselves, that Jesus Christ is in you—unless indeed you fail the test?" (2 Cor. 13:5).

Titus 2:11

Is Paul suggesting the doctrine of universalism, that all people, regardless of their relationship with Christ, are saved?

According to the apostle Paul, there are two kinds of people on this earth—those who are "dead" in their trespasses and sins (Eph. 2:1) and those who have been made "alive together with Christ" (v. 5). The only way to move out of the first state and into the second is through the divine work of regeneration, brought about by God's grace and appropriated by personal faith. People who do not personally respond to God's provision stand condemned in their sins (Rom. 3:23). It is only when people "believe" that they enter into the experience of personal salvation (10:10).

Jesus did not believe in universalism (John 14:6). Neither did Peter (Acts 4:12) or Paul (1 Tim. 2:5). It is only by being justified by His grace that we have the "hope of eternal life" (Titus 3:7).

PHILEMON

Philemon 1

Who was Philemon?

Paul's shortest letter is addressed to Philemon, "our beloved brother and fellow worker." This book is the only source of information about Philemon. It is evident from the context that he was a slaveholder (vv. 15–16) who had been converted, possibly as a result of Paul's ministry. Verse 19 indicates that Philemon is at least indebted to Paul in some way. Philemon was beloved by Paul and had worked with him or helped him with his ministry. He was acquainted with Epaphras, Mark, Aristarchus, Demas, and Luke (vv. 23–24). Since the church met at Philemon's house, he may have been a person of substance and influence.

Philemon 16

What was Paul's view on slavery?

Neither the teachings of Jesus nor the teachings of Paul condemn slavery. Rather than trying to overthrow the cultural institution of slavery, Paul sought to work within the system, requiring that slaves obey their masters (Eph. 6:5; Col. 3:22–24) and that masters not mistreat their slaves (Col. 4:1; 1 Peter 2:18–20). Paul recognized that what matters most is not one's status as enslaved or free but whether or not one knows Christ (Gal. 3:28). According to Paul, a slave is free in Christ, and a free man or woman is Christ's slave (1 Cor. 7:22). And yet Paul does write, concerning the believing slave, "if you are able also to become free, rather do that" (v. 21). And while he insists that Onesimus, the runaway slave, return to his master, Philemon (Philem. 12), he asks Philemon to forgive him and accept him as a brother (vv. 16–18). He may even allude to the possibility of granting Onesimus his freedom when he writes, "I know that you will do even more than what I say" (v. 21). For additional comments, see Ephesians 6:5.

HEBREWS

Authorship

Who wrote the book of Hebrews?

There has been much debate over the authorship of Hebrews. Many have ascribed it to Paul, but Hebrews 2:3 presents a major problem for this viewpoint. There the writer indicates that he received the message concerning salvation from "those who heard." It is very unlikely that Paul would have placed himself as a second hand recipient of the Gospel (compare Gal. 1:12). Suggested authors include Barnabas, Apollos, Clement of Rome, Luke, Silas, Philip, Priscilla, and John Mark. We can't go far beyond Origen's comment on this subject. He wrote, "Who the author of Hebrews is, God truly knows."

Hebrews 2:1–4

Does this passage teach that Christians can lose their salvation? To whom is this warning addressed?

Hebrews 2:1–4 is the first of five warning passages (compare 3:7–4:13; 5:11–6:20; 10:26–31; 12:25–29). These passages raise some difficult questions. Are the warnings addressed to believers? Do they teach that salvation can be lost through disobedience? If not, how can such severe warnings be addressed to true believers?

The key to answering these questions is to decide the identity of the readers of this letter. Although not without debate, most scholars agree on the basis of internal evidence that Hebrews was written to Hebrew Christians. That they are Hebrews is reflected in comments regarding the prophets, angels, Moses, Aaron, and the tabernacle. That they are believers is evidenced by the fact that they are called "holy brethren" (3:1), "brethren" (v. 12), "partakers of Christ" (v. 14). If the readers are believers, it seems logical to conclude that the warnings are addressed to believers. There is no indication that a different group is addressed in the five warning passages.

Arminians have taken the warnings to be addressed to saved people who are subsequently lost. At first glance, this viewpoint seems to be supported by the warning passages. But careful exegesis proves the theory wrong. John 10:28–29 teaches the perseverance of true saints and refutes this viewpoint.

Calvinists have taken the warnings to refer to those who have made an outward profession of faith but have never been genuinely saved. While this view can be supported by Scripture (compare Titus 1:16), it is inconsistent with internal indicators regarding the readers. This letter is written to saved individuals. And the warnings are also given to genuinely saved people. They have "tasted of the heavenly gift and have been made partakers of the Holy Spirit" (6:4). They are the "sanctified" (10:29) and are "His [God's] people" (v. 30).

Based on evidence from within the book, it seems that the readers were true believers who were in danger of drifting from Christ back to the shadows of Jewish ceremonies and legalism (2:1). This view has the advantage of consistency. It is consistent with the Bible's teaching regarding the believers' security and is consistent with internal indicators suggesting that the readers are believers.

In Hebrews 2:1–4, the author argues that since disobedience to the revelation mediated by angels was duly punished, those who disobey the Christian message of salvation will not go unpunished. The readers were in danger of drifting from the substance, Christ, to the shadows of Judaism. They were not in danger of losing their salvation. The danger was in failing to appropriate its provisions. Accordingly, the term "salvation" (v. 3) must be understood as a reference to sanctification rather than to justification. The readers will not be saved from sin's power and influence by drifting from grace back to Jewish laws and ceremonies.

Hebrews 2:10

How could Jesus, the perfect Son of God, be made "more perfect"?

In Hebrews 2:10–18, the author deals with an objection to the point being made in 1:4–2:18, the superiority of Jesus over angels. The humiliating sufferings of Christ might make His superiority doubtful to some. But the author points out that this suffering was necessary to complete Christ's identification with humanity.

In Hebrews 2:10, the author states that it was fitting for God to "perfect" Jesus, the "author" of salvation, through sufferings. The word translated "perfect" *(teleioo)* means "to complete," "to perfect," or "to qualify." The idea here is that God wanted to make Jesus fully qualified as the Author of salvation. And this training involved the sufferings of humanity. Robertson comments, "One cannot know human life without living it. There was no moral imperfection in Jesus, but He lived His human life in order to be able to be a sympathizing and effective leader in the work of salvation."[1]

Hebrews 3:7–4:13

How should believers regard the warning given by the writer to the Hebrews?

Refer first to the answer on 2:1–4 regarding the warning passages of Hebrews. The writer warns that as the Israelites failed to enter Canaan because of unbelief (3:19), the readers will miss out on similar blessing if they do not continue on in the faith (vv. 12, 19). Unbelief is a serious matter. It will exclude millions from heaven and will prevent numerous Christians from enjoying all that God has for them.

For the illustration of unbelief, the author draws upon Psalm 95:7–11, in which David warns his own generation against the rebellion that characterized God's people in the wilderness. Their rebellion and unbelief did not result in the loss of their salvation. But they did forfeit God's rest—entrance into the Promised Land. And so too, the Hebrew Christians were exhibiting the same faithlessness toward God's revelation as their forefathers had. And the consequences could be equally disastrous!

Hebrews 4:11

Should Christians observe the Sabbath?

In presenting his case for the superior work of Christ, the writer of Hebrews shows that believers can "rest" in Christ's finished work. The author writes, in 4:9, "There remains therefore a Sabbath rest for the people of God." The word translated "sabbath rest" *(sabbatismos)* can better be rendered, "a Sabbath kind of rest." The word used here is different than the word for the Sabbath *(sabbaton)*. The writer is not requiring Christians to keep the Sabbath (Saturday), as Jewish people did under the old covenant. But there is a "rest" for believers that is reminiscent of God's rest after Creation (Gen. 2:2; Heb. 4:4). When Jesus completed His work on the cross, He declared, "It is finished!" (John 19:30). This means that redemption has been completely accomplished and believers can "rest" in our Savior's finished work. Whenever we pray to the Father in the name of Jesus, whenever we worship or have devotions, whenever we receive God's forgiveness and blessing, we are enjoying a "Sabbath kind of rest." We are resting in the finished redemption that Christ has accomplished.

The Sabbath observance as a day of rest was the sign of God's covenant with the nation of Israel (Exod. 31:13–17). Under the old covenant, the Israelites were required to rest from sunset on Friday until sunset on Saturday. The writer of Hebrews makes it quite clear that the old covenant was terminated at the Cross when Jesus inaugurated the new covenant (Heb. 8:6). Since we are not under the old covenant, we need not observe the covenant sign. Nowhere in the New Testament are believers instructed to observe the Sabbath. However, the principles of rest and worship have application for believers in every age. The church in Acts customarily met on Sunday in commemoration of our Lord's resurrection. But Paul insists that the Christian faith is not bound up with the observance of days (Rom. 14:5–6; Col. 2:16–17). On a personal level, I observe *every* day as a "Sabbath kind of rest," resting in the finished work of Christ as mediator of a new covenant.

Hebrews 6:1–4

How should Christians understand this warning?

Refer first to the answer 2:1–4 regarding the warning passages of Hebrews. In the third warning (5:11–6:20), the author rebukes the readers for their lack of spiritual progress and encourages them to press on to maturity. The failure of the readers was a departure from grace to Judaistic ordinances as a means of maintaining their relationship with God. Now they were seeking to get saved again by going back to the Cross—the ABCs of the faith.

The author warns of the danger of regressing to spiritual infancy instead of moving on to adulthood (6:1–2). The writer argues that there is no point in laying a foundation again since it has already been established (vv. 4–5). These verses make it clear that the writer is addressing saved people. Beginning the Christian life again is impossible. The only option for the Hebrew Christians is to press on to maturity.

Verse 6 has often been misinterpreted. The writer says that something is impossible. The modal participle *(anastaurountas)* is the key. The *New American Standard Bible* adds the word "since." The better rendering would be "by." Renewal is possible but not one that involves recrucifying Christ! To renew believers again to repentance *by* recrucifying Christ, thus bringing Him open shame, is impossible! Since the readers cannot start the Christian life over again, they must simply press on to maturity.

Hebrews 7:3

Was Melchizedek a theophany or a historical person?

Melchizedek is a fascinating figure that appears in only two texts of the Old Testament—Genesis 14:18–20 and Psalm 110:4. The writer of Hebrews draws from these passages to show that Christ is of the priesthood of Melchizedek, a priesthood superior to that of Aaron. The author of Hebrews is not interested in anything that might be known about Melchizedek outside the biblical record. When making a comparison with Christ, the writer appeals to what is true about Melchizedek in a limited, literary sense. When the author describes Melchizedek "without father, without mother, without genealogy, having neither beginning of days nor end of life" (Heb. 7:3), he is simply saying that Melchizedek, like Christ, stands alone. The Old Testament provides no record of his ancestry, progeny, birth, or death. The silence of Scripture, as well as the statements about him, provide a fitting analogy with the person of Christ. Since there is no record of Melchizedek's death, his priesthood appears to be perpetual (Ps. 110:4). There is nothing in the Old Testament record that requires interpreting Melchizedek as an angel or as an appearance of Christ. This viewpoint is derived from a mistaken interpretation of Hebrews 7:3. Melchizedek prefigures Christ in three ways. First, he was both a king and a priest. Second, he was a king of righteousness and a king of peace. Third, he is a picture of a priest who holds his priesthood forever.

Hebrews 8:6

Is the new covenant a future or a present provision for God's people?

Hebrews 8:6–13 presents Christ as the Mediator of a better covenant than the old covenant and one that is enacted on better promises. Scholars have debated whether the new covenant is provision for God's people today or whether it will be inaugurated when a remnant of Israel repents at the Second Coming (Zech. 12:10–13:1). The answer is found in the Greek grammar of Hebrews 8:6. The writer declares that the "better covenant . . . has been enacted." The perfect passive indicative of *nomotheteo* (to enact) means that the action of the verb has started and continues. This reveals clearly that the new covenant stands in force. It was "enacted" by the death of Christ, whose mediatorial work on the cross brought God and humankind together. Believers in Jesus Christ, whether Jew or Gentile, can enjoy the blessings of the new covenant today!

Hebrews 9:3–4

Was the altar of incense in the Holy Place or in the Most Holy Place behind the veil?

The altar of incense was made of acacia wood and overlaid with gold. It stood about three feet high and was used for daily offerings of incense by the priests. According to Exodus 30:6, this altar was located in the Holy Place directly in front of the curtain, or veil, that shielded the ark of the covenant from view. However, the writer of Hebrews seems to disagree. He refers to the Holy of Holies as "having a golden altar of incense" (Heb. 9:4). At first glance, this seems to suggest that there is a contradiction between Exodus and Hebrews. But there is another possibility. While the altar of incense stood in the Holy Place before the veil, its ritual use on the Day of Atonement was connected with the Holy of Holies. The high priest would take coals from the altar of incense to burn incense within the Holy of Holies (Lev. 16:12–13). In Hebrews 9:4, the writer uses the word "having" *(echousa)* instead of "in which" *(en he),* which seems to suggest association rather than location. I suggest that the writer of Hebrews is referring to the incense altar in terms of its liturgical function on the Day of Atonement rather than of its physical location in the Holy Place.

Hebrews 10:5

Does the writer of Hebrews misquote Psalm 40:6?

Psalm 40:6 quotes the Messiah as saying, "My ears Thou hast opened," while the writer of Hebrews quotes, "But a body Thou hast prepared for Me" (Heb. 10:5). It appears as though the text of the Old Testament has been distorted by a New Testament writer. Actually, the problem is not so much with the author as with the translation he was using. In Psalm 40:6, the Greek translation known as the Septuagint replaces the words, "My ears Thou hast opened" with "a body Thou didst prepare for Me." Bruce points out that the Greek version cannot be explained as representing a variant or corrupted Hebrew reading.[2]

It seems that the writer has given an interpretive paraphrase of the Hebrew text. It has been suggested that the Hebrew text of Psalm 40:6 might contain an allusion to the piercing of the slave's ear to signify willingness to serve the master permanently (Exod. 21:6). The writer of Hebrews interprets this to signify that Christ in His incarnation has taken on the "body" and role of a servant. Others suggest that the psalmist made reference to God making ears that are responsive and obedient. The writer of Hebrews interprets this to mean that God has prepared a body that will perform God's will. Either option would satisfy the difficulty. Geisler and Howe remind us that "NT citations need not be exact quotations as long as they are faithful to the truth contained in the OT text."[3]

Hebrews 10:11

If the old covenant sacrifices did not atone for sin, what did they accomplish?

In Hebrews 10:1–18, the writer demonstrates the effectiveness of Christ's sacrifice by comparing it with the inadequate sacrifices of the old covenant system. He points out that the old covenant sacrifices never make people perfect, ultimately satisfy God, or take away sins. He declares, in verse 11, that "every priest stands daily ministering and offering time after time the same sacrifices, which can never take away sins."

So what did the old covenant sacrifices accomplish? The old covenant sacrifices expressed a need that they did not actually fulfill. They pointed to the need for atonement, for the satisfaction of God's wrath, and for the removal of the defilement of sin. Ultimately, they could not accomplish these needs. But when the sacrifices were offered *by faith,* in keeping with God's commands, God accepted them as tokens of what Christ would finally accomplish. This is evident in Romans 3:25, where Paul writes that "in the forbearance of God He passed over the sins previously committed." This suggests that God, out of His patience and grace, was willing to overlook past sins because He knew they would be atoned for by Christ. When God saw the sacrifices offered on the temple altar, He said something like, "That's good enough for now. That sacrifice will make you acceptable until Jesus, My sacrificial Lamb, can offer the full and final sacrifice for all time."

Hebrews 10:26–31

How should a Christian regard this warning? It seems so severe.

Refer first to the answer on 2:1–4 regarding the warning passages of Hebrews. The fourth warning passage is probably the most difficult because of its severity. It would be easy to change one's view of the readers at this point and suggest that they are unsaved. But that is not a consistent approach to the epistle. And there are clear indications within this warning that the readers are saved. Notice the "we" (v. 26), "sanctified" (v. 29), and "His people" (v. 30). This warning is clearly addressed to believers, and it speaks of the seriousness of deliberate sin committed by those of the faith.

This warning is given to Christians who were reverting from grace to the requirements of Jewish ritualism. These believers were tempted to minimize Christ's sacrifice by turning back to Mosaic ritual. The writer responds, in verse 26, by pointing out that to minimize Christ's sacrifice is to reject the only sacrifice for sins. If there was severe judgment under the Mosaic Law (vv. 27–28), how much more severe will be God's discipline on those who minimize the work of His Son (v. 29)! The writer appeals to the Old Testament (Deut. 32:35; Ps. 135:4) to point out that God's people will reap what they sow.

Hebrews 11:21

Is there a discrepancy between this text and Genesis 47:31, regarding the death of Jacob?

Genesis 47:31 records that when Jacob died, he "bowed . . . at the head of the bed." The writer of Hebrews records that as Jacob was dying, he blessed each of the sons of Joseph and "worshiped, [leaning] on the top of his staff" (Heb. 11:21). This discrepancy arose from the fact that the original Hebrew text was written without vowels. And the Hebrew consonants for "staff" *(matteh)* and "bed" *(mittah)* are exactly the same *(mth)*. When the Masoretes standardized the text adding vowels, around A.D. 700, they pointed the Hebrew word as "bed." The Greek translators of the Septuagint had interpreted the word to be the word for "staff." Kent rightly points out that the conflict is actually between the Septuagint and the Masoretic pointing, not in the Hebrew text as such.[4] The writer of Hebrews follows the Septuagint rendering and reflects the earliest tradition among Jewish scholars. That Jacob worshiped, leaning on his staff, makes good sense in light of the context. I suspect, with other scholars, that the Masoretic pointing of the Hebrew text is in error.

Hebrews 11:32

What are people like Barak, Samson, and Jephthah doing in the "hall of fame" of faith?

I suppose we could ask this question of Noah (who got drunk), of Abraham (who lied about Sarah), of Isaac (who lied about Rebekkah), of Jacob (who cheated his brother and deceived his father), of Moses (who killed a man), of Rahab (who was a harlot), and of David (who was an adulterer). None of the people in Hebrews 11 appear there because of their exemplary conduct. On the other hand, they are listed in the hall of fame of faith because of their faith in God and His promise. And they did extraordinary things based on their faith in God's promise. Barak was unwilling to go into battle without Deborah; Samson did not achieve his maximum potential; Jephthah made a foolish vow. But their faith was undiminished by these noteworthy failures, and for this they are recognized.

Hebrews 12:17

Why couldn't Esau repent if he sought it with tears?

Hebrews 12:14–17 presents some of the dangers and difficulties of responding to God's discipline. Among the dangers is a godless attitude and refusal to repent of wrongdoing. As an example, the writer reminds us of Esau, who sold his birthright for a single meal. Verse 17 adds this comment, "For you know that even afterwards, when he desired to inherit the blessing, he was rejected, for he found no place for repentance, though he sought for it with tears." The exegetical question for the reader is, To what does the pronoun "it" *(auten)* refer? While the pronoun might refer to repentance—a change of mind on his part or his father's—it more likely refers to the "blessing." This latter view is more consistent with Genesis 27:34, 38. What Esau sought with tears was the blessing that he had so foolishly squandered. Yet there was no place for true repentance in his heart. He regretted what he had lost, not his foolish actions.

Hebrews 12:25–29

Is this warning for believers or for unbelievers? How does it apply to us?

Refer first to the answer on 2:1–4 regarding the warning passages of Hebrews. The fifth and final warning urges the readers to think seriously about the importance of heeding what God has spoken. A reminder of the awesome scene at Sinai is used to emphasize the importance of absolute compliance with God's Word. Verse 25 reveals the principle that greater privilege means greater responsibility. If God judged the disobedient at Sinai, certainly He will judge those who are the recipients of greater privilege under grace! Believers must not take lightly the truth of God's fiery holiness, which was demonstrated at Mount Sinai. We must serve God "with reverence and awe; for our God is a consuming fire" (vv. 28–29).

The five warnings in the book of Hebrews remind us that sin is a serious matter. Being the recipients of God's grace should not cause us to take sin lightly. Schoonhoven remarks:

> The recipients are warned not to sin because when they do sin, they at that very moment and in that very act are violating the holiness of God and living in discord with the reality of the grace into which they have entered. The threats are so grave because the act of sin is so serious. It partakes of a realm that is wholly contrary to God; it is in another sphere of existence, the demonic sphere. And to the extent that it is participated in, even though it be slight, it is an offense to the holiness of God.[5]

Endnotes

1. A. T. Robertson, *Word Pictures in the New Testament*, vol. 5 (Nashville: Broadman Press, 1932), 347.
2. F. F. Bruce, *The Epistle to the Hebrews* (Grand Rapids: Eerdmans, 1964), 232.

3. Norman Geisler and Thomas Howe, *When Critics Ask* (Wheaton: Victor Books, 1992), 521.
4. Homer A. Kent Jr., *The Epistle to the Hebrews* (Grand Rapids: Baker Book House, 1972), 233.
5. Calvin R. Schoonhoven, "The 'Analogy of Faith'" in *Scripture, Tradition, and Interpretation* (1978): 98.

JAMES

James 1:13

If God does not tempt anyone, why did Jesus instruct His disciples to pray, "Do not lead us into temptation" (Matt. 6:13)?

Some of James's readers thought that as God brought trials, He also brought temptation. This could lead to blaming God for temptation and sin! Such a suggestion is absolutely inconsistent with God's character. James responds by making it very clear that God is not a source of solicitation to evil. He never tempts someone to do what is morally wrong.

So what did Jesus mean in His instruction to His disciples in Matthew 6:13? Jesus is suggesting that we pray for deliverance from situations in which we might be enticed and overcome by sin. Paul directs us to "make no provision for the flesh" (Rom. 13:14). Jesus is simply asking that we request God's help in accomplishing this. And this is the kind of prayer that God will be sure to answer!

James 1:25; 2:12

What does James mean by the "perfect law, the law of liberty"?

Many suggestions have been offered as answers to this major interpretive question in James. Some have suggested that James has in mind the Law of Moses, which the psalmist regards as "perfect" (Ps. 19:7). Others suggest that James is referring to Jesus' reinterpretation and explanation of the law (Matt. 5:21–48; compare James 2:8). Hiebert argues that the context suggests James is referring to "the word" of God (1:21–22). He presents the view that James refers to that "authoritative body of truth that is the foundation of the Christian faith."[1] This law is "perfect" in that it is final and complete, embodying the full and effective revelation of God in Christ Jesus. It can be designated "the law of liberty" because it produces liberty, setting believers free in Christ (John 8:32).

James 2:14–26

Does James contradict Paul on the doctrine of justification when he insists that we are "justified by works, and not by faith alone"?

At first glance it appears that James is in flat contradiction with Paul on the doctrine of justification. Paul insists that "a man is not justified by the works

310

of the Law but through faith in Christ Jesus" (Gal. 2:16; compare Rom. 3:20; Eph. 2:8–9). James, however, argues that "a man is justified by works, and not by faith alone" (James 2:24). Is it possible to reconcile these apparently contradictory viewpoints?

Some scholars have argued that James was familiar with Galatians and Romans and was deliberately refuting Paul. If that be the case, James completely misunderstood Paul and appears to have been quite unaware of the issue of circumcision (Rom. 2:25–29; compare Gal. 5:2–11). There is a better alternative.

James and Paul were confronting different issues. Their words are similar, but their concepts are very different. Paul was refuting those who advocated works—circumcision and the observance of Jewish ceremonial law—as necessary for justification. James, on the other hand, was challenging those who presumed the adequacy of mere intellectual assent to orthodox doctrine. Ladd remarks, "In brief, James and Paul are dealing with two different situations: Paul with the self-righteousness of Jewish legal piety and James with dead orthodoxy."[2] It is enlightening to see how differently James and Paul use certain Greek words.

Pistis (faith). Paul uses this term to denote personal acceptance (trust) of the Gospel and commitment to Christ. James acknowledges this meaning (2:1), but in 2:14–26 uses *pistis* and *pisteuo* referring to mere intellectual assent to doctrine. Note his emphasis on faith "alone" (v. 24). "The argument is that verbal, intellectual assent to doctrine is meaningless unless an altered lifestyle reveals a truly salvific commitment."[3]

Erga (works). Paul uses this term in refuting the Judaizers to denote the works of the law—ceremonial rites added to the work of Christ. In James, *erga* are moral deeds, such as acts of charity, that flow naturally from a genuine faith. Paul also recognizes such works as evidences of a true faith (Gal. 6:6, 10; Eph. 2:10; Titus 1:16).

Dikaioo (to justify). Paul uses this term in a forensic or legal way, "to declare to be just or righteous." James, however, uses the term in a manner more in keeping with the Septuagint's usage, "show to be righteous."

Paul and James illustrate their respective points from two different incidents in the life of Abraham. Paul highlights Genesis 15:6, showing that Abraham was justified by faith before being circumcised (Rom. 4:9–13; Gal. 3:6–7). James highlights Genesis 22, showing the testing of Abraham's faith by which his righteousness was proven. Both agree that the faith that saves is not *alone*.

James 3:1

Why do teachers incur a stricter judgment?

Teachers had a high status in Jewish society and in the early church. Consequently, some sought the position who were not qualified. James warns that one should not seek this office who is not properly qualified. Teachers are subject to a stricter judgment for two reasons. First, they will be judged for leading others into error (Matt. 18:6–7). Second, they will be judged on the basis of their greater accountability. The Bible clearly teaches that greater opportunity means greater accountability (Rom. 2:12). To whom much is given, much will be required (Luke 12:48). Those who have had great privilege to study will be judged for their greater knowledge of God's truth.

James 5:1–6

Is James addressing believers or unbelievers in these verses?

In this text James warns wealthy oppressors of coming judgment for mistreating the poor. Some suggest that these oppressors are Christians. James apparently knew some rich believers (James 1:10). Yet the words "you have fattened your hearts in a day of slaughter" (5:5) seem to be rather strong if describing Christians. Another possibility is that they are non-Christians. They may have professed faith in Christ, but their conduct makes their profession of faith suspect (Titus 1:16). But why would James include such a reference to readers generally considered to be believers?

Perhaps the safest approach is to regard the words of James 5:1–6 as a general warning to *all* who misuse their wealth. God holds people accountable for the use of their temporal resources. Those who use their resources for selfish purposes, ignoring the needs of the oppressed, will be judged. For believers, this will take place as the judgment seat of Christ (2 Cor. 5:10). For the unbeliever, this will occur before the Great White Throne (Rev. 20:11–15).

James 5:12

Does the Bible forbid solemn oaths?

Swearing an oath may be defined as an appeal to God or to something held sacred to support the truthfulness of a statement, promise, or vow.[4] It was common practice among Jewish people in ancient times to support statements of truth with an oath. The Old Testament condemned false oaths (Exod. 20:7). But frequently Jewish people made oaths with subtle distinctions between those considered binding and those that were not. In the Mishnah, the tractate *Shebuoth* is devoted to the topic of oaths. The rabbis held that oaths made "by Shaddai" or "by Sabaoth" or "by the Merciful and Gracious" are binding. But oaths made "by heaven and earth" are not (4.13). Jesus denounced such hypocrisy (Matt. 5:33–37).

James nicely summarizes the teaching of Jesus. His command is "do not swear, either by heaven or by earth or with any other oath" (5:12). The present imperative of prohibition commands that this practice be stopped. He appeals to the Christians' reputation for constant honesty, "Let your yes be yes, and your no, no; so that you may not fall under judgment."

While flippant oaths are certainly condemned by this text, the church has long debated whether a Christian should ever use a solemn oath. Is it appropriate for a Christian to give an oath as a witness in a court of law? This might qualify as an area of conscience where Christians may have different opinions. Sensitive to this concern, many courts now ask witnesses to swear or affirm that their testimony is true. The best policy is to always speak the truth (Eph. 4:25) so that no one will find it necessary to suggest that you confirm your word with an oath.

James 5:14–18

Does this text provide instruction for receiving physical healing?

Several years ago I read of a father and a church official who were sent to jail for refusing to divulge the whereabouts of the man's sick daughter. They said that they would "abide by their church's tenet regarding treatment of the sick by prayer, the laying on of hands and anointing with oil" (*Oregonian*, 17 June, 1989). In rejecting medical treatment for the sick child they said that the church's healing practices were based on James 5:14.

Many people have refused medical treatment on the basis of this text. Many of these have prayed faithfully for the sick and their prayers for healing have not been answered. Could it be that this passage has been misinterpreted? There is an alternative that should be considered.[5]

The key words. To understand what James is referring to in this text, we must carefully examine several of the key words.

5:14 *astheneo* (sick): From *sthenoo* (strengthen) and the prefix *a* (not), meaning weakness. This word is used of physical weakness twenty times in the New Testament, of spiritual weakness fourteen times.

aleipho (anointing): Not a "sacred" *(chrio)*, but a common anointing; to bestow honor (Luke 7:38) and to refresh (Matt. 6:17; Luke 7:46).

5:15 *kamno* (sick): Used only here and in Hebrews 12:3–4, where it speaks of growing weary. It can carry the idea of physical illness, but the primary usage means to grow weary or fatigued.

5:16 *iaomai* (healed): Used elsewhere of healing the heart (Heb. 12:12–13), a spiritual healing.

The context. These readers were at the point of emotional and spiritual exhaustion in their deep struggle with temptation (1:13–15) and sin (5:16). The reference to Elijah in 5:17 adds support to this view. He found himself spiritually weak and weary after his encounter with Jezebel (1 Kings 19:3–4).

The promise in 5:15 seems more consistent with our Christian experience. Many have prayed for physical healing and encountered disappointment. But there is no question that God wants to bring spiritual healing to the weak and weary saint.

The exposition. Catholics use this text as a justification for "extreme unction," also known as the "last rites." Protestants have tried to relate the process outlined by James to the modern practice of using prayer plus medicine as a means for healing. Yet careful study of the text does not lead to such conclusions. James 5:14–18 does not teach that divine healing is available through anointing the sick by the church elders. Rather, the elders have a ministry of bringing refreshment and encouragement to the spiritually weak and weary saints.

The spiritually weak and weary are to call for the elders for assistance. The elders are spiritual leaders who exercise oversight in the church family (1 Tim. 3:1). The call is to be initiated by the struggling saint. There may also be occasion when the elders initiate the visit. The elders are invited to pray for the believer. There is an effective ministry of prayer that many of us neglect. Christian leaders should always take the opportunity to pray when making a pastoral call.

The anointing with oil does not refer to a ceremonial or ritual anointing with oil as a means of divine healing. James is referring to the common practice of using oil as a means of bestowing honor and refreshment. The term is used of anointing the feet (Luke 7:38) and the head (v. 46). The "anointing" here is metaphorical. It speaks of bringing encouragement.

James declares that the prayer offered in faith will be answered (5:15). Those who are spiritually weary will be refreshed and encouraged. God will lift up their spirits! While it is not always God's will for us to be healed physically, it is His will for us to be in good health spiritually.

James makes it clear that sin is an issue that must be dealt with (vv. 15–16). Believers are to confess their sins to one another, bringing them before the Lord for forgiveness and cleansing. Finally, believers are instructed to appropriate God's resources through prayer (vv. 16–18). James reminds his readers of the example of Elijah, whose unusual prayer was specifically answered.

James 5:17

Was the drought in the time of Elijah three years or three and a half?

Some have seen James as contradicting the Old Testament in stating that the drought lasted three years and six months. Actually, there is no time period for the drought recorded in the book of Kings. First Kings 18:1 simply says that "in the third year" God told Elijah to go and show himself to Ahab. After the contest on Mount Carmel, the drought ended. It is possible that a three-year drought was preceded by Israel's dry season (mid-May through mid-October), during which there is no rainfall. In that case the drought would have totaled three and one-half years. This time period is well established in Jewish tradition and is confirmed by Jesus in Luke 4:25.

Endnotes

1. D. Edmond Hiebert, *The Epistle of James* (Chicago: Moody Press, 1979), 136.
2. George Eldon Ladd, *A Theology of the New Testament* (Grand Rapids: Eerdmans, 1974), 593.
3. Peter Davids, *Commentary on James* (Grand Rapids: Eerdmans, 1982), 50.
4. Hiebert, *The Epistle of James*, 310.
5. For a thorough explanation of this viewpoint, consult Daniel R. Hayden, "Calling the Elders to Pray," *Bibliotheca Sacra* 138 (July–September 1981): 258–66.

1 PETER

1 Peter 1:11

Did God reveal mysteries beyond the comprehension of those who recorded the revelation in Scripture?

First Peter 1:11 clearly indicates that the prophets made predictions by the Spirit about things they did not fully comprehend. Isaiah, for example, predicted both the sufferings of Christ (Isa. 53) and the glories of His kingdom (11), although he did not understand every detail. Daniel was told things that were beyond his immediate comprehension, words that were "concealed and sealed up until the end time" (Dan. 12:9). Peter goes on to say that the prophets ministered not so much for themselves but for those living in the day of fulfillment (1 Peter 1:12).

Often times the meaning placed in the text by the Spirit of God is revealed by a later prophet or author of Scripture. In the field of hermeneutics, this is called *sensus plenior* (full sense). *Sensus plenior* may be defined as the divinely intended meaning not clearly intended by the human author but made evident by subsequent revelation. This is a function of inspiration, not of illumination. The full meaning is made known by the writers of Scripture, not discovered by the modern interpreter.

1 Peter 2:8

To what have the unbelievers been "appointed"?

In 1 Peter 2:8, Peter appeals to Psalm 118:22 and Isaiah 8:14 to show that Christ is a stone of stumbling to those who refuse to believe in Him. Those who are "disobedient to the Word" stumble with regard to Christ. Then Peter adds the problematic phrase, "And to this . . . they were also appointed." To what are these unbelievers appointed? Are they appointed to disobedience? Disbelief? Destruction?

The first two options are essentially the same. Disobedience to the Word results in disbelief in Jesus. Is Peter saying that some were appointed to belief while others to disbelief? The predestination of the elect is explicit in Scripture (Eph. 1:5, 11). The predestination of unbelievers sounds logical and may be biblical. However, as I pointed out in commenting on Romans 9:22, while God is sovereign over the destinies of both the elect and the nonelect, He is not behind the destiny of the nonelect in the same way He is behind the destiny of the elect. The problem with "double predestination" is that it gives the idea that the two predestinations are of equal character when they are not.

Bigg argues that "Their disobedience is not ordained, but the penalty . . . is."[1] This seems to be the best explanation in light of the context and other biblical teaching. Those who stumble over Jesus because of their disobedience to the Word face a divinely ordained judgment. It is to this judgment that unbelievers are most certainly "appointed."

1 Peter 3:7

In what way is the wife "a weaker vessel"?

In discussing the respective responsibilities of the husband and wife in marriage, Peter explains that the husband should be guided by a proper understanding of the wife's needs and responsibilities. Husbands are to "live with your wives in an understanding way, as with a weaker vessel, since she is a woman." There has been much debate over what Peter means by the words, "a weaker vessel" *(astheneteros skeuos).*

Did Peter mean that women are *physically* weaker than men? This doesn't seem to match with reality. Female marathoners, weight lifters, and swimmers have demonstrated physical strength beyond that of many men. Did Peter mean that women are *spiritually* weaker than men? This view does not seem to work either. Many godly women have demonstrated their spiritual capacity as Christian leaders and Bible teachers. Are women weaker *emotionally*? Some have argued that they are more prone to responding emotionally. But while this is true for some, it is not for others.

I would like to suggest that the woman is not "weaker" because of some intrinsic difference between female and male. Rather, a wife is weak in the sense that she is more *vulnerable* because of her position under the authority of her husband (compare 3:1). Because of her responsibility to be submissive, she is vulnerable to abuse by a thoughtless or insensitive husband. Husbands need to take this into consideration in their exercise of leadership within the home. A husband must honor his wife lest his own spiritual life be negatively affected.

1 Peter 3:18–20

Who are the "spirits now in prison," and when did Christ preach to them?

In the midst of his discussion on suffering (3:13–4:19), the apostle Peter presents the supreme example of undeserved suffering—the passion of Christ. In the illustration we are confronted with an intriguing interpretive problem (3:18–20). Who are the "spirits now in prison"? Where is this prison? When did Christ preach to them?

Christ's Triumph Over Suffering (3:18). In verse 18, Peter reminds the believers of the suffering of Christ and what it accomplished. Christ's death for *(peri)* sins constituted a substitutionary judgment in behalf of sinners, "the unjust." His death prepared the way for sinners' reconciliation with God (compare 2 Cor. 5:18).

But Christ's death was not a defeat. "Having been put to death in the flesh," He was "made alive in the spirit." The two participles (aorist actives) are simultaneous with the main verb "died." There is a balance and correspondence between the two terms "flesh" *(sarx)* and "spirit" *(pneuma).* Both terms are used without the article to emphasize quality and to denote two contrasted modes of Christ's existence—His earthly sphere of existence as human, "flesh," and His heavenly sphere of existence as divine spirit, "spirit."

The point of verse 18 is that Christ's death was not a defeat, but a triumph. While Christ died to His earthly sphere of existence, by resurrection, "made alive," He entered into a fuller life and was liberated for greater ministry (Matt. 28:20; John 14:12).

Christ's Preaching to Spirits in Prison (3:19–20). There are several different viewpoints with regard to the spirits in prison and when Christ preached to them.

The earliest view identifies the "spirits now in prison" with the fallen angels, the "sons of God," in Genesis 6. The view is supported by 2 Peter 2:4 and Jude 6. But for what purpose would such a proclamation be made?

Some see the reference to unbelievers to whom the Gospel was preached by Christ through the apostles after Pentecost. The "prison" would refer to their bondage to sin and Satan. This viewpoint fails to adequately explain the reference to Noah.

Others understand the spirits in prison to refer to those of Noah's day now in hades. According to this viewpoint, Christ descended to hell between His death and resurrection. His preaching is viewed as being either condemnatory, "I told you so!" or conciliatory, offering the antediluvians a second chance for salvation. Ephesians 4:9 is appealed to for support of such a descent into hell. Some believe that Christ took this opportunity to clarify the means of salvation for the Old Testament saints and then took them to heaven, "led captive a host of captives." Problems with this view include the following: (1) There is no evidence in Scripture that anyone is offered a "second chance" after death (compare Heb. 9:27). (2) Why would Peter single out the antediluvians to be the recipients of this preresurrection ministry of Jesus? (3) Ephesians 4:9 simply refers to Christ's descent to the earth, "the lower parts" of the universe, at His incarnation. The descent is in contrast to His ascension. (4) The viewpoint is quite complex and requires a great deal of hypothesis and speculation. A good rule of hermeneutics is to prefer the clear and simple view over the complex and obscure interpretation.

A view that can be traced as far back as Augustine holds that verses 19–20 refer to the preincarnate preaching of Christ through Noah (compare 1:11; Neh. 9:30). The preaching was accomplished by Christ's divine spirit—the immaterial aspect of His person. The "spirits now in prison" are the souls of those who heard the message, rejected it, and now find themselves in judgment.

This view has the strength of eliminating references to the obscure "doctrine" of Christ's descent into hell and the question of what His preaching might accomplish there. It also has the advantage of clarity and simplicity.

The point of the illustration is that Christ's ministry in His divine Spirit that preceded His incarnation (as the angel of Yahweh) resumed at His death. Christ's death was a victory, not a defeat! While death ended the physical, earthly dimension of His life and ministry, it inaugurated once again His ministry as Divine Spirit.[2]

1 Peter 4:1

Does physical suffering deter one's response to temptation and sin?

In 1 Peter 4:1, the apostle Peter draws an implication based upon 3:18–22, where he discussed Christ's sufferings and death. Christ's death was a fatal blow to the power and penalty of sin, bringing salvation to those who accept His provision. Now Peter draws a spiritual lesson for the believer. As Christ's death meant an end of sin, so our identification with Christ's redemptive sufferings provide a basis for victory over sin. Paul says a very similar thing in Romans 6:7, "for he who has died [that is, was crucified with Christ, v. 6] is freed from sin."

Identification with Christ and His death arms the believer with spiritual resources to deal with the issue of sin. As Mounce comments, "To be joined to the One who died for sins is to have given up sin as a way of life."[3]

1 Peter 4:6

When is the Gospel preached to "those who are dead"? What did Peter mean by this?

First Peter 4:6 presents the interpreter with two key exegetical questions. First, what is the meaning of the words, "those who are dead"? Does this refer to those who are spiritually dead, physically dead, or dead in hades (compare 3:19–20)? The reference in verse 5 to the "living and the dead" seems to exclude the first option. Since those in the grave do not receive a second chance to receive the Gospel (Heb. 10:27), there is no need to preach to them. This would exclude the last option. It is probable, then, that the "dead" refers to those who have died physically, probably since receiving the Gospel.

The second key question concerns the meaning of the phrase, "judged in the flesh." Does this refer to the judgment that Christ bore because of our sins or to those condemned to martyrdom? The theme of suffering being developed in this section (3:14; 4:1, 13) suggests that the latter is the case.

Peter is saying that those who have died for their faith, "those who are dead," enjoy life forever because of Christ's work. Although they suffered physical death, "judged in the flesh," they have entered into eternal life, "live in the spirit."

1 Peter 5:13

To whom is Peter referring by the words, "She who is in Babylon"?

There is much debate regarding Peter's reference to "she who is in Babylon." Some suggest, based on the appearance of the term "Babylon" in Revelation

17–18, that Peter is referring to Rome. Others say that he had in mind the Mesopotamian Babylon made so famous by its illustrious builder, Nebuchadnezzar. Since Babylon was already destroyed by the time when Peter wrote, it has been suggested that he was referring to a city of the same name located in Egypt. Another intriguing possibility is that Peter is using the term "Babylon" as a cryptogram or code name for "a place of exile." Babylon was the place of exile for the Judeans of the southern kingdom. As scattered aliens, the readers of 1 Peter had much in common with their Judean ancestors and with other Jewish believers of the Diaspora.

The reference in the verse to the greeting sent by "Mark" may be our best clue as to the identity of "she who is in Babylon." We do know that John Mark, Barnabas's nephew, was in Rome toward the end of Paul's imprisonment in A.D. 62 (Col. 4:10). According to Eusebius, Mark was in Rome serving as Peter's interpreter just before his death in A.D. 64 (*Historia Ecclesiastica* 2:25; 3:39; 5:8; 6:14). If Mark sent his greetings from Rome, perhaps "she who is in Babylon" represents the church at Rome. Peter may have adopted this term because of the idolatry and corruption characteristic of both ancient Babylon and Rome.

Endnotes

1. Charles Bigg, *Epistles of St. Peter and St. Jude* (Edinburgh: T. & T. Clark, 1901), 133.
2. For further study, see William Joseph Dalton, *Christ's Proclamation to the Spirits: A Study of 1 Peter 3:18–4:6* (Rome: Pontifical Biblical Institute, 1965); also, D. Edmond Hiebert, "The Suffering and Triumphant Christ: An Exposition of 1 Peter 3:18–22" *Bibliotheca Sacra* (April–June 1982): 146–158.
3. Robert H. Mounce, *A Living Hope: A Commentary on 1 & 2 Peter* (Grand Rapids: Eerdmans, 1982), 62.

2 PETER

2 Peter 1:1

Can we be sure that Peter actually wrote this book?

Differences in style between 1 and 2 Peter and the lack of external evidence for Petrine authorship have led to questions regarding the authenticity of this epistle. But there is no doubt that the author intended to identify himself as the apostle Peter. He refers to himself as "Simon Peter" (1:1). He writes of his approaching death (v. 14), which was predicted by Jesus (John 21:18–19). He claims to be a witness of Jesus' Transfiguration (2 Peter 1:16–17), as was Peter (Matt. 17:1–4). The evidence points to this epistle being a genuine work of the apostle Peter.

2 Peter 1:19

How can God's prophetic word be "made more sure"?

Having recounted his experience on the Mount of Transfiguration (1:16–18), Peter declares that "we have the prophetic word made more sure." There is some difficulty in interpreting the phrase "made more sure" *(bebaioteron)*.

It is possible that Peter is saying that the testimony of the prophets has been confirmed by the apostle's experience at the Transfiguration. Bigg suggests that Peter is appealing to the principle of a second witness.[1] We have the Prophets (1 Peter 1:10). And now we have the testimony of the apostles! This view, however, seems to undermine the integrity and authority of the Prophets as if they need a second witness to confirm their truth.

It seems better within this context to understand that Peter is referring to a *more sure* prophetic word.[2] Having shared his personal experience on the Mount of Transfiguration, Peter announces that there is something more certain—the prophetic word. In other words, Peter is saying, "If you don't believe our testimony about Jesus, look at the Scriptures!"

2 Peter 2:4

Who are the "angels" who "sinned"?

The "angels" who sinned appear to refer to the "sons of God" (angels) who took on human bodies to intermarry with the human race (see on Gen. 6:2). As a result of this sin God brought the judgment of the Flood and condemned some of these wicked angels to immediate judgment. Those that remain free function as demons, seeking to thwart God's purposes and work. While they are presently free, these demons are aware that they face future judgment (Matt. 8:29). Believers apparently have a part in executing this judgment (1 Cor. 6:3). With Satan, the Beast, and the False Prophet, they are destined for the lake of fire (Rev. 20:10, 15).

2 Peter 2:18–20

To whom is Peter referring by the pronouns "they," "those," and "the ones"?

In 2 Peter 2:10, Peter begins a description of the character of the false teachers (v. 1) who had infiltrated the church. Peter describes their arrogance, ignorance, immorality, and greed. He reveals, in verse 18, that these false teachers are carried away by their own sin and entice others to follow them.

The pronoun "they" in verse 19 refers to the false teachers whom Peter has been describing. "Those who barely escape" appear to refer to new converts who have recently escaped from the darkness of unbelief. The "ones who live in error" are certainly a reference to the unbelievers from whom the new converts have escaped.

Peter goes on in verse 20 to describe those who have "escaped the defilements of the world by the knowledge of the Lord and Savior Jesus Christ." This is certainly not a reference to the false teachers or to the unbelievers. Peter would never describe them in this way (compare vv. 10–17). The pronoun "they" in verse 20 must refer to the new converts who have escaped from bondage by their knowledge of the Savior.

2 Peter 2:20

If Peter is talking about believers, how can their last state (saved) be worse than their first (unsaved)?

The answer to this question is found in the next verse. Here Peter builds on the principle that the greater the light, the greater the accountability. As believers, the new converts are more accountable before God than unbelievers. Having received the light of the Gospel, more is expected of them.

Peter explains, in verse 21, "For it would be better for them not to have known the way of righteousness, than having known it, to turn away from the holy commandment delivered to them." The words translated, "would be better" reflect a "tendential imperfect" in which the action tends toward the realization but falls short.[3] Peter is not saying that it would have been better for these people to have remained unsaved. He is saying, "It would just about have been better." Saved sinners may be almost worse off than unsaved sinners because of their accountability to the light and resources of the Gospel.

Endnotes

1. Charles Bigg, *Epistles of St. Peter and St. Jude* (Edinburgh: T. & T. Clark, 1901), 268.
2. F. Rienecker, *Linguistic Key to the Greek New Testament* (Grand Rapids: Zondervan, 1976), 772.
3. H. E. Dana and J. R. Mantey, *A Manual Grammar of the Greek New Testament* (Toronto: Macmillan, 1927), 189.

1 JOHN

1 John 1:9

Is this verse intended for believers or unbelievers? Must Christians confess their sins to be assured of God's forgiveness?

The apostle John wrote his first epistle to combat false teaching (1 John 4:1) with a clear presentation of the truth and to promote fellowship in the family of God (1:3). In 1 John 1:6–2:2, the apostle presents three tests designed to answer those who claim to have fellowship with God but who live in disobedience—the tests of conduct (vv. 6–7), confession (vv. 8–9), and creed (vv. 10–2:2). Apparently there were those in the church who denied the existence of sin in their lives (v. 8). John points out that if, instead of denying their sin, they acknowledge it, this will lead to forgiveness and cleansing.

It has been argued that this text applies only to unbelievers, who must confess their sins in order to become saved and to appropriate God's forgiveness. It is implied that confession is unnecessary for Christians because they have already been justified—declared righteous—in Christ (Rom. 5:1).

I certainly agree that Christians are declared righteous in Christ and that a personal act of sin cannot change their righteous standing or position. However, a personal act of sin can change how we relate to God in terms of fellowship. Here it is helpful to distinguish between *positional* and *relational* truth. A believer's position in Christ is based on justification. That position can never change (Rom. 8:31–39). But sin does affect how we relate to God in terms of fellowship and intimacy. It is hard, if not impossible, to experience personal intimacy with my Lord when I am unwilling to acknowledge and repent from known sin. First John 1:9 deals with how Christians relate to God after they have been declared righteous by faith. When they confess their sins, God is faithful to His promises and righteous in His dealings, providing forgiveness and cleansing for the repentant. Confession is not so much a requirement for believers as it is an opportunity for restoration of fellowship after offending our holy God. Christians are a confessing people. And as we confess, God forgives and cleanses.

1 John 2:12–14

Why does John change from the present tense, "I am writing," to the past tense, "I wrote"?

In presenting some warnings against worldliness, John applies his teaching to three groups—children, fathers, and young men (1 John 2:12–13). Here he uses the present tense, "I am writing." Then he repeats himself with slight variation, using the aorist tense, "I have written" (John 2:13–14). Bruce points out that "no completely satisfying explanation has been given for the duplication of this three–fold encouragement."[1] As for the change in tense, it seems that John first contemplates the letter as incomplete, using the present tense, "I am writing." He then contemplates the letter from the viewpoint of completion, using the aorist tense, "I have written."

1 John 3:6, 9

Is John teaching that a believer never sins?

John makes a rather startling statement in 1 John 3:6: "No one who abides in Him sins; no one who sins has seen Him or knows Him." When we contemplate our own lives and consider the evidence of our many sins, we are left a bit puzzled and perhaps concerned. "John seems to be saying that believers don't sin. Maybe I'm not a true believer?"

The key to this difficulty is to recognize the nature of the present tense of the verb. In the Greek language, the present tense is used to signify action in progress. It is used to denote what "habitually occurs" or "recurs at successive intervals."[2] John uses the present tense in 1 John 3:6, 9 to refer to people who sin repeatedly as characteristic of their lifestyle.

John is not saying that it is impossible for a Christian to sin. He is simply saying that it is not characteristic of believers to persist in sin. Christians will sin, and they will often repeat their sins as they struggle to find Christ's victory in a particular area. But a true believer is not going to practice sin as a lifestyle. According to John, new birth involves a radical change that brings into the believer's life new resources and motivation to live a life that is pleasing to God. Whereas sin is the natural way of life for unbelievers, sin is unnatural and contrary to the lifestyle of God's children.

1 John 4:18

Does this verse contradict the biblical teaching that we are to fear God?

In Deuteronomy 10:20, Moses declares, "You shall fear the LORD your God." Why then, in discussing the love of God, does John write, "There is no fear in love; but perfect love casts out fear" (1 John 4:18). Are love and fear incompatible in our relationship with God?

The fear of the Lord is an important concept that is taught throughout the Bible (compare Deut. 6:13; Prov. 9:10; 31:30; Eccl. 12:13; Heb. 10:30–31; 1 Peter 2:17). In Proverbs 2:5, fearing God is equated with knowing God. If you truly know God and appreciate His attributes, you can't help but have a healthy respect for His person. If you know that He is holy, righteous, and just, you can't help but want to honor and please Him. Fearing God means departing from evil (Job 28:28), doing His commandments (Ps. 111:10), and hating evil (Prov. 8:13). The fear of the Lord is an action-oriented response to God based on a reverent appreciation of His majestic person.

Now, is John suggesting that God's love is incompatible with all of this? Not at all. John is talking in the context of judgment (1 John 4:17). The believer's confidence "in the day of judgment" is that there will be nothing to fear. Believers can approach the judgment seat of Christ (2 Cor. 5:10) without fear since God, in love, has provided redemption from sins. Fear is associated with deserved punishment. With guilt removed by Christ, the fear of punishment is gone. It is in this sense that God's "perfect love casts out fear."

1 John 5:6–8

What three witnesses is John referring to in these verses?

The apostle John declares, "For there are three that bear witness, the Spirit and the water and the blood; and the three are in agreement." Throughout the history of the church, there has been debate regarding the identity of these witnesses. The "Spirit" is clearly identified within the context (v. 7) as the Holy Spirit. No problem here. The debate begins when we ask what John meant by "the water." Did John refer to the baptism of Christ (Matt. 3:13–17) or to the water (and blood) that flowed from His side (John 19:34)? John's mention of the "blood and water" that came from Jesus' side, when pierced by the soldier, might lead us to conclude that he is referring to the same thing here. But in this text the order is reversed—"water and blood"—and we wonder how these body fluids that flowed from Christ served as a witness.

The "blood" was interpreted by Luther to refer to the Lord's Supper, whereas Augustine argued that John was referring to the blood from Christ's side. Tertullian thought it was a general reference to the death of Christ.

Although the terms "water" and "blood" may seem to be rather unusual symbols, they do aptly describe the two key events in Jesus' career—His baptism by water and His inauguration of the new covenant. At His baptism the Father witnessed from heaven, "This is My beloved Son, in whom I am well-pleased" (Matt. 3:17). At His death, Jesus inaugurated the new covenant by the shedding of blood (Heb. 8:6; 9:11–22). These two events, along with the ministry of the Holy Spirit (Matt. 12:31–32; Acts 10:38) unite as three grand witnesses to the truth of Christ's person and work.

1 John 5:8

Part of this verse is missing from modern translations. How do we explain this change in the Bible?

The Textus Receptus, used in the King James translation of the Bible, reads as follows: "For there are three that bear witness *in heaven, the Father, the Word, and the Holy Spirit, and these three are one. And there are three that bear witness on earth*, the Spirit and the water and the blood; and the three are in agreement." A serious textual question is raised with regard to the words in italics. The following evidences lead us to conclude that these words were not a part of John's original text.[3] First, the passage is absent from every known Greek manuscript except four very late manuscripts. Second, the passage is quoted by none of the church fathers, who would certainly have appealed to it in their debate with anti-Trinitarians. Third, the passage is absent from the manuscripts of all ancient versions. Fourth, the passage makes an awkward break in the flow of John's statement about the witnesses.

It seems that these words were probably added by someone who thought that this verse provided an occasion to support the orthodox teaching on the Trinity. If they were original to the text, there is no good reason why they would be missing from so many manuscripts. Translators have recognized this text as spurious and have excluded it from recent translations.

1 John 5:16–17
What is the "sin leading to death"?

In 1 John 5:14–17, the apostle discusses the matter of answered prayer. He promises that God will answer believers' prayers when they pray according to God's will (vv. 14–15). He then proceeds to give an example of effective intercessory prayer. A believer may successfully pray for someone sinning a sin "not leading to death." However, there is a "sin leading to death." John does not forbid us to pray for a person committing this sin. But neither does he request that we pray for those in this condition.

Students of the Bible have long debated the identity of the "sin leading to death." Stott provides us with the most complete discussion of this interpretive problem.[4]

A Specific Sin. It has been suggested that John is referring to one of the specific sins in the Bible for which the death penalty applied (Lev. 20:1–27) —adultery, incest, homosexuality, bestiality, etc.

Apostasy. Some have argued that John is referring to Christians who renounce their faith and deny Christ. But we have pointed out from other texts that a true believer is not going to do this (John 10:28). A true believer will not persist in sin (1 John 3:9).

Blasphemy. When the religious leaders of Christ's day deliberately ascribed to Satan the miracles that He did by the Holy Spirit, Jesus said that they committed a sin that "shall not be forgiven" (Matt. 12:31–32). Yet in studying this text, we discover that the unusual circumstances of this cannot be reproduced today. The "unpardonable sin" was a unique, first-century occurrence.

A State of Persistent Sin. Some scholars have appealed to 1 Corinthians 11:30 to suggest that John's "sin leading to death" refers to a state of persistent sin that is judged with physical death. But, one wonders, at what point do we cease praying for the sinner? At what point is it determined that the sin is one "leading to death"?

Persistent Rejection of the Gospel. Within the context of 1 John, Stott argues that the apostle is referring to the persistent rejection of the Gospel by antichrists.[5] He points out that the spiritual life mentioned within this context is contrasted with spiritual death (5:13, 16). Stott explains that the term "brother" is used here in the broad sense of "neighbor," as in 1 John 2:9, 11; 3:16–17 and Matthew 5:22–24. Accordingly, John is referring to those "antichrists" who had passed as brothers but were counterfeits who did not have a life-giving relationship with God. As false teachers, they were spiritually dead and were leading others to death. By rejecting the Life, they sinned "leading to death."

Endnotes

1. F. F. Bruce, *The Epistles of John* (Grand Rapids: Eerdmans, 1970), 57.
2. H. E. Dana and J. R. Mantey, *A Manual Grammar of the Greek New Testament* (Toronto: MacMillan, 1927), 184–85.
3. Bruce M. Metzger, *A Textual Commentary on the Greek New Testament* (London: United Bible Societies, 1971), 716–17.
4. John R. W. Stott, *The Epistles of John* (Grand Rapids: Eerdmans, 1964), 186–90.
5. Ibid., 189–90.

2 JOHN

2 John 1

Who is the "chosen lady" to whom John addresses this epistle?

It is debated as to whether John has reference to a church or to an individual. The use of the second person plural rather than the singular, in verses 8, 10, and 12, might suggest that a community of believers is in mind. The personification of the church in a feminine form would be in harmony with the feminine noun *ekklesia* (church). This would also be consistent with the metaphor of the church as the bride of Christ (Eph. 5:29–32). However, such an involved metaphor that includes the concept of "children" (2 John 1, 13) seems out of harmony with the simplicity of the message.

It is probably best to understand the "lady" to refer to an individual Christian woman and her family. Perhaps a local body of believers met in her home and would have benefited from the letter. She apparently had a sister whose children (v. 13) were in Ephesus and had contact with John's ministry there.

2 John 10

How do we reconcile John's instruction in verse 10 with Paul's instructions to practice hospitality (Rom. 12:13; 1 Tim. 3:2)?

In John's day, false teachers were circulating among the churches taking advantage of Christian hospitality to propagate their heresies. While hospitality should be extended to strangers as a general principle, John admonishes the believers to refuse hospitality to confirmed heretics who come to their houses for the purpose of disseminating false doctrine. John's words in verse 8 give the reason for this. Even strong Christians are susceptible to being misled, and John doesn't want to see God's work undermined.

3 JOHN

3 John 7

Is it wrong for churches and Christian organizations to receive financial support from unbelievers?

In 3 John 7–8, the apostle John encourages believers to support the work of traveling missionaries and teachers. He commends these Christian workers because of their dedication to Christ and separation from the world. John notes that they took no support for their ministry from unbelievers. They did not want it to appear that they were selling salvation or compromising the Gospel.

The Christian workers John is referring to were operating by the principle that God's people should support God's work. That is a good principle to follow. And yet there are times when God has used unbelievers as channels of blessing for His people. The Israelites received silver, gold, and clothing from the Egyptians when they left Egypt (Exod. 12:35–36). Solomon received help in terms of workers and materials from the Gentile king Hiram when building God's temple (1 Kings 5:1–10; 7:13–14; 9:14).

It should be noted that 3 John 7 does not *prohibit* Christian workers from receiving financial support from unbelievers. It simply reports that these particular individuals did not. As a general principle, believers should not seek support for God's work from unbelievers. But if a developer wants to donate some property for a church in the community, we need not refuse the offer unless it would somehow compromise our testimony for Christ. God owns all the silver and gold in the universe (Hag. 2:8), and He can disperse it for the needs of His people at His own discretion.

JUDE

Jude 1

Who was Jude?

The author identifies himself as "Jude [Greek, *Judas*], a bond-servant of Jesus Christ, and brother of James." It is unlikely that the author was Judas the apostle (Luke 6:16), for he seems to distinguish himself from the apostles (Jude 17). Both internal evidence and the testimony of the church fathers (Clement of Alexandria; Epiphanius, Bishop of Salamis) indicate that the epistle was written by Jude (or Judas), the half brother of Jesus (Matt. 13:55; Mark 6:3), who came to faith after the Resurrection (John 7:5; Acts 1:14).

Jude 9

Did Jude get his information about the dispute between Michael and the Devil from an apocryphal story?

Many scholars have suggested that Jude drew his information about the dispute between Michael, the archangel, and the Devil from an ancient book called the Testament of Moses or the Assumption of Moses. This book is part of the Pseudepigrapha, a collection of books falsely ascribed to eminent biblical figures of the past such as Enoch, Noah, and Moses. These are Jewish writings from the second-temple period (538 B.C.–A.D. 70), resembling the Apocrypha in general character but not included in the Hebrew Bible, the fourteen books of the Apocrypha, or other rabbinic literature.

The Testament of Moses is a retelling of the events of Deuteronomy 31–34. The book records Moses' farewell address to Joshua and foretells the history of Israel from the entrance into the land to the end of the age. The only extant copy today, discovered in 1861, is a Latin translation of the Greek. This copy is incomplete, corrupt, and illegible in some places. The church fathers were familiar with the entire book.

The dispute between Michael and the Devil over the body of Moses is nowhere mentioned in the Hebrew Bible (compare Deut. 34:5–6). Where did Jude get this information? The Fathers (Clement, Origen, and Didymus) all state that the Testament of Moses was Jude's source. Their testimony, however, cannot be validated since the only extant copy of the testament breaks off before the death of Moses.

Did Jude draw his information from a pseudepigraphal book? It is impossible to know for sure. Jude may have known of this incident from another source and was led by the Holy Spirit to refer to it. By divine inspiration this account has been recorded in Scripture. But even if Jude drew his material from the Testament of Moses, it is not necessary to conclude that he accepted the book as an inspired work. He may have simply affirmed the truth of this particular incident. In any case, the Holy Spirit chose to include this material as part of the inspired writings of Jude.

Jude 14–15

Did Jude believe that the book of Enoch was divinely inspired?

In verses 14–15, Jude interprets a prophecy in the book of Enoch to predict the judgment that will fall upon false teachers at the second coming of Christ. Although Enoch is known from the Old Testament (Gen. 5:18–24), his prophecy does not appear in Scripture. It is found, however, in the book of 1 Enoch (1:9; 5:4).

First Enoch is a pseudepigraphal book falsely attributed to the biblical Enoch. It is a composite book written by many authors during the three centuries before Christ. Fragments of the book have been found among the Dead Sea Scrolls. First Enoch purports to record what was revealed to Enoch concerning the mysteries of the universe, the future of the world, and the course of human history. The book was well known to Jews of the first century and to the early church fathers.

How should we deal with Jude's quotation from the Pseudepigrapha? It would be wrong to assume that just because Jude quotes the book that he believed 1 Enoch to be an inspired writing. Nor should we assume that Jude is not inspired simply because he appears to have quoted this noninspired source. It could be that Jude quoted 1 Enoch because he knew that the prophecy was true. Quoting Thomas Jefferson does not demand the conclusion that everything Jefferson said was true. So quoting 1 Enoch does not require us to accept the whole book as inspired.

It is also possible that both Enoch and Jude quoted a common source that is not preserved for us today. One way or another, God chose to record this prophecy in Jude because it is divinely inspired and true.

REVELATION

Revelation 1:4

Who are the "seven Spirits" that are before God's throne?

In his greeting to the churches, John acknowledges that the blessings of grace and peace are from God the Father, from "the seven Spirits who are before His throne," and "from Jesus Christ." We have heard of the Holy Spirit, but who are the "seven Spirits"?

Some have suggested that the "seven Spirits" are seven angels (1:20). It is pointed out that according to Jewish tradition, there are seven archangels who serve the throne of God (1 Enoch 20:1–8). Others have argued that the word *seven* should be understood figuratively as the number associated with the idea of completion. Accordingly, the "seven Spirits" is interpreted to refer to the Holy Spirit in the fullness or completeness of His ministry. This view fits nicely in what may be a Trinitarian reference to the Father, Son, and Holy Spirit in Revelation 1:4–5. Noting the other references to the "seven Spirits" (3:1; 4:5; 5:6), Mounce concludes that the "seven Spirits" represent a "heavenly entourage that has a special ministry in connection with the Lamb."[1]

Three of the references use the expression, "the seven Spirits of God." If this is interpreted as a genitive of relationship, then the words "of God" would speak of the close relationship the Spirits have with God. Revelation 5:6 identifies the seven Spirits with the "seven eyes" of the Lamb. John records that the seven Spirits have been "sent out into all the earth." This would be consistent with Christ's promise of the Holy Spirit (Acts 1:8; Rev. 16:7). It seems from these references that the "seven Spirits" refers to the second person of the Trinity, the Holy Spirit in the completeness of His ministry.

Revelation 1:20

Who are the seven angels of the seven churches (compare 2:1, 8, 12, etc.)?

In Revelation 1:20, the "seven stars" in John's vision are interpreted to be "the angels of the seven churches." Each of the seven letters that follow in chapters 2–3 are addressed to "the angel of the church in. . . ." How should we understand this term "angel"?

The Greek *aggelos* literally means "messenger" or "envoy." It refers to one who is "sent." The term is used of John the Baptizer, who announced the coming of Jesus (Matt. 11:10), and of the disciples sent out by Christ (Luke 9:52). The word can also be used of a divine messenger, an angel (Matt. 4:6; Luke 1:11). What did John have in mind when he used the term *aggelos*?

Most translations translated *aggelos* by the term "angel" in Revelation 1:20. While it is possible that John had in mind the angels associated with the churches, we have only one cryptic allusion to this in 1 Corinthians 11:10. I suggest that the more natural rendering of *aggelos* in Revelation 1:20 is "messengers." These messengers are associated with and may represent the seven churches. They had heard of John's imprisonment on Patmos and were concerned for his well-being. They may have been sent as messengers by their respective churches to attend to John's needs. Perhaps they came with some questions. John seems to have sent all the messengers home with letters for their churches. These are the seven letters of Revelation 2–3.

Revelation 2–3

Are the churches of Revelation 2–3 to be understood literally?

It has been suggested that the seven churches represent types of churches throughout all generations or that they represent periods of church history. These viewpoints are quite speculative and subjective. Each of the churches in Revelation 2–3 had a historical setting and specific needs. John responded to those needs within the individual letters. There is no basis for departing from a historical, grammatical interpretation of the seven churches. As we study these letters, we learn from the problems that John addressed, and we can make relevant application to our own church situations.

Revelation 4:4

Who are the "twenty-four elders" sitting around the throne of God?

John describes twenty-four elders sitting on thrones around the throne of God. They are clothed in white and wear golden crowns on their heads. Later John describes them prostrating themselves before God's throne in an act of worship (Rev. 4:10). What or who are these twenty-four elders?

Angels. Some have suggested that these are angels who are associated in some way with God's rule or government. But angels customarily *stand* before the throne of God (Luke 1:19).

Redeemed. Others have argued that these are the redeemed—both Old Testament and New Testament saints. One problem with this view is that Israel's resurrection as a redeemed people takes place at the Second Coming (Dan. 12:2), which appears to be future from the standpoint of this text (Rev. 19).

Church-age Saints. It has been suggested that the number "twenty-four" represents the priesthood, since there were twenty-four groups of priests in ancient times (1 Chron. 24). These, then, are believer priests (compare 1 Peter 2:9). While possible, this interpretation seems to be a bit of a stretch.

Human or Angelic Beings. Since the text does not identify the twenty-four elders, perhaps it is best for us to avoid speculating about their identity. Based upon the references in Revelation 4:9–11 and 5:8–12, we may conclude that they are either human or angelic beings who worship God and have some responsibility for leading in heavenly worship.

Revelation 6:9–11

If the church is raptured before the Tribulation, who are these martyrs that are slain during the Tribulation?

Those who espouse the pretribulation rapture viewpoint believe that all Christians will be removed from the earth before the seven-year Tribulation (see on 2 Thess. 2:3). Does this mean that there will be no Christians on the earth during the Tribulation?

The rapture of the church will not terminate God's plan for world evangelism! God will bring about many conversions through the ministry of the Holy Spirit and the Word of God. During the Tribulation, the Gospel will be preached to all nations (Matt. 24:14). Those who respond will experience the same salvation as those who were raptured. But they will suffer persecution as no saints have in the history of the church (vv. 21–22). As in the early days of the church, many believers living during the Tribulation will bear witness by their deaths to the truth of their faith in Christ.

Revelation: 7:3–8

Who are the 144,000 who are sealed as "bond-servants" of God?

Revelation 7 records the manifestation of God's grace as the seven seals (6:1–8:1) are unfolding. Here John describes the sealing of 144,000 "bond-servants" of God. Exactly who are these people?

In verses 4–8, they are listed as coming from the twelve tribes of Israel—twelve thousand from each tribe. We note that the tribes of Dan and Ephraim are missing, but Levi and Joseph take their place. Many commentators interpret the tribal references figuratively and conclude that these saints are Christians—the Israel of God. But we are left to wonder why John would list the tribes by name and with such detail if the text is merely symbolic.

Following a more literal, historical hermeneutic, I suggest that the 144,000 are Jewish believers—part of the remnant of those who will come to faith during the Tribulation (Zech. 13:8–9). Gundry argues that they are preserved through the Tribulation and converted at the end.[2] I suggest that they are converted at the beginning of the Tribulation and serve as evangelists throughout the period. This seems to be supported in the verses that follow (7:9–17). There we have a description of a great company of Gentiles who have come to faith during the Tribulation. They were probably saved through believing the message of the 144,000. Perhaps it is during this time that Israel will begin to fulfill its destiny as a light to the Gentiles (Isa. 42:6).

Revelation 9:1–12

What is the nature of the locust swarm that will torment people for five months during the Tribulation?

The "locusts" described here do not appear to be ordinary locusts. Instead of eating grass and leaves, they torment people (9:4–5). Their place of origin, "the bottomless pit" (v. 2), and their king, "the angel of the abyss" (v. 11), suggest that these "locusts" may actually be demons that have taken the appearance of locusts. Their attacks are limited to unbelievers, those "who do not have the seal of God on their foreheads" (v. 4). John uses similes and metaphors to describe these supernatural "locusts" in terms we can understand (vv. 7–10).

Revelation 11:3–14

Who are the two witnesses that are killed and then translated to heaven?

In Revelation 11:3–14, John describes the ministry of two witnesses who will prophesy for 1,260 days—the last half of the Tribulation. Their ministry will be much like that of John the Baptizer, calling out a believing remnant from the Tribulation to prepare for Messiah's (second) coming. They have supernatural power to protect themselves during their mission (v. 5) and are given authority to perform miracles (v. 6). The witnesses will be invincible until their work is done. Only then will God allow them to be killed by the Beast—the Antichrist (v. 7).

Many commentators have speculated regarding the identity of the two witnesses. Some suggest that they are Elijah and Enoch, men who never died. It is believed that Hebrews 9:27 means that everyone must die. Since they did not experience death, these men will return during the Tribulation and fulfill the role of the two witnesses. Others identify the two witnesses as Elijah and Moses because of their similar powers—calling down fire, stopping rainfall, and turning water to blood (11:5–6).

I take a more cautious approach on this subject. The text does not identify the witnesses. Similarities to leaders of the past does not demand that the witnesses be men of the past. Hebrews 9:27 states a general truth and does not demand that raptured saints of the past return to experience death. It is quite speculative to attempt an identification of the witnesses. Their identities will be clear enough during the Tribulation.

Revelation 12:1–6

Who are the participants in the conflict described here?

Revelation 12 looks back to the past and ahead to the future to reveal the root cause of the persecution of Israel and of the Tribulation saints. There are three main participants in the conflict:

The woman (vv. 1–2). The woman is described as giving birth to a child who is to rule the nations (v. 5). One might easily jump to the conclusion that the woman is Mary, mother of Jesus. But verse 6 describes this woman as fleeing to the wilderness where she might be protected and nourished for 1,260 days—a time period that coincides with the last half of the Tribulation (v. 3). This woman is not a person of the past but represents a people of the future. I identify the woman as Israel who gave the Messiah to the world and who will be severely persecuted during the last half of the Tribulation (Matt. 24:15–22; Rev. 12:13–14).

The dragon (vv. 3–4). The red seven-headed dragon is identified in verse 9 as Satan. The first sentence of verse four appears to take us back to Satan's beginnings. Satan swept "a third of the stars of heaven" to the earth. The term "stars" may be understood literally, as in Revelation 8:12. But the term can also refer to angelic beings (compare Job 38:7; Rev. 9:1, 11). This verse may refer to Satan's original fall, when a third of the angels joined him in rebellion and were cast out of heaven (2 Peter 2:4). Satan's ultimate objective is to destroy the woman's child. This reflects Satan's role in antisemitic activity since Israel's beginning as a people. Satan would like to destroy the people that Christ is destined to rule. Much of his activity during the Tribulation reflects this purpose.

The Son (vv. 5–6). The Son of the woman is Christ (v. 5), who is destined to rule the nations. Since Satan failed in his attempt to destroy Christ at His birth (v. 4), he turned his attention to the woman (Israel) to persecute her (v. 6). The most intense period of this persecution occurs during the last 1,260 days (three and one-half years) of the Tribulation.

The earth (vv. 15–16). Having fled to the wilderness, the woman (Israel) will find some respite from the persecution of Satan. But then the Serpent (Satan) will send a flood to wipe out God's people, Israel. But the "earth" responded, coming to the woman's assistance. The "earth" refers to the Gentile nations, which will demonstrate their faith in Christ by coming to Israel's aid during the persecutions of the Tribulation (compare Matt. 25:31–46).

Revelation 13:1–18

Who are the "beast" and the "false prophet" described by John in chapter 13?

Revelation 13 describes Satan's counterpart to what God offers us in Christ and in the Holy Spirit. The "beast" is a political figure who represents a federation of ten kings (compare 17:12). His power, throne, and authority come from the "dragon," Satan himself (13:2). A study of the character and activity of this individual leads us to identify him with the "little horn" of Daniel 7:8, the last Gentile world ruler (Dan. 7:20–26; 9:26–27; 11:36–45). Although John does not use the term in Revelation, many have referred to the "beast" as the Antichrist. Certainly, as one who opposes Christ by seeking to take His place, the "beast" fits this description.

The second "beast" in Revelation 13 is a religious authority who becomes the chief promoter of the Beast (vv. 11–18). In Revelation 19:20 this individual is called "the false prophet." The main goal of the False Prophet is to promote the worship of the first beast (13:12). To accomplish this, the False Prophet will perform deceptive signs (vv. 14–15).

With his associates the Beast and the False Prophet, Satan has sought to counterfeit the Holy Trinity. But in this case, we have an unholy trinity—Satan, Antichrist, and False Prophet.

Revelation 14:4–5

What does John mean when he refers to those who were "not defiled with women"?

Revelation 13 may lead us to conclude that the evil on earth is out of God's control. But chapter 14 gives us another picture. There are many who will refuse to involve themselves in Satan's corrupt religious system during the Tribulation.

In a vision of the future, John describes a scene in which the Lamb is standing with the 144,000 (compare 7:4–8). These saints are identified as "the ones who have not been defiled with women." He further describes them as "celibates" (14:4). One might jump to the conclusion that celibacy is a more holy state than marriage or that marital relationships are somehow defiling. This, of course, is completely contrary to the Bible's teaching on marriage (Gen. 2:24; 1 Cor. 7:3–5, 25–28).

The text in question must be understood in light of John's teaching about a religious and political center described in Revelation 17:1 as the "great harlot." The great harlot is further described as "the mother of harlots and of the abominations of the earth." What we see in this description is a corrupt and immoral administration that is associated with the empire of the Beast. I suggest that those who have not been "defiled by women" are those who have not prostituted themselves by association and involvement with the "harlot" of Babylon and those allied with that corrupt place. While it would be normal to take the word "women" literally, it seems that both the context and the Scriptures cited above dictate a metaphorical meaning.

Revelation 17:1–6

What does John mean by the "great harlot," later identified as "Babylon"?

The destruction of Babylon has been predicted in Revelation 14:8 and 16:19. In Revelation 17–18 John describes this event in fuller detail. There is considerable debate among scholars regarding the interpretation of the term "Babylon." Is John referring to the city of Babylon or to some kind of economic or religious system? There are two basic interpretations:

Babylon is a system. According to this view, the "Babylon" of Revelation 17–18 represents the religious, political, and commercial aspects of the Beast's revived empire. The name "Babylon" stands for a system just as "Wall Street" stands for the American financial enterprises.

Babylon is a city. According to Dyer, Babylon is a "brick-and-mortar city . . . that will exist geographically and politically" during the future Tribulation.[3] Four key observations can be made about Babylon: First, Babylon is a literal city that will dominate the world (17:18). Second, it will be characterized as a harlot that prostitutes its moral values for material luxury (v. 1). Third, the entire city is viewed as a mystery in that its future position, relationship to the Antichrist, and ultimate destruction were unknown before John's vision (vv. 5, 7). Fourth, the city will gain control over seven nations, the Antichrist's growing empire, and eventually the entire earth (vv. 1, 5, 9–10).

Support for the viewpoint that "Babylon" should be interpreted as the literal city is seen in the fact that John's description of the judgment on Babylon is based on Jeremiah's prophecy of the same event (Jer. 50–51).

- compared to a golden cup   (Jer. 51:7a; Rev. 17:3–4)
- dwells on many waters   (Jer. 51:13; Rev. 17:1)
- involved with the nations   (Jer. 51:7b; Rev. 17:2)
- named the same   (Jer. 50:1; Rev. 17:5; 18:10)

That Babylon must be rebuilt and destroyed is suggested by five unfulfilled prophecies regarding the city in Jeremiah 50–51:

1. Babylon will be destroyed suddenly (51:8).
2. Babylon will be destroyed completely (50:3).
3. Building materials will never be reused (51:26).
4. Believers will flee from the city (50:8; 51:6).
5. Judah and Israel will be reunited (50:4–5).

Since these predictions have not been fulfilled, Jeremiah must be describing a yet future (eschatological) destruction of the literal city of Babylon. Dyer concludes, "The Babylon in Revelation 17–18 is the future rebuilt city of Babylon on the Euphrates. It will once again be restored and will achieve a place of worldwide influence only to be destroyed by the Antichrist in his thirst for power."[4]

Incredibly, the city of Babylon is rising again on the plain of Shinar! The government of Iraq has spent millions of dollars reconstructing the site. In 1987 and 1988 Dyer participated in the annual Babylon Festival and witnessed firsthand the work being done to restore the glory of ancient Babylon. One might wonder how the current reconstruction of Babylon relates to Bible prophecy. The extent of destruction predicted in the Bible (Isa. 13–14; Jer. 50–51) never took place historically. Therefore, the rebuilding of Babylon is necessary in order for these predictions to be fulfilled literally. While the rebuilding of Babylon is not the fulfillment of Bible prophecy, it is possible that God will use this to help set the stage for the final events of world history.[5]

Revelation 20:4

Who are those who shall reign with Christ during the thousand-year kingdom?

With Satan bound (Rev. 20:1–3), the kingdom of Christ may at last begin. This literal kingdom will be established in fulfillment of God's promise to David (2 Sam. 7:12–16; Luke 1:32–33). John describes those who "came to life and reigned with Christ for a thousand years." The immediate context identifies these resurrected saints as Tribulation martyrs, who had been "beheaded" because they had refused to worship the Beast and to receive his mark (compare Rev. 6:9; 13:15). But these saints will not reign alone. Jesus promised His apostles a place in His kingdom government (Matt. 19:27–28). And Paul declared that "we shall also reign with Him" (2 Tim. 2:12).

Revelation 20:8–9

Why is this final war called the battle of "Gog and Magog"?

Revelation 20:7–10 describes a final battle following the one-thousand-year kingdom that will give Satan and his followers one final chance to show their true character. Satan will gather his followers and converge on Christ and His people in Jerusalem (v. 9). But the battle is soon over as fire from heaven devours the Enemy. John calls this battle "Gog and Magog" since this rebellion is very similar in purpose to the one in Ezekiel by this name. The differences between these two events are greater than the similarities between them (see on Ezek. 38–39).

Revelation 22:3

How does the reference to the "curse" fit here?

The reference to the "curse" ties together a great theme of Scripture. The Bible begins with a curse that came as a result of sin (Gen. 3:14–19). But it ends with an announcement that "there shall no longer be any curse." In the eternal state, the curse, which came as a result of the Fall, will be removed. No longer will all creation groan under the bondage of sin (Rom. 8:20–22). John announces that the trees will be so revived that they will bear their fruit year round. The world will return to the sin-free state of pre-Fall Eden. God's great plan for the ages is simply to reverse the curse. We see the culmination of that plan in Revelation 22:3.

Revelation 22:11

What is the meaning of this enigmatic statement?

You won't find this verse in a memory verse packet! What did the Lord have in mind: "Let the one who does wrong, still do wrong; and let the one who is filthy, still be filthy"? This statement simply means that when Christ returns, destinies are fixed. Once you enter into eternity, there will be no further opportunity to change your status. What you are at that time, you will be forever! These words remind us that our decision regarding Christ has eternal consequences.

Revelation 22:18–19

How do we interpret this warning in light of the Bible's teaching on the perseverance of the saints?

The Revelation concludes with a warning against tampering with the text. Additions to or subtractions from the Revelation are said to have weighty consequences. Similar warnings are found in the Old Testament as well (Deut. 4:2; 12:32; Prov. 30:6).

Christians wonder about the warning that God will "take away his part from the tree of life." Does this mean that a true believer might lose his or her salvation? We have found the biblical evidence for the perseverance of the saints quite strong and convincing (compare John 10:28; Rom. 8:29–30). We must interpret the obscure statements of Scripture in light of what is very clear. I suggest that the warning assumes that a genuine child of God will not tamper with the Scripture. Only an unbeliever would presume to do so. That person will have no part in "the tree of life," which the redeemed will enjoy for eternity.

Endnotes

1. Robert H. Mounce, *The Book of Revelation* (Grand Rapids: Eerdmans, 1977), 70.
2. Robert H. Gundry, *The Church and the Tribulation* (Grand Rapids: Zondervan, 1973), 81–82
3. Charles H. Dyer, "The Identity of Babylon," *Bibliotheca Sacra* (October–December 1987): 440.
4. Ibid., 449.
5. For further study, see Charles H. Dyer, *The Rise of Babylon* (Wheaton: Tyndale House, 1991).

INDEX